AUTOBIOGRAPHY OF
PARLEY P. PRATT

AUTOBIOGRAPHY OF
PARLEY P. PRATT

One of the Twelve Apostles of the Church of Jesus Christ of
Latter-day Saints, Embracing His Life, Ministry and
Travels, With Extracts, in Prose and Verse,
From His Miscellaneous Writings

Edited by his son
PARLEY P. PRATT

Deseret Book Company
Salt Lake City, Utah

First printing in paperbound edition, May 1994

Library of Congress Cataloging-in-Publication Data

Pratt, Parley P. (Parley Parker), 1807–1857.
   Autobiography of Parley P. Pratt.

   (Classics in Mormon literature)
   Includes index.
   1. Pratt, Parley P. (Parley Parker), 1807–1857.
2. Mormon Church—Apostles—Biography. 3. The Church of Jesus Christ of Latter-day Saints—Apostles—Biography.
I. Pratt, Parley P. (Parley Parker), 1837–1897.
II. Title. III. Series.
BX8695.P7A295   1985   289.3'32'0924   [B]   85-10264
ISBN 0-87747-740-X (Classics in Mormon literature)
ISBN 0-87579-841-1 (paper)

Printed in the United States of America   72082-4640
10   9   8   7   6   5

CONTENTS

PREFACE TO THE FIRST EDITION

In publishing this volume I am discharging a duty solemnly imposed upon me by my lamented father, just before his departure on his last mission to the United States.

It affords me great pleasure to present the Autobiography of the late Author to his relatives, his numerous friends, and to the general reader.

The writer is well and favorably known through his *Voice of Warning,* his *Key to Theology,* and other productions of his pen, as well as through his personal labors. He was one of the first Apostles of the Church of Jesus Christ of Latter-day Saints, having been called by revelation and ordained to that office by the Prophet Joseph Smith and Oliver Cowdery. He was intimately associated with the martyrs Joseph and Hyrum, with Presidents B. Young and H. C. Kimball, and other leading men, almost from the first rise of the Church: his history, therefore, was so interwoven with that of the Church, that many of the most interesting sketches of Church history will be found therein.

The following pages, which embrace his life, ministry and travels, and some of his best miscellaneous writings in prose and verse, are the productions of his own pen.

He spared no pains to make the work a reliable record, and one that would be acceptable to all lovers of truth. It is written in the author's happiest style. He was an early pioneer of the Great West, and travelled extensively in different countries.

His life was one of indefatigable labor, varied and complicated, crowded with public labors and responsibilities, and full of strange and extraordinary events—a life mingled with the extremes of joy and sorrow—or, in the writer's own words, "a truly eventful one."

With confidence and satisfaction I submit this work to the reader, feeling assured that it will stand upon its own merits. I also have an earnest and sincere desire that it may be the means, through the blessing of God, of accomplishing much good.

In editing the work I have been kindly assisted by the author's personal friend, Elder John Taylor, to whom I feel deeply indebted.

The work embraces a period of history of fifty years—from the author's boyhood to the time of his betrayal, by apostates, into the hands of his enemies, and martyrdom.

The writer, in his second preface to his *Voice of Warning,* in 1846, gave expression to the following sentiment: "Should the author be called to sacrifice his life for the cause of truth, he will have the consolation that it will be said of him, as it was said of Abel, *"He being dead yet speaketh."*

EDITOR.

Salt Lake City, Dec., 1873.

TO THE PUBLIC

The circumstances attending the death of our beloved and much esteemed Apostle, Parley Parker Pratt, rendered it impossible for him to complete and prepare for publication the work in which he had for many years been engaged, which is now presented to the public.

The general history and incidents were recorded in various forms of manuscript, some in book form, some in loose leaves, whilst others were extracts from the *Millennial Star* and other publications, yet they needed collating and revising preparatory to their publication.

The deceased, as appears above, had laid upon his eldest son, P. P. Pratt, the responsibility of publishing his history in case anything should happen to prevent himself from doing it.

At the solicitation of Brother Pratt I undertook the task of assisting to collate and revise the work preparatory to publication. I found, as I expected it to be, quite an undertaking. But, as Bro. Parley brought the gospel to and baptized me, and as I have always entertained for him the most profound regard, I esteemed it a duty, due alike to gratitude and respect, to assist in having him properly presented before the community.

In the revision the changes are very few and unimportant, the meaning being rigidly adhered to, and the original, so far as possible, preserved intact. His doctrines and general views are left unchanged, as he was always considered sound in doctrinal points.

The multitudinous reminiscences manifested in his eventful life exhibit a true and living faith in God and his religion—an honesty of purpose, an inflexible will, and an unflagging, indefatigable industry and perseverance. He possessed a comprehensive mind, coupled with a sound judgment. He manifested an indomitable fortitude under the most trying circumstances, and in adversity and trials, as well as in prosperity, exhibited an example worthy of praise and emulation. He was indeed a true Latter-day Saint, an honorable Apostle, a good and kind husband, an affectionate father, a true friend, and an honest man.

From various premonitions which he had during his last visit with me in New York, I was satisfied that, when I took my last sad leave of him in that city, I should never see his face again in the flesh. These presentiments were but too speedily and sadly fulfilled. He has gone— but has left a name and a fame that will live throughout time and burst forth in eternity; and in the morning of the first resurrection, when the opening heavens shall reveal the Son of God, and he shall proclaim, "I am the resurrection and the life," when Death shall deliver up the dead, I expect to meet Bro. Parley in the resurrection of the just.

JOHN TAYLOR.

Preface to Classics in Mormon Literature Edition

One of the most significant of the Mormon proselyters, writers, and thinkers to emerge during the early years of the Restoration was Parley Parker Pratt. In that initial period of Church growth and development, a body of sacred literature, unique in its dimensions, was generated. Elder Pratt was a central figure in expounding the doctrines of the faith as introduced by the Prophet Joseph Smith. He published some thirty-one separate works during his lifetime (1807-1857). Of this number his two primary texts, A Voice of Warning and Key to the Science of Theology, are still in print. After Elder Pratt's untimely death in 1857, his son Parley Parker Pratt, Jr., published his father's autbiographical materials as they appear in this singular volume, The Autobiography of Parley Parker Pratt.

Publication of A Voice of Warning in 1837 set the standard for future Mormon pamphleteers. The textual format, which employed descriptions of basic Mormon doctrines and biblical references, arguments, and examples, was utilized as a guide by virtually all Latter-day Saint writers during the century that followed. A Voice of Warning can be classified as the first use of a book other than the standard works to spread the Latter-day Saint message. It was probably the most effective nineteenth century Mormon missionary tract and acted as a catalyst for the conversion of thousands. The tract continued to serve as a basic proselyting tool well into the twentieth century.

Elder Pratt began work on Key to the Science of Theology while he was in San Francisco, just prior to departing for his mission to Chile in the latter part of 1851. By March 1855 the volume was available for public sale. It is considered Mormonism's earliest comprehensive and synthetical text. Commencing with a definition of theology, it examines the loss of the true gospel, the nature of the Godhead, the origin of the universe, the Restoration, how to gain the presence of God, the Resurrection, degrees of glory, and the ultimate status of exalted men and women. Key to the Science of Theology proved to be Elder Pratt's last major work, published just two years before his assassination. (Peter Crawley, "Parley

P. Pratt: Father of Mormon Pamphleteering," *Dialogue* 15 [Autumn 1982]: 13-31.)

In company with William W. Phelps and Eliza R. Snow, Parley P. Pratt was one of the most important and fruitful writers of verse in the early Church. He wrote verses to commemorate many signal events in the history of Mormondom and in his own personal life. His most frequent themes were the restoration of the gospel and the eventual millennial reign of Jesus Christ. When Emma Smith compiled the first LDS hymnal, *A Collection of Sacred Hymns, for the Church of the Latter Day Saints,* in 1835, the work included three hymns written by Elder Pratt. At the time of his mission to the eastern states with the Twelve in the summer of 1835, he published eleven of his hymns in conjunction with a long narrative poem in six chapters entitled "The Millennium." This volume became the first book of Mormon poetry in the Church. (*The Millennium, a Poem. To Which Added Hymns and Songs,* Boston: Printed for Elder Parley P. Pratt, Author and Proprietor, 1835.) Eight of the eleven hymns later appeared in the first Mormon hymnal published in Europe, *A Collection of Sacred Hymns,* published at Manchester in 1840.

The printed wrapper of the initial issue of the *Millennial Star* in 1840 carried one of his most powerful hymns, "The Morning Breaks":

> The morning breaks; the shadows flee;
> Lo! Zion's standard is unfurled.
> The dawning of a brighter day
> Majestic rises on the world.
>
> The clouds of error disappear
> Before the rays of truth divine;
> The glory, bursting from afar,
> Wide o'er the nations soon will shine.

These two verses from that immortal hymn are indelibly set for all generations not only on the hearts of the Saints, but they also grace the monument erected at Elder Pratt's gravesite near Van Buren, Arkansas. Among other Pratt hymns still readily recognizable in today are "An Angel from on High," "Come, O Thou King of Kings," "Jesus, Once of Humble Birth," and "As the Dew from Heaven Distilling." One of Parley's grandsons, Samuel Russell, collected a majority of his progenitor's verses on restoration themes and set fifty of them to traditional hymn tunes. These were published by Cambridge University Press in 1913 in a work entitled *The Millennial Hymns of Parley Parker Pratt.*

Immediately prior to his leaving for his last mission, Parley met with his twenty-year-old son and namesake, Parley P. Pratt, Jr., for some final words of counsel. Of that event Parley stipulated, "[I] gave instructions and strict charge to my son . . . concerning my business, and the duties that would devolve upon him in my absence." (*Autobiography*, p. 000.) Included in those directions was the solemn duty for the son to publish Elder Pratt's autobiography should the author be unable to do so himself. His announced premonitions to his family and friends were realized. Parley did not live to finish his autobiography or to make revisions in the later notes that appeared under the editorship of Parley P. Pratt, Jr., in 1874. The last eight chapters appear to be journal entries added by his son.

Parley said that he was attracted to the gospel through reading the Book of Mormon. In 1857 he narrated an account of the witness that came to him while reading that sacred scripture for the first time years before: "As I read, I was convinced that it was true; and the Spirit of the Lord came upon me, while I read, and enlightened my mind, convinced my judgment, and rivetted the truth upon my understanding, so that I knew that the book was true, just as well as a man knows the daylight from the dark night, or any other thing that can be implanted in his understanding. I did not know it by any audible voice from heaven, by any ministration of an angel, by any open vision; but I knew it by the spirit of understanding in my heart—by the light that was in me. I knew it was true, because it was light, and had come in fulfilment of the Scriptures; and I bore testimony of its truth to the neighbours that came in during the first day that I sat reading it, at the house of an old Baptist deacon, named Hamblin." (*Journal of Discourses* 5:194.)

On a very hot August day in 1830 Elder Pratt wore blisters on his feet in an attempt to reach the Prophet at Manchester, New York. He felt compelled to meet the proprietor of the Book of Mormon. Instead, he found Hyrum Smith, who reported that Joseph was away in Harmony, Pennsylvania. Soon after their first meeting, Hyrum presented Parley with a copy of the Book of Mormon and took him home to the Peter Whitmer farm in Fayette, New York. There he was introduced to the Three Witnesses and also the Eight Witnesses. The day following this meeting, September 1, 1830, Parley was baptized in Seneca Lake by Oliver Cowdery, was confirmed a member of the Church, and was ordained an elder. That same month he went on to Canaan, Columbia County, New York, where he presented the gospel message to his family and was successful in converting his brother, Orson Pratt, on September 19, 1830.

The conversion of Parley Parker Pratt to the gospel of Jesus Christ added a veritable giant to Mormon leadership. His exceptional character traits manifested themselves in a literal galaxy of personal endowments. Andrew Love Neff observed: "Parley's soul was full of romance, poetry and song, imagery, delight and enthusiasm. Emotionalism here found its exemplar. . . . Deeds of romance and achievement exuded from his knightly spirit. Gracious Parley P. was one of the most brilliant as well as one of the most exotic characters of Mormonism." (Andrew Love Neff, *History of Utah, 1847 to 1869*, Salt Lake City: Deseret News Press, 1940, p. 577.)

John Henry Evans stylized Parley's abilities in these superlatives: "Abounding in vital energy, . . . Parley possessed a vivid imagination, was addicted to Popean cuplet and florid prose, had a vocabulary equal to his fancy, [and] kept himself always on the frontiers of life and thought." (John Henry Evans, *Joseph Smith, An American Prophet*, New York: The Macmillan Company, 1946, p. 60.)

While describing her husband's public stance "as an Orator, Author, Statesman and able expounder of the Gospel," Ann Agatha Pratt also shared a glimpse into Parley's private nature as a householder. She affirmed:

"He had an inate reverence and respect for woman as the mother of the souls of men. . . . As a father he was kind and gentle and hailed each new comer with as much pleasure and delight as if it were the only one. One of the greatest pleasures of his life was to gather them around his knees, holding as many as he could, and have them sing their sweet childish songs, often trying to join in with them as he dearly loved music and singing and always when possible he would have his family gather together for family worship; we would sing a suitable hymn then kneel down and dedicate his family, himself and all he had to the Lord. . . .

"His confidence in God was unbounded and he would go to Him and ask Him for what he needed, as a child would go to the father, with the same childlike simplicity. I have seen his prayers answered almost before he had finished his supplication." ("Reminiscences of Mrs. A. Agatha Pratt, January 07," F564, #16, LDS Church Archives.)

From 1830 to 1857, Elder Pratt was constantly engaged in a variety of missionary assignments. During this period he experienced more than a score of specific calls to the field. Among his areas of labor was a fifteen-hundred-mile journey to the western boundaries of Missouri (the Lamanite Mission). He was among the first of the Saints to stand upon the land where the City of Zion was to be built. In the summer of 1831

Parley served a mission in Ohio, Indiana, Illinois, and Missouri, and on February 21, 1835, he was ordained one of the original Twelve Apostles in this dispensation. Serving in that capacity, he became one of the chosen few who were ready to spend their time, their means, and even their lives, to assist in the establishment of the kingdom and spread the gospel at home and abroad as special witnesses. His brother Orson was likewise ordained to the Twelve a short time later, April 26, 1835. That same year saw the brothers expounding the gospel through Pennsylvania, New York, and several of the New England states.

Parley performed extensive proselyting in Canada. While working in Toronto and vicinity during 1836, he was successful in the conversion of such respected individuals as John and Leonora Taylor, Joseph Fielding, and Joseph's sisters, Mary and Mercy Fielding. Elder Pratt founded a large branch of the Church in New York during 1837. In 1838 he was caught up in the dreadful persecution of the Saints in Missouri. As a participant in the Battle of Crooked River, he was committed to prison for trial, along with other leading brethren who were being detained on a variety of charges.

During the committing trial before Judge Austin King, Parley was incarcerated with the Prophet Joseph at Richmond, Missouri. He was a witness to the Prophet's stinging reproof of the guards as with a voice of thunder Joseph cried, *"SILENCE, ye fiends of the infernal pit. In the name of Jesus Christ I rebuke you, and command you to be still; I will not live another minute and hear such language. Cease such talk, or you or I die THIS INSTANT!"* Greatly moved by that exalting experience, Elder Pratt responded, "Dignity and majesty have I seen but *once*, as it stood in chains, at midnight, in a dungeon in an obscure village of Missouri." (*Autobiography,* p. 180.)

In fulfillment of Joseph's prophetic revelation to the Twelve contained in Doctrine and Covenants, section 118, Parley and Orson Pratt started from Nauvoo on August 29, 1839, for the British Isles. At a conference of the Church held in the Temperance Hall at Preston, Lancashire, England, on April 15, 1840, authorization was given for the publication of a monthly periodical under the "direction and superintendence of the Twelve." Parley was to be the editor and publisher of the newly created *Latter-day Saints Millennial Star.* Initially the publication was printed in the town of Manchester at No. 47 Oxford Street. Elder Pratt's first issue, dated May 1840, is indicative of the millennial perspective that dominated his thinking and the entire missionary thrust in England. The prospectus of the *Star* stipulated:

"Its columns will be devoted to the spread of the fulness of the gospel—the restoration of the ancient principles of Christianity—the gathering of Israel—the rolling forth of the kingdom of God among the nations—the signs of the times—the fulfilment of prophecy—recording the judgments of God as they befall the nations, whether signs in the heavens or in the earth, 'blood, fire, or vapour of smoke'—in short whatever is shown forth indicative of the coming of the Son of Man, and the ushering in of his universal reign on the earth." (*Latter-day Saints Millennial Star* 1:5.)

Parley P. Pratt had given birth to what would evolve as the Church's oldest continuous periodical, enduring from 1840 until its discontinuation at the end of 1970 (the *Deseret News* now excepted). When other of the Twelve returned to America in 1841, Elder Pratt stayed on in his new appointment as "President over all the British Conferences," holding this post until the autumn of 1842.

Early in 1845 Elder Pratt was again called to leave Nauvoo and preside over branches of the Church in New England and the mid-Atlantic states with headquarters in New York City. Here he worked on the publication of a periodical entitled *The Prophet*. That summer he returned to Nauvoo and completed preparations for the mass exodus of the Saints from the City of Joseph. February 1846 found him in the vanguard of Mormons as they strung out across Iowa in a forced move from Illinois. At Council Bluffs, President Brigham Young assigned Elder Pratt to perform a short-term mission to England, where he was to regulate some important matters among the branches and to strengthen the Saints throughout the British Isles. By April 1847, Elder Pratt had returned to America and rejoined his family "dwelling in tents, in the Camp of Israel, at Council Bluffs." During the summer and autumn he and his household immigrated to the Salt Lake Valley.

In March 1851 the First Presidency directed Elder Pratt to preside over a "General Mission to the Pacific." He established his headquarters in San Francisco. While he was there, a sense of duty to the peoples of South America drew his attention to the prospects of a proselyting endeavor in that land. With his wife Phebe Soper and Elder Rufus Allen, he set sail for Valparaiso, Chile, on September 5, 1851. During a lengthy voyage of sixty-four days on the ship *Henry Kelsey*, Elder Pratt found time to do some writing. One item of correspondence, a letter to his family, might be singled out, as its contents demonstrate his extraordinary sensitivity and is a sample of the finest quality of composition. He mused:

"Just imagine sundown, twilight, the shades of evening, the curtains of the solitary night gathering in silent gloom and lone melancholy around a father who loves his home and its inmates; his fireside and the family altar! Behold him standing leaning over the vessel's side as it glides over waters of the lone and boundless Pacific, gazing for hours in succession into the bosom of its dark abyss, or watching its white foam and sparkling spray! What are his thoughts? Can you divine them? Behold, he prays! For what does he pray? For every wife, for every child, for every near and dear friend he has on earth, he prays most earnestly! most fervently! He calls each by name over and over again, before the altar of remembrance. And when this is done for all on earth, he remembers those in Heaven; calls their names; communes with them in spirit; wonders how they are doing; whether they think of him. He calls to mind their acts and sufferings in life, their death, and the grave where sleeps their precious dust." (*Autobiography*, p. 000.)

Frustrated by language difficulties, financial poverty, the death of an infant son born to Phebe, and the state of the religion and politics in Chile, the missionaries returned to San Francisco in March 1852.

After more than twenty-five years of constant missionary labors, Elder Pratt had some personal expectations of remaining closer to home and family for a season. Such imaginations were short-lived. In 1856 President Brigham Young directed him to carry out an extended proselyting tour in the eastern states. Elder Pratt's love of the Lord and respect for priesthood authority generated philosophical—even prophetic—reflections, as he gave his last discourse to the Saints assembled at the Bowery, Great Salt Lake City, September 7, 1856:

"I am now about to start to the States, to preach the Gospel of Jesus Christ and bear testimony of those things which I most assuredly do know; for this is my calling. I have desired, after travelling for twenty-five or twenty-six years, mostly abroad, to stay at home and minister among the people of God, and take care of my family; but God's will be done, and not mine. If it is the will of God that I should spend my days in proclaiming this Gospel and bearing testimony of these things, I shall think myself highly privileged and honoured. And when the Spirit of God is upon me, I think it matters but very little what I suffer, what I sacrifice—whether I secure the honour or dishonour of men, or where I die, if it so be that I can keep the faith, fight the good fight, and finish my course with joy.

"I have all eternity before me, in which to enjoy myself; and though I am a stranger and a pilgrim on this earth, and whether I be rich or poor, or live long or short, I shall yet plant gardens and eat the fruit of them, plant vineyards and drink the wine thereof, build houses and inhabit them, and, as one of the elect of God, shall long enjoy the works of my hands. All this shall I do, though worms eat the body that I now have." (*Journal of Discourses* 5:196-97.)

Leaving Salt Lake City on September 11, 1856, Elder Pratt traveled extensively among the branches in Philadelphia, New York City, Cincinnati, and elsewhere. While he was engaged in that calling, a man by the name of Hector McLean actively began to trace his whereabouts, blaming Elder Pratt for the estrangement between him (McLean) and his former wife, Eleanor. McLean nearly caught him in St. Louis. Fortunately, Elder Pratt eluded the man and managed to escape to Indian Territory (Oklahoma), where Elder George B. Higginson was working among the Indians of the Creek and Cherokee nations. Here Elder Pratt was arrested by a Captain Little of the U.S. Cavalry on a warrant emerging from the charges filed by Hector McLean at Fort Gibson (Oklahoma).

Elder Pratt was transferred under guard to Van Buren, Crawford County, Arkansas, where the nearest federal court convened. Judge John B. Ogden, U.S. Commissioner, presided over the examining session on Tuesday, May 12, 1857. Evidence presented against Elder Pratt was not considered sufficient to warrant holding him, and he was acquitted. However, the judge purposely did not announce the decision to release Elder Pratt at that time, hoping to dissuade McLean from his avowed determination to kill him. Elder Pratt was kept at the jailhouse overnight in protective custody. Early the next morning Judge Ogden brought his horse to him at the jail, saw that he was discharged, and at the same time offered him a knife and a pistol as a means of self-defense. But Elder Pratt declined, saying, "Gentlemen, I do not rely on weapons of that kind, my trust is in my God. Good-bye, gentlemen."

Although Elder Pratt rode a circuitous route to escape his pursuers, a light rain allowed Hector McLean and two accomplices, James Cornell and Amasa Howell, to track him. They caught up with the fleeing man some twelve miles northeast of Van Buren (near Alma, Arkansas) in front of the Winn farm. Shots were fired by McLean, but they failed to take effect. Riding up to Elder Pratt, McLean stabbed him in the left breast with his bowie knife. The wounded man fell from his horse while his assailants rode off. About ten minutes later McLean returned and, placing a gun next to Elder Pratt's neck, deliberately fired into the prostrate figure. Mr. Winn was a witness to the entire scene. He and some of his neighbors attended to the apostle in his dying moments. Before Elder Pratt died approximately two and a half hours later, he instructed those gathered about him on how to notify his family and the disposition of his personal effects. He then shared his final testimony: "I die a firm believer in the Gospel of Jesus Christ as revealed through the Prophet Joseph Smith, and I wish you to carry this my dying testimony. I know that the Gospel is true and that Joseph Smith was a prophet of the living God, I am dying a martyr to the faith." (Steven Pratt, "Eleanor McLean and the Murder of Parley P. Pratt," *BYU Studies* 15 [Winter 1975]: 248.)

While imprisoned at Richmond, Missouri, Joseph Smith had spoken of being bound to Parley P. Pratt "in chains as well as the cords of everlasting love." (Letter of Joseph Smith to Emma Smith, November 12, 1838.) With his dying breath, he reaffirmed that love and devotion to the Prophet.

Elder Pratt's body was "shrouded in fine linen" and placed in a pine casket prepared by William T. Steward. The remains were then driven by John B. Steward to Sterman's graveyard (now known as Fine Springs), where Elder George Higginson buried them at about ten o'clock on the evening of Thursday, May 14, 1857, "without the presence of a brother or a sister." (Steven Pratt, *op. cit.*; letter of George B. Higginson to Andrew Kimball, March 1892, LDS Church Archives; Journal of James Duffin, "Journal History," May 16, 1857.)

At the time of his death, Elder Pratt was fortified with a more certain knowledge that robbed death of its sting. He had affirmed on numerous occasions the fact that "man is an eternal being, both in regard to his material organization, and his mind and affections. The resurrection from the dead (if quickened by the celestial glory) restores him to life with all his bodily and mental powers and faculties, and consequently associates him with his family, friends, and kindred, as one of the necessary links of the chain which connects the great and royal family of heaven and earth, in one eternal body of kindred affection, and association." (Parley P. Pratt, "Celestial Family Organization," *The Prophet* [New York City], March 1, 1845, p. 1.)

In the Territory of Utah, Brigham Young declared, concerning Elder Pratt's death, "Nothing has happened so hard to reconcile my mind to since the death of Joseph." ("Reminiscences of Mrs. A. Agatha Pratt, January 07," F564, #16, LDS Church Archives.) Elder Pratt was just one month over fifty years of age when he died. Nearly thirty of those years had been spent in the selfless service of preaching the gospel of

Jesus Christ. His careful chronicling of associated events makes the *Autobiography* one of the most valuable works extant on the subject of Mormon missions.

Through the great and enduring legacy of his writings, hymns, songs, and poems, Parley Parker Pratt continues to inspire each new generation with the image of his indominable spirit. The vibrancy of his testimony and the motivational factors that shaped his life are captivatingly expressed in this particular work. The reader will discover an example of living faith personified in Elder Pratt that is both uplifting and worthy of emulation.

DR. LARRY C. PORTER
Director of Church History
Religious Studies Center
Brigham Young University

Chapter 1

PARENTAGE—CHILDHOOD—YOUTH—EDUCATION—EARLY IMPRESSIONS—JOURNEY WESTWARD—MAKING A NEW FARM IN THE WILDERNESS OF OSWEGO.

Parley Parker Pratt, the subject and author of these sketches, and third son of Jared and Charity Pratt, of Canaan, Columbia County, New York, was born April 12, 1807, in Burlington, Otsego County, N.Y.*

Of my early youth I shall say but little. My father was a hard working man, and generally occupied in agricultural pursuits; and, although limited in education, he sometimes taught school, and even vocal music.

He was a man of excellent morals; and he exerted himself diligently, by stern example as well as precept, to instill into the minds of his children every principle of integrity, honesty, honor and virtue.

He taught us to venerate our Father in Heaven, Jesus Christ, His prophets and Apostles, as well as the Scriptures written by them; while at the same time he belonged to no religious sect, and was careful to preserve his children free from all prejudice in favor of or against any particular denomination, into which the so-called Christian world was then unhappily divided.

We frequently attended public worship, with Presbyterians, Baptists and Methodists in turn, or, as circumstances rendered convenient—having equal respect for these several forms of worship and their adherents. Though my father did sometimes manifest a decided disapprobation of a hireling clergy, who seemed, in his estimation, to prefer the learning and wisdom of man to the gifts and power of the Holy Ghost.

His means to educate his children were very limited; but that excellent system of common school education early established in the Eastern and Middle States afforded to them, in common with others, an opportunity to learn, and even to become familiar with the four great branches, which are the foundation of literature and the sciences.

---

*For genealogy in full, see Appendix.

1

My opportunity, even in these institutions, was far more limited than most of the youths of my country, on account of my time being mostly required in physical exertion to assist in sustaining the family of my father.

But I always loved a book. If I worked hard, a book was in my hand in the morning while others were sitting down to breakfast; the same at noon; if I had a few moments, *a book!* a BOOK! A book at evening, while others slept or sported; a book on Sundays; a book at every leisure moment of my life.

At the age of seven years my mother gave me lessons to read in the Scriptures; I read of Joseph in Egypt,—his dreams, his servitude, his temptation and exaltation; his kindness and affection for his father and brethren. All this inspired me with love, and with the noblest sentiments ever planted in the bosom of man.

I read of David and Goliath; of Saul and Samuel; of Samson and the Philistines—all these inspired me with hatred to the deeds of evil doers and love for good men and their deeds.

After this I read of Jesus and his Apostles; and O, how I loved them! How I longed to fall at the feet of Jesus; to worship him, or to offer my life for his.

At about twelve years of age I read of the first resurrection, as described by John the Apostle, in the 20th chapter of his Revelation; how they, martyrs of Jesus, and those who kept His commandments would live and reign with Christ a thousand years, while the rest of the dead lived not again till the thousand years were ended. O, what an impression this made on my mind; I retired to rest after an evening spent in this way; but I could not sleep. I felt a longing desire and an inexpressible anxiety to secure to myself a part in a resurrection so glorious. I felt a weight of worlds,—of *eternal* worlds resting upon me; for fear I might still remain in uncertainty, and at last fall short and still sleep on in the cold embrace of death; while the great, the good, the blessed and the holy of this world would awake from the gloom of the grave and be renovated, filled with life and joy, and enter upon life with all its joys: while for a thousand years their busy, happy tribes should trample on my sleeping dust, and still my spirit wait in dread suspense, impatient of its doom. I tried to pray; but O, how weak!

At the age of fifteen I was separated from my father's house, and placed as an assistant on a farm, with a gentleman by the name of William S. Herrick.

This gentleman and his family were exemplary members of the Presbyterian Church; and better, kinder, or more agreeable people are seldom met with in this wicked world. They treated me as if I had been an only son, instead of a hired servant.

I was with them eight months, during which time our mutual affection for each other increased; and I felt grieved when my time expired and duty called me elsewhere.

During the winter following, being in the sixteenth year of my age, I boarded with one of my aunts (my father's sister), named Van Cott; she was an excellent and kind-hearted woman, and acted as a mother to me. This winter I spent mostly at school, and it was my last opportunity to improve my education by any means, except my own unaided exertion—at least for many years.

In this school, by close application, I made such extraordinary progress that the teacher often spoke of me to the whole school, and exhorted them to learn as Parley Pratt did;—said he (to some of them who were more fond of mischief than of study), if you would learn as he does, you would become men of wisdom and talent in the world; but if you continue the course you have done you will remain in obscurity and unknown; while he will be known, and fill important stations in society. I do not mention these circumstances by way of boasting; but simply because they are true. How little did I then realize, or even dream of the station I should be called to fill.

Again the spring returned; I was sixteen years of age. I left the school of my boyhood forever, and commenced again a life of toil. I assisted my cousin, William Pratt, in the cultivation of the farm of my aunt (where I had boarded the previous winter) until September, when I started a journey to the West, in company with my brother William, in search of some spot of ground in the wilderness which we might prepare as our future home.

We travelled about two hundred miles on foot, and at length selected a spot for a farm in the woods, about two miles from Oswego, a small town situated on Lake Ontario, in the State of New York. We purchased seventy acres of land, which was covered with an immense growth of timber, principally beech, maple and hemlock. For this we bargained with one Mr. Morgan, and agreed to pay four dollars per acre, in four annual payments with interest— paying some seventy dollars in hand.

We then repaired again to the East, and, by dint of hard labor, endeavored to earn the money. Wages were very low, and at length my brother William entirely failed in raising his part of the money for our next installment.

The next spring found me in the employment of a wealthy farmer, by the name of Eliphet Bristol, in the neighborhood of my aunt Van Cott's. Here I experienced no kindness; no friendship from my employer or his family. I always commenced work before sunrise, and continued till dark; losing only three days in eight months. I was then but a lad—being only seventeen years of age—and stood in need of fatherly and motherly care and comfort. But they treated a laborer as a machine; not as a human being, possessed of feelings and sympathies in common with his species. *Work!* WORK! WORK! you are hired to work. A man that paid for his work should never be weary, faint, or sick; or expect a kind look or word. He agrees to work; we agree to pay him; that is sufficient. He needs no kindness, no affection, no smiles, no encouragement of any kind. Such was their spirit towards me during this eight months of toil. I was glad when the time expired; I felt like one released from prison. I took my wages, and was accompanied by my father to our place in Oswego. Here I paid all my hard earnings to meet the yearly installment due on the land—reserving merely enough to purchase two axes. We then commenced to chop and clear the heavy timber all the time that we could command, extra of earning our board. It was a cold, snowy winter, such as is usual in the northern part of New York. But we earned our living, and chopped and cleared ten acres during the winter and spring; this we surrounded with a fence of rails, and planted with wheat and Indian corn, being in hopes to meet the next payment with the avails of our harvest.

Orchard of forest home of Lovina
Van Cott, where Parley spent
many pleasant hours as a child in
New York State

Aunt Lovina Van Cott, born 1786

The old home in New York of
Lovina Van Cott

Chapter 2

It was during these toils in the wilderness that my mind was drawn out from time to time on the things of God and eternity. I felt deeply anxious to be saved from my sins, and to secure an interest in that world "where the wicked cease from troubling, and the weary are at rest." I attended public worship with a society of Baptists who had employed one W. A. Scranton for their minister; he was a scholar from Hamilton Seminary (an institution where young men are educated for the ministry).

I said to my father one day while we were laboring together in the forest: "Father, how is it there is so manifest a difference between the ancient and modern disciples of Jesus Christ and their doctrines? If, for instance, I had lived in the days of the Apostles, and believed in Jesus Christ, and had manifested a wish to become his disciple, Peter or his brethren would have said to me, *'Repent and be baptized in the name of Jesus Christ for* REMISSION OF SINS, *and you* SHALL *receive the gift of the Holy Ghost.'* I should then have known definitely and precisely what to do to be saved. Whereas, *now* we go to the religious minister for instruction, and he tells us we must experience a mysterious, indefinite and undefinable something called religion before we can repent and be baptized acceptably. But, if we inquire how, or by what means we are to come at this experience, he cannot tell us definitely; but will tell us that it is the work of God in the soul; which he will accomplish in his own due time, for his own elect; and that we can do nothing acceptably till this is done. That even our prayers and repentance, and all our good works are sin; so long as this work of God is not done within us.

"Now, father," said I, "how is this? I believe in Jesus; I wish to serve him and keep his commandments; I love him: He has commanded all men to repent and be baptized, and has promised to remit the sins of all those who obey the gospel ordinances, and to pour out the Holy Spirit

6

upon them. Yet, if I apply to the Presbyterians they will sprinkle some water in my face instead of baptizing me. If I go to the Methodists it is the same. And if I go to the Baptists they will not baptize me for *remission of sins,* that I may receive the gift of the Holy Ghost; but they will require of me to relate *an experience,* and to tell of some time and place where I had already experienced that which I am only seeking for, and have not found. This, of course, I cannot do; and, therefore, they will not receive me unto baptism. How, then, can I observe the ordinances of God and keep his commandments?"

To these inquiries my father could give no satisfactory answer; but observed that times and circumstances had changed. With this I was not satisfied, of course; for who had a right to change the ordinances, transgress the law, or break the covenant of the everlasting gospel? Such were my thoughts.

I still continued to ponder upon these things, and to search the Scriptures to learn how to be saved. I found the same principles and practice throughout the history of the Apostles, the Jews, Samaritans, Gentiles, Ephesians, Corinthians, Romans, the Ethiopian eunuch, Saul of Tarsus, the jailer and his household, all were baptized when they believed in Jesus Christ and repented of their sins; and this as an ordinance connected with remission of their sins and the gift of the Holy Ghost. What, then, should I do? Where find one who was commissioned from heaven, and would administer salvation to me? I could only go to the Baptists; but I lacked that *"experience of religion"* which they always required. However, I resolved to try.

I accordingly appeared before them at their monthly meeting, or council, and requested to be baptized; they inquired into my experience; I related to them my firm belief in Christ, and my wish to serve God, without being able to tell them of any particular experience of religion. They finally consulted together; and came to the conclusion that I had been converted, whether I knew it myself or not, and a time was appointed for my baptism—a month or two thence. Here I again realized the difference. In ancient times persons were baptized immediately on profession of their faith; now they were subjected to a delay of weeks or months.

At length the time arrived, and I was baptized by Mr. Scranton, and duly initiated into the Baptist society; being about eighteen years of age. I felt some satisfaction in obeying this one ordinance; but still I was aware that all was not right,—that much was wanting to constitute a Christian, or a Church of Christ.

I endeavored to pray much, and to attend meetings strictly; I also endeavored to keep the commandments of Jesus as well as I could.

Mr. Scranton came to the house where I boarded to preach at a certain time, and I inquired of him what Jesus meant when he said, "these signs shall follow them that believe." He replied, that it meant these signs should follow the Apostles only.

This did not satisfy me; for it was plain and manifest perversion of common sense and language easy to be understood. It was as much as to say: Go ye into all the world and preach the gospel to the Apostles; and the Apostles that believe and are baptized shall be saved; and the Apostles that believe not shall be damned; and these signs shall follow the Apostles that believe. Thus, by logical consistency, confining the whole commission and gospel to the Apostles, with all its benefits, by the same rule that we would confine the promise of the signs following to them.

Chapter 3

Time passed; harvest came; a fine crop, but no market; and consequently the payment came due on our land and there was no means of payment.

The winter rolled round; spring came again; and with it a prosecution on the part of Mr. Morgan for money due on land.

The consequence was that all our hard earnings, and all our improvements in the wilderness, were wrested from us in a moment. Mr. Morgan retained the land, the improvements and the money paid.

Weary and disconsolate, I left the country and my father, who took charge of our crops and all unsettled business.

I spent a few months with my uncles, Ira and Allen Pratt, in Wayne County, N. Y., and in the autumn of 1826 I resolved to bid farewell to the civilized world—where I had met with little else but disappointment, sorrow and unrewarded toil; and where sectarian divisions disgusted and ignorance perplexed me—and to spend the remainder of my days in the solitudes of the great West, among the natives of the forest.

There, at least, thought I, there will be no buying and selling of lands,—no law to sweep all the hard earnings of years to pay a small debt,—no wranglings about sects, and creeds, and doctrines. I will win the confidence of the red man; I will learn his language; I will tell him of Jesus; I will read to him the Scriptures; I will teach him the arts of peace; to hate war, to love his neighbor, to fear and love God, and to cultivate the earth. Such were my resolutions.

In October, 1826, I took leave of my friends and started westward. I paid most of my money in Rochester for a small pocket Bible, and continued my journey as far as Buffalo. At this place I engaged a passage for Detroit, on board a steamer; as I had no money, I agreed to work for the same.

After a rough passage and many delays, I was at length driven by stress of weather to land at Erie, in Pennsylvania; from whence I travelled by land till I came to a small settlement about thirty miles west of Cleveland, in the State of Ohio. The rainy season of November had now set in; the country was covered with a dense forest, with here and there a small opening made by the settlers, and the surface of the earth one vast scene of mud and mire; so that travelling was now very difficult, if not impracticable.

Alone in a land of strangers, without home or money, and not yet twenty years of age, I became discouraged, and concluded to stop for the winter; I procured a gun from one of the neighbors; worked and earned an axe, some breadstuff and other little extras, and retired two miles into a dense forest and prepared a small hut, or cabin, for the winter. Some leaves and straw in my cabin served for my lodging, and a good fire kept me warm. A stream near my door quenched my thirst; and fat venison, with a little bread from the settlements, sustained me for food. The storms of winter raged around me; the wind shook the forest, the wolf howled in the distance, and the owl chimed in harshly to complete the doleful music which seemed to soothe me, or bid me welcome to this holy retreat. But in my little cabin the fire blazed pleasantly, and the Holy Scriptures and a few other books occupied my hours of solitude. Among the few books in my cabin, were McKenzie's travels in the Northwest, and Lewis and Clark's tour up the Missouri and down the Columbia rivers.

Spring came on again; the woods were pleasant, the flowers bloomed in their richest variety, the birds sung pleasantly in the groves; and, strange to say, my mind had become attached to my new abode. I again bargained for a piece of forest land; again promised to pay in a few years, and again commenced to clear a farm and build a house.

I was now twenty years of age.

I resolved to make some improvements and preparations, and then return to my native country, from which I had been absent several years. There was one there whom my heart had long loved, and from whom I would not have been so long separated, except by misfortune.

Chapter 4

It was the Fourth of July, 1827. The morning was beautiful and gay, the sun rose without a cloud over the pine-clad hills of my native land, where in boyhood I had often toiled and sported, just as I came within a mile of the farm of my good old aunt Van Cott, of Canaan, Columbia County, after an absence of three years. I had, during this time, exchanged the features of the bashful boy for those of the man; and, instead of a laughing, careless countenance, a forehead of marble and a cheek of rose, stern care had marked me as her child, and the sun had given a shade of brown to my features; these, added to a heavy growth of beard and whiskers, disguised me so far that I could pass through the neighborhood of people, known and familiar to me, unnoticed and unknown.

With a quick step, a beating heart, and an intense, indescribable feeling of joy, sorrow, hope, despondency and happiness, I approached the door of Mr. Halsey, and knocked; it was opened by an aged female, a stranger to me; I entered and inquired for Miss Thankful Halsey—in a moment more she had me by the hand, with a look of welcome which showed she had not forgotten me.

I spent the day and evening with her; explained to her all my losses, my poverty and prospects, and the lone retreat where I had spent the previous winter; and the preparations I had made for a future home. I also opened my religious views to her, and my desire, which I sometimes had, to try and teach the red man.

"In view of all these things," said I to her, "If you still love me and desire to share my fortune you are worthy to be my wife. If not, we will agree to be friends forever; but part to meet no more in time." "I have loved you during three years' absence," said she, "and I never can be happy without you."

Forest home

I repaired to my aunt's—found the usual welcome. After visiting my mother and kindred, for a few days, I saw my old friend, William S. Herrick, where I had been employed five years before. He was very anxious to employ me again; and finding I was willing, he discharged a hand he had already, and gave me double wages. I remained in his employ till October, and found the same kind reception as formerly.

On the 9th of September, 1827, Parley P. Pratt and Thankful Halsey were solemnly united in the bonds of matrimony, by Elder Palmer, Minister of the Baptist Church, in Canaan, Columbia County, N. Y.

In October we took leave of our friends in Canaan and took passage for the West. We hired a conveyance to Albany, and then took passage for Buffalo on a canal boat; and from there on board a schooner; passing up Lake Erie we landed in safety at the mouth of Black River, in Ohio, and within ten miles of my place. My wife had some money, which we paid in for the land I had purchased. The following spring found me 21 years of age, married and settled in a log dwelling, in the midst of a small clearing made with my own hands, in the place where I had spent the previous winter in solitude.

Chapter 5

Eighteen months had passed since our settlement in the wilderness. The
forest had been displaced by the labors of the first settlers for some distance around our cottage. A small frame house was now our dwelling, a
garden and a beautiful meadow were seen in front, flowers in rich profusion were clustering about our door and windows; while in the back-
ground were seen a thriving young orchard of apple and peach trees, and
fields of grain extending in the distance, beyond which the forest still
stood up in its own primeval grandeur, as a wall to bound the vision and
guard the lovely scene. Other houses and farms were also in view, and
some twenty children were returning from the school actually kept by
my wife, upon the very spot where two years before I had lived for
months without seeing a human being. About this time one Mr. Sidney
Rigdon came into the neighborhood as a preacher, and it was rumored
that he was a kind of Reformed Baptist, who, with Mr. Alexander
Campbell, of Virginia, a Mr. Scott, and some other gifted men, had dis-
sented from the regular Baptists, from whom they differed much in doctrine. At length I went to hear him, and what was my astonishment
when I found he preached faith in Jesus Christ, repentance towards
God, and baptism for remission of sins, with the promise of the gift of the
Holy Ghost to all who would come forward, with all their hearts, and
obey this doctrine!

Here was the *ancient gospel* in due form. Here were the very principles which I had discovered years before; but could find no one to
minister in. But still one great link was wanting to complete the chain of
the ancient order of things; and that was, the *authority* to minister in
holy things—the apostleship, the power which should accompany the
form. This thought occurred to me as soon as I heard Mr. Rigdon make
proclamation of the gospel.

Peter proclaimed this gospel, and baptized for remission of sins, and promised the gift of the Holy Ghost, because he was commissioned so to do by a crucified and risen Saviour. But who is Mr. Rigdon? Who is Mr. Campbell? Who commissioned them? Who baptized them for remission of sins? Who ordained them to stand up as Peter? Of course they were baptized by the Baptists, and ordained by them, and yet they had now left them because they did not administer the true gospel. And it was plain that the Baptists could not claim the apostolic office by succession, in a regular, unbroken chain from the Apostles of old, preserving the gospel in its purity, and the ordinances unchanged, from the very fact that they were now living in the perversion of some, and the entire neglect of others of these ordinances; this being the very ground of difference between the old Baptists and these Reformers.

Again, these Reformers claimed no new commission by revelation, or vision from the Lord, while they had not the least shadow of claim by succession.

It might be said, then, with propriety: "Peter I know, and Paul I know, but who are ye?"

However, we were thankful for even the forms of truth, as none could claim the power, and authority, and gifts of the Holy Ghost—at least so far as we knew.

After hearing Mr. Rigdon several times, I came out, with a number of others, and embraced the truths which he taught. We were organized into a society, and frequently met for public worship.

About this time I took it upon me to impart to my neighbors, from time to time, both in public and in private, the light I had received from the Scriptures concerning the gospel, and also concerning the fulfilment of the things spoken by the holy prophets. I did not claim any authority as a minister; I felt the lack in this respect; but I felt in duty bound to enlighten mankind, so far as God had enlightened me.

At the commencement of 1830, I felt drawn out in an extraordinary manner to search the prophets, and to pray for an understanding of the same. My prayers were soon answered, even beyond my expectations; the prophecies of the holy prophets were opened to my view; I began to understand the things which were coming on the earth—the restoration of Israel, the coming of the Messiah, and the glory that should follow. I was so astonished at the darkness of myself and mankind on these subjects that I could exclaim with the prophet: surely, *"darkness covers the earth, and gross darkness the people."*

I was all swallowed up in these things. I felt constrained to devote

Jared Pratt, father of
Parley P. Pratt

William Dickinson Pratt, born
1802, brother of Parley P. Pratt

Apostle Parley P. Pratt

Apostle Orson Pratt Sr.,
brother of Parley P. Pratt

Nelson Pratt, brother
of Parley P. Pratt

my time in enlightening my fellow men on these important truths, and in warning them to prepare for the coming of the Lord.

My brother William, who journeyed to the West with me in my seventeenth year, had now been missing to the family for five years, and was supposed to be dead. About the time he disappeared and was lost sight of, he was known to leave the city of New York, where he had been employed, and to pass up the Hudson on a steamer. He was heard of no more; and, as a notice appeared in the papers of the same date that a young gentleman by the name of William Pratt was drowned in the Hudson, on his way up the river, our parents and the family had given him up for lost.

One morning, as I was absent from home on business, about two miles distant, I heard of him; and that he was then residing about ten miles from me. On hearing this I ran nearly the whole distance on foot, and in about two hours had him by the hand. He was much surprised, although he had heard of a man of my name living in the neighborhood; but could not believe it was me. We had each of us taken our chance amid the hardships and toils of a new country for years, and at last found ourselves together about six hundred miles from our starting point.

This was a joyful and unexpected meeting of two brothers. He immediately accompanied me home, and was introduced to my wife and our little farm in the wilderness, where we spent some days together. He admired my wife; but above all my farm. "Brother Parley," said he, "how have you done all this? When we were last together you had no wife, no farm, no house, no orchard, and now you are here with everything smiling around you." I replied that hard work had accomplished it all. And, continued I, we are now about to leave this quiet home which we have toiled so hard to make, and perhaps, never see it again. "How so?" said he, with much surprise, and somewhat of disappointment. I then unfolded to him the gospel and prophecies as they had been opened to me, and told him that the spirit of these things had wrought so powerfully on my mind of late that I could not rest; that I could no longer be contented to dwell in quiet and retirement on my farm, while I had light to impart to mankind, of which I knew they were in a great measure ignorant. "But," said he, "if I had fifty acres of land, a comfortable house, a fine orchard, a beautiful garden, with meadow land, grain, and above all, such beautiful flowers and so valuable a housekeeper as you have, and all these things the work of our own hands, I am sure I would stay and enjoy the same while I lived; and the world might go on its own jog, and its own way, for all me. Besides, how are you to get your living? This is your all; you have toiled for years to obtain it, and why not now continue to enjoy it?" "William," said I, "I see plainly you know but little of my circumstances—of the changes which have taken place with me since we parted five years ago, nor how vastly wealthy I have become within that time. Why, sir, I have bank bills enough, on the very best institutions in the world, to sustain myself and family while we live."

"Indeed," said he, "well, I should like to see some of them; I hope they are genuine." "Certainly," I replied, "there is no doubt of that. They are true bills and founded on capital that will never fail, though heaven and earth should pass away. Of this I will convince you in a moment."

I then unlocked my treasury and drew from thence a large pocket book, full of promissory notes like the following: "*Whoever shall forsake father or mother, brethren or sisters, houses or lands, wife or children, for my sake and the gospel's, shall receive an hundred fold in this life, and in the world to come life everlasting.*" "*If ye abide in me, and my words abide in you, you shall ask what you will in my name and I will give it you.*" "*All things are possible to him that believeth.*"

"Now, William," said I, "are these the words of Jesus Christ, or are they not?" "They certainly are," said he, "I always believed the New Testament."

"Then you admit they are genuine bills?"

"I do."

"Is the signer able to meet his engagements?"

"He certainly is."

"Is he willing?"

"He is."

"Well, then, I am going to fulfil the conditions to the letter on my part. I feel called upon by the Holy Ghost to forsake my house and home for the gospel's sake; and I will do it, placing both feet firm on these promises with nothing else to rely upon."

"If I sink, they are false."

"If I am sustained, they are true. I will put them to the test. Experiment shall now establish the truth of Christ's promises, or the truth of infidelity."

"Well," said he, "try it, if you will; but, for my part, although I always believed the Bible, I would not dare believe it *literally*, and really stand upon its promises, with no other prop."

We parted. He to his business, I to my preparations for a mission which should only end with my life.

In August, 1830, I had closed my business, completed my arrangements, and we bid adieu to our wilderness home and never saw it afterwards.

On settling up, at a great sacrifice of property, we had about ten dollars left in cash. With this small sum, we launched forth into the wide world, determining first to visit our native place, on our mission, and then such other places as I might be led to by the Holy Spirit.

We made our way to Cleveland, 30 miles. We then took passage on a schooner for Buffalo, a distance of 200 miles. We had a fair wind, and the captain, being short of hands, gave me the helm, the sails being all set, and turned in. I steered the vessel the most of the day, with no other person on deck. Of course, our passage cost us little besides my labor. Landing in Buffalo, we engaged our passage for Albany on a canal boat, distance 360 miles. This, including board, cost all our money and some articles of clothing.

Arriving at Rochester, I informed my wife that, notwithstanding our passage being paid through the whole distance, yet I must leave the boat and her to pursue her passage to our friends; while I would stop awhile in this region. Why, I did not know; but so it was plainly manifest by the Spirit to me. I said to her, "we part for a season; go and visit our friends in our native place; I will come soon, but how soon I know not; for I have a work to do in this region of country, and what it is, or how long it will take to perform it, I know not; but I will come when it is performed."

My wife would have objected to this; but she had seen the hand of God so plainly manifest in His dealings with me many times, that she dare not oppose the things manifest to me by His spirit.

She, therefore, consented; and I accompanied her as far as Newark, a small town upwards of 100 miles from Buffalo, and then took leave of her, and of the boat.

It was early in the morning, just at the dawn of day, I walked ten miles into the country, and stopped to breakfast with a Mr. Wells. I proposed to preach in the evening. Mr. Wells readily accompanied me through the neighborhood to visit the people, and circulate the appointment.

We visited an old Baptist deacon by the name of Hamlin. After hearing of our appointment for evening, he began to tell of a *book*, a STRANGE BOOK, a VERY STRANGE BOOK! in his possession, which had been just published. This book, he said, purported to have been originally written on plates either of gold or brass, by a branch of the

The Three Witnesses to the Book of Mormon. An angel of God came down from heaven and presented before these three men the plates of the Book of Mormon and commanded that they give their testimony as a witness to the world that the Book of Mormon is true.

tribes of Israel; and to have been discovered and translated by a young man near Palmyra, in the State of New York, by the aid of visions, or the ministry of angels. I inquired of him how or where the book was to be obtained. He promised me the perusal of it, at his house the next day, if I would call. I felt a strange interest in the book. I preached that evening to a small audience, who appeared to be interested in the truths which I endeavored to unfold to them in a clear and lucid manner from the Scriptures. Next morning I called at his house, where, for the first time, my eyes beheld the "BOOK OF MORMON"—that book of books—that record which reveals the antiquities of the "New World" back to the remotest ages, and which unfolds the destiny of its people and the world for all time to come;—that Book which contains the fulness of the gospel of a crucified and risen Redeemer;—that Book which reveals a lost remnant of Joseph, and which was the principal means, in the hands of God, of directing the entire course of my future life.

I opened it with eagerness, and read its title page. I then read the testimony of several witnesses in relation to the manner of its being found and translated. After this I commenced its contents by course. I read all day; eating was a burden, I had no desire for food; sleep was a burden when the night came, for I preferred reading to sleep.

As I read, the spirit of the Lord was upon me, and I knew and comprehended that the book was true, as plainly and manifestly as a man comprehends and knows that he exists. My joy was now full, as it were, and I rejoiced sufficiently to more than pay me for all the sorrows, sacrifices and toils of my life. I soon determined to see the young man who had been the instrument of its discovery and translation.

I accordingly visited the village of Palmyra, and inquired for the residence of Mr. Joseph Smith. I found it some two or three miles from the village. As I approached the house at the close of the day I overtook a man who was driving some cows, and inquired of him for Mr. Joseph Smith, the translator of the "Book of Mormon." He informed me that he now resided in Pennsylvania; some one hundred miles distant. I inquired for his father, or for any of the family. He told me that his father had gone a journey; but that his residence was a small house just before me; and, said he, I am his brother. It was Mr. Hyrum Smith. I informed him of the interest I felt in the Book, and of my desire to learn more about it. He welcomed me to his house, and we spent the night together; for neither of us felt disposed to sleep. We conversed most of the night, during which I unfolded to him much of my experience in my search after truth, and my success so far; together with that which I felt was lacking,

Hyrum Smith, brother of the Prophet and the first Church member with whom Parley P. Pratt was privileged to converse on the restored gospel

viz: a commissioned priesthood, or apostleship to minister in the ordinances of God.

He also unfolded to me the particulars of the discovery of the Book; its translation; the rise of the Church of Latter-day Saints, and the commission of his brother Joseph, and others, by revelation and the ministering of angels, by which the apostleship and authority had been again restored to the earth. After duly weighing the whole matter in my mind I saw clearly that these things were true; and that myself and the whole world were without baptism, and without the ministry and ordinances of God; and that the whole world had been in this condition since the days that inspiration and revelation had ceased—in short, that this was a *new dispensation* or *commission*, in fulfilment of prophecy, and for the restoration of Israel, and to prepare the way before the second coming of the Lord.

In the morning I was compelled to take leave of this worthy man and his family—as I had to hasten back a distance of thirty miles, on foot, to fulfil an appointment in the evening. As we parted he kindly presented me with a copy of the Book of Mormon. I had not yet completed its perusal, and was glad indeed to possess a copy of my own. I travelled on a few miles, and, stopping to rest, I commenced again to read the book. To my great joy I found that Jesus Christ, in his glorified resurrected body, had appeared to the remnant of Joseph on the continent of America, soon after his resurrection and ascension into heaven; and that he also administered, in person, to the ten lost tribes; and that through his personal ministry in these countries his gospel was revealed and written in countries and among nations entirely unknown to the Jewish apostles.

Thus revealed, written, handed down and preserved, till revealed in this age by the angels of God, it had, of course, escaped the corruptions of the great and abominable church; and been preserved in purity.

This discovery greatly enlarged my heart, and filled my soul with joy and gladness. I esteemed the Book, or the information contained in it, more than all the riches of the world. Yes; I verily believe that I would not at that time have exchanged the knowledge I then possessed, for a legal title to all the beautiful farms, houses, villages and property which passed in review before me, on my journey through one of the most flourishing settlements of western New York.

Surely, thought I, Jesus had *other sheep*, as he said to his Apostles of old; and here they were, in the wilderness of the world called new. And they heard the voice of the Good Shepherd of Israel; and he brought them to his fold. Truly, thought I, he was not sent (in person) save to the lost sheep of the house of Israel, as he told the woman of Canaan; and here were a portion of them. Truly, thought I, the angels sung with the spirit and with the understanding when they declared: "*We bring you glad tidings of great joy, which shall be to* ALL PEOPLE."

In his mortal tabernacle he confined his ministry and that of his Apostles to the land of Judea; but afterwards, released from the bonds of mortal life, or rather death, and clothed with an immortal body, and with organs strong and lasting as the immortal mind, he possessed all power in heaven and on earth; he was then enabled to extend his ministry to heaven, earth or hell. He could take the wings of the morning, and, with the speed of light, make his way to the Heaven of Heavens; and converse and counsel among the sons of God; or receive counsel from his Father in Heaven; or, leaving again the starry worlds, he could descend to the dark and gloomy abodes of the spirits in prison and preach to them the gospel—bursting off their shackles and unlocking their prison doors; while these once dark abodes were now brilliant with light, and, instead of prison groans, were heard joyful acclamations of deliverance to the captive, and the opening of the prison to them that are bound; or coming again to visit the earth, he could soar away beyond the waves and tempests, which had before set bounds to the geographical knowledge of man, and stood up as an impregnable barrier to the intercourse of nations; and there, in other tribes and tongues, make known the riches of his grace, and his *triumph* over death.

And when ages had passed, and nations slumbered in the dust—when cruelty and bloodshed had blotted almost every trace of priesthood and apostleship from the earth; when saints had been worn out and overcome; times, laws and ordinances changed; the Bible itself robbed of its plainness; and all things darkened and corrupted; a pure and faithful record of his ministry to other nations is forthcoming from among the archives of the dead, to reveal the "*mystery of iniquity;*" to speak, as with a voice of thunder, in rebuking the evil and revealing the fulness of the gospel. Such was the Book of Mormon—such its effect upon the startling nations.

Chapter 6

Having rested awhile and perused this sacred book by the roadside, I again walked on.

In the evening I arrived in time to fill my appointment. I met a crowded house, and laid before them many interesting truths, which were listened to with deep interest.

The next evening I had another appointment, and the people came out in great numbers, and were filled with the spirit of interest and inquiry.

They urged me very much to continue my discourses among them; but I felt to minister no more till I had attended to some important duties for myself. I had now found men on earth commissioned to preach, baptize, ordain to the ministry, etc., and I determined to obey the fulness of the gospel without delay. I should have done so at the first interview with Elder Hyrum Smith; but these two appointments were already out, and thirty miles' travel required all the time I had.

I now returned immediately to Hyrum Smith's residence, and demanded baptism at his hands. I tarried with him one night, and the next day we walked some twenty-five miles to the residence of Mr. Whitmer, in Seneca County. Here we arrived in the evening, and found a most welcome reception.

This was the family, several of whose names were attached to the Book of Mormon as witnesses—Mr. Joseph Smith having translated much of the book in Whitmer's chamber.

I found the little branch of the Church in this place full of joy, faith, humility and charity. We rested that night, and on the next day, being

Oliver Cowdery, who received his apostleship from Peter, James, and John, and who acted as scribe for Joseph Smith the Prophet in the translation of the Book of Mormon. Parley P. Pratt was baptized by and received the priesthood from Oliver Cowdery.

Orson Pratt, Sr.

Apostle Orson Pratt, brother and convert of Parley P. Pratt

about the lst of September, 1830, I was baptized by the hand of an Apostle of the Church of Jesus Christ, by the name of Oliver Cowdery. This took place in Seneca Lake, a beautiful and transparent sheet of water in Western New York.

A meeting was held the same evening, and after singing a hymn and prayer, Elder Cowdery and others proceeded to lay their hands upon my head in the name of Jesus, for the gift of the Holy Ghost. After which I was ordained to the office of an Elder in the Church, which included authority to preach, baptize, administer the sacrament, administer the Holy Spirit, by the laying on of hands in the name of Jesus Christ and to take the lead of meetings of worship.

I now felt that I had authority in the ministry.

On the next Sabbath I preached to a large concourse of people, assembled at the house of a Mr. Burroughs. The Holy Ghost came upon me mightily. I spoke the word of God with power, reasoning out of the Scriptures and the Book of Mormon. The people were convinced, overwhelmed in tears, and four heads of families came forward expressing their faith, and were baptized.

My work was now completed, for which I took leave of my wife and the canal boat some two or three weeks previous.

I now took leave of the little branch of the church with which I had been associated, and pursued my journey to the land of my fathers and of my boyhood.

I found my wife in health and spirits, enjoying herself with her friends. I also found my father and mother, friends and kindred, and, among others, my good old aunt and cousins, at the old homestead, where I always found a welcome reception.

This was a pleasant and retired mountain valley, consisting of a beautiful farm and a small and convenient house, out-buildings, orchard, meadow, etc., encircled on the south, west and north with a curve of hills, consisting of farming lands and pasture, and their summits and bosoms partially clothed with a beautiful forest of pine and chestnut; while the scene opened to the southeast in a descending landscape to a beautiful vale of some miles in extent, filled with flourishing farms and dwellings, and watered by a winding stream; while far beyond stretched other hills and pine-clad mountains, and the spire of a church and a small town were seen nestling among the hills at two miles distance.

This was the residence of my aunt Van Cott, and the place where I had spent some of the happiest seasons of my youth. My aunt had three children—an only son, and two daughters. These were now in the bloom of early youth, and were fast advancing to a state of maturity. Her husband had died at an early day, after an illness of seven years; and here lived the widow and orphans, surrounded with peace and plenty, blooming with health, and smiling with innocence and joy. Retired from the throng of busy, boisterous life, and strangers to most of its woes, ills and corruptions, the stranger who happened there was welcome; the hungry were fed, the naked were clothed, and, above all, the kindred found a hearty reception. In short, it was a spot, in all respects, adapted to retirement and contemplation, where the poet and the novelist would find a thousand things to please the imagination, and to swell their favorite volumes.

In this visit to my native place, there was one family greatly missed by me. I felt keenly the disappointment at not seeing them—that of my old employer, Wm. S. Herrick. He had moved to the West, and his house was occupied by strangers.

I now commenced my labors in good earnest. I addressed crowded audiences almost every day, and the people, who had known me from a child, seemed astonished—knowing that I had had but little opportunity of acquiring knowledge by study; and while many were interested in the truth, some began to be filled with envy, and with a lying, persecuting spirit. My father, mother, aunt Van Cott, and many others, believed the truth in part; but my brother Orson, a youth of nineteen years, received it with all his heart, and was baptized at that time, and has ever since spent his days in the ministry.

It was during my labors in these parts, in the autumn of 1830, that a very singular and extraordinary sign was shown in the heavens, which I will here describe.

I had been on a visit to a singular people called Shakers, at New Lebanon, about seven miles from my aunt Van Cott's, and was returning that distance, on foot, on a beautiful evening of September. The sky was without a cloud; the stars shone out beautifully, and all nature seemed reposing in quiet, as I pursued my solitary way, wrapt in deep meditations on the predictions of the holy prophets; the signs of the times; the approaching advent of the Messiah, to reign on the earth, and the important revelations of the Book of Mormon; my heart filled with gratitude to God that He had opened the eyes of my understanding to receive the truth, and with sorrow for the blindness of those who lightly rejected the same, when my attention was aroused by a sudden appear-

Joseph Smith, the Prophet, Seer, and Revelator, and martyr, who received the apostleship from Peter, James, and John, and with whom Parley P. Pratt lay in chains while held prisoner in Richmond jail in Missouri

*The Sacred Grove in New York State, where God the Father and Jesus Christ
appeared to Joseph Smith when he was a boy of fourteen years of age*

ance of a brilliant light which shone around me, above the brightness of the sun. I cast my eyes upward to inquire from whence the light came, when I perceived a long chain of light extended in the heavens, very bright, and of a deep fiery red. It at first stood stationary in a horizontal position; at length bending in the center, the two ends approached each other with a rapid movement, so as to form an exact square. In this position it again remained stationary for some time, perhaps a minute, and then again the ends approached each other with the same rapidity, and again ceased to move, remaining stationary, for perhaps a minute, in the form of a compass; it then commenced a third movement in the same manner, and closed like the closing of a compass, the whole forming a straight line like a chain doubled. It again remained stationary for a minute, and then faded away.

I fell upon my knees in the street, and thanked the Lord for so marvelous a sign of the coming of the Son of Man.

Some persons may smile at this, and say that all these exact movements were by chance; but, for my part, I could as soon believe that the letters of the alphabet would be formed by chance, and be placed so as to spell my name, as to believe that these signs (known only to the wise) could be formed and shown forth by chance.

Renewed in spirit and filled with joy I now pursued my way, and arrived at my aunt Van Cott's, not weary, but refreshed with a long walk, and deep communion with myself and God.

Having lifted a warning voice to multitudes in all this region of country, I now took leave, and repaired again to the western part of New York, and to the body of the Church.

On our arrival, we found that brother Joseph Smith, the translator of the Book of Mormon, had returned from Pennsylvania to his father's residence in Manchester, near Palmyra, and here I had the pleasure of seeing him for the first time.

He received me with a hearty welcome, and with that frank and kind manner so universal with him in after years.

On Sunday we held meeting at his house; the two large rooms were filled with attentive listeners, and he invited me to preach. I did so, and afterwards listened with interest to a discourse from his own mouth, filled with intelligence and wisdom. We repaired from the meeting to the water's edge, and, at his request, I baptized several persons.

President Joseph Smith was in person tall and well built, strong and active; of a light complexion, light hair, blue eyes, very little beard, and of an expression peculiar to himself, on which the eye naturally rested with interest, and was never weary of beholding. His countenance was ever mild, affable, beaming with intelligence and benevolence; mingled with a look of interest and an unconscious smile, or cheerfulness, and entirely free from all restraint or affectation of gravity; and there was something connected with the serene and steady penetrating glance of his eye, as if he would penetrate the deepest abyss of the human heart, gaze into eternity, penetrate the heavens, and comprehend all worlds.

He possessed a noble boldness and independence of character; his manner was easy and familiar; his rebuke terrible as the lion; his benevolence unbounded as the ocean; his intelligence universal, and his language abounding in original eloquence peculiar to himself—not polished—not studied—not smoothed and softened by education and refined by art; but flowing forth in its own native simplicity, and profusely abounding in variety of subject and manner. He interested and edified, while, at the same time, he amused and entertained his audience; and none listened to him that were ever weary with his discourse. I have even known him to retain a congregation of willing and anxious listeners for many hours together, in the midst of cold or sunshine, rain or wind, while they were laughing at one moment and weeping the next. Even his most bitter enemies were generally overcome, if he could once get their ears.

I have known him when chained and surrounded with armed murderers and assassins who were heaping upon him every possible insult and abuse, rise up in the majesty of a son of God and rebuke them, in the name of Jesus Christ, till they quailed before him, dropped their weapons, and, on their knees, begged his pardon, and ceased their abuse.

In short, in him the characters of a Daniel and a Cyrus were wonderfully blended. The gifts, wisdom and devotion of a Daniel were united with the boldness, courage, temperance, perseverance and generosity of a Cyrus. And had he been spared a martyr's fate till mature manhood and age, he was certainly endued with powers and ability to have revolutionized the world in many respects, and to have transmitted to posterity a name associated with more brilliant and glorious acts than has yet fallen to the lot of mortal. As it is, his works will live to endless ages, and unnumbered millions yet unborn will mention his name with honor, as a noble instrument in the hands of God, who, during his short and youthful career, laid the foundation of that kingdom spoken of by

The Hill Cumorah, where the plates of the Book of Mormon were delivered by the Angel Moroni to the Prophet Joseph Smith

Daniel, the prophet, which should break in pieces all other kingdoms and stand forever.

But I will not forestall the reader. I have yet to speak of him in my history, under many and varying circumstances, in which I have necessarily been associated with him, up to the latest year of his life.

Chapter 7

It was now October, 1830. A revelation had been given through the mouth of this Prophet, Seer and Translator, in which Elders Oliver Cowdery, Peter Whitmer, Ziba Peterson and myself were appointed to go into the wilderness, through the western States, and to the Indian territory. Making arrangements for my wife in the family of the Whitmers, we took leave of our friends and the church late in October, and started on foot.

After travelling for some days we called on an Indian nation at or near Buffalo; and spent part of a day with them, instructing them in the knowledge of the record of their forefathers. We were kindly received, and much interest was manifested by them on hearing this news. We made a present of two copies of the Book of Mormon to certain of them who could read, and repaired to Buffalo. Thence we continued our journey, for about two hundred miles, and at length called on Mr. Rigdon, my former friend and instructor, in the Reformed Baptist Society. He received us cordially and entertained us with hospitality.

We soon presented him with a Book of Mormon, and related to him the history of the same. He was much interested, and promised a thorough perusal of the book.

We tarried in this region for some time, and devoted our time to the ministry, and visiting from house to house.

At length Mr. Rigdon and many others became convinced that they had no authority to minister in the ordinances of God; and that they had not been legally baptized and ordained. They, therefore, came forward and were baptized by us, and received the gift of the Holy Ghost by the laying on of hands, and prayer in the name of Jesus Christ.

The news of our coming was soon noised abroad, and the news of the discovery of the Book of Mormon and the marvelous events connected with it. The interest and excitement now became general in Kirtland, and in all the region round about. The people thronged us night and day, insomuch that we had no time for rest and retirement. Meetings were convened in different neighborhoods, and multitudes came together soliciting our attendance; while thousands flocked about us daily; some to be taught, some for curiosity, some to obey the gospel, and some to dispute or resist it.

In two or three weeks from our arrival in the neighborhood with the news, we had baptized one hundred and twenty-seven souls, and this number soon increased to one thousand. The disciples were filled with joy and gladness; while rage and lying was abundantly manifested by gainsayers; faith was strong, joy was great, and persecution heavy.

We proceeded to ordain Sidney Rigdon, Isaac Morley, John Murdock, Lyman Wight, Edward Partridge and many others to the ministry; and, leaving them to take care of the churches and to minister the gospel, we took leave of the saints and continued our journey.

Fifty miles west of Kirtland, we had occasion to pass through the neighborhood where I first settled in the wilderness, after my marriage. We found the people all excited with the news of the great work we had been the humble instruments of doing in Kirtland and vicinity. Some wished to learn and obey the fulness of the gospel—were ready to entertain us and hear us preach. Others were filled with envy, rage and lying.

We had stopped for the night at the house of Simeon Carter, by whom we were kindly received, and were in the act of reading to him and explaining the Book of Mormon, when there came a knock at the door, and an officer entered with a warrant from a magistrate by the name of Byington, to arrest me on a very frivolous charge. I dropped the Book of Mormon in Carter's house, and went with him some two miles, in a dark, muddy road; one of the brethren accompanied me. We arrived at the place of trial late in the evening; found false witnesses in attendance, and a Judge who boasted of his intention to thrust us into prison, for the purpose of testing the powers of our apostleship, as he called it; although I was only an Elder in the Church. The Judge boasting thus, and the witnesses being entirely false in their testimony, I concluded to make no defense, but to treat the whole matter with contempt.

I was soon ordered to prison, or to pay a sum of money which I had not in the world. It was now a late hour, and I was still retained in court, tantalized, abused and urged to settle the matter, to all of which I made

Sidney Rigdon, counselor of Joseph Smith the Prophet and convert of Parley P. Pratt.

no reply for some time. This greatly exhausted their patience. It was near midnight. I now called on brother Petersen to sing a hymn in the court. We sung, "O how happy are they." This exasperated them still more, and they pressed us greatly to settle the business, by paying the money.

I then observed as follows: "May it please the court, I have one proposal to make for a final settlement of the things that seem to trouble you. It is this: if the witnesses who have given testimony in the case will repent of their false swearing, and the magistrate of his unjust and wicked judgment and of his persecution, blackguardism and abuse, and all kneel down together, we will pray for you, that God might forgive you in these matters."

"My big bull dog pray for me," says that Judge.

"The devil help us," exclaimed another.

They now urged me for some time to pay the money; but got no further answer.

The court adjourned, and I was conducted to a public house over the way, and locked in till morning; the prison being some miles distant.

In the morning the officer appeared and took me to breakfast; this over, we sat waiting in the inn for all things to be ready to conduct me to prison. In the meantime my fellow travellers came past on their journey, and called to see me. I told them in an undertone to pursue their journey and leave me to manage my own affairs, promising to overtake them soon. They did so.

After sitting awhile by the fire in charge of the officer, I requested to step out. I walked out into the public square accompanied by him. Said I, "Mr. Peabody, are you good at a race?" "No," said he, "but my big bull dog is, and he has been trained to assist me in my office these several years; he will take any man down at my bidding." "Well, Mr. Peabody, you compelled me to go a mile, I have gone with you two miles. You have given me an opportunity to preach, sing, and have also entertained me with lodging and breakfast. I must now go on my journey; if you are good at a race you can accompany me. I thank you for all your kindness—good day, sir."

I then started on my journey, while he stood amazed and not able to step one foot before the other. Seeing this, I halted, turned to him and again invited him to a race. He still stood amazed. I then renewed my exertions, and soon increased my speed to something like that of a deer. He did not awake from his astonishment sufficiently to start in pursuit till I had gained, perhaps, two hundred yards. I had already leaped a fence, and was making my way through a field to the forest on the right of the road. He now came hallooing after me, and shouting to his dog to seize me. The dog, being one of the largest I ever saw, came close on my footsteps with all his fury; the officer behind still in pursuit, clapping his hands and hallooing, "stu-boy, stu-boy—take him—watch—lay hold of him, I say—down with him," and pointing his finger in the direction I was running. The dog was fast overtaking me, and in the act of leaping upon me, when, quick as lightning, the thought struck me, to assist the officer, in sending the dog with all fury to the forest a little distance before me. I pointed my finger in that direction, clapped my hands, and shouted in imitation of the officer. The dog hastened past me with redoubled speed towards the forest; being urged by the officer and myself, and both of us running in the same direction.

Gaining the forest, I soon lost sight of the officer and dog, and have not seen them since. I took a back course, crossed the road, took round into the wilderness, on the left, and made the road again in time to cross a bridge over Vermilion River, where I was hailed by half a dozen men, who had been anxiously waiting our arrival to that part of the country, and who urged me very earnestly to stop and preach. I told them that I could not then do it, for an officer was on my track. I passed on six miles further, through mud and rain, and overtook the brethren, and preached the same evening to a crowded audience, among whom we were well entertained.

The Book of Mormon, which I dropped at the house of Simeon Carter, when taken by the officer, was by these circumstances left with him. He read it with attention. It wrought deeply upon his mind, and he went fifty miles to the church we had left in Kirtland, and was there baptized and ordained an Elder. He then returned to his home and commenced to preach and baptize. A church of about sixty members was soon organized in the place where I had played such a trick of deception on the dog.

We now pursued our journey for some days, and at length arrived in Sandusky, in the western part of Ohio. Here resided a tribe, or nation of Indians, called Wyandots, on whom we called, and with whom we spent several days. We were well received, and had an opportunity of laying before them the record of their forefathers, which we did. They rejoiced in the tidings, bid us God speed, and desired us to write to them in relation to our success among the tribes further west, who had already removed to the Indian territory, where these expected soon to go.

Taking an affectionate leave of this people, we continued our journey to Cincinnati. In this city we spent several days, and preached to many of the people, but without much success. About the 20th of December we took passage on a steamer for St. Louis. In a few days we arrived at the mouth of the Ohio, and finding the river blocked with ice, the boat did not proceed further. We therefore landed and pursued our journey on foot for two hundred miles, to the neighborhood of St. Louis.

We halted for a few days in Illinois, about twenty miles from St. Louis, on account of a dreadful storm of rain and snow, which lasted for a week or more, during which the snow fell in some places near three feet deep. Although in the midst of strangers, we were kindly entertained, found many friends, and preached to large congregations in several neighborhoods.

In the beginning of 1831 we renewed our journey; and, passing through St. Louis and St. Charles, we travelled on foot for three hundred miles through vast prairies and through trackless wilds of snow—no beaten road; houses few and far between; and the bleak northwest wind always blowing in our faces with a keenness which would almost take the skin off the face. We travelled for whole days, from morning till night, without a house or fire, wading in snow to the knees at every step, and the cold so intense that the snow did not melt on the south side of the houses, even in the mid-day sun, for nearly six weeks. We carried on our backs our changes of clothing, several books, and corn bread and raw pork. We often ate our frozen bread and pork by the way, when the bread would be so frozen that we could not bite or penetrate any part of it but the outside crust.

After much fatigue and some suffering we all arrived in Independence, in the county of Jackson, on the extreme western frontiers of Missouri, and of the United States.

This was about fifteen hundred miles from where we started, and we had performed most of the journey on foot, through a wilderness country, in the worst season of the year, occupying about four months, during which we had preached the gospel to tens of thousands of Gentiles and two nations of Indians; baptizing, confirming and organizing many hundreds of people into churches of Latter-day Saints.

This was the first mission performed by the Elders of the Church in any of the States west of New York, and we were the first members of the same which were ever on this frontier.

Chapter 8

Two of our number now commenced work as tailors in the village of Independence, while the others crossed the frontier line and commenced a mission among the Lamanites, or Indians.

Passing through the tribe of Shawnees we tarried one night with them, and the next day crossed the Kansas river and entered among the Delawares. We immediately inquired for the residence of the principal Chief, and were soon introduced to an aged and venerable looking man, who had long stood at the head of the Delawares, and been looked up to as the Great Grandfather, or Sachem of ten nations or tribes.

He was seated on a sofa of furs, skins and blankets, before a fire in the center of his lodge; which was a comfortable cabin, consisting of two large rooms.

His wives were neatly dressed, partly in calicoes and partly in skins; and wore a vast amount of silver ornaments. As we entered his cabin he took us by the hand with a hearty welcome, and then motioned us to be seated on a pleasant seat of blankets, or robes. His wives, at his bidding, set before us a tin pan full of beans and corn boiled up together, which proved to be good eating; although three of us made use alternately of the same wooden spoon.

There was an interpreter present and through him we commenced to make known our errand, and to tell him of the Book of Mormon. We asked him to call the council of his nation together and give us a hearing in full. He promised to consider on it till next day, in the meantime recommending us to a certain Mr. Pool for entertainment; this was their blacksmith, employed by government.

The man entertained us kindly and comfortably. Next morning we again called on Mr. Anderson, the old chief, and explained to him something of the Book. He was at first unwilling to call his council; made several excuses, and finally refused; as he had ever been opposed to the introduction of missionaries among his tribe.

We continued the conversation a little longer, till he at last began to understand the nature of the Book. He then changed his mind; became suddenly interested, and requested us to proceed no further with our conversation till he could call a council. He despatched a messenger, and in about an hour had some forty men collected around us in his lodge, who, after shaking us by the hand, were seated in silence; and in a grave and dignified manner awaited the announcement of what we had to offer. The chief then requested us to proceed; or rather, begin where we began before, and to complete our communication. Elder Cowdery then commenced as follows:

"Aged Chief and Venerable Council of the Delaware nation; we are glad of this opportunity to address you as our red brethren and friends. We have travelled a long distance from towards the rising sun to bring you glad news; we have travelled the wilderness, crossed the deep and wide rivers, and waded in the deep snows, and in the face of the storms of winter, to communicate to you great knowledge which has lately come to our ears and hearts; and which will do the red man good as well as the pale face.

"Once the red men were many; they occupied the country from sea to sea—from the rising to the setting sun; the whole land was theirs; the Great Spirit gave it to them, and no pale faces dwelt among them. But now they are few in numbers; their possessions are small, and the pale faces are many.

"Thousands of moons ago, when the red men's forefathers dwelt in peace and possessed this whole land, the Great Spirit talked with them, and revealed His law and His will, and much knowledge to their wise men and prophets. This they wrote in a Book; together with their history, and the things which should befall their children in the latter days.

"This Book was written on plates of gold, and handed down from father to son for many ages and generations.

"It was then that the people prospered, and were strong and mighty; they cultivated the earth; built buildings and cities, and abounded in all good things, as the pale faces now do.

"But they became wicked; they killed one another and shed much blood; they killed their prophets and wise men, and sought to destroy the Book. The Great Spirit became angry, and would speak to them no more; they had no more good and wise dreams; no more visions; no more angels sent among them by the Great Spirit; and the Lord commanded Mormon and Moroni, their last wise men and prophets, to hide the Book in the earth, that it might be preserved in safety, and be found and made known in the latter day to the pale faces who should possess the land; that they might again make it known to the red man; in order to restore them to the knowledge of the will of the Great Spirit and to His favor. And if the red man would then receive this Book and learn the things written in it, and do according thereunto, they should cease to fight and kill one another; should become one people; cultivate the earth in peace, in common with the pale faces, who were willing to believe and obey the same Book, and be good men and live in peace.

"Then should the red men become great, and have plenty to eat and good clothes to wear, and should be in favor with the Great Spirit and be his children, while he would be their Great Father, and talk with them, and raise up prophets and wise and good men amongst them again, who should teach them many things.

"This Book, which contained these things, was hid in the earth by Moroni, in a hill called by him, Cumorah, which hill is now in the State of New York, near the village of Palmyra, in Ontario County.

"In that neighborhood there lived a young man named Joseph Smith, who prayed to the Great Spirit much, in order that he might know the truth; and the Great Spirit sent an angel to him, and told him where this Book was hid by Moroni; and commanded him to go and get it. He accordingly went to the place, and dug in the earth, and found the Book written on golden plates.

"But it was written in the language of the forefathers of the red man; therefore this young man, being a pale face, could not understand it; but the angel told him and showed him, and gave him knowledge of the language, and how to interpret the Book. So he interpreted it into the language of the pale faces, and wrote it on paper, and caused it to be printed, and published thousands of copies of among them; and then sent us to the red men to bring some copies of it to them, and to tell them this news. So we have now come from him, and here is a copy of the Book, which we now present to our red friend, the chief of the Delawares, and which we hope he will cause to be read and known among his tribe; it will do them good."

We then presented him with a Book of Mormon.

There was a pause in the council, and some conversation in their own tongue, after which the chief made the following reply:

"We feel truly thankful to our white friends who have come so far, and been at such pains to tell us good news, and especially this new news concerning the Book of our forefathers; it makes us glad in here"—placing his hand on his heart.

"It is now winter, we are new settlers in this place; the snow is deep, our cattle and horses are dying, our wigwams are poor; we have much to do in the spring—to build houses, and fence and make farms; but we will build a council house, and meet together, and you shall read to us and teach us more concerning the Book of our fathers and the will of the Great Spirit."

We again lodged at Mr. Pool's, told him of the Book, had a very pleasant interview with him, and he became a believer and advocate for the Book, and served as an interpreter.

We continued for several days to instruct the old chief and many of his tribe. The interest became more and more intense on their part, from day to day, until at length nearly the whole tribe began to feel a spirit of inquiry and excitement on the subject.

We found several among them who could read, and to them we gave copies of the Book, explaining to them that it was the Book of their forefathers.

Some began to rejoice exceedingly, and took great pains to tell the news to others, in their own language.

The excitement now reached the frontier settlements in Missouri, and stirred up the jealousy and envy of the Indian agents and sectarian missionaries to that degree that we were soon ordered out of the Indian country as disturbers of the peace; and even threatened with the military in case of non-compliance.

We accordingly departed from the Indian country, and came over the line, and commenced laboring in Jackson County, Missouri, among the whites. We were well received, and listened to by many; and some were baptized and added to the Church.

Thus ended our first Indian Mission, in which we had preached the gospel in its fulness, and distributed the record of their forefathers among three tribes, viz: the Catteraugus Indians, near Buffalo, N. Y., the Wyandots of Ohio, and the Delawares west of Missouri.

We trust that at some future day, when the servants of God go forth in power to the remnant of Joseph, some precious seed will be found growing in their hearts, which was sown by us in that early day.

It was now the 14th of February, 1831. The cold north wind which had blown for several weeks, accompanied with very severe weather, had begun to give place to a milder breeze from the south; and the deep snows were fast settling down, with every prospect of returning spring.

Elders Cowdery, Whitmer, Peterson, myself, and F. G. Williams, who accompanied us from Kirtland, now assembled in Independence, Jackson County, Missouri, and came to the conclusion that one of our number had better return to the church in Ohio, and perhaps to head-quarters in New York, in order to communicate with the Presidency, report ourselves, pay a visit to the numerous churches we had organized on our outward journey, and also to procure more books.

For this laborious enterprise I was selected by the voice of my four brethren. I accordingly took leave of them, and of our friends in that country, and started on foot.

In nine days I arrived at St. Louis, distance three hundred miles. It was now the latter part of February; the snow had disappeared, the rivers were breaking up, and the whole country inundated as it were with mud and water. I spent a few days with a friend in the country, at the same place we had tarried on the way out; and then took a steamer in St. Louis bound for Cincinnati, where I landed in safety after a passage of one week. From Cincinnati I travelled on foot to Strongville, Ohio, forty miles from Kirtland.

This last walk consisted of some two hundred and fifty miles, over very bad, muddy road; and for some days I had found myself much fatigued, and quite out of health. Hearing of some brethren in Strongville, I determined to inquire them out, and try their hospitality to a sick and weary stranger without making myself known.

I accordingly approached the house of an old gentleman by the name of Coltrin, about sundown, and inquired if they could entertain a weary stranger who had no money. The old gentleman cast his eyes upon me, and beheld a weary, weather-beaten traveller; soiled with the toil of a long journey; besmeared with mud, eyes inflamed with pain, long beard, and a visage lengthened by sickness and extreme fatigue. After a moment's hesitation he bade me welcome, and invited me into his house. Several ladies were at tea. I addressed them as a stranger who had come to partake of their hospitality for the night.

They received me with a smile of welcome, and immediately insisted on my sitting down to tea, during which something like the following conversation took place:

"Stranger, where are you from? you certainly look weary; you must have travelled a long distance!"

"Yes; I am from beyond the frontiers of Missouri; a distance of twelve hundred miles."

"Ah, indeed! Did you hear anything of the four great prophets out that way?"

"Prophets! What prophets?"

"Why, four men—strange men—who came through this country and preached, and baptized hundreds of people; and, after ordaining Elders and organizing churches, they continued on westward, as we suppose, to the frontiers on a mission to the Indians; and we have never heard from them since. But the great work commenced by them still rolls on. It commenced last fall in Kirtland, and has spread for a hundred miles around; thousands have embraced it, and among others ourselves and many in this neighborhood."

"But what did they preach? And why do you call them prophets?"

"Why they opened the Scriptures in a wonderful manner; showed the people plainly of many things to come; opened the doctrine of Christ, as we never understood it before; and, among other things, they introduced a very extraordinary Book, which, they said, was an ancient record of the forefathers of the Indian tribes."

"How were they dressed, and in what style did they travel?"

"They were dressed plainly and comely, very neat in their persons, and each one wore a hat of a drab color, low round crown and broad brim, after the manner of the Shakers, so it is said; for we had not the privilege of seeing them ourselves.

"However, these fashioned hats were not a peculiarity of this people; but were given to each of them by the Shakers, at the time they passed through this country; so they wore them. As to their style of travelling, they sometimes go on foot, sometimes in a carriage, and sometimes, perhaps, by water; but they provide themselves with neither purse nor scrip for their journey, neither shoes nor two coats apiece."

"Well, from your description of these four men I think I have seen them on the frontiers of Missouri. They had commenced a mission in the Indian territory; but were compelled by the United States agents, influenced, no doubt, by missionaries, to depart from the Indian country, although well received by the Indians themselves."

"You saw them, then?"

"I did."

"Were they well?"

"I believe they were all in good health and spirits."

"Will they return soon? O, who would not give the world to see them!"

"Well, I am one of them, and the others you may, perhaps, see."

"You one of them! God bless you. What is your name?"

"My name is Parley P. Pratt, one of the four men you have described, but not much of a prophet; and as to a sight of me in my present plight, I think it would not be worth half a world."

The rest of the conversation I cannot write, for all spoke, all laughed, and all rejoiced at once.

The next morning I found myself unable to rise from my bed, being severely attacked with the measles.

I came near dying, and was confined for one or two weeks among them, being scarcely able to raise my head. I was watched over night and day, and had all the care that a man could have in his father's house.

As I recovered in part, being still very weak, I was provided with a horse, on which I arrived at Kirtland.

Hundreds of the saints now crowded around to welcome me, and to inquire after my brethren whom I had left in Missouri.

Here also I again met President Joseph Smith, who had, during our absence, come up from the State of New York.

I found the churches in Ohio had increased to more than a thousand members, and those in New York to several hundred.

I also heard from my wife, from whom I had been absent about six months. The news was that the whole Church in the State of New York, including herself (for she had joined during my absence), was about to remove to Ohio in the opening spring. I, therefore, was advised to proceed no farther eastward, but to await their arrival.

After visiting the saints a few days, I commenced to labor with my hands; but the Lord would not suffer me to continue long in this occupation.

Some time in March, I was commanded of the Lord, in connection with S. Rigdon and L. Copley, to visit a people called the Shakers,* and preach the gospel unto them.

We fulfilled this mission, as we were commanded, in a settlement of this strange people, near Cleveland, Ohio; but they utterly refused to hear or obey the gospel. After this I paid a visit to the churches round about Kirtland.

See Doctrine and Covenants, section 49.

As I went forth among the different branches, some very strange spiritual operations were manifested, which were disgusting, rather than edifying. Some persons would seem to swoon away, and make unseemly gestures, and be drawn or disfigured in their countenances. Others would fall into ecstacies, and be drawn into contortions, cramp, fits, etc. Others would seem to have visions and revelations, which were not edifying, and which were not congenial to the doctrine and spirit of the gospel. In short, a false and lying spirit seemed to be creeping into the Church.

All these things were new and strange to me, and had originated in the Church during our absence, and previous to the arrival of President Joseph Smith from New York.

Feeling our weakness and inexperience, and lest we should err in judgment concerning these spiritual phenomena, myself, John Murdock, and several other Elders, went to Joseph Smith, and asked him to inquire of the Lord concerning these spirits or manifestations.

After we had joined in prayer in his translating room, he dictated in our presence the following revelation:—(Each sentence was uttered slowly and very distinctly, and with a pause between each, sufficiently long for it to be recorded, by an ordinary writer, in long hand.

This was the manner in which all his written revelations were dictated and written. There was never any hesitation, reviewing, or reading back, in order to keep the run of the subject; neither did any of these communications undergo revisions, interlinings, or corrections. As he dictated them so they stood, so far as I have witnessed; and I was present to witness the dictation of several communications of several pages each.

This inquiry was made and the answer given in May, 1831.)

Chapter 9

REVELATION ON FALSE SPIRITS—MINISTRY AMONG THE CHURCHES—REMARKABLE MIRACLE OF HEALING—ARRIVAL OF EMIGRANT SAINTS FROM NEW YORK—SEVERE DISAPPOINTMENT.

"Hearken, O ye Elders of my Church, and give ear, to the voice of the living God; attend to the words of wisdom which shall be given unto you, according as ye have asked and are agreed, as touching the Church, and the spirits which have gone abroad in the earth. Behold, verily I say unto you, that there are many spirits which are false spirits, which have gone forth in the earth, deceiving the world; and also Satan hath sought to deceive you, that he might overthrow you.

"Behold, I, the Lord, have looked upon you, and have seen abominations in the Church that possess my name; but blessed are they who are faithful and endure, whether in life or in death; for they shall inherit eternal life. But woe unto them that are deceivers and hypocrites, for, thus saith the Lord, I will bring them to judgment.

"Behold, I say unto you, there are hypocrites among you, who have deceived some, which has given the adversary power; but, behold, such shall be reclaimed; but the hypocrites shall be detected and cut off, either in life or in death, even as I will; and woe unto them who are cut off from my Church, for the same are overcome of the world; wherefore, let every man beware, lest he do that which is not in truth and righteousness before me.

"And now come, saith the Lord, by the Spirit, unto the Elders of His Church, and let us reason together, that ye may understand: Let us reason—even as a man reasoneth—one with another, face to face; now, when a man reasoneth, he is understood of man, because he reasoneth as a man; even so will I, the Lord, reason with you, that you may understand: wherefore, I, the Lord, asketh you this question, unto what were ye ordained? To preach my gospel by the Spirit, even the Comforter which was sent forth to teach the truth; and then received ye spirits

49

which ye could not understand, and received them to be of God, and in this are ye justified? Behold, ye shall answer this question yourselves; nevertheless, I will be merciful unto you; he that is weak among you, hereafter, shall be made strong.

"Verily, I say unto you, he that is ordained of me and sent forth to preach the word of truth by the Comforter, in the spirit of truth, doth he preach it by the spirit of truth, or some other way? And if it be by some other way, it be not of God. And, again, he that receiveth the word of truth, doth he receive it by the spirit of truth, or some other way? If it be some other way, it be not of God; therefore, why is it that ye cannot understand, and know that he that receiveth the word by the spirit of truth, receiveth it as it is preached by the spirit of truth?

"Wherefore, he that preacheth and he that receiveth, understandeth one another, and both are edified and rejoice together; and that which doth not edify, is not of God, and is darkness; that which is of God is light, and he that receiveth light and continueth in God, receiveth more light; and that light groweth brighter and brighter until the perfect day. And, again, verily I say unto you, and I say it that you may know the truth, that you may chase darkness from among you; for he that is ordained of God and sent forth, the same is appointed to be the greatest, notwithstanding he is least, and the servant of all; wherefore, he is possessor of all things, for all things are subject unto him, both in Heaven and on the earth; the life and the light, the spirit and the power sent forth by the will of the Father through Jesus Christ, His Son; but no man is possessor of all things, except he be purified and cleansed from all sin; and if ye are purified and cleansed from all sin, ye shall ask whatsoever you will in the name of Jesus, and it shall be done; but, know this, it shall be given you what you shall ask, and as ye are appointed to the head, the spirits shall be subject unto you.

"Wherefore, it shall come to pass, that if you behold a spirit manifested that you cannot understand, and you receive not that spirit, ye shall ask of the Father in the name of Jesus, and if he give not unto you that spirit, that you may know that it is not of God; and it shall be given unto you power over that spirit, and you shall proclaim against that spirit with a loud voice, that it is not of God; not with railing accusation, that ye be not overcome; neither with boasting, nor rejoicing, lest you be seized therewith; he that receiveth of God, let him account it of God, and let him rejoice that he is accounted of God worthy to receive, and by giving heed and doing these things which ye have received, and which ye shall hereafter receive, and the kingdom is given you of the

Father, and power to overcome all things which is not ordained of Him; and, behold, verily I say unto you, blessed are you who are now hearing these words of mine from the mouth of my servant, for your sins are forgiven you.

"Let my servant, Joseph Wakefield, in whom I am pleased, and my servant, Parley P. Pratt, go forth among the churches and strengthen them by the word of exhortation; and also my servant, John Corrill, or as many of my servants as are ordained unto this office, and let them labor in the vineyard; and let no man hinder them of doing that which I have appointed unto them; wherefore, in this thing, my servant, Edward Partridge, is not justified; nevertheless, let him repent and he shall be forgiven. Behold, ye are little children, and ye cannot bear all things now; ye must grow in grace and in the knowledge of the truth. Fear not, little children, for you are mine, and I have overcome the world, and you are of them that my Father hath given me; and none of them that my Father hath given me shall be lost; and the Father and I are one. I am in the Father and the Father in me; and, inasmuch as ye have received me, ye are in me and I in you; wherefore, I am in your midst, and I am the good Shepherd (and the stone of Israel; he that buildeth upon this rock shall never fall), and the day cometh that you shall hear my voice and see me, and know that I am. Watch, therefore, that ye may be ready; even so. Amen."

In obedience to the foregoing, Joseph Wakefield and myself visited the several branches of the Church, rebuking the wrong spirits which had crept in among them, setting in order things that were wanting; ordaining Elders and other officers; baptizing such as believed and repented of their sins; administering the gift of the Holy Ghost by the laying on of hands, in the name of Jesus Christ; laying hands on little children and blessing them; praying for the sick, and comforting the afflicted, etc. On some occasions we assembled fifty or sixty little children in one circle, in the midst of the assembly of the saints, and laid our hands upon them all, and prayed for them, and blessed them in the name of Jesus.

Thus my time passed sweetly and swiftly away for some weeks. I was sometimes in the society of President Smith, in Kirtland, and of the saints in that place, and sometimes in the branches abroad.

About this time a young lady, by the name of Chloe Smith, being a member of the Church, was lying very low with a lingering fever, with a family who occupied one of the houses on the farm of Isaac Morley, in Kirtland. Many of the Church had visited and prayed with her, but all to no effect; she seemed at the point of death, but would not consent to have a physician. This greatly enraged her relatives, who had cast her out because she belonged to the Church, and who, together with many of the people of the neighborhood, were greatly stirred up to anger, saying, "these wicked deceivers will let her lie and die without a physician, because of their superstitions; and if they do, we will prosecute them for so doing." Now these were daily watching for her last breath, with many threats.

Under these circumstances, President Smith and myself, with several other Elders called to see her. She was so low that no one had been allowed for some days previous to speak above a whisper, and even the door of the log dwelling was muffled with cloths to prevent a noise.

We kneeled down and prayed vocally all around, each in turn; after which President Smith arose, went to the bedside, took her by the hand, and said unto her with a loud voice, "in the name of Jesus Christ arise and walk!" She immediately arose, was dressed by a woman in attendance, when she walked to a chair before the fire, and was seated and joined in singing a hymn. The house was thronged with people in a few moments, and the young lady arose and shook hands with each as they came in; and from that minute she was perfectly restored to health.

Some time in May, 1831, the Church arrived with their families from the State of New York, to settle in Kirtland; but, to my unexpressible disappointment, my wife had not come with them, but had gone to spend the summer in the East with her friends. It was now too late to go to her, as the time was near when I was in duty bound to return to my fellow laborers in Missouri. To be so long absent from her, and then undertake a second journey without seeing her, was a severe trial, but God gave me grace to overcome my feelings, for his sake and the gospel's.

Chapter 10

On the sixth of June, 1831, a general conference was convened at Kirtland, consisting of all the Elders, far and near, who could be got together. In this conference much instruction was given by President
Smith, who spake in great power, as he was moved by the Holy Ghost;
and the spirit of power and of testimony rested down upon the Elders in
a marvelous manner. Here also were some strange manifestations of false
spirits, which were immediately rebuked.

Several were then selected by revelation, through President Smith,
and ordained to the High Priesthood after the order of the Son of God;
which is after the order of Melchizedek. This was the first occasion in
which this priesthood had been revealed and conferred upon the Elders
in this dispensation, although the office of an Elder is the same in a certain degree, but not in the fulness. On this occasion I was ordained to
this holy ordinance and calling by President Smith.

After these things, and the business of the conference was over, myself and Orson Pratt were appointed by revelation to perform a mission
together, through the Western States, and to meet the brethren I had
left in Jackson County, Missouri; and many others also who were sent in
a similar manner, two and two through the Western States, and who
were all appointed to meet in Jackson County, Missouri, and hold the
next conference. *

Soon after the conference my brother and myself commenced our
journey without any means to bear our expenses. We travelled through
the States of Ohio, Indiana, Illinois and Missouri, in the midst of the
heat of summer on foot, and faithfully preached the gospel in many parts

---

*See Doctrine and Covenants, section 52.

of all these States. We suffered the hardships incident to a new and, in many places, unsettled country, such as hunger, thirst, fatigue, etc. We arrived in upper Missouri in September, having baptized many people and organized branches of the Church in several parts of Ohio, Illinois and Indiana. On our arrival we found a considerable settlement of the brethren from Ohio, who had immigrated during the summer and taken up their residence in Jackson County. President Smith, and many of the Elders, had been there and held a conference, and, having organized a Stake of Zion, pointed out and consecrated certain grounds for a city and temple, they had again returned to the East. With them, the brethren whom I had left there the previous winter, had also returned.

I felt somewhat disappointed in not meeting with the brethren; but was consoled with the reflection that I had been diligent in preaching the gospel on my journey, while others had hurried through the country, perhaps, without tarrying to do much good.

I was now taken sick with the fever and ague, owing to the exposures of the climate through which we had travelled. I suffered extremely for several months; being brought very low with fever, and with other afflictions.

I tarried mostly with a branch of the Church commonly called the Colesville branch. They had removed from Colesville, in the State of New York, and settled on the borders of a fertile prairie, about twelve miles west of the village of Independence, and near the boundaries which divide the State of Missouri from the Indian Territory. They consisted of about sixty souls, and were under the presidency of a faithful and zealous Elder by the name of Newel Knight—an account of whose miraculous conversion we here record, as extracted from the life of Joseph Smith, published in the *Millennial Star*, Vol. 4, p. 116:

"During this month of April, I (Joseph Smith) went on a visit to the residence of Mr. Joseph Knight, of Colesville, Broom County, N.Y., with whom and his family I had been previously acquainted, and whose name I have above mentioned as having been so kind and thoughtful towards us while translating the Book of Mormon. Mr. Knight and his family were Universalists; but were willing to reason with me upon my religious views, and were, as usual, friendly and hospitable. We held several meetings in the neighborhood; we had many friends and some enemies. Our meetings were well attended, and many began to pray fervently to Almighty God that He would give them wisdom to understand the truth. Among those who attended our meetings regularly was Newel

Knight, son of Joseph Knight. He and I had many serious conversations on the important subject of man's eternal salvation. We were in the habit of praying much at our meetings, and Newel had said that he would try and take up his cross and pray vocally during meeting; but when we again met together he rather excused himself. I tried to prevail upon him, making use of the figure, supposing that he should get into a mud hole would he not try to help himself out? And that we were willing now to help him out of the mud hole. He replied, 'that provided he had got into a mud hole through carelessness, he would rather wait and get out himself than have others to help him, and so he would wait until he should get into the woods by himself and there he would pray.' Accordingly he deferred praying until next morning, when he retired into the woods, where, according to his own account afterwards, he made several attempts to pray, but could scarcely do so—feeling that he had not done his duty, but that he should have prayed in the presence of others. He began to feel uneasy, and continued to feel worse both in mind and body until, upon reaching his own house, his appearance was such as to alarm his wife very much. He requested her to go and bring me to him. I went and found him suffering very much in his mind, and his body acted upon in a very strange manner. His visage and limbs distorted and twisted in every shape and appearance possible to imagine; and finally, he was caught up off the floor of the apartment and tossed about most fearfully. His situation was soon made known to his neighbors and relatives, and in a short time as many as eight or nine grown persons had got together to witness the scene. After he had thus suffered for a time, I succeeded in getting hold of him by the hand, when almost immediately he spoke to me, and with very great earnestness requested of me that I should cast the devil out of him; saying, 'that he knew that he was in him, and that he also knew that I could cast him out.' I replied, 'if you know that I can it shall be done,' and then, almost unconsciously, I rebuked the devil, and commanded him in the name of Jesus Christ to depart from him; when immediately Newel spoke out and said, 'that he saw the devil leave him and vanish from his sight.'*

"The scene was now entirely changed; for as soon as the devil had departed from our friend his countenance became natural; his distor-

---

*This was the first miracle which was done in this Church, or by any member of it, and it was done not by man nor the power of man, but it was done by God, and by the power of godliness; therefore, let the honor and the praise, the dominion and the glory, be ascribed to the Father, Son and Holy Spirit, for ever and ever. Amen.

tions of body ceased; and almost immediately the Spirit of the Lord descended upon him, and the visions of eternity were opened to his view. He afterwards related his experience as follows:

"'I now began to feel a most pleasing sensation resting upon me, and immediately the visions of Heaven were opened to my view. I felt myself attracted upward, and remained for some time enrapt in contemplation, insomuch that I knew not what was going on in the room. By-and-by I felt some weight pressing upon my shoulder and the side of my head, which served to recall me to a sense of my situation, and I found that the Spirit of the Lord had actually caught me up off the floor, and that my shoulder and head were pressing against the beams.'

"All this was witnessed by many, to their great astonishment and satisfaction, when they saw the devil thus cast out and the power of God and His Holy Spirit thus made manifest. So soon as consciousness returned, his bodily weakness was such that we were obliged to lay him upon his bed and wait upon him for some time. As may be expected, such a scene as this contributed much to make believers of those who witnessed it; and, finally, the greater part of them became members of the Church."

This Colesville branch was among the first organized by Joseph Smith, and constituted the first settlers of the members of the Church in Missouri. They had arrived late in the summer, and cut some hay for their cattle, sowed a little grain, and prepared some ground for cultivation, and were engaged during the fall and winter in building log cabins, etc. The winter was cold, and for some time about ten families lived in one log cabin, which was open and unfinished, while the frozen ground served for a floor. Our food consisted of beef and a little bread made of corn, which had been grated into coarse meal by rubbing the ears on a tin grater. This was rather an inconvenient way of living for a sick person; but it was for the gospel's sake, and all were very cheerful and happy.

We enjoyed many happy seasons in our prayer and other meetings, and the Spirit of the Lord was poured out upon us, and even on the little children, insomuch that many of eight, ten or twelve years of age spake, and prayed, and prophesied in our meetings and in our family worship. There was a spirit of peace and union, and love and good will manifested in this little Church in the wilderness, the memory of which will be ever dear to my heart.

It was during my long illness in this dreary winter that I had the following dream or vision: I thought I saw myself dressed in a clean and

beautiful linen robe, white as snow, and extending from the neck down-
ward in beautiful folds. On either breast were lines of golden writing, in
large Roman letters, about a third of an inch in length, and the lines extending from the center of the breast on each side six or eight inches
long. The upper line on each side appeared larger and more beautiful or
conspicuous than the others; one of these lines was: "HOLY PROPHET,"
and the other was: "NEW JERUSALEM."

On awaking from this dream I immediately called to mind the words
of the Saviour to John the Revelator: *"He that overcometh will I make a pillar in the temple of my God, and he shall go no more out; and I will write upon
him the name of my God, and the name of the City of my God, which is New
Jerusalem."*

This dream certainly encouraged me, and enabled me to bear my
sickness, privation and long absence from my wife and former friends
more patiently.

Chapter 11

Some time in February, 1832, a Conference was held by Bishop Partridge and the Elders remaining in this part of the country. To this Conference I was determined to go, though very feeble and almost unable to sit up. I was assisted on to a horse, and rode twelve miles. I kept my bed during the Conference; but at the close, several Elders being about to take their journey to Ohio, I determined to go with them. I requested the Elders, therefore, to lay their hands on me and pray. They did so. I was instantly healed, and the next morning started in company with Elder Levi Hancock, a journey of twelve hundred miles on foot.

I gained strength at every step, and the second evening, after wading through the snow about six inches deep for some ten miles, I was enabled to address a congregation for the first time in several months.

I now parted with Levi Hancock, and had John Murdock for a fellow traveller. We passed down the south side of the Missouri river, among a thin settlement of people—mostly very ignorant but extremely hospitable. Some families were entirely dressed in skins, without any other clothing; including ladies young and old. Buildings were generally without glass windows, and the door open in winter for a light. We preached, and warned the people, and taught them as well as we could.

While ministering in these settlements, and exposed to a heavy snow storm, brother John Murdock was taken sick with a heavy fever; this caused us to stop early in the day among strangers, in a small log cabin consisting of one room; we held a meeting in the evening, and then had a bed made down on the floor, before the fire. Before morning brother Murdock was much better, but I was seized with a most dreadful chill, followed by a heavy turn of fever; morning found me unable to rise or speak. As the bed was in the way, they lifted it by the four corners, with me on it, and placed it in the back part of the room, on another bed. Here I lay, entirely helpless with a burning fever, during which I distinctly heard a dialogue between John Murdock and the lady of the house; she upbraiding us as imposters thrown upon them at this inclement season, while they were out of milling and of wood, and but illy prepared for such a burden; that one was sick the night before, and now the other was taken down; that it was six miles to the next house, deep snow and no road broke, and we would probably be on their hands for weeks.

To these inhospitable remarks brother Murdock mildly replied, trying to soothe the woman; reasoning with her, and telling her that brother Parley would soon be better, and then we would go our way.

This dialogue gave me such a sense of unwelcome, and I pitied brother Murdock to that degree for having to stay with such spirits on my account, that I felt I could endure it no longer. With the utmost effort I roused myself sufficiently to call brother Murdock to my bed, whispering to him to lay hands on me unobserved, so as not to be seen or overheard. He did so; I then asked him to give me a drink of water. The effort had been too much, I swooned away while he was gone for the water; he could hardly arouse me sufficiently to drink of it; it was like waking from the dead. I drank of it, bounded on my feet, dressed myself, put on my shoes and hat, and told him I was ready to start. The family all marvelled; one exclaimed, "what a strange disease; it could not be fever, and then be cured in an instant." We gave no explanations, but started on our journey up a steep hill, in the deep snow, in the midst of their urgings to stay to breakfast, or at least have a cup of coffee. I said nothing, but thought to myself: ye hypocrites, to murmur as you have, and then ask me to stay and eat.

We travelled on for some miles nearly in silence—I waiting all the while for brother Murdock to make some remarks referring to our inhospitable treatment, and the dialogue with the mistress of the house.

At last I broke silence. Said I, "Brother Murdock, how did you feel to be so talked to by that woman? I thought you bore it with great patience, and I pitied you from my heart, or I never should have had faith and courage to be thus healed and start my journey."

He replied that no such conversation had occurred between him and the lady, nor had she uttered one word indicative of any such inhospitable feeling.

"Well," said I, "I heard it articulated in plain English by some two persons, perfectly imitating her voice and yours; it was no imagination, or raging delirium of a fever. I can swear I heard a conversation to that effect for a length of time.

"If it was not the lady and yourself, then it was something from an invisible world, which clearly revealed to me the spirit of our hostess."

We reached the next house; I was a well man; found good quarters, and we were kindly and hospitably entertained for some days.

Pursuing our journey, we arrived at St. Louis, were kindly received by some citizens of that place, and held meeting with them. They conveyed us over the Mississippi free of charge, and we continued our journey, preaching by the way. We arrived at length at Vandalia, the then capital of Illinois. Here we were invited to a hotel, where we sojourned free of charge, and preached to a good audience in the Presbyterian meeting house. Next morning resuming our journey, we crossed the Okah river on a bridge, but the bottoms for two or three miles were overflowed to various depths, from six inches to three or four feet, and frozen over, except in the main channels, with a coat of ice, which we had to break by lifting our feet to the surface at every step. This occupied some hours and called into requisition our utmost strength, and sometimes we were entirely covered with water. At length we got through in safety and came to a house where we warmed and dried our clothes and took some whiskey. Our legs and feet had lost all feeling, became benumbed, and were dreadfully bruised and cut with the ice.

On the next day we had to cross a plain fifteen miles in length, without a house, a tree, or any kind of shelter; a cold northwest wind was blowing, and the ground covered with snow and ice. We had made two or three miles into the plain when I was attacked with a severe return of my old complaint, which had confined me so many months in Jackson County, and from which I had recovered by a miracle at the outset of this journey—I mean the fever and ague.

I travelled and shook, and shook and travelled, till I could stand it no longer; I vomited severely several times, and finally fell down on the snow, overwhelmed with fever, and became helpless and nearly insensible. This was about seven or eight miles from the nearest house.

Brother John Murdock laid his hands on me and prayed in the name of Jesus; and, taking me by the hand, he commanded me with a loud voice, saying: "In the name of Jesus of Nazareth arise and walk!" I attempted to arise, I staggered a few paces, and was about falling again when I found my fever suddenly depart and my strength come. I walked at the rate of about four miles per hour, arrived at a house, and was sick no more.

We continued our journey, preaching by the way, and crossing the Wabash at Vincennes, we stopped in that vicinity for several days, drawing crowded houses. Here we met with Elders Dustin and Bebee, who left Jackson County, Missouri, when we did, and for the same purpose.

"Well, brethren, how do you do?" said we to them.

"Tolerably well; only we have spent ten dollars each which was given us by the Bishop when we started, and we have sold books and spent the avails of them; and besides this we have been compelled to borrow money in a certain branch of the Church, and have spent that also; and we think it hard to travel for the public good and this at our own charges."

"Ah!" said I, "and how is this? we have not yet spent the first cent since we left the Church in Jackson County; nor shall we have any occasion for any spending money for weeks to come. Where did you stay last night?"

"In the large village of Washington."

"Did you preach to the people?"

"Yes; in the Court House."

"Did they charge you for your keeping?"

"Yes. A dollar and a quarter."

"Well, we are going there tonight, and, although entire strangers, we shall be well entertained free of charge, preach or no preach."

"How do you do it?" said they.

"O, we hold up our heads like honest men; go to the best houses, call for the best they have, make known our calling, pray with, or preach to them, ask for their bill on taking leave, but they will take nothing from us; but always invite us to call again."

"Well, they will not treat you so in Washington tonight; you will have to pay a good round sum."

"Well, we shall see."

We took leave of them and of the good people where we had been preaching, having first sent an appointment by the mail carrier, that if the inhabitants of Washington would get together we would address them that evening.

We entered the town at dark, stopped at a hotel, called for lodging and supper and a room for ourselves; and asked the landlord if a meeting had been got up for us. He said the mail carrier brought the news of our appointment, but he believed it had been neglected to be given out; was very sorry, made many apologies, and still offered to have the bell rung and the people assembled if we wished. We told him we were glad of an opportunity to rest, and did not wish a meeting at so late an hour.

We retired to our room and made no further acquaintance. Next morning on taking leave, we asked what was to pay. He answered, "not anything," said we were welcome to his hospitality at any time, and bid us call again.

Giving out an appointment

Leaving Washington, we were next entertained by a very hospitable preacher of the Christian order, whose name I have forgotten. We tarried at his house a week or two, and preached to crowded congregations in all the region; he frequently going with us to introduce us and open the way. While here, having a little leisure between appointments, I went alone and on foot to the town of Madison, about nine miles from his house. My design was to get out an appointment and preach, which came to pass the same evening in the following manner: I stepped into a hotel, they were all at dinner, I placed the Book of Mormon on a public table and sat down to read a newspaper; soon the boarders came out, and one by one looked at the Book, and inquired whose it was; soon the landlord came out, who I learned was so very deaf that one could only be heard by placing mouth to ear and shouting at the very top of the voice. He caught up the Book and inquired, "Whose is this?" I arose, placed my arm round his neck, and my mouth close to his ear, and shouted, "IT IS MINE, AND I HAVE COME TO PREACH!!" This was so loud that it almost alarmed the town. He welcomed me to entertainment free of charge, had the Court House opened, the town notified, and evening found me in the judge's seat, a reporter in the clerk's desk, and a crowded audience. I had good liberty and all seemed much interested.

After a few days we resumed our journey, and in May arrived in Kirtland, where I again met my wife after an absence of one year and seven months.

Chapter 12

I shall not attempt to describe our feelings or our joy; these things are known by experience, not by language. I found her health much impaired, and she had long suffered from complaints of the nature of consumption; but she was now reduced still further by her anxious solicitude about my long absence.

When she found herself once more in the quiet enjoyment of my society, she gradually resumed her wonted cheerfulness, and began to enjoy better health; but still she was far from being well.

After spending a few weeks at home, I performed a short mission in the southeastern part of Ohio, and again returned, having travelled on foot in the heat of summer about three hundred miles. In this mission I met with no success in the ministry, owing to the prejudice, ignorance and bigotry of the people, who either would not hear at all, or else heard in a careless manner, and went away with the same indifference as they came.

I now determined to take my wife and our little effects and remove to Western Missouri. To bear the expenses of this long journey my wife had some sixty dollars, which she brought with her from the East, and certain men also put into my hands sums of money to be expended in lands and improvements in that country. With brother Joseph's counsel and blessing I bade farewell to Kirtland.

We took a stage coach for the Ohio River, thence by steamer to St. Louis, and again by steamer up the Missouri. I took a steerage passage among the poorer class, and was dressed more like a laborer than a public minister. However, the throng of passengers on the boat learned by

64

some means that I was a preacher, and on the 4th of July they pressed me very hard to address them in the cabin in honor of our national anniversary. I refused for awhile; but at length complied, on conditions that steerage passengers, boat hands, firemen, and all classes, black or white, should have the privilege of assembling in the cabin to hear the discourse.

This was readily complied with, and very soon a large assembly was convened and in waiting, consisting of ladies and gentlemen, lawyers, merchants, farmers, servants, waiters and colored gentlemen.

I presented myself before this motley assembly in a plain coat of gray satinet, and bowed respectfully. All tried to be grave, but a smile, a sneer, a look of contempt would now and then escape from some of the more genteel portion of the assembly, as if they would say, "Can any good thing come out of Nazareth," or, in other words, can so plain a man be possessed of knowledge sufficient to entertain such an assembly on so important an occasion as the 4th of July, and this, too, without preparing a discourse beforehand?

I read a chapter; all was serious attention. I offered up a prayer; all was deep interest. I commenced a discourse, and nearly all were in tears. I introduced the Book of Mormon as a record of ancient America; I dwelt upon its history and prophetic declarations, now being verified by the erection of free institutions in this great country, and their growing influence. I spoke of the general prosperity and resources of the country, acknowledging the hand of Providence in the same; warned them against national pride, ambition, and injustice; exhorted them, in common with all citizens, to use the utmost diligence to preserve the general peace and the pure influence of our national institutions; and to improve in light, intelligence and love, without which we, too, might be brought down to destruction like the Israelites and Nephites of old; and our bones and ruined cities and monuments alone be left to other people, as theirs were left to us, as a testimony of our greatness which would have passed away. I also showed them from the Book of Mormon that we were destined to remain forever as a blessed and free people on this land, on conditions of keeping the commandments of Jesus Christ, and that our settlements and commerce would soon extend to the vast shores of the Pacific ocean, and our ensign stand out to the nations as a standard inviting them to a banquet of freedom, peace and plenty.

After meeting I was pressed upon to come into the cabin for the rest of the passage. And even when we changed boats at Louisville, such was the influence of my fellow passengers, that the gentlemen's and also the ladies' cabin and board was free to me without money or price. One gentleman offered as high as ten dollars for a copy of the Book of Mormon; but, unluckily, I had none with me.

Arriving at the Colesville branch, on the western boundaries of the State (where I had spent the previous winter in sickness and poverty), about the 1st of August, 1832, we commenced cutting hay, building, purchasing and planting land, and making every preparation to receive those who had sent funds for this purpose. During the months of August and September I had, with a little help, secured about fifteen tons of hay, and put into the ground fifteen acres of wheat, besides building a log house and doing something at fencing, etc. These exertions in the heat of the season brought on a severe illness, in which I was nigh unto death; but I was again restored in a few days by the laying on of hands and prayer in the name of Jesus.

About this time Lewis Abbott arrived with his family from Kirtland, and having sent some money by me, partly to aid in my expenses, and partly for the purpose of making improvements, he became dissatisfied and demanded the utmost farthing. This took everything I had done;— my wheat on the ground, my hay, my cows all but one, and left me entirely destitute, after all my laborious exertions. At this brother Abbott seemed satisfied, and thought he had got quite rich, and turned his money to good advantage; but the curse of God rested upon all his property as was soon manifest.

The next winter I took a mission in company with Elder William E. McLellin down through the State of Missouri and into Illinois, crossing the Mississippi at Clarksville.

As we approached Clarksville, we were told by several of the inhabitants near, not to attempt a meeting or any religious instruction there, for they were a hardened and irreclaimable set of blasphemers and infidels, given to gambling, drinking and cursing, etc.; and that many different orders of the clergy had attempted in vain to reclaim them, or even to get a hearing. Before entering the town we ascended a mountain and cried mightily unto the Lord that He would open our way, and move upon the hearts of the people to receive us and hear the Word.

We then entered the town and called at a hotel. We told the landlord that we had come in the name of Jesus Christ to preach the gospel to the people, being sent by him without purse or scrip. "Well," said he, "you are welcome to my house and such fare as we have; and we will meet together and hear your religion, and if it proves to be better than ours we will embrace it; for we confess that our religion is to fiddle and dance, and eat and drink, and be merry, and gamble and swear a little; and we believe this is better than priestcraft."

We replied that we would try them anyhow. So a meeting was convened; we preached, had good attention, and much of a candid spirit of inquiry was manifest, and we were treated with hospitality and friendship, and even ferried over the river free; and this was more than those religious sectaries would do, who had warned us against them.

Passing over the river, the next day we came to Green County, Illinois; and as the day drew to a close we began to circulate an appointment as we travelled along a thick settlement of thrifty farmers, for preaching in a school house in the neighborhood that evening.

As we sat by the highway side to rest ourselves, an old farmer rode past on horseback, and halted to ask if we were travellers. We replied that we were travelling to preach the gospel, and had an appointment that evening at the school house just ahead, and invited him to come and hear.

"No," said he, "I have not attended a religious meeting this five years; I have long been disgusted and tired of priestcraft and religious ignorance and division, and have concluded to stand aloof from it all."

"Well, we are as much opposed to these things as you can be, and, therefore, have come to preach the gospel, and show the knowledge of God in its ancient purity, being instructed and sent of Him without purse or scrip. So come and hear us."

"O! indeed, if that is the case, I will."

So he came; the house was crowded with Baptists, Methodists, Universalists, Non-professors, Infidels, etc.

We preached. After meeting, a Baptist minister by the name of John Russell, a very learned and influential man, invited us to tarry in the neighborhood and continue to preach; he said his house should be our home, and he called a vote of the people whether they wished us to preach more. The vote was unanimous in the affirmative.

We tarried in the neighborhood some two months, and preached daily in all that region to vast multitudes, both in town and country, in the grove, and in school houses, barns and dwellings.

All parties were our hearers and friends, and contributed liberally to our wants; and the old farmer, whose name was Calvin, who had not been to meeting before for five years, became a constant hearer, and opened his house for our home. He was very wealthy, and bade us welcome to shoes, clothing, or anything we needed; many Infidels, Universalists, etc., did the same.

In this neighborhood there lived a Baptist minister by the name of Dotson, who opposed us with much zeal, from time to time, both in public and in private, and from house to house.

He said the Book of Mormon was a fable; a silly, foolish mixture of matter, possessing no interest, and that he could write a better book himself. However, his principal objection was, that God could give no *new* revelation—the New Testament contained all the knowledge that God had in store for man, and there was nothing remaining unrevealed.

We asked him to open the New Testament and read to us the history and destiny of the American continent and its inhabitants, and the origin and lineage of the same; also, the history of the ten tribes of Israel, and where they now were. We also asked him to read to us from that book his own commission, and that of other ministers of this age to preach the gospel. But he could do none of these things; but still insisted that there was no subject worthy of new revelation, and that no revelation could be given.

Said I, "Mr. Dotson, relate to me your experience and call to the ministry."

"Well," he replied, "I will do so, seeing that it is you, friend Pratt; for you are able to bear it, and to comprehend something about it; but I have never told it to my own members; and I dare not, for they would not believe me."

"Well, Mr. Dotson, be particular on the manner and means by which you were called to the ministry."

"Why, sir, said he, *"I was called by a vocal voice from Heaven."*

"Well, Mr. Dotson, *there* is one exception to your general rule. We come to you with a new revelation, and you reject it, because there can be no new revelation; and yet you profess to have a new revelation, God having spoken from the heavens and called *you,* and commissioned *you* to preach eighteen hundred years after the New Testament was written, and all revelation finished! How is this?

"The New Testament no where calls you by name; neither makes mention of you as a minister of the gospel; but new revelation does, if we are to believe you. And yet you would teach your hearers and us, and all the world, to disbelieve all modern revelation merely because it is new. Consequently, we are all bound by your own rule to reject your call to the ministry, and to believe it is a lie."

He could say no more.

At another time he was at Mr. Russell's with us, and, in presence of

Mr. R. and others, was opposing the Book of Mormon with all his power.

We asked him to listen while we read a chapter in it. He did so, and was melted into tears, and so affected and confounded that he could not utter a word for some time. He then, on recovering, asked us to his house, and opened the door for us to preach in his neighborhood. We did so, and were kindly entertained by him.

But after this, he again hardened his heart, and finding his opposition all in vain, he wrote a letter to the Rev. Mr. Peck, of Rock Spring, some sixty miles distant, informing him that the "Mormons" were about to take Green County, and requesting his immediate attendance.

This Mr. Peck was a man of note, as one of the early settlers of Illinois, and one of its first missionaries. He had labored for many years in that new country and in Missouri, and was now Editor of a paper devoted to Baptist principles.

This gentleman was soon forthcoming, and commenced his public addresses among the people, to try to convince them of the great errors we had taught.

He said there were no antiquities in America; no ruined cities, buildings, monuments, inscriptions, mounds, or fortifications, to show the existence of such a people as the Book of Mormon described.

He also said, that there were no domestic animals such as the cow, the ox, or the horse, found here when Europeans first discovered the country. He then inquired how these animals became extinct since the destruction of the Nephites.

He said further, that the fortifications and mounds of this country were nothing more than the works of Nature.

He then warned the people against the study of the prophetic parts of the Old and New Testaments, observing that these mysterious prophecies were directly calculated to lead them into delusion and bewilderment; that the best way to read and understand prophecy was, to read it backwards—that is to say, after it is fulfilled; that it was never designed to be understood before it came to pass.

He also taught that the Millennium was already commenced, and that Jesus Christ would not come, in person, till the great and last judgment; and that the Millennium must first continue a year for each day of the thousand years, spoken of by John the Revelator, etc.

A meeting was held for the purpose of replying to him; the people came out in great numbers.

I then replied in substance as follows:

"My hearers:—The Rev. Mr. Peck is a great man. He is a man of age and varied experience and learning. I am but a youth, inferior to him in all these respects. I reverence his gray hairs; I respect his learning; I admire his talents and ingenuity; and I feel a delicacy in replying to him; and nothing but a love for the truth and a hatred of error and falsehood, could induce me to come in contact with him before the public; but where truth and salvation are at stake I cannot shrink from duty, in consideration of age or talent; I cannot spare the man, even if he were my father.

"To do away the Book of Mormon, we are called upon to believe that the temples, statues, pyramids, sculptures, monuments, engravings, mounds and fortifications, now in ruins on the American continent, are all the works of Nature in her playful moments; that the bones of slumbering nations were never clothed upon with flesh, and that their sleeping dust was never animated with life.

"This is too monstrous; it is too marvelous, too miraculous for our credulity; we can never believe that these things are the works of Nature, unaided by human art; we are not so fond of the marvelous.

"Again, we are told that no cows or oxen were here when Europeans first came to the country. I would ask what the wild buffalo are, if they are not the cattle of the ancient inhabitants? I would ask how horse tracks came to be imbedded in the petrified rock of Kentucky, without a horse to make them? And if no race of animals could become extinct, which once existed here, I would ask Mr. Peck either to produce a living mammoth, or annihilate his bones. But, perhaps, the reverend gentleman would say that those bones, too, were the works of Nature, and that the huge animal they seem to represent never existed.

"Again, my hearers, we are warned against the study of prophecy. We are told that a careful perusal of the prophecies, which the reverend gentleman is pleased to call '*mysterious*,' is a principal cause of our delusion and blindness; and that the prophecies were only designed to be read and understood after they were fulfilled.

"We will apply this rule, and learn its workings by practical experience.

"The people at the time of the flood adopted this rule, all save eight souls. Mr. Peck's theology was then almost catholic. The universal world (save eight) were disposed to remain in ignorance as to the meaning of prophecy till after its fulfilment. The result was that they knew not until the flood came and swept them all away; then they could understand.

"The people of Sodom were all of Mr. Peck's faith—all save Lot and his family; they also perished unawares.

"The Jews also were of this same school—I mean those who perished in the siege of Jerusalem, in fulfilment of the prophecy of Jesus Christ, recorded in the 21st chapter of Luke.

"And permit me here to remind my hearers that this ancient system of theology, will certainly prevail to an almost universal extent at the time of the coming of the Son of Man. For Jesus himself testified that, as it was in the days of Noah and in the days of Lot, so should it be in the days of the coming of the Son of Man. I would here pause and congratulate my reverend friend on the glorious and popular prospects before him. Certain it is that most of the world will, at some future day, be of his faith in this respect; they will let the prophecies of the Holy Scriptures alone, and not attempt to understand them until after their fulfilment.

"But we are of another school.

"We believe in Jesus, who said 'search the Scriptures;' we believe with Peter, that we have a more sure word of prophecy, unto which we do well to take heed, as unto a light shining in a dark place; until the day dawn, and the day star arise in our hearts.

"We believe the Apostle when he says that, 'whatsoever was written aforetime was written for our profit and learning; that, we through patience and comfort of the Scriptures, might have hope.' We wish to be children of the light and not of darkness; that that day come not upon us unawares. In short we wish, like Timothy of old, to understand the Scriptures from our very childhood; considering that they are able to make us wise unto salvation, through faith in Christ Jesus.

"Again, we are told that the world is in the enjoyment of the Millennium, or thousand years of rest, spoken of by John, the Revelator.

"Of course then Satan is bound, and does not tempt any man. The martyrs of Jesus, and those who kept His commandments are raised from the dead, and are now present on the earth reigning with Jesus Christ. The nations learn war no more, none are in ignorance, none in darkness, the knowledge of God covers the earth as the waters do the seas. The cow and the leopard, the kid and the bear, the wolf and the lamb, the lion, the serpent and the little child, all dwell together in peace. For such events the prophets have described in connection with the Millennium.

"But the great announcement of all—the most important communication made to us by Mr. Peck is concerning the time of the second coming of Jesus Christ. It was now ascertained by him to be postponed till the great and last day; and that we are to have a Millennium of *three hundred and sixty-five thousand years* first, before Christ comes. Only think! *'three hundred and sixty-five thousand!'* Why, according to this calculation the world is yet in its infancy; we are early in the morning of creation. The great day of the existence of the world has only dawned; a long and glorious race is yet before the generations of man. What is the age of Adam or Methuselah! What the few fleet years of the earth's existence, compared to the time yet to come before its end!

"O, ye holy prophets and saints of old, had you been in possession of the knowledge of the astounding facts now announced by this reverend gentleman, you would never have warned mankind so repeatedly to be ready for the great day of the Lord, for it was soon at hand.

"And had Jesus Christ known this fact, he would never have warned the world of the danger of that day coming on them unawares. He and His Apostles would have said: it is yet far—very far off. The Millennium must first dawn, and then continue three hundred and sixty-five thousand years; and then, behold, I will come to judge the world.

"But, my hearers, please read the prophet Zechariah on this subject, chapter 14.

"We were there informed that 'Jesus Christ will come, and all the saints with him,'—that he will 'set his feet on the Mount of Olives;' that he will 'deliver the Jews and Jerusalem from their enemies;' that he will 'destroy those who are in the siege against that city;' and that he will 'reign as a king over all the earth, from that time forth; and there shall be one Lord and his name one.'

"Now, if he comes and all the saints with him, it cannot be his first coming. If he comes to fight for the Jews and overthrow their enemies, it cannot be his first coming. If the Mount of Olives rends in twain at the same time, and opens so as to form a great valley in the place thereof, it has no connection with his first coming.

"Again, if he comes to reign as a *'King over all the earth,'* it can have no allusion to the last judgment,—the end of the earth. Consequently, if Zechariah has told the truth, we are to expect the coming of Jesus Christ distinct from his first coming; unconnected with the last judgment, at the very commencement of his reign of a thousand years, which we call the Millennium; but which, Mr. Peck says, has commenced, entirely independent of any such event. But what can we expect of a man when he comments upon the prophecies, while at the same time he contends that none can understand them until after their fulfilment.

"Of course, my hearers, he himself acts upon the principle which he lays down to others; and if he does, he never studies, never searches the prophecies, acknowledges himself in darkness on all subjects connected with unfulfilled prophecy; expects to remain so, and expects his hearers to do the same.

"O, my beloved friends, have the people of this western country been led in darkness for so many years by learned and reverend gentlemen? are they willing to remain in darkness now, when the veil is withdrawn, and his folly made manifest before all the people, and this too by his own words, uttered in presence of you all?

"If so, follow him, and cleave to him as your teacher. But if not, we exhort you to hold fast the truth as we have delivered it to you; come forward this day, and obey the ordinances of God; seek for the Holy Spirit to guide you into all truth, and continue to search the Scriptures for more light, and God will bless you forever. Amen."

After this meeting some of the Baptists and others came forward and were baptized, and joined the Church of the Saints; and the people in general remained steadfast in the faith, and were unmoved by the exertions of Messrs. Peck and Dotson.

This filled them with envy, and they soon began to manifest a lying and abusive spirit to such a degree that all the people could see and distinguish plainly between the spirits of truth and error.

Mr. Peck soon took leave and retired home, and we continued our mission.

Hundreds of the people were convinced of the truth, but the hearts of many were too much set on the world to obey the gospel; we, therefore, baptized only a few of the people, and organized a small society, and about the first of June took leave and returned home.

Having rested myself a few days, I now commenced again to cultivate the earth. I plowed about six acres of ground for wheat, and was busy from day to day in the woods, preparing timber to fence the same, when the following dream, or night vision, was given me:

A man came to me and called me with a loud voice: "Parley, Parley." I answered, "Here am I." Said he, "Cease splitting rails, for the Lord has prepared you for a greater work." I answered, "Whereby shall I know that this message is from the Lord?" He replied, "Follow me, and I will show you."

I followed him for some distance along a long path, and at last came to a place of ancient sepulchres, where many of the Nephites of old had been buried. One of these opened,—the flesh of the man withered away; he became like a skeleton, and passed down into the grave. I understood and knew by the spirit, that this signified that it was the voice of one from the dead which had spoken to me. I therefore exclaimed, "It is enough; I know the message is of the Lord; return unto me, that we may converse together." He then came forth out of the grave, was again clothed upon with a body like a man, and he talked with me, and told me many things.

I awoke the next morning, and thought of my dream, but I was necessitated, as I thought, to finish my fence and sow my crop before I ceased to labor with my hands. I, therefore, continued to make and haul rails from the woods. I perfected my fence and sowed my crop, but I never reaped; I never saw the wheat after it was more than three inches high.

Chapter 13

It was now the summer of 1833. Immigration had poured into the County of Jackson in great numbers; and the Church in that county now numbered upwards of one thousand souls. These had all purchased lands and paid for them, and most of them were improving in buildings and in cultivation. Peace and plenty had crowned their labors, and the wilderness became a fruitful field, and the solitary place began to bud and blossom as the rose.

They lived in peace and quiet; no lawsuits with each other or with the world; few or no debts were contracted; few promises broken; there were no thieves, robbers, or murderers; few or no idlers; all seemed to worship God with a ready heart. On Sundays the people assembled to preach, pray, sing, and receive the ordinances of God. Other days all seemed busy in the various pursuits of industry. In short, there has seldom, if ever, been a happier people upon the earth than the Church of the Saints now were.

In the latter part of summer and in the autumn, I devoted almost my entire time in ministering among the churches; holding meetings; visiting the sick; comforting the afflicted, and giving counsel. A school of Elders was also organized, over which I was called to preside. This class, to the number of about sixty, met for instruction once a week. The place of meeting was in the open air, under some tall trees, in a retired place in the wilderness, where we prayed, preached and prophesied, and exercised ourselves in the gifts of the Holy Spirit. Here great blessings were poured out, and many great and marvelous things were manifested and taught. The Lord gave me great wisdom, and enabled me to teach and edify the Elders, and comfort and encourage them in their preparations for the great work which lay before us. I was also much edified and strengthened. To attend this school I had to travel on foot, and sometimes with bare feet at that, about six miles. This I did once a week, besides visiting and preaching in five or six branches a week.

While thus engaged, and in answer to our correspondence with the Prophet, Joseph Smith, at Kirtland, Ohio, the following revelation was sent to us by him, dated August, 1833:

"Verily I say unto you, my friends, I speak unto you with my voice, even the voice of my Spirit; that I may show unto you my will concerning your brethren in the land of Zion; many of whom are truly humble, and are seeking diligently to learn wisdom and to find truth; verily, verily I say unto you, blessed are such for they shall obtain; for I, the Lord, showeth mercy unto all the meek, and upon all whomsoever I will, that I may be justified when I shall bring them into judgment.

"Behold, I say unto you, concerning the school in Zion, I the Lord am well pleased that there should be a school in Zion; and also with my servant, Parley P. Pratt, for he abideth in me; and inasmuch as he continueth to abide in me, he shall continue to preside over the school in the land of Zion until I shall give unto him other commandments; and I will bless him with a multiplicity of blessings in expounding all Scriptures and mysteries to the edification of the school and of the Church in Zion, and to the residue of the school I, the Lord, am willing to show mercy; nevertheless, there are those that must needs be chastened, and their works shall be made known. The axe is laid at the root of the trees, and every tree that bringeth not forth good fruit, shall be hewn down and cast into the fire; I, the Lord have spoken it. Verily I say unto you, all among them who know their hearts are honest, and are broken, and their spirits contrite, and are willing to observe their covenants by sacrifice; yea, every sacrifice which I, the Lord, shall command, they are all accepted of me, for I, the Lord will cause them to bring forth as a very fruitful tree which is planted in a goodly land, by a pure stream that yieldeth much precious fruit.

"Verily I say unto you, that it is my will that an house should be built unto me in the land of Zion, like unto the pattern which I have given you; yea, let it be built speedily by the tithing of my people; behold, this is the tithing and the sacrifice which I, the Lord, require at their hands; that there may be an house built unto me for the salvation of Zion, for a place of thanksgiving for all saints, and for a place of instruction for all those who are called to the work of the ministry in all their several callings and offices, that they may be perfected in the understanding of their ministry in theory, in principle, and in doctrine; in all things pertaining to the kingdom of God on the earth, the keys of which kingdom have been conferred upon you.

"And inasmuch as my people build an house unto me in the name of the Lord, and do not suffer any unclean thing to come into it that it be not defiled, My glory shall rest upon it; yea, and my presence shall be there; for I will come into it, and all the pure in heart that shall come into it shall see God; but if it be defiled I will not come into it, and my glory shall not be there for I will not come into unholy temples.

"And now behold, if Zion do these things she shall prosper and spread herself and become very glorious, very great, and very terrible; and the nations of the earth shall honor her and shall say, surely Zion is the city of our God; and surely Zion cannot fall, neither be moved out of her place; for God is there, and the hand of the Lord is there, and He hath sworn by the power of His might to be her salvation and her high tower; therefore, verily thus saith the Lord, let Zion rejoice, for this is Zion, THE PURE IN HEART; therefore let Zion rejoice while all the wicked shall mourn; for behold, and lo! vengeance cometh speedily upon the ungodly as the whirlwind, and who shall escape it? The Lord's scourge shall pass over by night and by day, and the report thereof shall vex all people; yet it shall not be stayed until the Lord come; for the indignation of the Lord is kindled against their abominations and all their wicked works; nevertheless, Zion shall escape if she observe to do all things whatsoever I have commanded her; but if she observes not to do whatsoever I have commanded her, I will visit her, according to all her works, with sore affliction; with pestilence; with plague; with sword; with vengeance; with devouring fire; nevertheless, let it be read this once in their ears, that I, the Lord, have accepted of their offering; and if she sin no more none of these things shall come upon her, and I will bless her with blessings, and multiply a multiplicity of blessings upon her and upon her generations forever and ever, saith the Lord your God. Amen."

This revelation was not complied with by the leaders and Church in Missouri, as a whole; notwithstanding many were humble and faithful. Therefore, the threatened judgment was poured out to the uttermost, as the history of the five following years will show.

That portion of the inhabitants of Jackson County which did not belong to the Church, became jealous of our growing influence and numbers. Political demagogues were afraid we should rule the county; and religious priests and bigots felt that we were powerful rivals, and about to excel all other societies in the State in numbers, and in power and influence.

These feelings, and the false statements and influences growing out of them, gave rise to the organization of a company of outlaws, whose avowed object was to drive the Church of the Saints from the county.

These were composed of lawyers, magistrates, county officers, civil and military; religious ministers, and great numbers of the ignorant and uninformed portion of the population, whose prejudices were easily aroused.

They commenced operations by assembling in great numbers, destroying a printing office and its materials; demolishing dwellings and stores, and plundering the contents and strewing them in the street; cutting open feather beds, breaking furniture, destroying fences and crops, whipping, threatening and variously abusing men, women and children, etc.

The saints submitted to these outrages for a time in all patience, without defence or resistance of any kind, supposing that the public authorities would of course put a stop to them, as in duty bound.

But they were soon convinced to the contrary, and were compelled to take up arms for defence; and also to make the most vigorous exertions to prosecute according to law. We assembled in small bodies in different neighborhoods, and stood on guard during the nights, being ready to march in a moment to any place of attack.

I had the command of about sixty men who were thus assembled in the Colesville branch; and rendezvoused in some log buildings during a very rainy time.

It was evening. I was out in the act of posting guards a short distance from the dwellings, when two men assailed us, armed with guns and pistols; and supposing it against our principles to make any defence, they attacked the guards. I was without arms, but stepped forward to interfere between them, when one of them drew his gun backwards, and, with both hands, struck the barrel of it across the top of my head. I staggered back, but did not fall; the blood came streaming down my face, and I was for an instant stunned by the blow; But, recovering myself, I called help from the house and disarmed them, and put them under guard till morning. Their arms were then restored, and they let go in peace.

The taking of these two men proved a preventive against an attack that night. They were the advance of a party of men who were about to come upon the settlement, but were disconcerted by this means.

On the next day, about sunset, myself and a Mr. Marsh set out on horseback to visit the Circuit Judge at Lexington, a distance of some forty miles. We were under the necessity of travelling the most private paths across the country, in order to avoid our enemies; but we had a most faithful pilot, an old resident of the country, who knew every crook and turn of the different paths.

We had ridden but a few miles when it became so excessively dark that we could not see each other, or distinguish any object. Our pilot dismounted several times and tried to feel his way. We were at last compelled to halt for some time, until it cleared and became a little lighter; but the rain began to fall in torrents, and continued all the latter part of the night. We soon became drenched, and every thread about us perfectly wet; but still we dare not stop for any refreshment or shelter, until day dawned, when we found ourselves forty miles from home and at the door of a friend, where we breakfasted and refreshed ourselves.

We then repaired to Lexington, and made oath before Judge Ryland of the outrages committed upon us, but were refused a warrant. The Judge advised us to fight and kill the outlaws whenever they came upon us. We then returned to the place where we breakfasted, and, night coming on, we retired to bed. Having been without sleep for the three previous nights, and much of the time drenched with rain, this, together with the severe wound I had received, caused me to feel much exhausted. No sooner had sleep enfolded me in her kind embrace than a vision opened before me.

I was in Jackson County; heard the sound of firearms, and saw the killed and wounded lying in their blood. At this I awoke from slumber, and awaking Mr. Marsh and the family with whom we lodged, I told them what I had seen and heard in my dream, and that I was sure a battle had just occurred.

Next morning we pursued our journey homeward with feelings of anxiety indescribable. Every officer of the peace had abandoned us to our fate; and it seemed as if there was no alternative but for men, women and children to be exterminated. As we rode on, ruminating upon these things, a man met us from Independence, who told us there was a battle raging when he left; and how it had terminated he knew not.

This only heightened our feelings of anxiety and suspense. We were every instant drawing nearer to the spot where we might find our friends alive and victorious, or dead, or perhaps in bondage, in the hands of a worse than savage enemy.

On coming within four miles of Independence, we ventured to inquire the distance at a certain house; this we did in order to pass as strangers, and also, in hopes to learn some news; the man seemed frightened, and inquired where we were from. We replied, from Lexington. Said he, "Have you heard what has happened?" We replied, "That we had heard there was some difficulty, but of all the participants we had not been informed." "Why," said he, "the Mormons have *riz*, and have killed six men."

We then passed on, and as soon as we were out of sight we left the road and took into the woods.

Taking a circuitous route, through thickets of hazel interwoven with grape vine, we came in sight of Independence, after some difficulty and entanglement, and advanced towards it; but seeing parties of armed men advancing towards us, we wheeled about, and retreating a distance, turned again into the woods, and galloping about a half mile, reached the tents of our friends.

But what was our astonishment when we found our brethren without arms, having surrendered them to the enemy!

The truth was this: The same evening that I dreamed of the battle, a large body of the outlaws had marched to a certain settlement, where they had before committed many outrages, and commenced to unroof dwellings, destroy property, and threaten and abuse women and children. While some sixty men were thus engaged, and their horses quietly regaling themselves in the cornfields of the brethren, about thirty of our men marched upon them, and drove them from the field. Several were severely if not mortally wounded on both sides; and one young man of the Church died of his wounds the next day—his name was Barber.

In the battle brother Philo Dibble, of Ohio, was shot in the body through his waistband; the ball remained in him. He bled much inwardly, and, in a day or two his bowels were so filled with blood and so inflamed that he was about to die, or, rather, he had been slowly dying from the time he was wounded. The smell of himself had become intolerable to him and those about him. At length Elder Newel Knight administered to him, by the laying on of hands, in the name of Jesus; his hands had scarcely touched his head when he felt an operation penetrating his whole system as if it had been a purifying fire. He immediately discharged several quarts of blood and corruption, among which was the

ball with which he had been wounded. He was instantly healed, and
went to work chopping wood. He remained an able bodied man, a hard
worker, and even did military duty for many years after. He is still living
in Davis County, Utah.

The next morning, Nov. 5, armed men were assembled in Independence from every part of the county. These joined the outlaws, and
called themselves militia, and placed themselves under the command of
Lieutenant-Governor Boggs and a colonel by the name of Pitcher. Thus
organized, manned and officered, they were a formidable band of outlaws; capable of murder, or any other violence or outrage which would
accomplish their purpose; which was to drive the people of the Church
from the county, and plunder their property and possess their lands.

Very early the same morning, several volunteers united their forces
from different branches of the Church and marched towards Independence, in order to defend their brethren and friends. When within a
short distance from the town they halted, and were soon informed that
the militia were called out for their protection; but in this they did not
place confidence; for they saw that the armed body congregated had
joined with the mobbers and outlaws, and were one with them to carry
out their murderous purposes. On communicating with the leaders,
Boggs and Pitcher, it was found that there was no alternative but for the
Church to leave the county forthwith, and deliver up their arms, and
certain men to be tried for murder, said to have been committed in the
battle the previous evening.

Rather than have submitted to these outrageous requirements the
saints would willingly have shed their blood; but they knew that if they
resisted this mob, the lies of the designing and the prejudice of the ignorant would construe their resistance into a violation of law, and thus
bring certain destruction upon them; therefore, they surrendered their
arms and agreed to leave the county forthwith. The men who were demanded as prisoners were also surrendered and imprisoned, but were dismissed in a day or two without trial.

A few hours after the surrender we arrived at the camp of our brethren on our return from Lexington.

The struggle was now over, our liberties were gone, our homes to be
deserted and possessed by a lawless banditti; and all this in the United
States of America.

The sun was then setting, and twelve miles separated me from my
family; but I determined to reach home that night. My horse being
weary I started on foot, and walked through the wilderness in darkness;

avoiding the road lest I should fall into the hands of the enemy.

I arrived home about the middle of the night, and furnishing my wife with a horse, we made our escape in safety.

When night again overtook us we were on the bank of the Missouri River, which divided between Jackson and Clay Counties. Here we camped for the night, as we could not cross the ferry till morning. Next morning we crossed the river, and formed an encampment amid the cottonwoods on its bank.

While we thus made our escape companies of ruffians were ranging the county in every direction; bursting into houses without fear, knowing that the people were disarmed; frightening women and children, and threatening to kill them if they did not flee immediately. At the head of one of these parties appeared the Rev. Isaac McCoy (a noted Baptist missionary to the Indians), with gun in hand, ordering the people to leave their homes immediately and surrender everything in the shape of arms.

Other pretended preachers of the gospel took part in the persecution—speaking of the Church as the common enemies of mankind, and exulting in their afflictions. On Tuesday and Wednesday nights, the 5th and 6th of November, women and children fled in every direction. One party of about one hundred and fifty fled to the prairie, where they wandered for several days, mostly without food; and nothing but the open firmament for their shelter. Other parties fled towards the Missouri River. During the dispersion of women and children, parties were hunting the men, firing upon some, tying up and whipping others, and some they pursued several miles.

Thursday, November 7. The shore began to be lined on both sides of the ferry with men, women and children; goods, wagons, boxes, provisions, etc., while the ferry was constantly employed; and when night again closed upon us the cottonwood bottom had much the appearance of a camp meeting. Hundreds of people were seen in every direction, some in tents and some in the open air around their fires, while the rain descended in torrents. Husbands were inquiring for their wives, wives for their husbands; parents for children, and children for parents. Some had the good fortune to escape with their families, household goods, and some provisions; while others knew not the fate of their friends, and had lost all their goods. The scene was indescribable, and, I am sure, would have melted the hearts of any people on the earth, except our blind oppressors, and a blind and ignorant community.

Next day our company still increased, and we were principally engaged in felling cottonwood trees and erecting them into small cabins. The next night being clear, we began to enjoy some degree of comfort.

The exodus

About two o'clock the next morning we were called up by the cry of signs in the heavens. We arose, and to our great astonishment all the firmament seemed enveloped in splendid fireworks, as if every star in the broad expanse had been hurled from its course, and sent lawless through the wilds of ether. Thousands of bright meteors were shooting through space in every direction, with long trains of light following in their course. This lasted for several hours, and was only closed by the dawn of the rising sun. Every heart was filled with joy at this majestic display of signs and wonders, showing the near approach of the coming of the Son of God.

All our goods were left behind; but I obtained some of them afterwards at the risk of my life. But all my provisions for the winter were destroyed or stolen, and my grain left growing on the ground for my enemies to harvest. My house was afterwards burned, and my fruit trees and improvements destroyed or plundered. In short, every member of the society was driven from the county, and fields of corn were ravaged and destroyed; stacks of wheat burned, household goods plundered, and improvements and every kind of property destroyed. One of this banditti afterwards boasted to one of the brethren that, according to their own account of the matter, the number of houses burned was two hundred and three.

The Saints who fled took refuge in the adjoining counties, mostly in Clay County, which received them with some degree of kindness. Those who fled to the county of Van Buren were again driven and compelled to flee; and those who fled to Lafayette County were soon expelled, or the most part of them, and had to move to wherever they could find protection.

When the news of these outrages reached the Governor of the State, courts of inquiry, both civil and military, were ordered by him, but nothing effectual was ever done to restore our rights, or to protect us in the least. It is true the Attorney-General, and a military escort under Colonel, afterwards General Doniphan, and our witnesses went to Jackson County and demanded indictments; but the court refused to do anything in the case, and the military, Attorney-General and witnesses were mobbed out of the county; and thus that matter ended.

The Governor also ordered them to restore the arms of which they robbed us, but they never were restored. Even our lands were robbed of their timber, and either occupied by our enemies for years or left desolate. Soon after Jackson County had rebelled against the laws and constitution of the General and State governments, several of the adjacent counties followed the example, by justifying her proceedings, and by opposing the Saints in settling among them. The counties of Clay, Ray, Clinton and various others, held public meetings, the tenor of which was to deprive the members of our society of the rights of citizenship, drive them from among them, and to compel them to settle only in such places as these outlaws should dictate; and even at that time some of their proceedings went so far as to publicly threaten to drive the whole society from the State. The excuses they offered for these outrages were:

First: The society were guilty principally of being eastern or northern people.

Secondly: They were guilty of some slight variations in manners and language from the other citizens of the State, who were mostly from the South.

Thirdly: Their religious principles differed in some important particulars from most other societies.

Fourthly: They were guilty of immigrating rapidly from the different States, and of purchasing large quantities of land, and of being more enterprising and industrious than their neighbors.

Fifthly: Some of them were guilty of poverty—especially those who had been driven, from time to time, and robbed of their all. And,

Lastly: They were said to be guilty of believing in the present Government administration of Indian affairs, viz: that the land west of the Mississippi, which Government had deeded in fee simple to the immigrating tribes, was destined by Providence for their permanent homes.

All these crimes were charged upon our society, in the public proceedings of the several counties, and were deemed sufficient to justify their unlawful proceedings against us. The reader may smile at this statement, but the public journals of Upper Missouri in 1835, actually printed charges and declarations against us, of the tenor of the foregoing.

By these wicked proceedings our people were once more compelled to remove, at a great sacrifice of property, and were at last permitted to settle in the north of Ray County, where, by the next legislature, they were organized into the counties of Caldwell and Davies. Here again they exercised the utmost industry and enterprise, and these wild regions soon presented a more flourishing aspect than the oldest counties of the State.

In the meantime, the majority of the State so far countenanced these outrages that they actually elected Lilburn W. Boggs (one of the oldest actors in the scenes of Jackson County, who had assisted in murder and plunder, and the expulsion of twelve hundred citizens, in 1833) for Governor of the State, and placed him in the executive chair, instead of suspending him by the neck, between the heavens and the earth, as his crimes justly merited. This movement may be said to have put an end to liberty, law and government in that State. About this time, Colonel Lucas, a leader of the banditti, was elected Major-General, instead of being hung for treason and murder. And Moses Wilson, another leader of the mob, was elected Brigadier-General; and others were advanced accordingly. These all very readily received their commissions from their accomplice, Governor Boggs, and thus corruption, rebellion and conspiracy had spread on every side, being fostered and encouraged by a large majority of the State; and thus the treason became general.

In the meantime, our society had greatly increased by a rapid immigration, and having long felt the withering hand of oppression from so corrupt an administration, they had endeavored to organize themselves, both civil and military, in the counties where they composed the majority, by electing such officers as they thought would stand for equal rights, and for the laws and Constitution of the country. In this way they hoped to withstand the storm which had so long beaten upon them, and whose black clouds now seemed lowering in awful gloom, preparing to burst with overwhelming fury upon all who dared to stand for liberty and law.

Chapter 14

As the history of this horrible persecution of the Church was interwoven with my own, I have traced it for a few years in connection; in which
I have of necessity digressed from the main thread of my own personal
narrative, to which I must return.

After making our escape into the county of Clay—being reduced to
the lowest poverty—I made a living by day labor, jobbing, building, or
wood cutting, till some time in the winter of 1834, when a general Conference was held at my house, in which it was decided that two of the Elders should be sent to Ohio, in order to counsel with President Smith
and the Church at Kirtland, and take some measures for the relief or restoration of the people thus plundered and driven from their homes. The
question was put to the Conference: "Who would volunteer to perform
so great a journey?"

The poverty of all, and the inclement season of the year made all
hesitate. At length Lyman Wight and myself offered our services, which
were readily accepted. I was at this time entirely destitute of proper
clothing for the journey; and I had neither horse, saddle, bridle, money
nor provisions to take with me; or to leave with my wife, who lay sick
and helpless most of the time.

Under these circumstances I knew not what to do. Nearly all had
been robbed and plundered, and all were poor. As we had to start without delay, I almost trembled at the undertaking; it seemed to be all but
an impossibility; but "to him that believeth all things are possible." I
started out of my house to do something towards making preparation; I

hardly knew which way to go, but I found myself in the house of brother John Lowry, and was intending to ask him for money; but as I entered his miserable cottage in the swamp, amid the low, timbered bottoms of the Missouri river, I found him sick in bed with a heavy fever, and two or three others of his family down with the same complaint, on different beds in the same room. He was vomiting severely, and was hardly sensible of my presence. I thought to myself, "well, this is a poor place to come for money, and yet I must have it; I know of no one else that has got it; what shall I do?" I sat a little while confounded and amazed. At length another Elder happened in; at that instant faith sprung up in my heart; the Spirit whispered to me, "is there anything too hard for the Lord?" I said to the Elder that came in: "Brother, I am glad you have come; these people must be healed, for I want some money of them, and must have it."

We laid hands on them and rebuked the disease; brother Lowry rose up well; I did my errand, and readily obtained all I asked. This provided in part for my family's sustenance while I should leave them. I went a little further into the woods of the Missouri bottoms, and came to a camp of some brethren, by the name of Higbee, who owned some horses; they saw me coming, and, moved by the Spirit, one of them said to the other, "there comes brother Parley; he's in want of a horse for his journey—I must let him have old Dick;" this being the name of the best horse he had. "Yes," said I, "brother, you have guessed right; but what will I do for a saddle?" "Well," says the other, "I believe I'll have to let you have mine." I blessed them and went on my way rejoicing.

I next called on Sidney A. Gilbert, a merchant, then sojourning in the village of Liberty—his store in Jackson County having been broken up, and his goods plundered and destroyed by the mob. "Well," says he, "brother Parley, you certainly look too shabby to start a journey; you must have a new suit; I have got some remnants left that will make you a coat," etc. A neighboring tailoress and two or three other sisters happened to be present on a visit, and hearing the conversation, exclaimed, "Yes, brother Gilbert, you find the stuff and we'll make it up for him." This arranged, I now lacked only a cloak; this was also furnished by brother Gilbert.

Brother Wight was also prospered in a similar manner in his preparations. Thus faith and the blessings of God had cleared up our way to accomplish what seemed impossible. We were soon ready, and on the first of February we mounted our horses, and started in good cheer to ride one thousand or fifteen hundred miles through a wilderness country. We had not one cent of money in our pockets on starting.

We travelled every day, whether through storm or sunshine, mud, rain or snow; except when our public duties called us to tarry. We arrived in Kirtland early in the spring, all safe and sound; we had lacked for nothing on the road, and now had plenty of funds in hand. President Joseph Smith and the Church in Kirtland received us with a hospitality and joy unknown except among the Saints; and much interest was felt there, as well as elsewhere, on the subject of our persecution.

The President inquired of the Lord concerning the matter, and a further mission was appointed us. * In fulfilment of which we continued our journey eastward, in connection with President Joseph Smith, S. Rigdon, Hyrum Smith, Frederick G. Williams, Orson Hyde and Orson Pratt.

We journeyed two and two in different routes, visiting the churches and instructing the people as we travelled. President Joseph Smith and myself journeyed together. We had a pleasant and prosperous mission among the churches, and some very interesting times in preaching to the public. We visited Freedom, Catteraugus County, N. Y.; tarried over Sunday, and preached several discourses, to which the people listened with great interest; we were kindly and hospitably entertained among them. We baptized a young man named Heman Hyde; his parents were Presbyterians, and his mother, on account of the strength of her traditions, thought that we were wrong, and told me afterwards that she would much rather have followed him to an earthly grave than to have seen him baptized.

Soon afterwards, however, herself, her husband, and the rest of the family, with some thirty or forty others, were all baptized and organized into a branch of the Church—called the Freedom branch—from which nucleus the light spread and souls were gathered into the fold in all the regions round. Thus mightily grew the word of God, or the seed sown by that extraordinary personage, the Prophet and Seer of the nineteenth century.

As we journeyed day after day, and generally lodged together, we had much sweet communion concerning the things of God and the mysteries of His kingdom, and I received many admonitions and instructions which I shall never forget.

---

*See Revelation, *Book of Doctrine and Covenants,* Section 101. [Now Section 103.]

Arriving in Geneseo, we met with the other Elders who had started from Kirtland on the same mission, and with others who were local, and held a general Conference. Among those whose hospitality we shared in that vicinity was old father Beeman and his amiable and interesting family. He was a good singer, and so were his three daughters; we were much edified and comforted in their society, and were deeply interested in hearing the old gentleman and brother Joseph converse on their early acquaintance and history. He had been intimate with Joseph long before the first organization of the Church; had assisted him to preserve the plates of the Book of Mormon from the enemy, and had at one time had them concealed under his own hearth.

At this Conference we had an interesting time; public meetings were convened; multitudes assembled to hear, and Presidents Joseph Smith and S. Rigdon addressed the crowds in great plainness of speech with mighty power. At the close of this Conference we again parted company, President Smith and most of the Elders returned home to Kirtland.

I then journeyed in connection with a young Elder, named H. Brown, as far as Henderson County, in northern New York, where lived Elder Brown's father, and where there was quite a branch of the Church. I visited with them for a few days, resting from my toils and ministering among them. Taking leave of these friends, I went to Sackett's Harbor, where all were yet strangers to the fulness of the gospel. Leaving an appointment at a hotel that I would return in a few days thence, and address the people wherever they saw fit to assemble, I crossed over the bay to a country neighborhood, called Pillar Point. In this neighborhood there had been some preaching by our Elders; but no branch of the Church organized, though there had been one or two instances of healing, and some few were believing. Here I appointed a meeting for evening in a school house; it was crowded full of people; indeed, all could not get in.

As the meeting closed a man named William Cory stepped forward, and earnestly begged of me to go home with him and minister to his wife, as she was lying at the point of death in consequence of a lingering sickness, not having risen up in her bed for six days without swooning or going into fits. He further said that he was worn out by being up with her every night, and that his neighbors were weary with watching, and it was doubted whether she could survive through the night without relief.

The Spirit would not suffer me to go with him that night, but I promised to call in the morning. At this many voices were heard, saying:

"Yes, yes, there's a case in hand; let him heal her and we'll all believe." Others exclaimed: "I wonder if she'll be at his meeting tomorrow! We shall see, and if so, we'll all believe." Expressions like these, joined with my own weakness, only tended to dampen my courage and confidence in the case.

I went home with a friend who invited me to partake of his hospitality for the night. As we entered his house, we found one of his children very sick with a violent pain in the head, to which it had been subject from its birth, and which came at regular periods, and was never relieved till it gathered and broke at his ear—so said his parents. The little fellow was rolling from side to side in his bed, and screeching and screaming with pain. I stepped to the bedside, and laid my hands upon his head in the name of Jesus Christ; he was instantly made whole and went to sleep. Next morning he got up well, and continued so; he said that the pain all left him as soon as my hands touched his head.

In the morning, before I arose, I had a vision, as follows: I saw a log house, and entered it through a door at the northwest corner; in the northeast corner lay a woman sick in bed; in the southeast corner was a small door opening into an adjoining room, and near it a stairway, where stood a ladder; the fireplace being in the south end. As I entered the house and laid my hands on the woman, she rose up and was made whole; the house being crowded, she took her seat near the fire and under the ladder, or near by it, and she praised God with a shout of glory, clapping her hands for joy, and exclaimed: "Thank God, I'm every whit whole." I awoke from my vision and related the same to the family where I stayed.

The man harnessed his horses, and with seven or eight persons in the wagon, including myself, we started for meeting, intending to call and see Mrs. Cory on our way, as I had appointed the previous evening. On alighting at her house I saw it was the same that I had seen in the vision; there were the doors, the stairway, ladder, fireplace, bed, and sick woman, just as I had seen and described.

I laid my hands upon the woman, and said: "In the name of Jesus Christ, be thou made whole this instant." I then commanded her to arise and walk. Her husband burst into tears; the people looked surprised; but the woman arose and walked to the fire, and happened to take her seat near the ladder, as I had related in the vision before I saw her. She then clapped her hands for joy, gave a shout of "Glory to God in the highest," and testified that she was every whit whole. We invited her to accompany us to the meeting; she immediately made ready, walked out, helped herself into the wagon, and rode some two miles over a very rough road. She then got out of the wagon, and walked with a strong and quick step into the meeting, where she sat till the discourse was over; when she arose and testified what the Lord had done for her. She then rode home, and was baptized in connection with several others, who came forward and obeyed the fulness of the gospel. We afterwards laid our hands on them for the gift of the Holy Ghost, when it fell upon them in great power, insomuch that all in the room felt its power and influence and glorified God; some spake in tongues, others prophesied and bore testimony to the truth.

The next evening I went over to Sackett's Harbor in order to preach; many of the people from Pillar Point, who had witnessed these things, went with me, and, among others, Mr. Cory with his wife, who had been so miraculously healed. A great rabble came out to hear, or rather to disturb the meeting; and among others, some half dozen clergymen of different orders, who were loud in their challenges and calls for miracles; "give us a miracle—we want a miracle—heal the sick—raise the dead, and then we'll believe." The lying, rage, and confusion excited by these wicked spirits, broke up the meeting, and I had much ado to get out of the crowd without being stoned or torn to pieces.

After tarrying a few days in this region, I took leave and continued my journey as far as Columbia County, east of the Hudson. I arrived at my Aunt Van Cott's, and found them all well; paid a visit to my father and mother; gave them money sufficient to enable them to remove to Kirtland, Ohio, and then commenced my return. I had started from the frontiers of Missouri and ridden on horseback fifteen hundred miles.

As I returned towards the West, I came to the town of Freedom, Catteraugus County, N. Y., where President Joseph Smith and myself had preached on our outward journey, a few weeks previously, and where we had baptized a young man by the name of Heman Hyde, as the first fruits in that place. As I called for the night, I found that a large church had been gathered during my absence, consisting of some forty members or more, principally through the labors of my brother Orson. The new members, and the people in general, rejoiced to see me, and aided me on my journey; and Heman Hyde accompanied me to Kirtland, where we arrived the latter part of April, and were kindly and hospitably entertained by President Joseph Smith.

Chapter 15

It was now the first of May, 1834, and our mission had resulted in the assembling of about two hundred men at Kirtland, with teams, baggage,
provisions, arms, etc., for a march of one thousand miles, for the purpose of carrying some supplies to the afflicted and persecuted Saints in
Missouri, and to reinforce and strengthen them; and, if possible, to influence the Governor of the State to call out sufficient additional force
to cooperate in restoring them to their rights. This little army was led by
President Joseph Smith in person. It commenced its march about the
first of May; passing through Ohio, Indiana, and Illinois, it entered Missouri some time in June.

I was chiefly engaged as a recruiting officer, and, not being much
with the camp, can give but little of its history. I visited branches of the
Church in Ohio, Indiana, Illinois and Missouri, and obtaining what
men and means I could, fell in with the camp from time to time with additional men, arms, stores and money. On one occasion, I had travelled
all night to overtake the camp with some men and means, and having
breakfasted with them and changed horses, I again started ahead on express to visit other branches, and do business to again overtake them. At
noon I had turned my horse loose from the carriage to feed on the grass
in the midst of a broad, level plain. No habitation was near; stillness and
repose reigned around me; I sank down overpowered with a deep sleep,
and might have lain in a state of oblivion till the shades of night had
gathered about me, so completely was I exhausted for want of sleep and

rest; but I had only slept a few moments till the horse had grazed
sufficiently, when a voice, more loud and shrill than I have ever before
heard, fell on my ear, and thrilled through every part of my system; it
said: *"Parley, it is time to be up and on your journey."* In the twinkling of
an eye I was perfectly aroused; I sprang to my feet so suddenly that I
could not at first recollect where I was, or what was before me to perform. I related the circumstance afterwards to brother Joseph Smith, and
he bore testimony that it was the angel of the Lord who went before the
camp, who found me overpowered with sleep, and thus awoke me.

Arriving in the Allred settlement, near Salt River, Missouri, where
there was a large branch of the Church, the camp rested a little, and despatched Elder Orson Hyde and myself to Jefferson City, to request of His
Excellency, Governor Daniel Dunklin, a sufficient military force, with
orders to reinstate the exiles, and protect them in the possession of their
homes in Jackson County.

We had an interview with the Governor, who readily acknowledged the justice of the demand, but frankly told us he dare not attempt
the execution of the laws in that respect, for fear of deluging the whole
country in civil war and bloodshed. He advised us to relinquish our
rights, for the sake of peace, and to sell our lands from which we had
been driven. To this we replied with firmness, that we would hold no
terms with land pirates and murderers. If we could not be permitted to
live on lands which we had purchased of the United States, and be protected in our persons and rights, our lands would, at least, make a good
burying ground, on which to lay our bones; and, like Abraham's possession in Canaan, we should hold on to our possessions in the county of
Jackson, for this purpose, at least. He replied that he did not blame us in
the least, but trembled for the country, and dare not carry out the plain,
acknowledged and imperative duties of his office. We retired, saying to
ourselves: "That poor coward ought, in duty, to resign; he owes this,
morally at least, in justice to his oath of office."

We returned to the camp, which was then on the march, somewhere below the county of Ray. President Joseph Smith, his brother
Hyrum, L. Wight and others, repaired with us into a solitary grove,
apart, to learn the result of our mission.

After hearing our report, the President called on the God of our
fathers to witness the justice of our cause and the sincerity of our vows,
which we engaged to fulfill, whether in this life or in the life to come.
For, as God lives, truth, justice and innocence shall triumph, and iniquity shall not reign.

Pursuing our journey, we arrived at Fishing River, Ray County, and encamped for the night on a hill between its forks. This stream was then about six inches deep in each of its branches where the road crossed it. We had but just camped, when there arose such a storm as has been seldom witnessed on our earth; the wind blew, the vivid lightning flashed, the thunder rolled, the earth trembled, and the floods descended in a manner never before witnessed by us. Our tents were blown down, and some of us lay six or eight inches deep in water. There was a large meeting house there with the door open, into which many of us gathered for shelter, after being nearly drowned.

Next morning the fords of Fishing River were said to be twenty to forty feet deep. We afterwards learned that an army of outlaws were in our neighborhood, and would have attacked us that night but for the storm; the floods in the river each side of us prevented a hostile meeting, until certain citizens made the acquaintance of our leaders, and learned their intentions. Thus the excitement was allayed, and the outlaws finally disbanded.

About this time, owing to some murmurings and insubordination in the camp, the cholera broke out among them, in fulfilment of the word of the Lord, by the mouth of His servant Joseph, and resulted in the death of some fifteen or twenty of the camp, or of others connected with the Saints. Finally, the camp was by the word of the Lord, disbanded; some remained as settlers in that country, and others returned to their homes and families in Ohio.

I left the camp at Fishing River, and arrived home in Clay County, where my family resided, late in July. I found my wife still afflicted, and on account of long sickness, was reduced to greater poverty than before, and I was somewhat embarrassed with debts on account of her board, etc., while I was absent.

About the time of the arrival of the camp at Fishing River, the mob of Jackson County sent a committee of twelve of their leaders, to confer with the authorities of the exiled Church in Clay County, to make proposals for the settlement of the whole matter, by purchasing the lands from which they had been driven. The Saints would not sell their lands to their murderers and the land pirates who had driven and plundered them; therefore the mob's representatives were unsuccessful.

As this committee of twelve returned, and were crossing the Missouri River at evening, their boat sank in an instant in the middle of the stream, and only about half of the committee ever reached the shore alive. Brother Joseph said it was the angel of the Lord who sank the boat.

Having no means of support except by the labor of my hands, I now commenced again to exert myself at hard labor. In this I continued till October of the same year, when, being counselled by the Presidency to remove to Ohio, I started a journey of one thousand miles with my wife, in a wagon drawn by two horses. We had not a single dollar in money, but we trusted in God, and lacked for nothing. During this journey my wife continued in a very feeble state of health.

After a journey of near one thousand miles, we arrived at New Portage, fifty miles from Kirtland, early in the winter, and finding a large society of the Saints who welcomed us among them, we stopped for the winter. I now commenced to preach, both in that place and in all the region round, to multitudes who turned out to hear the Word. Many embraced the gospel, and enjoyed the gifts of God; instances of healing were of almost daily occurrence, and the people waxed strong in the faith and in the gifts and power of God. I also labored with my hands with all diligence, when time would permit; thus the winter passed away.

While laboring here, letters were received from W. W. Phelps, then President of the Church in Missouri, suspending my papers because I had gone away in debt; which debt had been contracted in behalf of my sick wife while I had been away in the service of the Conference, as recorded in the previous chapter. I had once offered the money on the same, but the person to whom it was due, in view of my public services, refused to take it; nevertheless, President Phelps now censured me severely, observing in his letter that such conduct was not the way of the pure in heart.

Under this censure I ceased to officiate, at which both the Church and people in general in and about New Portage were much grieved. In the fore part of February, 1835, I repaired to Kirtland, laid the case before President Smith, with my defence in writing, in which is stated the true circumstances. I proceeded to plead the injustice of the accusation, when the President arose to his feet, lifted his hand to heaven, and with a voice, and energy, and power of the Holy Spirit which thrilled the inmost soul, and would have raised the dead, he exclaimed: "Brother Parley, God bless you, go your way rejoicing, preach the gospel, fill the measure of your mission, and walk such things under your feet; it was a trick of Satan to hinder your usefulness; God Almighty shall be with you, and nothing shall stay your hand."

I was comforted, encouraged, filled with new life, thanking God that there was one noble spirit on the earth who could discern justice and equity, appreciate the labors of others, and had boldness of soul to judge and act accordingly.

In accordance with one of the early revelations to the Church concerning the calling and ordination of Twelve Apostles,* this quorum was now being filled. Among those chosen for this high and holy calling was my brother Orson and myself. He being still absent, and the other members having been already ordained, a meeting was convened at Kirtland, and very numerously attended, in which, on the 21st day of February, 1835, I took the oath and covenant of apostleship, and was solemnly set apart and ordained to that office; and as a member of that quorum under the hands of Joseph Smith, Oliver Cowdery and David Whitmer; the minutes of which in the Church History are as follows:

"Kirtland, February 21st, 1835. Pursuant to adjournment, a meeting of the Church was held, and, after prayer by President David Whitmer, and a short address by President Oliver Cowdery to the congregation, Elder Parley P. Pratt was called to the stand, and ordained one of the Twelve by President Joseph Smith, Jr., David Whitmer and Oliver Cowdery. 'O, Lord, smile from heaven upon this thy servant; forgive his sins, sanctify his heart, and prepare him to receive the blessing. Increase his love for thee and for thy cause; increase his intelligence, communicate to him all that wisdom, that prudence and that understanding which he needs as a minister of righteousness, and to magnify the apostleship whereunto he is called. May a double portion of that Spirit which was communicated to the disciples of our Lord and Saviour, to lead them to all truth, rest down upon him, and go with him where he goes, that nothing shall prevail against him; that he may be delivered from prisons, from the power of his enemies, and from the adversary of all righteousness. May he be able to mount up on wings as an eagle; to run and not be weary, to walk and not to faint; may he have great wisdom and intelligence, and be able to lead thine elect through this thorny maze. Let sickness and death have no power over him; let him be equal with his brethren in bringing many sons and daughters to glory, and many nations to a knowledge of the truth. Great blessings shall rest upon thee; thy faith shall increase, thou shalt have great power to prevail. The veil of the heavens shall be rolled up, thou shalt be permitted to gaze within it, and receive instructions from on high. No arm that is formed and lifted against thee shall prosper, no power shall prevail, for thou shalt have power with God, and shalt proclaim His gospel.

---

*See Revelation, *Book of Doctrine and Covenants*, Section 43. [Now Section 18.]

Thou wilt be afflicted, but thou shalt be delivered, and conquer all thy foes. Thine office shall never be taken from thee, thou shalt be called great, angels shall carry thee from place to place. Thy sins are forgiven, and thy name written in the Lamb's Book of Life; even so. Amen.'

CHARGE GIVEN BY OLIVER COWDERY TO P. P. PRATT

"I am aware, dear brother, that the mind naturally claims something new; but the same thing rehearsed frequently profits us. You will have the same difficulties to encounter in fulfilling this ministry that the ancient Apostles had. You have enlisted in a cause that requires your whole attention; you ought, therefore, to count the cost; and to become a polished shaft, you must be sensible, requires the labor of years, and your station requires a perfect polish. It is required not merely to travel a few miles in the country, but in distant countries; you must endure much toil, much labor, and many privations to become perfectly polished. Your calling is not like that of the husbandman, to cultivate a stinted portion of the planet on which we dwell, and when Heaven has given the former and the latter rain, and mellow autumn ripened his fruits, gather it in, and congratulate himself for a season in the remission of his toils, while he anticipates his winter evenings of relaxation and fireside enjoyments. But, dear brother, it is far otherwise with you. Your labor must be incessant, and your toil great; you must go forth and labor till the great work is done. It will require a series of years to accomplish it; but you will have this pleasing consolation, that your Heavenly Father requires it; the field is His; the work is His; and He will not only cheer you, animate you, and buoy you up in your pilgrimmage, in your arduous toils; but when your work is done and your labor o'er, he will take you to himself. But before this consummation of your felicity, bring your mind to bear upon what will be imperiously required of you to accomplish the great work that lies before you. Count well the cost. You have read of the persecutions and trials of ancient days. Has not bitter experience taught you that they are the same now? You will be dragged before the authorities for the religion you profess; and it were better not to set out than to start, look back, or shrink when dangers thicken upon, or appalling death stares you in the face. I have spoken these things, dear brother, because I have seen them in visions. There are strong dungeons and gloomy prisons for you. These should not appall you. You must be called a good or bad man. The ancients passed through the same. They had this testimony, that they had seen the Saviour after he rose from the dead. You must bear some testimony, or your mission, your labor, your toil will be in vain. You must bear the same testimony that there is but one God, one Mediator; he that has seen Him will know Him, and testify of Him. Beware of pride; beware of evil; shun the very appearance of it; for the time is coming when, if you do not give heed to these things, you will have a fall. Among your many afflictions you will have many blessings also; but you must pass through many afflictions in order to receive the glory that is in reserve for you. You will see thousands who, when they first see you, will know nothing about salvation by Jesus Christ; you shall see a nation born in a day. A great work lies before you, and the time is near when you must bid farewell to your native land, cross the mighty deep, and sound the tocsin of alarm to other nations, kindreds, tongues and people. Remember, that all your hopes of deliverance from danger and from death will rest upon your faithfulness to God; in His cause you must necessarily serve Him with a perfect heart and a willing mind. Avoid strife and vain glory; think not yourself better than your brethren, but pray for them as well as for yourself; and if you are faithful, great will be your blessings; but if you are not, your stewardship will be taken from you and another appointed in your stead.

"Elder Pratt gave his hand to President O. Cowdery, and said he had received ordination, and should fulfil the ministry according to the grace given him; to which the President replied: 'Go forth, and angels shall bear thee up, and thou shalt come forth at the last day, bringing many with thee.'"

Thomas B. Marsh and Orson Pratt were absent on a mission. Elder Marsh returned to Kirtland on the 25th of April, and Elder Pratt on the 26th, and received their ordinations and blessing.

The following charge was given to the Twelve by President O. Cowdery:

"Dear Brethren: Previous to delivering the charge, I shall read a part of a revelation. It is known to you that, previous to the organization of this Church, in 1830, the Lord gave revelations, or the Church could not have been organized. The people of this Church were weak in faith compared with the ancient. Those who embarked in this cause were desirous to know how the work was to be conducted. They read many things in the Book of Mormon concerning their duty, and the way the great work ought to be done; but the minds of men are so constructed that they will not believe without a testimony of seeing or hearing. The Lord gave us a revelation that, in process of time, there should be twelve men chosen to preach His gospel to Jew and Gentile.

"Our minds have been on a constant stretch to find who these twelve were, when the time should come we could not tell; but we sought the Lord by fasting and prayer to have our lives prolonged to see this day; to see you; and to take a retrospect of the difficulties through which we have passed; but, having seen the day, it becomes my duty to deliver to you a charge; and first, a few remarks respecting your ministry. You have many revelations put into your hands; revelations to make you acquainted with the nature of your mission; you will have difficulties by reason of your visiting all the nations of the world. You will need wisdom in a ten-fold proportion to what you have ever had; you will have to combat all the prejudices of all nations."

He then read the revelation and said: "Have you desired this ministry with all your hearts? If you have desired it, you are called of God, not of man, to go into all the world." He then read again from the revelation what the Lord said to the Twelve. "Brethren, you have your duty presented in this revelation. You have been ordained to the holy priesthood; you have received it from those who have their power and authority from an angel; you are to preach the gospel to every nation. Should you in the least degree come short of your duty, great will be your condemnation; for the greater the calling the greater the transgression. I, therefore, warn you to cultivate great humility, for I know the pride of the human heart. Beware, lest the flatterers of the world lift you up; beware, lest your affections are captivated by worldly objects. Let your ministry be first. Remember, the souls of men are committed to your charge, and, if you mind your calling, you shall always prosper.

"You have been indebted to other men in the first instance for evidence; on that you have acted; but it is necessary that you receive a testimony from Heaven for yourselves; so that you can bear testimony to the truth of the Book of Mormon, and that you have seen the face of God. That is more than the testimony of an angel. When the proper time arrives, you shall be able to bear this testimony to the world. When you bear testimony that you have seen God, this testimony God will never suffer to fall, but will bear you out; although many will not give heed, yet others will. You will, therefore, see the necessity of getting this testimony from Heaven.

"Never cease striving till you have seen God face to face. Strengthen your faith; cast off your doubts, your sins, and all your unbelief, and nothing can prevent you from coming to God. Your ordination is not full and complete till God has laid His hands upon you. We require as much to qualify us as did those who have gone before us; God is the

Four pictures of Parley P. Pratt

Thomas B. Marsh

David W. Patten

Brigham Young

Heber C. Kimball

Orson Hyde

William E. McLellin

Parley P. Pratt

Luke S. Johnson

William B. Smith

Orson Pratt

John F. Boynton

Lyman E. Johnson

same. If the Saviour in former days laid his hands on his disciples, why not in latter days?

"With regard to superiority I must make a few remarks. The ancient Apostles sought to be great; but lest the seeds of discord be sown in this matter, understand particularly the voice of the Spirit on this occasion. God does not love you better or more than others. You are to contend for the faith once delivered to the saints. Jacob, you know, wrestled till he obtained. It was by fervent prayer and diligent search that you have obtained the testimony you are now able to bear. You are as one; you are equal in bearing the keys of the kingdom to all nations. You are called to preach the gospel of the Son of God to the nations of the earth; it is the will of your Heavenly Father that you proclaim His gospel to the ends of the earth, and the islands of the sea.

"Be zealous to save souls. The soul of one man is as precious as the soul of another. You are to bear this message to those who consider themselves wise; and such may persecute you; they may seek your life. The adversary has always sought the life of the servants of God; you are, therefore, to be prepared at all times to make a sacrifice of your lives, should God require them in the advancement and building up of His cause. Murmur not at God. Be always prayerful; be always watchful. You will bear with me while I relieve the feelings of my heart. We shall not see another day like this; the time has fully come; the voice of the Spirit has come to set these men apart.

"You will see the time when you will desire to see such a day as this, and you will not see it. Every heart wishes you peace and prosperity; but the scene with you will inevitably change. Let no man take your bishopric; and beware that you lose not your crowns. It will require your whole souls; it will require courage like Enoch's.

"The time is near when you will be in the midst of congregations who will gnash their teeth upon you. This gospel must roll, and will roll until it fills the whole earth. Did I say congregations would gnash upon you? Yea, I say nations will gnash upon you; you will be considered the worst of men. Be not discouraged at this. When God pours out His Spirit the enemy will rage; but God, remember, is on your right hand and on your left. A man, though he be considered the worst, has joy, who is conscious that he pleases God. The lives of those who proclaim the true gospel will be in danger; this has been the case ever since the days of righteous Abel. The same opposition has been manifest whenever men came forward to publish the gospel. The time is coming when you will be considered the worst by many, and by some the best of men. The time is coming when you will be perfectly familiar with the things of God. This testimony will make those who do not believe your testimony seek your lives; but there are whole nations who will receive your testimony. They will call you good men. Be not lifted up when you are called good men. Remember you are young men, and you shall be spared. I include the other three. Bear them in mind in your prayers; carry their cases to a throne of grace; although they are not present, yet you and they are equal. This appointment is calculated to create an affection in you for each other stronger than death. You will travel to other nations; bear each other in mind. If one or more is cast into prison, let the others pray for him, and deliver him by their prayers. Your lives shall be in great jeopardy; but the promise of God is, that you shall be delivered.

"Remember you are not to go to other nations till you receive your endowment. Tarry at Kirtland until you are endowed with power from on high. You need a fountain of wisdom, knowledge and intelligence, such as you never had. Relative to the endowment, I make a remark or two, that there be no mistake. The world cannot receive the things of God. He can endow you without worldly pomp or great parade. He can give you that wisdom, that intelligence and that power which character- ized the ancient saints, and now characterizes the inhabitants of the upper world. The greatness of your commission consists in this: You are to hold the keys of this ministry; you are to go to the nations afar off; na- tions that sit in darkness. The day is coming when the work of God must be done. Israel shall be gathered. The seed of Jacob shall be gathered from their long dispersion. There will be a feast to Israel, the elect of God. It is a sorrowful tale, but the gospel must be preached, and God's ministers rejected; but where can Israel be found and receive your tes- timony and not rejoice? Nowhere! The prophecies are full of great things that are to take place in the last days. After the elect are gathered out, destruction shall come on the inhabitants of the earth; all nations shall feel the wrath of God, after they have been warned by the saints of the Most High. If you will not warn them others will, and you will lose your crowns.

"You must prepare your minds to bid a long farewell to Kirtland, even till the great day come. You will see what you never expected to see; you will need the mind of Enoch or Elijah, and the faith of the brother of Jared; you must be prepared to walk by faith, however appal- ling the prospect to human view; you, and each of you, should feel the force of the imperious mandate, 'Son, go labor in my vineyard,' and cheerfully receive what comes; but in the end you will stand while others will fall. You have read in the revelation concerning ordination: 'Beware how you ordain, for all nations are not like this nation; they will willingly receive the ordinances at your hands to put you out of the way. There will be times when nothing but the angels of God can deliver you out of their hands.'

"We appeal to your intelligence, we appeal to your understanding, that we have so far discharged our duty to you. We consider it one of the greatest condescensions of our Heavenly Father in pointing you out to us; you will be stewards over this ministry; you have a work to do that no other men can do; you must proclaim the gospel in its simplicity and purity, and we commend you to God and the word of His grace. You have our best wishes, you have our most fervent prayers, that you may be able to bear this testimony,—that you have seen the face of God. Therefore, call upon Him in faith and mighty prayer, till you prevail; for it is your duty and privilege to bear such testimony for yourselves. We now exhort you to be faithful to fulfil your calling,—there must be no lack here; you must fulfil in all things, and permit us to repeat, all nations have a claim on you; you are bound together as the three witnesses were; you, notwithstanding, can part and meet, and meet and part again, till your heads are silvered o'er with age."

He then took them separately by the hand, and said, "Do you with full purpose of heart take part in this ministry, to proclaim the gospel with all diligence, with these your brethren, according to the tenor and intent of the charge you have received?" Each of whom answered in the affirmative.

Chapter 16

After this solemn ordinance was completed, together with the blessings, charges and instructions connected therewith, I was instructed to
prepare for a mission in the coming spring, in connection with my brethren of the quorum.

I now returned home to New Portage, and began to make preparations for my mission, but the state of my affairs was such that it seemed
almost impossible for me to leave home; my wife was sick, my aged
mother had come to live with me, and looked to me for support—age
and infirmity having rendered my father unable to do for himself or family. I was also engaged in building a house, and in other business, while
at the same time I was somewhat in debt, and in want of most of the
necessaries of life.

Under these embarrassed circumstances, I hesitated for a while
whether to attempt to perform the mission assigned me, or stay at home
and finish my building and mechanical work. While I pondered these
things, with my mind unsettled, and continued my work, with a feeling
of hesitation whether it was a duty to sacrifice all the labor and expense
to which I had been in my preparations and unfinished work, or whether
it was a duty to stay and complete it, I was called very suddenly to administer to a brother by the name of Matthews, who was taken suddenly
and dangerously ill. I found him writhing and groaning in the utmost
agony, being cramped and convulsed in a horrible manner, while the
family were in great consternation, and weeping around him. I kneeled
down to pray, but in the midst of my prayer we were interrupted by the
cry of *fire! fire!! fire!!!* We sprang from our knees, and ran towards my

house, which was all in a blaze, being an unfinished, two story frame building, open to the fresh breeze and full of shavings, lumber, shingles, etc., while a family occupied a small apartment of the same, and no water near.

Our utmost exertions barely accomplished the removal of the family and their goods; the building, tools, boards, shingles, building materials, all were consumed in a few moments. Thus closed all my hesitation; my works of that nature were now all completed, and myself ready to fill my mission. One gave me a coat; another a hat; a third, house room; a fourth, provisions; while a fifth forgave me the debts due to them; and a sixth bade me God speed to hasten on my mission.

Taking an affectionate leave of my family and friends in New Portage, I repaired to Kirtland, ready to accompany my brethren. While they made ready I paid a visit to an adjoining township called Mentor; and visiting from house to house, I attempted to preach to them; but they were full of lying and prejudice, and would not hear the Word. I then appointed a meeting in the open air, on the steps of a meeting house owned by a people called "Campbellites," one Mr. Alexander Campbell being their leader; they having refused to open the house to me. Some came to hear, and some to disturb the meeting; and one Mr. Newel soon appeared at the head of a mob of some fifty men and a band of music. These formed in order of battle and marched round several times near where I stood, drowning my voice with the noise of their drums and other instruments. I suspended my discourse several times as they passed, and then resumed. At length, finding that no disturbance of this kind would prevent the attempt to discharge my duty, they rushed upon me with one accord at a given signal, every man throwing an egg at my person. My forehead, bosom, and most of my body was completely covered with broken eggs. At this I departed, and walked slowly away, being insulted and followed by this rabble for some distance. I soon arrived in Kirtland, and was assisted by my kind friends in cleansing myself and clothes from the effects of this Christian benevolence.

All things being in readiness, and the spring fairly opened, the Twelve took their journey down Lake Erie, and landed at Dunkirk, in the neighborhood of which we had appointed to hold a conference. The members of the Church assembled from the region round, and the people turned out in great numbers. We addressed them in several interesting discourses, and had a good time; many seemed to receive the Word with joy, and some were baptized and added to the Church.

From thence we continued our journey through the Eastern States, holding conferences in every place where branches of the Church had been organized, ordaining and instructing Elders and other officers; exhorting the members to continue in prayer and in well doing; ministering to the sick and instructing the ignorant. We also preached the Word, and baptized such as desired to be obedient to the faith; confirming them by the laying on of hands and prayer in the name of Jesus Christ; thus the Holy Ghost and the gifts thereof were shed forth among the people, and they had great joy. The month of August 1835, found us in the State of Maine, and the mission completed.

We now returned to Boston, and from thence home to Kirtland, where we arrived sometime in October. After spending a few days in the society of the Saints in Kirtland, I repaired to New Portage, where I found my wife and mother in usual health, and was received with joy by them and the Saints. I now made preparation and removed to Kirtland, in order to be with the body of the Church at headquarters; and to improve every opportunity of obtaining instruction.

A portion of the Temple at Kirtland was now finished, and schools were opened in several apartments. The Presidency of the Church, the Twelve, and many others were organized into a school for the purpose of studying the Hebrew language. This study, and the meetings of the several quorums for instruction and endowment, occupied most of the winter.

The ordinances of the priesthood were revealed to a greater extent than had been known among men since the prophets and Apostles of old fell asleep; and many were anointed to their holy calling, and were instructed in principles which were great and glorious in themselves, and calculated to enlarge the mind and prepare the chosen servants of God for the great work before them. Many great and marvelous things were prophesied, which I am not at liberty to record, and many of which have since been fulfilled to the very letter. Many persons were carried away in the visions of the Spirit, and saw and heard unspeakable things; and many enjoyed the ministering of angels, and the gift of healing and of speaking in tongues.

Spring at length returned, and the Elders prepared to take leave of each other, and to go on their several missions. As to myself, I was deeply in debt for the expenses of life during the winter, and on account of purchasing a lot, and building thereon. I, therefore, knew not what to do, whether to go on a mission or stay at home, and endeavor by industry to sustain my family and pay my debts.

It was now April; I had retired to rest one evening at an early hour,

Kirtland Temple

and was pondering my future course, when there came a knock at the door. I arose and opened it, when Elder Heber C. Kimball and others entered my house, and being filled with the spirit of prophecy, they blessed me and my wife, and prophesied as follows:

"Brother Parley, thy wife shall be healed from this hour, and shall bear a son, and his name shall be Parley; and he shall be a chosen instrument in the hands of the Lord to inherit the priesthood and to walk in the steps of his father. He shall do a great work in the earth in ministering the Word and teaching the children of men. Arise, therefore, and go forth in the ministry, nothing doubting. Take no thoughts for your debts, nor the necessaries of life, for the Lord will supply you with abundant means for all things.

"Thou shalt go to Upper Canada, even to the city of Toronto, the capital, and there thou shalt find a people prepared for the fulness of the gospel, and they shall receive thee, and thou shalt organize the Church among them, and it shall spread thence into the regions round about, and many shall be brought to the knowledge of the truth and shall be filled with joy; and from the things growing out of this mission, shall the fulness of the gospel spread into England, and cause a great work to be done in that land.

"You shall not only have means to deliver you from your present embarrassments, but you shall yet have riches, silver and gold, till you will loath the counting thereof."

This prophecy was the more marvelous, because being married near ten years we had never had any children; and for near six years my wife had been consumptive, and had been considered incurable. However, we called to mind the faith of Abraham of old, and judging Him faithful who had promised, we took courage.

I now began in earnest to prepare for the mission, and in a few days all was ready. I took an affectionate leave of my wife, mother and friends, and started for Canada in company with a brother Nickerson, who kindly offered to bear my expenses. After a long and tedious passage in a public coach (the roads being very bad and the lake not open), we arrived at the Falls of Niagara sometime in the month of April, 1836.

As this was my first visit to this place it made a deep and awful impression on my mind. We halted a short time to view this wonder of nature, and to adore that God who had formed a world so sublimely grand. The leaping of a mighty river of waters over a perpendicular fall of one hundred and sixty feet, the foaming and dashing of its white spray upon the rocks beneath; the rising cloud of mist with its glittering rainbow, the yawning gulf with its thousand whirlpools; all conspired to fill the contemplative mind with wonder and admiration, and with reverence to the Great Author of all the wonders of creation; while its everlasting roar which may be heard for many miles distant, seemed a lively emblem of eternity.

While musing on this spot, I fell into the following train of reflection: O, Niagara! Generations may pass in long succession; ages may roll away and others still succeed; empires may rise and flourish, and pass away and be forgotten; but still thy deafening, thy solemn and awful voice is heard in one eternal roar. The temples of marble may moulder to dust, the monuments of the great may crumble to decay, the palaces of kings fall to ruin and their very place become unknown, their history forgotten in the almost countless ages of antiquity; and still thy sound is heard in everlasting moan, as if mourning over the ruins of by-gone years.

With deepest eloquence thou seemest to speak in awful pride, saying: "Before Abraham was, I am;" and with mingled feelings of pity and contempt thou seemest to inquire:—

> Where now is Nimrod's mighty tower? Where the
> Majestic walls, the warlike battlements,
> The splendid palaces, the hanging gardens
> Of Babylon?
> Where the proud Nebuchadnezzar, who, with
> Golden sceptre, swayed the world, and made
> The nations tremble? Where the proud Nineveh,—
> The strong Thebes, with its hundred gates?
> The golden Tyre, the splendid Athens, the
> Majestic Rome, with all their works of art—
> Their monuments of fame, once the pride
> And glory of the world?
> Where the mighty Pharaoh's, the terrible
> Alexanders, the invincible Cesars,
> The warlike Hannibal? Tyrants in turn.
> Where now the gifted poets, the splendid
> Orators, the profound philosophers
> Of Greece and Rome, whose mighty genius
> Hurled royal tyrants headlong from their thrones,—
> Made senates weep or laugh at will, and ruled
> The nations? They are swept away by time;
> Their beauty, like the morning flower, is withered
> Their pride and glory gone like leaves of autumn;—
> Their grandest works are fast decaying,
> Mouldering to ruin, soon to be forgotten.

But still my store house is unexhausted,
My fountain full and overflowing—my
Solid munitions of rocks stand secure.—
My voice as mighty as when the beauteous
Colors of the rainbow first sported in
The sunbeams:—
As when the intelligences of olden worlds
First gazed with admiration upon my
Expanded waters; or, animated at
The music of my voice joined in the chorus,
And all the sons of God shouted for joy.

But, boast not, O proud Niagara! Though
Thou mayest withstand the ravages of time,—
While countless millions, swept away with all
Their mighty works, are lost in following years.—
Yet there is a voice to speak, long and loud;
'Tis Michael's trump, whose mighty blast shall rend
Thy rocks, and bow thy lofty mountains in the dust,
Before whose awful presence thy waters
Blush in retiring modesty; and in
Respectful silence thou shalt stand in listening
Wonder, and admire, while thunders roll
Majestic round the sky, the lightnings play,—
The mountains sink—the valleys rise—till Earth,
Restored to its original, receives
Its final rest, and groans and sighs no more.

Till then, weep on, and let thy voice ascend
In solemn music to the skies,—'tis like
A funeral dirge,—'tis fit to weep o'er the miseries
Of a fallen world in anguish deep.

Chapter 17

Leaving the Falls we continued our journey for a day or two on foot, and as the Sabbath approached we halted in the neighborhood of Hamilton, and gave out two or three appointments for meetings. Brother Nickerson now left me to fill these appointments, and passed on to his home, in a distant part of the province.

I preached to the people, and was kindly entertained till Monday morning, when I took leave and entered Hamilton, a flourishing town at the head of Lake Ontario; but my place of destination was Toronto, around on the north side of the lake. If I went by land I would have a circuitous route, muddy and tedious to go on foot. The lake had just opened, and steamers had commenced plying between the two places; two dollars would convey me to Toronto in a few hours, and save some days of laborious walking; but I was an entire stranger in Hamilton, and also in the province; and money I had none. Under these circumstances I pondered what I should do. I had many times received answers to prayer in such matters; but now it seemed hard to exercise faith, because I was among strangers and entirely unknown. The Spirit seemed to whisper to me to try the Lord, and see if anything was too hard for him, that I might know and trust Him under all circumstances. I retired to a secret place in a forest and prayed to the Lord for money to enable me to cross the lake. I then entered Hamilton and commenced to chat with some of the people. I had not tarried many minutes before I was accosted by a stranger, who inquired my name and where I was going. He also asked me if I did not want some money. I said yes. He then gave me ten dollars and a letter of introduction to John Taylor, of Toronto, where I arrived the same evening.

Mrs. Taylor received me kindly, and went for her husband, who was busy in his mechanic shop. To them I made known my errand to the city, but received little direct encouragement. I took tea with them, and then sought lodgings at a public house.

In the morning I commenced a regular visit to each of the clergy of the place, introducing myself and my errand. I was absolutely refused hospitality, and denied the opportunity of preaching in any of their houses or congregations. Rather an unpromising beginning, thought I, considering the prophecies on my head concerning Toronto. However, nothing daunted, I applied to the Sheriff for the use of the Court House, and then to the authorities for a public room in the market place; but with no better success. What could I do more? I had exhausted my influence and power without effect. I now repaired to a pine grove just out of the town, and, kneeling down, called on the Lord, bearing testimony of my unsuccessful exertions; my inability to open the way; at the same time asking Him in the name of Jesus to open an effectual door for His servant to fulfil his mission in that place.

I then arose and again entered the town, and going to the house of John Taylor, had placed my hand on my baggage to depart from a place where I could do no good, when a few inquiries on the part of Mr. Taylor, inspired by a degree of curiosity or of anxiety, caused a few moments' delay, during which a lady by the name of Walton entered the house, and, being an acquaintance of Mrs. Taylor's, was soon engaged in conversation with her in an adjoining room. I overheard the following:

"Mrs. Walton, I am glad to see you; there is a gentleman here from the United States who says the Lord sent him to this city to preach the gospel. He has applied in vain to the clergy and to the various authorities for opportunity to fulfil his mission, and is now about to leave the place. He may be a man of God; I am sorry to have him depart."

"Indeed!" said the lady; "well, I now understand the feelings and spirit which brought me to your house at this time. I have been busy over the wash tub and too weary to take a walk; but I felt impressed to walk out. I then thought I would make a call on my sister, the other side of town; but passing your door, the Spirit bade me go in; but I said to myself, I will go in when I return; but the Spirit said: go in now. I accordingly came in, and I am thankful that I did so. Tell the stranger he is welcome to my house. I am a widow; but I have a spare room and bed, and food in plenty. He shall have a home at my house, and two large rooms

John Taylor, who later became President of the Church, and who was converted by Parley P. Pratt while on a mission to Canada

to preach in just when he pleases. Tell him I will send my son John over
to pilot him to my house, while I go and gather my relatives and friends
to come in this very evening and hear him talk; for I feel by the Spirit
that he is a man sent by the Lord with a message which will do us good."

The evening found me quietly seated at her house, in the midst of a
number of listeners, who were seated around a large work table in her
parlor, and deeply interested in conversation like the following:

"Mr. Pratt, we have for some years been anxiously looking for some
providential event which would gather the sheep into one fold; build up
the true church as in days of old, and prepare the humble followers of the
Lamb, now scattered and divided, to receive their coming Lord when He
shall descend to reign on the earth. As soon as Mrs. Taylor spoke of you
I felt assured, as by a strange and unaccountable presentiment, that you
were a messenger, with important tidings on these subjects; and I was
constrained to invite you here; and now we are all here anxiously waiting to hear your words."

"Well, Mrs. Walton, I will frankly relate to you and your friends the
particulars of my message and the nature of my commission. A young
man in the State of New York, whose name is Joseph Smith, was visited
by an angel of God, and, after several visions and much instruction, was
enabled to obtain an ancient record, written by men of old on the American continent, and containing the history, prophecies and gospel in
plainness, as revealed to them by Jesus and his messengers. This same
Joseph Smith and others, were also commissioned by the angels in these
visions, and ordained to the apostleship; with authority to organize the
Church, to administer the ordinances, and to ordain others, and thus
cause the full, plain gospel in its purity to be preached in all the world.

"By these Apostles thus commissioned, I have been ordained as an
Apostle, and sent forth by the word of prophecy to minister the baptism
of repentance for remission of sins, in the name of Jesus Christ; and to
administer the gift of the Holy Ghost, to heal the sick, to comfort the
mourner, bind up the broken in heart, and proclaim the acceptable year
of the Lord.

"I was also directed to this city by the Spirit of the Lord, with a
promise that I should find a people here prepared to receive the gospel,
and should organize them in the same. But when I came and was rejected
by all parties, I was about to leave the city; but the Lord sent you, as a
widow, to receive me, as I was about to depart; and thus I was provided
for like Elijah of old. And now I bless your house, and all your family and
kindred in His name. Your sins shall be forgiven you; you shall under-

stand and obey the gospel, and be filled with the Holy Ghost; for so great faith have I never seen in any of my country."

"Well, Mr. Pratt, this is precisely the message we were waiting for; we believe your words and are desirous to be baptized."

"It is your duty and privilege," said I, "but wait yet a little while till I have an opportunity to teach others, with whom you are religiously connected, and invite them to partake with you of the same blessings."

After conversing with these interesting persons till a late hour, we retired to rest. Next day Mrs. Walton requested me to call on a friend of hers, who was also a widow in deep affliction, being totally blind with inflammation in the eyes; she had suffered extreme pain for several months, and had also been reduced to want, having four little children to support. She had lost her husband, of cholera, two years before, and had sustained herself and family by teaching school until deprived of sight, since which she had been dependent on the Methodist society; herself and children being then a public charge. Mrs. Walton sent her little daughter of twelve years old to show me the way. I called on the poor blind widow and helpless orphans, and found them in a dark and gloomy apartment, rendered more so by having every ray of light obscured to prevent its painful effects on her eyes. I related to her the circumstances of my mission, and she believed the same. I laid my hands upon her in the name of Jesus Christ, and said unto her, "your eyes shall be well from this very hour." She threw off her bandages; opened her house to the light; dressed herself, and walking with open eyes, came to the meeting that same evening at sister Walton's, with eyes as well and as bright as any other person's.

The Methodist society were now relieved of their burden in the person of this widow and four orphans. This remarkable miracle was soon noised abroad, and the poor woman's house was thronged from all parts of the city and country with visitors; all curious to witness for themselves, and to inquire of her how her eyes were healed.

"How did the man heal your eyes?" "What did he do?—tell us," were questions so oft repeated that the woman, wearied of replying, came to me for advice to know what she should do. I advised her to tell them that the Lord had healed her, and to give Him the glory, and let that suffice. But still they teased her for particulars. "What did this man do?" "How were your eyes opened and made well?"

"He laid his hands upon my head in the name of Jesus Christ, and rebuked the inflammation, and commanded them to be made whole and restored to sight; and it was instantly done."

"Well, give God the glory; for, as to this man, it is well known that he is an impostor, a follower of Joseph Smith, the false prophet."

"Whether he be an impostor or not, I know not; but this much I know, whereas I was blind, now I see! Can an impostor open the eyes of the blind?"

"Perhaps, then, you intend to be his disciple, to join the 'Mormons?'"

"He said nothing to me about joining the 'Mormons,' but taught me the gospel, and bore testimony that God had restored its power to the earth. Would you like to be partakers thereof? Or why do you inquire so earnestly about my eyes being healed?"

"Oh, we are John Wesley's disciples. We are the Christian Church. We know John Wesley, but as to this man, we know not whence he is."

"How is this that you know not whence he is, and yet he hath opened my eyes? Did John Wesley open the eyes of the blind? Can an impostor do it?"

"Ah, we see how it is. You are determined to forsake the Christian Church, the good old way, for the sake of these fools, these weak impostors—the Mormons. Well, farewell. But remember, you will have no more support from our society, no more encouragement of any kind; you shall not even teach a school for us. How then will you live?"

Such contentions and discouragement as these, poured into the ears of a poor mother from day to day, together with railings, lyings, and various sophistry and slander, soon caused her to waver, and like thousands of other poor, weak mortals, she shrank back into the net of sectarian delusion, and was seen by the Saints no more. In the meantime our meetings commenced at Mrs. Walton's. At first very few attended, but they gradually increased till her rooms, and sometimes her yard, were well filled with attentive hearers.

Sunday at length arrived, and, not wishing to show opposition, or to set up a separate standard without cause, I appointed no meeting, but accompanied a friend who invited me to hear a preacher in a certain chapel. After the discourse, I was introduced to the speaker by my friend, who invited us both to dine at his house. After much interesting conversation, I was invited to accompany them to another meeting, held at the residence of a Mr. Patrick, a wealthy, aristocratic gentleman, who held an office in the government.

In a large apartment, well furnished, was soon convened a solemn, well dressed, and, apparently, serious and humble people, nearly filling the room. Each held a bible, while Mr. Patrick presided in their midst, with a bible in his hand and several more lying on the table before him. With one of these I was soon furnished, as was any other person present who might lack this, apparently, necessary article. In this manner these people had assembled twice each week for about two years, for the professed purpose of seeking truth, independent of any sectarian organization to which any of them might nominally belong.

Here had assembled John Taylor, his wife, Mrs. Walton and some others who now knew me, although to the president and most of the congregation I was entirely unknown, and, from my appearance, was supposed to be some farmer from the country, who had dropped in by invitation.

Meeting was soon opened by singing and prayer in a fervent manner, after which each one was at liberty to introduce such subject of investigation as he might think proper. John Taylor arose, and read in the New Testament the account of Philip going to Samaria and preaching the gospel, and what followed. Closing the book, he remarked that the Samaritans received the Word with joy; and were then baptized, both men and women; after which the two Apostles, Peter and John, came from Jerusalem, and laid their hands on them in the name of Jesus, and prayed that they might receive the Holy Ghost; and they received it, and spake with tongues, and prophesied. "Now," said he, "where is our Philip? Where is our receiving the Word with joy, and being baptized *when we believed?* Where is our Peter and John? Our apostles? Where is our Holy Ghost by the laying on of hands? Where are our gifts of the Holy Ghost? Echo answers, where?

"Is this the pattern of the Christian Church, the model for the organization in all after times? If so, we, as a people, have not the ministry, the ordinances, the gifts which constitute the Church of Jesus Christ. We are told that we were sprinkled in our infancy, but this was not baptism; and if it was, we neither believed nor rejoiced at the time, nor did we act in the matter at all, but were acted upon. How different from the Samaritans, who were baptized *when they believed, and received the Word with joy.*

"Again, Peter and John were commissioned as Apostles, and they administered the Holy Spirit by the laying on of hands in the name of Jesus. Instead of which, we have had ministers commissioned by the King and Parliament of England, or by John Wesley and his successors, without any pretence of a word from the Lord or his angels to commission them. Again, the Samaritans had spiritual gifts. We have none. If, then, we differ entirely from the pattern in all things, what claim have we, or any of the Christian world, to be considered the Church of Christ? If we are not members of the Church of Christ, wherein do we differ from the heathen, whom we affect to despise or pity? We even shudder for nations or individuals grown up without baptism, while at the same time it would appear that we are all without it,—that we are all heathen, so far as the Christian Church is concerned, as we have not even the shadow of anything according to the pattern. We cannot boast of even an approach to a base resemblance or counterfeit. What say you to this, my brethren?"

The subject now opened gave rise to a most candid investigation. Several spoke to the point. Some were of the opinion that the principles, being lost, were never to be restored. Others suggested that it was their privilege to pray that the heavens might be opened and men commissioned by new revelation. Others, again, hinted that the Lord might, perhaps, have commissioned men already in some part of the world; and, if so, why not pray that he would send them to us.

Nothing definite was concluded on when the old preacher who invited me arose and said: "There is a stranger present who, perhaps, might wish to speak."

The chairman observed that he was not aware of the presence of a stranger, but if such was the case he was at liberty, as were all persons in these meetings, to make remarks. I arose, and observed that I was a stranger from the United States; but not a stranger to the great principles under investigation in this meeting. I was prepared to speak on the subject at some length; but should not do so then, as the time had been well occupied and the people edified.

My credentials were then presented to the meeting through the chairman, and a special appointment given out for me at evening.

However they might differ as to the means of restoration of the Christian Church, certain it is that they appeared at the close to unite, with one voice, in acknowledgment of their destitution. "O Lord," said the chairman, in his closing prayer, "we have neither apostles, visions, angels, revelations, gifts, tongues, ordinances, nor a Christian ministry; we acknowledge that we are destitute of everything like the pattern of the true Church, as laid down in thy holy Word, and we pray thee to send whom thou wilt." At this all seemed to say Amen, while tears and sobs attested their sincerity.

Chapter 18

In the evening Mr. Patrick's large rooms were crowded to excess with anxious listeners. I then addressed them on the subject they had been investigating. The following is an outline of the discourse, which occupied from two to three hours:

"Friends, I am aware that the subject now under consideration is one of the most vital importance to the Christian world, and, though it may seem to be new to most persons, it is familiar to me. I have traced it in all its bearings, weighed it in every possible light, and am prepared to impart to others that which, I trust, will satisfy and enlighten the inquiring mind.

"It appears from our text, as well as from the general tenor of the New Testament, that certain definite principles existed, which, acted upon and enjoyed, constituted the Christian Church, or body of Christ, viz:

"First. An inspired priesthood or apostleship, authorized to administer salvation in the name of Jesus.

"Second. Faith in their words and testimony, on the part of those who heard them.

"Third. Reformation of life.

"Fourth. Obedience to certain ordinances, as baptism and the laying on of hands in the name of Jesus Christ, in order to the remission of sins and the gift of the Holy Ghost.

"Fifth. The spiritual gifts imparted to the body thus organized, in order to its edification, growth and perfection.

"It may be presumed that every portion of the professed Christian Church, without any exception—I mean those who admit the Scriptures to be a record of things as they existed—will readily agree, that the five principles just named did exist, and did constitute the Christian Church or body of Christ. This, then constitutes the model or pattern of the object of our present search.

"We have only to compare modern pretences with this ancient model, in order to judge of them at once. Either the same principles would be required to constitute the body of Christ in all succeeding ages, or else the New Testament must cease to be a standard, and be superseded by a dispensation of later origin; claiming power to nullify or make void the dispensation of Jesus Christ and his Apostles, and to introduce another order of things in its stead.

"This last alternative none are so bold as to claim. All agree that the gospel was a perfect system, an unchangeable and everlasting covenant, never to be changed or altered by the Lord, and only perverted or altered by man under a severe penalty—a dreadful anathema. In physical matters men are not easily deceived or duped; for instance, a man sees or hears an exact description of a human body as existing in the days of Socrates or Plato; it has head, eyes, ears, mouth, arms, hands, legs, feet, etc. Can an impostor impose upon that man in this age? Can he introduce a wild beast, a fowl, a serpent, a man dismembered of his head, eyes, ears, hands, or feet? Could he pass any of these upon his fellow men as constituting the human body; the model or pattern answering to the former description? No, he could not. He would be considered out of his senses, and would be laughed to scorn for attempting such a thing.

"Why, then, are we at a loss in judging of the various systems which, in modern times, claim to be the church of Christ? Why do we not compare them with the model, and reject or receive at once? Perhaps you will say that such a course leads to consequences and conclusions so awful, that it opens truths so unwelcome, that it is natural to shrink from the view; and, like the ostrich in the desert, when pursued too closely, hides the head and eyes in a false covering, while the body is exposed to certain destruction.

"Says one, 'if the ancient model or pattern is the standard, then the veil of modern Christendom is thrown off, and the entire world unchristianized—for we nowhere find such a pattern.' Well, admit then that there is no Christian church in existence among men, and that there has not been for many ages. What then? is it a truth? If so, truth will not harm anybody. If the whole world has been for ages wrapped in mystery

and deception, is it not better to find it out now than to continue in ignorance until Jesus reveals it at the judgment day, and sinks us in a moment from the highest pinnacle of hope and expectation to despair,
rendered a thousand-fold more painful by a sudden reverse?

"But suppose, on opening our eyes to this great discovery, we search
and find our observations and conclusions warranted by the whole tenor
of prophetic writ? Suppose Jesus Christ and his Apostles and prophets all
agree in bearing testimony, and foretelling the very order of things
which we find to exist; also, its final end or termination, and the restoration of his Church and the reign of his Saints? Would not our own observations of what actually exists, confirmed by the prophetic declarations of such a host of witnesses, all testifying that it would be so, be a
double assurance that we had opened our eyes to a snare in time to escape, and cause us to leap forward with a thrill of joy and faith to that
which is to come?

"We could then exclaim, in viewing the trumpery, pomp, splendor
and greatness of Catholicism, or the scarcely less false and glaring systems of absurdity and priestcraft under the name of Protestantism, in
their various forms, O, thou mystery of iniquity! thou art at last revealed, thou who deceivest all nations with thy sorcery, and with whom
the kings of the earth and the nobles and great men have committed for-
nication, and lived deliciously; thy covering is removed, and the people
shall see thy nakedness and abhor thee; and many shall be ready when
the proclamation is made, 'Come out of her, my people.'

"But suppose, on the other hand, we shut our eyes to these truths,
and hug to our bosoms those systems of falsehood and error, which claim
to be of Christ, but are not? The result will be a continuance on our part
to build up that which the Lord purposes in due time to tear down, and
to oppose that which the Lord will send into the world to accomplish his
purposes. We would in this case be his enemies, and be found fighting
against him.

"Let us look at the Jews in the glass of prophecy. Our own dear
selves not being in the scale, perhaps we can the more readily discern the
equity of the balance, and afterwards venture to be weighed in the same,
even though both Jew and Gentile should be found wanting.

"For nearly two thousand years we behold the Jews without a
prophet, inspired priest, king, ruler or teacher, to lead them to light, to
freedom, or to God. No voice from the burning bush; no thunderings
upon Sinai; no still small voice whispering of right and salvation; no call
from the eternal throne; no vision, angel or dream to light them on their

pathway, as they wander and are oppressed amid the darkness of Gentile dominion. Their temple is in ruins; their sacrifices have ceased; their priesthood is powerless; while their very city and country is desolate, or trodden under foot. We say to the Jew, why all this? Is it not possible that your fathers have rejected the Messiah and his holy Apostles and prophets; and these things been withheld from them in the anger of the Almighty? O, no, says the Jew, we are the true church and people of God; revelations, prophets, visions, angels and gifts were only given at first to establish the church of Israel, and the canon of Scripture being complete, there was no further need of these things; therefore, they ceased.

"Now, *you* know that this Jew is mistaken. You pity him. You wonder at his ignorance. You know that when in the days of Samuel's childhood there was no open vision from the Lord; it was because the priesthood, the proper communication between God and the people, was in transgression. The priests of the house of Eli were robbing the sacrifices for their own aggrandizement; and were committing whoredoms with the very women who came there to worship. *You* also know that when King Saul was no longer favored with revelation, when the heavens were shut against him, and the Lord answered him not, neither by vision, angel, dream, Urim and Thummim, nor prophet; it was because the Lord had forsaken him and had rent the kingdom from him, and had given it to David, dooming him to destruction, and withdrawing His spirit from him, abandoning him to a spirit of murder and persecution towards the chosen instruments of the Almighty. *You* also know that, when, before Christ, these gifts had ceased in the Jewish church (say from Malachi to John the Baptist), there were a multitude of sects, none of which were right. All had to come on a level and repent, and be baptized by John, in order to prepare the way of the Lord.

"You also know that the Jews were no longer favored with apostles and inspired men after they had rejected Christ and his Apostles, because they were rejected of the Lord; and the kingdom, according to the words of Jesus, was taken from them and given to a people who should bring forth the fruits of the same. You also know that the reason why a Jew to this day is without these things is, because his fathers, eighteen hundred years ago, rejected them.

"But the Jew knows none of these things. He is blinded with the vain and delusive thought that his race, being the chosen of the Lord, must forever remain in favor, whether they do iniquity or not. Why! exclaims the Jew, we dare not for a moment look at things in the light you suggest; it would disfranchise the whole nation for eighteen centuries, and count them as aliens from the covenant of their fathers, and from the commonwealth of Israel. Well, what if it does? Is it not better for them to know the worst in time to mend?

"Now, let us turn to the Gentile church. They, by the ministration of the Apostles, received the kingdom of God, and enjoyed its fruits. The natural branches were broken off, and they were grafted in; 'take heed,' says Paul, 'for if God spared not the natural branches, *take heed, lest he spare not thee.*'

"When the Gentile church received the kingdom, and became such, they were everywhere blessed with the ministry of inspired men, and were favored with revelations, visions, angels and prophets, as the New Testament bears witness. What became of these things? Under what circumstances, and in fulfilment of what Scriptures did they cease from among the Gentiles?

"The prophet Daniel had foretold of the several powers which would arise and bear rule in the earth. But the Roman, the most terrible power of all, should *'destroy the mighty and the holy people.'* This power should change the times and the laws, and wear out the Saints of the Most High, until the end, when the Saints should take the kingdom under the whole Heaven, and possess it. Such in substance is Daniel's testimony.

"John, in his revelations, bears the same testimony. He predicts that a certain power under the figure of a woman upon a beast, with Mystery written upon her forehead, should have dominion among all nations; have to do with all kings; and that all nations should be deceived by her, and their kings live deliciously with her, while she would be drunken with the blood of the saints and with the blood of the martyrs of Jesus.

"Paul also predicts a time when men *'would not endure sound doctrine, but would turn away their ears from the truth, and be turned unto fables, heaping to themselves, teachers.'* That they would *'have a form of godliness and deny the power.'* Paul also bears testimony that the Gentiles, if they abide not in faith, shall meet with a similar fall as did the Jews.

"Jesus Christ speaks of a time when the times of the Gentiles shall be fulfilled: their dominion come to an end with great judgment, and Jerusalem no longer be trodden under foot by them.

"Now the summary of these things is this:

"The Gentiles killed the Apostles and inspired men.

"The Gentiles ceased to bring forth the fruits of the kingdom.

"The Gentiles became drunken with the blood of the saints.

"The Gentiles destroyed the mighty and holy people.

"The Gentiles changed the times, and laws, and ordinances of God.

"The Gentiles turned away their ears from the truth, and were turned unto fables.

"The Gentiles would not endure sound doctrine, but heaped to themselves teachers.

"The Gentiles maintained a form of godliness without its miracles and powers.

"The Gentiles were *'full of names of blasphemy,'* and mystery was written as a frontispiece on all their institutions.

"The Gentiles deceived all nations, and drew kings and great men into the wake of their mysterious abominations and religious mummeries.

"The Gentiles continue to bear rule by these means till the judgments of the Almighty sweep them from the earth, and put an end to their dominion; and God restores Israel and Jerusalem, and gives the dominion to his Saints.

"How often the Lord may have restored the priesthood and ordinances, the true Church and its gifts to the earth, among the humble, is not known. But this much we know, there would be no peace nor security for men professing such institutions; they would be either hunted down and destroyed, or driven to the necessity of secluding themselves in the most secret recesses, where their history would never come down to us. As *Protestants,* we can make no pretences to a successive line of apostleship; for this would imply that we were never Roman Catholics; therefore, what need of protestation or dissent from that to which we never had belonged? Nothing short of a new dispensation—a new revelation to commission apostles as at the first, could give any religious body a claim, or a shadow of claim, to be the Church of Jesus Christ, or entitle them to the spiritual gifts.

"Such, my friends, is the deplorable picture of Gentile Christianity as presented before us, whether we look with the naked eye on facts around us, or, aided by the glass of prophecy and history, review the dim vista of successive generations in the mighty past. Yet in the midst of the reign of error and blood there have always been many individuals who desired to know and serve the Lord. They have desired to see the triumph of truth; but the time had not come; they died without the sight; but they will arise again to enjoy the triumph; they with us will rejoice when error is overthrown and the Saints possess the kingdom.

"I have now reviewed the past, my friends, and have shown by what means the Jews and Gentiles have lost the peculiar blessings which characterize the Church of God. I have detained you long, and am, as yet, only on the threshold of the great subject before me. In another discourse I might draw a brighter picture by setting before you the great and precious promises which ensure to the world a new dispensation, in which all these things will be restored, and the Church of the Saints grow, flourish and triumph in the earth.

"I must now close by blessing this people who have opened their hearts to listen with such attention. May the blessings of the Lord Jesus Christ and his spirit rest upon you, that you may receive and know the truth. Amen."

As I finished speaking the unanimous voice was for another meeting, which was finally given out for the next evening.

Evening came again. Crowds assembled.

I then went into detail with a chain of prophecy, beginning with Moses and the prophets, and ending with John's revelation; showing that the latter-day glory was to be ushered in by a new dispensation revealed from heaven; by the ministration of angels, and sustained by the marvelous power and gifts of God; till it resulted in the overthrow of all mystery, darkness, ignorance and corruption, and the ushering in of the universal reign of peace and truth.

This prophetic review occupied some two or three hours more. I then closed by saying that had I time I would give them the details of the commencement of this restoration by a new dispensation revealed from the heavens by the angels of God, and in exact and detailed fulfilment of some of the prophecies which I had been reviewing. All cried out for another meeting, which was appointed for the next night.

In the third evening I related the visions, manifestations and many of the details of the organization and movements of the Church of the Saints.

The truth was now plainly before this people, who had been in so wonderful a manner prepared for its reception, as predicted by brother Kimball on my head before leaving home. The man of the house now rejected me, and the meeting of seekers after truth left his house, and came and were baptized, and held their meetings at the house of the widow Walton, who had received me, and who was now baptized with all her household, who were of sufficient age to receive the gospel.

John Taylor and his wife, whose house I first entered in Toronto, were also baptized. He soon became an assistant in the ministry. This is that same John Taylor who is now one of the Twelve Apostles.

The work soon spread into the country and enlarged its operations in all that region; many were gathered into the Church, and were filled with faith and love, and with the Holy Spirit, and the Lord confirmed the Word with signs following. My first visit to the country was about nine miles from Toronto, among a settlement of farmers, by one of whom I had sent an appointment beforehand. John Taylor accompanied me—this was before he was baptized—we rode on horseback. We called at a Mr. Joseph Fielding's, an acquaintance and friend of Mr. Taylor's. This man had two sisters, young ladies, who seeing us coming ran from their house to one of the neighboring houses, lest they should give welcome, or give countenance to "*Mormonism.*" Mr. Fielding stayed, and as we entered the house he said he was sorry we had come, he had opposed our holding meeting in the neighborhood; and, so great was the prejudice, that the Methodist meeting house was closed against us, and the minister refused, on Sunday, to give out the appointment sent by the farmer.

"Ah!" said I, "why do they oppose Mormonism?" "I don't know," said he, "but the name has such a contemptible sound; and, another thing, we do not want a new revelation, or a new religion contrary to the Bible." "Oh!" said I, "if that is all we shall soon remove your prejudices. Come, call home your sisters, and let's have some supper. Did you say the appointment was not given out?" "I said, sir, that it was not given out in the meeting house, nor by the minister; but the farmer by whom you sent it agreed to have it at his house." "Come then, send for your sisters, we will take supper with you, and all go over to meeting together. If you and your sisters will agree to this, I will agree to preach the old Bible gospel, and leave out all new revelations which are opposed to it."

The honest man consented. The young ladies came home, got us a good supper, and all went to meeting. The house was crowded; I preached, and the people wished to hear more. The meeting house was opened for further meetings, and in a few days we baptized brother Joseph Fielding and his two amiable and intelligent sisters, for such they proved to be in an eminent degree. We also baptized many others in that neighborhood, and organized a branch of the Church, for the people there drank in truth as water, and loved it as they loved life.

After ministering in and about Toronto for about two months I found it necessary to return home, as some of my debts were pressing, and we needed a supply of our printed works to circulate among the people. I accordingly gave out word, in a meeting in Toronto one Sunday evening, that I should take boat for home next morning. Now all this time I had asked no man for money, nor had I explained my circumstances. However, on shaking hands at the close of the next meeting, several bankbills were secretly shaken into my hands, amounting in all to several hundred dollars—including subscriptions for books, periodicals, etc. I thanked the Lord God of Israel for the fulfilment of the first instalment of brother Kimball's prophecy, and went on my way rejoicing. On my arrival in Kirtland I was enabled to meet my most urgent debts, and to get time on the remainder.

I found my wife had been healed of her seven years' illness from the time brother Kimball had ministered unto her, and I began to realize more fully that every word of his blessing and prophecy upon my head would surely come to pass. After a pleasant visit with the Saints, I took my wife with me and returned again to Toronto, in June, 1836.

The work I had commenced was still spreading its influence, and the Saints were still increasing in faith and love, in joy and in good works. There were visions, prophesyings, speaking in tongues and healings, as well as the casting out of devils and unclean spirits. One remarkable circumstance, among many, I will relate in detail:

There was living within a short day's journey of Toronto, in a certain neighborhood where I ministered every two weeks (for the circuit of my labors had now so much enlarged that I had to travel continually from branch to branch and neighborhood to neighborhood), a man named Lamphere, who was noted for being the most irreligious man in all the country; he and the family were hardly ever known to attend a religious meeting; they would work on the Sabbath, and swear, curse, etc. This man and his family were so wrought upon by the power of truth that he opened his house for stated meetings, which I held there regularly every two weeks. He and the family always entertained me with every kindness and every demonstration of hospitality in their power. The people of the neighborhood always turned out to hear, and seemed to receive the Word with faith and joy, but as yet none of them had been baptized, or joined the Church of the Saints. All noticed the change in the Lamphere family, and all rejoiced, and even marvelled at so sudden a reformation in a family so *gospel hardened,* as they called it, though in truth none of them had ever heard the gospel in its power and fulness till my visits commenced there.

Now there was living in that neighborhood a young man and his wife, named Whitney; he was a blacksmith by trade; their residence was perhaps a mile or more from this Lamphere's, where I held my semimonthly meetings. His wife was taken down very suddenly about that time with a strange affliction. She would be prostrated by some power invisible to those about her, and, in an agony of distress indescribable, she would be drawn and twisted in every limb and joint, and would almost, in fact, be pulled out of joint. Sometimes, when thrown on to the bed, and while four or five stout men were endeavoring to hold her, she would be so drawn out of all shape as to only touch the bed with her heels and the back part of her head. She would be bruised, cramped and pinched, while she would groan, scream, froth at the mouth, etc. She often cried out that she could see two devils in human form, who were thus operating upon her, and that she could hear them talk; but, as the bystanders could not see them, but only see the effects, they did not know what to think or how to understand.

She would have one of these spells once in about twenty-four hours, and when a period of these spells were over she would lie in bed so lame, and bruised, and sore, and helpless that she could not rise alone, or even sit up, for some weeks. All this time she had to have watchers both night and day, and sometimes four and five at a time, insomuch that the neighbors were worn out and weary with watching. Mr. Whitney sent for me two or three times, or left word for me to call next time I visited the neighborhood. This, however, I had neglected to do, owing to the extreme pressure of labors upon me in so large a circuit of meetings—indeed, I had not a moment to spare. At last, as I came round on the circuit again, the woman, who had often requested to see the man of God, that he might minister to her relief, declared she would see him anyhow, for she knew she could be healed if she could but get sight of him. In her agony she sprang from her bed, cleared herself from her frightened husband and others, who were trying to hold her, and ran for Mr. Lamphere's, where I was then holding meeting. At first, to use her own words, she felt very weak, and nearly fainted, but her strength came to her, and increased at every step till she reached the meeting. Her friends were all astonished, and in alarm, lest she should die in the attempt, tried to pursue her, and they several times laid hold of her and tried to force or persuade her back. "No," said she, "let me see the man of God; I can but die, and I cannot endure such affliction any longer." On she came, until at last they gave up and said, "Let her go, perhaps it will be according to her faith." So she came, and when the thing was explained the eyes of the whole multitude were upon her. I ceased to preach, and, stepping to her in the presence of the whole meeting, I laid my hands upon her and said, "Sister, be of good cheer, thy sins are forgiven, thy faith hath made thee whole; and, in the name of Jesus Christ, I rebuke the devils and unclean spirits, and command them to trouble thee no more." She returned home well, went about her housekeeping, and remained well from that time forth.

Her neighbors watched to see if the trouble would return upon her, but, after a few days they gave up all their fears, and gave glory to God, saying that the ancient gospel had truly been restored.

About seven miles from this place lived a merchant by the name of Lamareux, who was a man of extended thought and general information; he sometimes preached or lectured to the people. This man, on hearing the strange reports of what was going on, sent for me. I visited him on a day appointed; he had shut up his store, suspended all business, dressed in his best, and prepared a dinner, while at the same time a general meeting of the people was convening in his large barn. He received us cordially, and after dinner accompanied us to the barn, where there was, indeed, a crowd of some hundreds of anxious listeners. We preached; after which the old merchant exclaimed to the meeting, that if this was Mormonism he was a Mormon.

He pressed us to tarry a few days, or rather go with him, to which we consented. So, next morning he furnished a horse and saddle for himself, and another for me. We mounted—he leading the way. We travelled through a fine settled country of villages and farms, where I had never been before, and where they were strangers to "Mormonism" and to me, but well acquainted with him.

As we went, he preached, saying to every man he met, and even crying aloud to those at a distance, and as we halted in each little village:

"Hear ye, my friends, the kingdom of Heaven is restored again to man, with the gospel in its ancient fulness and power. Turn out and hear this stranger who is with me, and do not gainsay him, for I testify to you that the sick are healed, the eyes of the blind are opened, and devils are cast out under his hand in the name of Jesus. And if you do not believe it we can give you names and particulars, and prove it by scores and hundreds of witnesses."

The more I tried to keep him still the more he proclaimed these things.

Leaving a chain of appointments, we travelled as far as Scarborough, and, preaching there, we returned the next day and filled the chain of appointments given out the day before. The excitement now became general, and a very learned clergyman, a Mr. Browning, of the Presbyterian order—announced himself as the people's chosen cham-

pion to meet us in public debate and put us down, or receive our doctrine, according as truth might appear on investigation.

A public discussion was at last agreed upon, to be held a few weeks
thence in the open air, as no building would hold the people. The pre-
liminaries were as follows:

The Bible to be recognized as a standard of truth.

We were to have the opening speech, in which we were to set forth
our principles; when the reverend gentleman was to have a certain
length of time to reply, and so on alternately.

The meeting at length came off. Thousands attended, and listened
with patience. Elder O. Hyde, who had now arrived from the States to
my assistance, took up the matter, as I was unavoidably engaged elsewhere. A large platform had been erected for the speakers, and while
Elder Hyde sat almost alone before that vast assemblage, the reverend
gentleman had five or six other clergymen beside him as helps.

In the opening speech Elder Hyde laid down the following principles, viz:

A true Church of Christ is composed of apostles, prophets, elders,
teachers and members, who have been baptized (immersed) in the name
of Jesus Christ, and who have received his spirit by the laying on of
hands of his apostles, or authorized servants.

A true Church of Christ believed in visions, angels, spirits, prophesyings, revelations, healings and miracles of every kind, as described in
the New Testament.

Any creed or religious body differing from this New Testament pattern could not be considered the Church of Christ, however sincere they
might be.

Having laid down these premises, he demanded of his opponent a
positive admission or denial of the premises, before he would allow himself to be drawn to a second question or point of debate. This took his
opponents all aback; they had sense enough to see that if they affirmed
these premises there was an end of Presbyterianism, and all other sectarian forms which have set aside these powers. On the other hand, if
they denied the premises laid down by Elder H., it would be denying the
Bible standard, by which both parties agreed to abide. For these reasons
the party of the opposition utterly refused to either affirm or deny. Attempts were made in every possible form to draw Elder H. to other points
of debate; but all in vain. Slanderous reports from the press, pamphlets,
and newspaper abuse, were offered in abundance; but were not suffered
to be introduced into the discussion, because both parties had agreed to

abide by the Bible as a standard. Thus, after a few hours of shuffling and trickery on the part of the opposition, and a few vain attempts to introduce the poisonous slanders which so often prevail in blinding the public mind, they were utterly silenced.

Elder Hyde then proceeded to address the vast assemblage at considerable length, congratulating them on the triumph of truth, and exhorting them to obey the gospel, and thus avail themselves of its blessings, after which the discussion closed; but the truth grew and prevailed.

Chapter 19

In July, 1836, while lodging at the house of brother Joseph Fielding, the voice of the Lord came unto me in a dream, saying: *"Parley!"* And I answered: "Here am I;" for I was in a vision of the Spirit and knew that it was the Lord who spake unto me. And he said: "When did I ever reveal anything unto you in a dream and it failed to come to pass?" And I answered: "Never, Lord." "Well, then," He continued, "go unto this people and cry unto them with a mighty voice that they repent, lest I smite them with a curse and they die; for, notwithstanding the present fruitfulness of the earth, there shall be a famine in the land; and not only a famine for bread, but a famine for the Word of the Lord; for I will call my servants out from their midst and send them to the nations afar off."

Having heard these words I took courage, and I continued to lift up my voice in the congregations, both in town and country, testifying of the gospel and warning the people of things to come. Many repented and were baptized, while many hardened their hearts and were filled with a contentious and lying spirit. But the Saints were filled with faith, joy, and love; and they met together oft, and had great union and peace, and were happy in the society of each other.

In the autumn of the same year—I think in September—I had preached on Sunday in the chapel, on the subject of the coming of the Son of Man and the signs which would precede his coming. I prophesied that they would see signs in the heavens very soon, such as were spoken of by Jesus Christ in the New Testament; and that when they should begin to see them they might know for themselves that His coming was nigh at hand.

After thus preaching I returned in the evening to the house of brother and sisters Fielding, at the hour of 9 p.m.; we sat up for an hour or two conversing on these important things and rejoicing, when, on going out at the door and looking abroad, we beheld a most wonderful scene in the heavens, and, as it continued for some time, we finally went to some of the nearest neighbors and called them out to behold it.

A wave of white light extended like a rainbow from east to west over the entire horizon, a little south of the meridian. It was in appearance about twenty feet wide, and seemed agitated in its motions like a wave of the sea; at length it removed like the motions of a great swell of the sea towards the south and disappeared; when lo! another similar light appeared immediately in the place of the former, and, after remaining stationary with agitated motions for some time, it rolled away to the south and disappeared like the former, and was replaced by a third. Thus the same scene was renewed and continued for hours. We finally all retired to rest, while it yet continued to be exhibited.

After spending the season in continued labors, and organizing the Church in many places, I was about to return in October to Kirtland, Ohio, to my home. Now, there was a man named Caird, who, previous to my visit to Canada, had been over from England as a preacher, who pretended to be sent of God by revelation. He had preached many things, and told the people that God had raised up apostles in England, and organized the true church, and was sending preachers from thence into all the world, to prepare the way for the coming of the Son of Man. This man held to the sprinkling of infants, which he called baptism. He also held that the church of which he was a representative and messenger, included the national Church of England; and all others who had been baptized (sprinkled), whether Catholic or Protestant. This great, universal church was the true church, only needing the restoration of apostles and gifts which had now commenced to be restored.

This man had great influence in Canada on his former visit, and he had long been looked for to return to Toronto on his second visit. The people were all expectation, and very anxious that he should arrive in time to meet me before I should return home; for many persons greatly wondered that there should arise about the same time one church in America and another in England, both professing apostolic power and universal jurisdiction. Some of those who had heard both of us, tried to think that both systems were one and would run together. Others said they would wait and see which serpent swallowed the other before they would join either. Some affirmed that Mr. Caird would never shrink from the investigation of anything, therefore, he must embrace "Mormonism;" for it has only to be investigated to be appreciated. Others equally affirmed that Mr. Pratt never shrank from investigation, and, therefore, they must meet each other; must come to an understanding; must become one, or else one of their systems must be shown to be very erroneous; for these men have neither of them ever found his master in any of the sects here in Canada at any rate. Such is a specimen of the sayings and feelings of an excited public, in view of the meeting of two such men. On my own part, although I knew his system was erroneous and not founded in truth, yet I had formed a very favorable opinion of the man, and had made up my mind to meet a fearless champion who would not shrink one moment from a full and free investigation. Believing this, I felt in high hopes that he would be an instrument in the hands of God to receive and spread the truth.

This man still lingered at Kingston, two hundred miles distant, and did not come up to Toronto as expected. To satisfy the anxiety of the people, I at length proposed in our meeting one Sabbath, that I would take steamer the next morning and go down to Kingston, and see this strange man.

That same night I had a dream, as follows: I thought I was in a vast wilderness of wild beasts of every description, among which was a species of elephant so large that its trunk reached nearly to the tops of the tall trees, and when he walked the earth trembled; the beasts of the field fled from before him, and the trees were swayed on either side of him as slender reeds. At this I was afraid, and I wafted myself up by the power of the Spirit, and sat in the top of a tall tree. As he approached, I reflected as follows: Why should such a man as I fear? I have any amount of power given me of God, I will, therefore, descend to earth before him; for he can never harm me. I accordingly descended. He considered this a defiance on my part, so he boasted that I had no power, and that I could not stand before him.

At this I put forth my hand and caught him by the trunk, and lifting him from the ground by the power of the Spirit, I dashed him to the ground a number of times; at this he seemed to dwindle down to about the size of a suckling calf, and finally turned into a serpent and swelled out to the length of about a hundred feet, and half the size of a man's body. He then spoke great swelling words in defiance of my power; said it was not the power of God, but only the power of a man; and he continued to mock and defy me, saying, "If you have the great power of God, why do you not pull me in pieces?"

At this I saw a great white stone, smooth and round at the top, in the shape of the half of an egg, and about six feet in diameter. The serpent coiled himself around this stone, and professed to be fastened to it. And he said: "Now I will remain fast to this rock, and give you a fair chance to pull me to pieces." I answered, "you are not fastened to the rock, but will slip from it the moment I pull." "Nay," said he, "try me, and see." I laid hold of him, and the same power came on me as before, but as I began to pull he slipped from the rock. I then tried to fasten him to some weeds or some rubbish which was near, but the moment I pulled he would slip from them; I could not, therefore, fasten him to anything. I said to him, "you will not remain fastened to anything; how, then, can I pull you to pieces?"

Being a little at a loss to know what to do, I turned to Elder Orson Hyde, who seemed to stand by, and said, "Brother Orson, see those wide jaws and that small neck; it is an excellent hold; seize him by the neck and hold him fast, and, in the name of Jesus, I will give an almighty pull." He did so, and I pulled; the serpent then dwindled down to the size of a small snake half a yard in length, and crawled off and hid among the grass.

I awoke under the strong impression that the great beast and the serpent represented Mr. Caird; and that the rock was the true gospel, to which he pretended to be fast. This impression was so different from the opinion I had formed of the man, that I felt greatly disappointed. I was not willing to believe the vision; I exclaimed in the bitterness of sorrow and disappointment: "Is it possible that this is Mr. Caird, so beloved, so revered as a great and good man?" I hardly dare believe it. "O Lord, if this vision is of thee and its application, please show me the interpretation of it in plainness, that I may not err." I immediately fell asleep again and dreamed as follows:

I thought I took a steamer and arrived in Kingston at early dawn. I thought I took up one of the principal streets, directly northward from the water, and put up at a house of entertainment. I then inquired for Mr. Caird, and was told that he was on the same street near to me. I saw him, and tried to tell him of the glorious fulness of the gospel. He immediately rejected, and refused to hear me, and commenced to speak reproachfully of me and the cause. I replied to him in the language of the New Testament: "Doth our law judge a man before it hear him?" He answered with a sneer: "I am perfectly willing to judge Mormonism without hearing it; I would not break my shins to hear it anyhow." I awoke a second time, feeling satisfied in regard to Mr. Caird.

I arose next morning and told the people that I now knew Mr. Caird; that he was false, and would bitterly and utterly refuse to investigate or hear the truth. I told them I had no desire to go to see him, for the Lord had shown him to me in a dream, and I knew more about him than all of them. This, however, they could not realize; they assured me that he was no such man; and, as they had found me the means to go and see him, and had chosen a man to go with me, they rather insisted on my going. "Well," said I, "I will go, but you will find the matter just as I tell you." So I went, accompanied by a Mr. Goodson.

We landed in Kingston at early dawn, went up the street as I had dreamed, took lodgings, and then inquired for Mr. Caird, and was answered that he was near us on the same street. I wrote him a line seeking an interview. No answer was returned. We waited all day, and then attended his meeting at evening. He preached well, and showed great intelligence. I could detect nothing to condemn. As he was about closing, I prayed the Lord to cause him to show himself, that I might discern his spirit. On a sudden he broke off from his subject, and commenced railing against Mormonism at a most horrible rate. He said he had that day received a line from one of these impostors, calling him brother, and professing to be of the new church, which had been lately organized in England by the spirit of revelation; "by this false profession," he said, "they had deceived some of his friends in Toronto." Now all these things were lies.

I arose in the meeting and asked to speak, but did not obtain privilege. I, however, told the people that Mr. Caird had lied; he had received no line from an Elder of the Church of the Saints calling him brother, or professing to be of his new church, organized in England; I defied him to produce such a line. All the answer the multitude returned to this was to hiss, and to cry, "Gold Bible! Gold Bible!—New Revelation!" etc.

Next morning we published a printed handbill with a statement of his lying, a copy of the line I had really sent to him, and a statement of our doctrine as Latter-day Saints. This we circulated freely in his next meeting, challenging him to refute the charge, or to meet us in debate.

We could draw no answer from him. We circulated the handbills in the streets by hundreds, and then sent plenty of them by mail to our friends in Toronto. The bill was headed: *"Doth our law judge a man before it hear him?"* Our friends in Toronto were astonished above measure at

the confirmation of the dream, in which God by his servant had revealed
a man's spirit, and clearly exposed the heart of a wicked man whom his
best acquaintances were unable to discern. Mr. Caird, on being exposed
at Kingston, fled to Toronto, and there commenced preaching to crowds
in the Court House; but there the newsboys met him in the face, and circulated the handbills which we had sent, showing him to be a liar, and
he utterly unable to refute or gainsay it. He threatened prosecution; but
the boys, nothing daunted, continued to offer the bills gratis in his face
to those who went in to hear.

We returned to Toronto, and his old friends urged him to meet me;
but he could not be prevailed on to do so, although his discourses were
full of opposition, and misrepresentation of the principles of the Saints.
I now applied to Wm. Lyon McKenzie, a printer and editor, in King
street, for some large public halls or rooms of his, which would hold hundreds of people. He gave us the use of them, and we put out a bill, adver-
tizing two meetings, and pledging to the public that we would prove to
a demonstration that Mr. Caird, who was now preaching in this city,
was a false teacher, whom God had never sent, and that no believer in
the Bible, who listened with attention, should go away unconvinced of
that fact, or the truth of the doctrine of the Church of Jesus Christ of
Latter-day Saints. In the handbill Mr. Caird was again invited to attend.

Long before the hour of the first appointment had arrived the house
was thronged to that degree that ten dollars was in vain urged upon any
one who would vacate their seat, even on the stairs which led to the
hall. I took for a text the saying of the Apostle John: "Whosoever trans-
gresseth, and abideth not in the doctrine of Christ, the same hath not
God." I then reviewed the doctrine of Christ and of His Apostles, in detail, showing what were the ordinances, gifts, powers, precepts, promises, and commandments of Jesus Christ, as contrasted with the public
teachings and doings of this man, Caird.

The people were astonished at the review and contrast, and were
apparently all satisfied that we had fulfilled the pledge to a demonstration. The next evening the house was as crowded as the first; all listened
with profound attention. We opened the Scriptures of the prophets, and
many were enlightened. In these two meetings Elder Hyde was present,
and presided as chairman. Thus was fulfilled to the letter this strange and
wonderful double dream. And thus the truth prevailed over the counterfeit, while the people's minds were settled as to which was the Moses and
which was the magician.

Mr. Caird retired from the country, returned home to Scotland, where I found him ten years afterwards living in private life and of no notoriety.

The truth had now triumphed in Canada, as was predicted on my head on starting from Kirtland, Ohio. Several branches of the Church had been organized, and Elders had been ordained to take care of the flocks and to continue the work. I took an affectionate leave of my friends in that country, and, with my wife, returned home. Where I had labored, the Lord had opened the hearts of the Saints sufficiently to pay up my debts, as had been predicted; and at the turn of the season, less than a twelvemonth from the date of brother Kimball's prophecy, my wife bore me a son, and we called his name Parley. He was born early in the morning of March 25th, 1837.

Chapter 20

There were but two points in this extraordinary prophecy which now remained unfulfilled. One of these was that from the results of this Canada Mission the work should spread into England, and a great work there would be the consequence. The other was that I should eventually be so rich and have so much money that I would loath the counting thereof.

My dear wife had now lived to accomplish her destiny; and when the child was dressed, and she had looked upon it and embraced it, she ceased to live in the flesh. Her death happened about three hours after the birth of this child of promise. A few days previous to her death she had a vision in open day while sitting in her room. She was overwhelmed or immersed in a pillar of fire, which seemed to fill the whole room, as if it would consume it and all things therein; and the Spirit whispered to her mind, saying: "Thou art baptized with fire and the Holy Ghost." It also intimated to her that she should have the privilege of departing from this world of sorrow and pain, and of going to the Paradise of rest as soon as she had fulfilled the prophecy in relation to the promised son. This vision was repeated on the next day at the same hour, viz:—twelve o'clock. She was overwhelmed with a joy and peace indescribable, and seemed changed in her whole nature from that time forth. She longed to be gone, and anticipated the time as a hireling counts the days of his servitude, or the prisoner the term of his imprisonment.

She was buried in the churchyard near the Temple in Kirtland, Ohio. Many hundreds attended the funeral and wept sorely, for she was

Photo not
available

Thankful Halsey, first wife of
Parley P. Pratt

Three pictures of Parley P. Pratt Jr., oldest son of Parley P. Pratt
and Thankful Halsey Pratt

extensively known. Her trials, for the gospel's sake, while her husband had been absent from time to time on distant missions, her lingering sickness of years, her barrenness, her miraculous cure, her conception of the promised child, were all matters of note in the Church far and near. But she had gone behind the veil to rest, where the wicked cease from troubling and the weary are at rest; while I was left to toil and struggle alone. My grief, and sorrow, and loneliness I shall not attempt to describe.

My son was put to nurse on the breast of a sister Allen, who had just then lost an infant. For the satisfaction of our posterity I will here attempt some description of my wife's person and qualities.

She was tall, of a slender frame, her face of an oval form, eyes large and of a dark color, her forehead lofty, clear complexion, hair black, smooth and glossy. She was of a mild and affectionate disposition and full of energy, perseverance, industry and cheerfulness when not borne down with sickness. In order, neatness and refinement of taste and habit she might be said to excel. She was an affectionate and dutiful wife, an exemplary Saint, and, through much tribulation, she has gone to the world of spirits to meet a glorious resurrection and an immortal crown and kingdom.

Farewell, my dear Thankful, thou wife of my youth, and mother of my first born; the beginning of my strength—farewell. Yet a few more lingering years of sorrow, pain and toil, and I shall be with thee, and clasp thee to my bosom, and thou shalt sit down on my throne, as a queen and priestess unto thy lord, arrayed in white robes of dazzling splendor, and decked with precious stones and gold, while thy queen sisters shall minister before thee and bless thee, and thy sons and daughters innumerable shall call thee blessed, and hold thy name in everlasting remembrance.

In the spring of 1837, soon after the death of my wife, I returned to Canada, to visit the Saints, and to confer on the subject of a mission to England. Several of the Saints in Canada were English, who had friends in England. Letters had already been sent to them with information of the rise of the Church, and of its principles. Several of the Canadian Elders felt a desire to go on a mission to their friends in that country.

At length, Joseph Fielding, Isaac Russell, John Goodson and John Snider, of the Canada Elders, were selected for a mission to England. Elders H. C. Kimball and Orson Hyde, of the quorum of the Twelve, were selected to go at the head of the mission, and Elder Willard Richards was appointed to accompany them.

About this time, after I had returned from Canada, there were jar-rings and discords in the Church at Kirtland, and many fell away and be-came enemies and apostates. There were also envyings, lyings, strifes and divisions, which caused much trouble and sorrow. By such spirits I was also accused, misrepresented and abused. And at one time, I also was overcome by the same spirit in a great measure, and it seemed as if the very powers of darkness which war against the Saints were let loose upon me. But the Lord knew my faith, my zeal, my integrity of purpose, and he gave me the victory.

I went to brother Joseph Smith in tears, and, with a broken heart and contrite spirit, confessed wherein I had erred in spirit, murmured, or done or said amiss. He frankly forgave me, prayed for me and blessed me. Thus, by experience, I learned more fully to discern and to contrast the two spirits, and to resist the one and cleave to the other. And, being tempted in all points, even as others, I learned how to bear with, and ex-cuse, and succor those who are tempted.

Late in July I arrived in the City of New York, on a mission, took lodgings, and commenced to preach and write. My first production in that city was a book of upwards of two hundred pages, entitled the "Voice of Warning." The first edition of this work consisted of four thousand copies; it has since been published and re-published in America and Europe, till some forty or fifty thousand copies have not been sufficient to supply the demand. Thousands date their conversion to the fulness of the gospel to the reading of that book.

While I was thus engaged, the English mission, under brothers Kim-ball and Hyde, began to prosper exceedingly. It first commenced in Pres-ton, where some of the friends of the Canada Elders had already had some information of it by letters from Canada. From this beginning it spread, till now, 1854, it shows for itself whether brother Kimball's prophecy was fulfilled, which said to me the year before, that a great work should be done in Canada under my hand, and that from thence it should spread into England, and a great work should be done there.

Thus is completed, all but one item, a chain of prophecy, which may, perhaps, be set down as one among the most extraordinary in the annals of history. It is extraordinary, whether we look at the varied scen-ery, the wide and complicated field of action, the clearness and precision of its numerous items and specifications, the lack of natural probability of its fulfilment, or the precision and exactness with which it was pro-gressively fulfilled in every item. Having thus proved the merits of brother Kimball as a prophet, I look for the time when I shall possess great riches, and even handle money till the counting thereof will be a burthen. I look for this with all the certainty with which any person can anticipate anything in the future.

But to return to my own narrative. Of all the places in which the English language is spoken, I found the City of New York to be the most difficult as to access to the minds or attention of the people. From July to January we preached, advertised, printed, published, testified, visited, talked, prayed, and wept in vain. To all appearance there was no interest or impression on the minds of the people in regard to the fulness of the gospel. There was one member of the Church of the Saints living there, whose name was Elijah Fordham; he was an Elder, and assisted me. We had baptized about six members, and organized a little branch, who were accustomed to meet in a small upper room in Goerck street; sometimes two or three others met with us. We had hired chapels and advertised, but the people would not hear, and the few who came went away without being interested. So we had been forced to give them up, after spending our money and strength in vain.

We had retired to our private room up stairs with the few members we had, to hold a last prayer meeting, as I was about taking leave for New Orleans. We had prayed all round in turn, when, on a sudden, the room was filled with the Holy Spirit, and so was each one present. We began to speak in tongues and prophesy. Many marvelous things were manifested which I cannot write; but the principal burthen of the prophesyings was concerning New York City, and our mission there.

The Lord said that He had heard our prayers, beheld our labors, diligence, and long suffering towards that city; and that He had seen our tears. Our prayers were heard, and our labors and sacrifices were accepted. We should tarry in the city, and go not thence as yet; for the Lord had many people in that city, and He had now come by the power of His Holy Spirit to gather them into His fold. His angels should go before us and cooperate with us. His Holy Spirit should give the people visions and dreams concerning us and the work of the Lord; and He would make bare his arm to heal the sick and confirm the Word by signs following; and from that very day forward we should have plenty of friends, money to pay our debts with the publishers; means to live, and crowds to hear us. And there should be more doors open for preaching than we could fill; crowds, who could not get in, should stand in the streets and about the entrance to try to hear us; and we should know that the Almighty could open a door and no man could shut it.

As these things were manifested in power and the demonstration of the Spirit, we could not doubt them. So we gave up going to New Orleans, and concluded to stay; but we were almost ready to say in our hearts, like one of old: "If the Lord should make windows in Heaven could these things be?"

Now there was in this little meeting a man named David Rogers, whose heart was touched. He, being a chairmaker, fitted up a large room, and seated it with the chairs of his ware house, and invited us to preach in the same. This room was crowded. He then joined with one of our members, who was a joiner, and rented a small place, and seated it for a regular place of meeting; this was generally crowded. In the meantime, a Methodist clergyman came to hear me, whose name was Cox. He invited me to his house to preach, near East River; he and household were obedient to the faith, with many of the members of his society. While preaching, a lady solicited me to preach in her house in Willett street; "for," said she, "I had a dream of you and of the new Church the other night." Another lady wished me to preach in her house, in Grant street.

In the meantime I was invited by the Free Thinkers to preach, or give a course of lectures, in Tammany Hall. In short, it was not three weeks from the delivery of the prophecies in the upper room till we had fifteen preaching places in the city, all of which were filled to overflowing. We preached about eleven times a week, besides visiting from house to house. We soon commenced baptizing, and continued doing so almost daily during the winter and spring. One lady, who had been four years under the doctor's care with a crippled leg, arose and walked, with her leg instantly restored whole, even as the other. Her physician was immediately dismissed, and was very angry, because we had spoiled his patronage. He even threatened to sue us. Another lady, who had lain in her bed four years with the dumb palsy, arose and walked. She had not, previous to our laying hands on her, been able to stir a finger, or a toe, on her right side for about four years; so said the family, and so she herself testified. In this case her physician, and also some religious ministers, who called to see her, glorified God, acknowledged His hand, and exhorted her to persevere in the faith.

A child of Mr. Wandle Mace, of No. 13 Bedford street, was healed of brain fever in the last stage, when the doctors had given it over, and the kindred and neighbors had gathered in to see it die. I laid my hands on it, in the presence of them all, and it was healed, and in a few hours took nourishment, and commenced to play and run about the floor. In

Mary Ann Frost Pratt, wife of Parley P.
Pratt and formerly the widow of
Nathan Stearns

Mary Ann Stearns Winters, mother of
Augusta Winters Grant, wife of
President Heber J. Grant

Three pictures of Olivia Pratt Driggs, daughter of Parley P. and
Mary Ann Frost Pratt

Three pictures of Moroni L. Pratt, son of Parley P. and
Mary Ann Frost Pratt

the same house, in an upper chamber, lay a woman, by the name of Dexter, sick, who had not left her room, nor scarcely her bed, for some six months; she was at the point of death, and her babe also, who had taken the disease from her. Her mother, who had the care of her, was present when the child was healed, and she ran up stairs and told the woman that there were men below who healed the sick, as in days of old, by the laying on of hands in the name of Jesus. The woman exclaimed: "Thank God, then I can be healed." She sent for us, and was from that hour restored to health, and the child also. She walked about two miles to the East River and was baptized, and then walked home again—it being a very wet day with snow and rain, and the sidewalks about shoe deep in snow and mud. After these three miracles of healing had been witnessed in that house in Bedford street, six persons who witnessed them were baptized, viz: Wandle Mace and wife, Theodore Curtis and wife, and the sick woman and her mother, before named.

During our stay in New York I made frequent visits to the country, and to other towns. Branches of the Church were formed at Sing Sing, and in Jersey, and also in Brooklyn and various other parts of Long Island. Some members were also baptized in Holiston, Mass.

On May 9th I received the hand of Mary Ann Frost, daughter of Aaron Frost, of Bethel, Oxford County, Maine, in marriage. She was the widow of Nathan Stearns, and had one daughter, about four years of age.

Chapter 21

In April, 1838, I took leave of New York, and, with a small colony, emigrated once more to Missouri. We settled in Caldwell County in May. Here I again commenced anew; built a house and made a farm. I also devoted much of my time to the ministry; I visited many different neighborhoods, and was everywhere received with hospitality, and listened to with interest and attention.

On the 4th of July, 1838, thousands of the citizens who belonged to the Church of the Saints assembled at the City of Far West, the county seat of Caldwell, in order to celebrate our nation's birth. We erected a tall standard, on which was hoisted our national colors, the stars and stripes, and the bold eagle of American liberty. Under its waving folds we laid the corner stone of a Temple of God, and dedicated the land and ourselves and families to Him who had preserved us in all our troubles. An address was then delivered by S. Rigdon, in which was portrayed in lively colors the oppression which we had suffered at the hands of our enemies. We then and there declared our constitutional rights as American citizens, and manifested our determination to resist, with our utmost endeavors from that time forth, all oppression, and to maintain our rights and our freedom, according to the holy principles of liberty, as guaranteed to every person by the Constitution and laws of our country.

This declaration was received with shouts of hosannah to God and the Lamb, and with many long cheers by the assembled thousands, who

were determined to yield their rights no more, unless compelled by
superior power.

Soon after these things the war clouds began again to lower with
dark and threatening aspect. Those who had combined against the laws
in the adjoining counties, had long watched our increasing power and
prosperity with jealousy, and with greedy and avaricious eyes. It was a
common boast that, as soon as we had completed our extensive improvements, and made a plentiful crop, they would drive us from the State,
and once more enrich themselves with the spoils.

Accordingly, at an election held in Davies County, a portion of
these bandits undertook to prevent the members of the Church of the
Saints from voting—forcing them from the poll box, and threatening to
kill whoever should attempt to vote. As some voters were attacked they
defended themselves, knocked down several of their opponents, gained
the victory, and cast in their votes.

This was a pretext for a general rising of the insurrectionists in all
the adjoining counties. They were alarmed for fear the "Mormons," as
they called them, should become so formidable as to maintain their
rights and liberties, insomuch that they could no more drive and plunder
them. Public meetings were held in Carroll, Saline, and other counties;
in which resolutions were passed and published, openly declaring the
treasonable and murderous intention of driving the citizens belonging to
the Church from their counties, and, if possible, from the State.

Resolutions to this effect were published in the journals of Upper
Missouri, and this without a single remark of disapprobation. Nay,
more: this murderous gang, when assembled in arms and painted like Indian warriors, and when openly committing murder, robbery, house
burning, and every crime known to the laws, were denominated citizens, whites, etc., in most of the journals of the State. While those who
stood firm to the laws of the land, and only defended themselves, and
their homes and country, were denominated "Mormons," in contradis-
tinction to the appellation of "citizens," "whites," etc., as if we had been
some savage tribe, or some colored race of foreigners.

In pursuance of the resolutions thus passed and published, a formidable banditti were soon assembled under arms, to the amount of several
hundred, and rendezvoused in Davies County. Here they commenced
firing upon our citizens, plundering, and taking peaceable citizens prisoners. The people of the Church made no resistance, except to assemble
on their own ground for defence. They also made oath before the District Judge, Austin A. King, to the above outrages.

One thousand men were then ordered into service, under the com-

mand of Major-General Atchison, and Brigadier-Generals Parks and
Doniphan. These marched to Davies County and remained in service
thirty days. But, judging from the result, they had no intention of coming in contact with the mob, but only to make a show of defending *one*
neighborhood, while the mob were allowed to attack *another*. The gang
now withdrew from Davies County and proceeded to De Witt, Carroll
County. Here they laid seige for several days, and subsisted by plunder
and robbery, watching every opportunity to fire upon our citizens.

At this time they had one or more pieces of artillery, in addition to
small arms and ammunition in abundance. A Presbyterian priest, *"Rev."*
Sashel Woods, served as chaplain to the gang, and said prayers in the
camp evening and morning. They succeeded in killing a number of citizens in and about De Witt. They also turned a gentleman, named Smith
Humphrey, and his wife and children out of doors, when sick, and setting fire to the house, burned it to ashes before their eyes. At length they
succeeded in driving every citizen from the place, at the sacrifice of
everything which they could not take with them.

This happened during a cold, stormy time in October; and, as many
of the citizens were sickly, and robbed of shelter and everything comfortable, they came near perishing. Some of them, in fact, did perish before
they arrived in Caldwell, a distance of sixty miles. Here the survivors
were hospitably taken in by their brethren. The militia, under General
Parks, made some show of trying to prevent these outrages; but all in
vain. At length the General informed the citizens that his forces were so
small, and many of them so much in favor of the insurrectionists, that it
was useless to look any longer to them for protection.

Several messages were also sent to the Governor, Lilburn W. Boggs,
the old mob-leader, imploring protection. But he was utterly deaf to everything which called for the protection of the *"Mormons,"* as he called
us. But, on the contrary, he harkened to the insinuations of the mob
which were without shadow of foundation. At one time he called out an
army, and put himself at their head to march against the *"Mormons."*
But, as he approached the upper country with this formidable force of
several thousand men, he was officially notified that the *"Mormons"*
were not in a state of insurrection, but were the victims of those who
were so, and that they needed his help.

His Excellency then disbanded his forces, and returned to Jefferson
City, to await till the mobs should compel the *"Mormons"* to some act
which might be considered illegal, which would give him some pretext
for driving them from the State.

After the evacuation of De Witt, when our citizens were officially notified that they must protect themselves, and expect no more protection from any department of the State Government, they assembled in Far West to the number of one thousand men, or thereabout, and resolved to defend their rights to the last. A call was made upon every person who could bear arms to come forward in defence of our houses, homes, wives and children, and the cause of our country and our God. In the meantime the bandits, elated with success and emboldened by the negligence of every department of the State Government, were increasing in numbers daily. They were concentrating in Davies County, with artillery and military stores, with open threats that they would now drive the citizens from Davies and Caldwell Counties.

In their marauding expeditions they took a number of citizens prisoners. Among these was Mr. Amasa Lyman, a minister of the gospel, and an excellent citizen of Caldwell County. They kept him prisoner for a number of days, while his family were in suspense and knew not his fate. They abused him in various ways, and held frequent consultations to kill him; but at length he was set at liberty.

The people of Davies County assembled several hundred men for defence. Several parties of the banditti were met, disarmed and dispersed. A detachment under Colonel D. W. Patten, marched against their main body with a *posse* of about one hundred men, met and dispersed them, with the loss of their artillery and some military stores. Another party were dispersed and disarmed by the Sheriff of Caldwell County and his *posse,* as they were on the march through that county to reinforce the banditti of Davies.

While these transactions were going forward, small parties of the enemy were busily engaged among the settlements, in plundering and burning houses; driving women and children from their homes to perish with hunger and cold, and robbing them of beds, bedding, furniture, wearing apparel, etc., etc. Hundreds were thus compelled to flee to the cities and strongholds. Many women and children came in at the dead hours of the night, and in the midst of dreadful storms of rain and snow, in which they came near perishing.

While these things were transpiring in Davies, Caldwell was threatened from every quarter. Her citizens were driven from her frontiers, and came pouring into the town of Far West, from day to day, with women, children, goods, provisions, etc.; in short, with everything moveable which they had time to bring. Lands and crops were abandoned to the enemy. The citizens were under arms from day to day, and a strict military guard was maintained every night. Men slept in their clothes, with arms by their sides, and ready to muster at a given signal at any hour of the night.

During this state of alarm guns were fired and the signal drum beat in the middle of a dark and gloomy night of October. The citizens came running together with arms in hand. An express had arrived from the south part of the county, stating that a party of the enemy were plundering houses, carrying off prisoners, killing cattle, and ordering families out of their houses, on pain of having them burned over their heads. A portion of the militia, under Captain Durphy, went with a deputy sheriff to the scene of the riot. I was one of the *posse,* the whole consisting of about sixty men.

This company was soon under way, having to ride through extensive prairies a distance of some twelve miles. The night was dark, the distant plains far and wide were illuminated by blazing fires, immense columns of smoke were seen rising in awful majesty, as if the world was on fire. This scene of grandeur can only be comprehended by those acquainted with scenes of prairie burning; as the fire sweeps over millions of acres of dry grass in the fall season, and leaves a smooth, black surface divested of all vegetation.

The thousand meteors, blazing in the distance like the camp-fires of some war host, threw a fitful gleam of light upon the distant sky, which many might have mistaken for the Aurora Borealis. This scene, added to the silence of midnight, the rumbling sound of the tramping steeds over the hard and dried surface of the plain, the clanking of swords in their scabbards, the occasional gleam of bright armor in the flickering firelight, the gloom of surrounding darkness, and the unknown destiny of the expedition, or even of the people who sent it forth; all combined to impress the mind with deep and solemn thoughts, and to throw a romantic vision over the imagination, which is not often experienced, except in the poet's dreams, or in the wild imagery of sleeping fancy.

In this solemn procession we moved on for some two hours, when it was supposed we were in the neighborhood of danger. We were then ordered to dismount and leave our horses with a guard. This done, we proceeded on foot for a mile or two in search of the enemy. We had not proceeded far when, as we entered the wilderness, we were suddenly fired upon by an unknown enemy in ambush. One of our little number fell at the first fire, being mortally wounded; his name was Obanyon. At a short distance we could now behold the camp-fires of the enemy. It was now dawn of day in the eastern horizon, but darkness still hovered over the scenes of conflict. Orders were issued to form in the brush, and under cover of the trees, which was instantly done. The fire now became general on both sides, and the whole wilderness seemed one continued echo of the report of the deadly rifle. After a few rounds of discharges, orders were given to charge the enemy in the camp. As we rushed upon them the strife became deadly, and several fell on both sides. At this instant a ball pierced the brave Colonel, David Patten, who was then at my side, and I saw him fall. Being on the eve of victory, I dared not stop to look after his fate, or that of others, but rushed into the enemy's camp. This was located on the immediate banks of Crooked River, which was here several rods wide, and not fordable. The enemy, being hard pushed, flung themselves into the stream, and struggled for the other shore. Those who reached it soon disappeared.

The firing now ceased, and the wilderness resounded with the watchword, *"God and Liberty."*

Our little band, which had been thrown into some disorder, were instantly formed, and their pieces reloaded. This done, a detachment surveyed the field, to look after the wounded. I turned to Gideon Carter, who was lying on his face, and saw him die. His face was so marred and disfigured with wounds and blood that I did not recognize him then, but learned afterwards that we had mistaken him for one of the enemy, and left him on the ground in mistake. I next found David Patten, whom, a few minutes previously, I had seen fall. He could speak, but was lying on his side, pale and almost dying, a ball having pierced the lower part of his body. Many others were wounded, and some dangerously.

The enemy had left their horses, saddles, camp and baggage, in the confusion of the flight. We harnessed some of their horses and placed them before a wagon, arranged blankets therein, on which we laid those who were not able to mount a horse; this done, our whole troop mounted the horses we had taken and formed in front and rear of the wagon which bore the wounded. We then moved slowly back to the guard and horses we had left. Here we halted and readjusted the wounded. It was an awful sight to see them pale and helpless, and hear their groans. There were about six of our men wounded, and one left dead on the ground. The enemy suffered a similar loss, besides their camp, and many of their arms and military stores.

We ascertained from the prisoners whom we rescued, that the enemy consisted of about sixty marauders, headed by a Methodist preacher, named Bogart. Our *posse* who were actually engaged, could not have been more than fifty. At the commencement of the engagement there were three of our fellow citizens held as prisoners in their camp; they had been kidnapped from their peaceful homes the day previous. Two of these made their escape at the commencement of the engagement; the third was shot through the body in attempting to run to our lines, but fortunately recovered.

Having now arranged everything to the best advantage for the wounded, we made slowly on towards Far West. When we came within five miles of the city our express had reached there with the news of the battle, and we were met by a surgeon and others for our relief. Among those who met us here was the wife of the pale and dying Patten. Our wounded were now taken into a house, and their wounds dressed. As Mrs. Patten entered the room, and cast her eyes upon the pale and ghastly features of her husband, she burst into tears, exclaiming: "O God! O my husband! How pale you look!"

He was still able to speak, but he died that evening in the triumphs of faith. The young Obanyon also died about the same time. The others recovered of their wounds, but one of them named Hendrix is still a cripple. Patten and Obanyon were buried together, under military honors; a whole people, as it were, followed them to the grave. All wept, whose feelings were not too intense to find vent in tears. He was the only member of the quorum of the Twelve who had as yet found a martyr's grave. He was a great and good man, and one who chose to lay down his life for the cause of truth and right; for this privilege he had diligently sought and prayed; "for," said he, "I had rather die than live to see it thus in my country."

But, to return to the main thread of my narrative: having conveyed the wounded to their place of hospitality, the *posse* hastened to Far West, and delivered the spoils of the enemy to the colonel of the regiment, who afterwards delivered them to the higher civil or military authorities of the State.

These several defeats of the insurrectionists in Davies County, as well as in Caldwell County, checked for a time their ruinous ravages. They saw that it was impossible to conquer a people who were fighting for their homes, their wives and children, as well as for their country and conscience, unless they could come against them with some show of authority; for it had become an established fact that the people of the Saints never resisted authority, however abused.

The next exertion of the enemy was to spread lies and falsehoods of the most alarming character. All our acts of defence were construed into insurrection, treason, murder and plunder. In short, the public were deceived by bigotry, priestcraft, and a corrupt press, and made to look upon all our acts of defence precisely as they would look upon the same acts performed, without cause or provocation, upon peaceable citizens. Murderous gangs were construed into peaceable militia in the State service, and to resist them was, on the part of the Saints, murder, treason and robbery. And, finally, the whole was treated abroad as the "*Mormon insurrection,*"—"*Mormon war,*" etc.

And, as if this were not enough, parties set fire to their own houses, or that of their neighbors, and then laid it to the Saints. Whole neighborhoods were falsely alarmed, or rather really alarmed, by the doings of these bandits; and in their fright they fled to more distant places of security, and clamored loudly to the State authorities for protection from the "*Mormons,*" whom they represented as burning, plundering, and destroying all before them. While they were simply standing on their own ground and maintaining the defensive, and this, too, in the last extreme, and not till they were abandoned by every department of the State Government.

This flame was greatly assisted by several dissenters from the Church through fear, or for love of power and gain. These dissenters became even more false, hardened, and bloodthirsty than those who had never known the way of righteousness. Many of them joined the enemy, and were the leaders in all manner of lying, murder and plunder. The Governor and ex-mobber, Lilburn W. Boggs, who had long sought some opportunity to destroy us, and drive us from the State, now issued an order for some ten thousand troops to be mustered into service and marched to the field against the "*Mormons.*" He gave the command of this formidable force to General Clark, who lived, perhaps, a hundred and fifty miles or more from the scene of trouble. The order was expressly to exterminate the "*Mormons,*" or drive them from the State.

It said nothing of criminals; it made no allusion to punishing crime and protecting innocence; it was sufficient to be called a "*Mormon.*" A peaceable family just emigrating, or passing through the country; a missionary going or coming on his peaceable errand of mercy; an aged soldier of the American revolution on his death bed, or leaning on his staff in the chimney corner; a widow with her babes; the tender wife, or helpless orphan; all were included in this order of wholesale extermination or banishment. It was enough that they believed as Mormon did; or that they were members of the Church of the Saints.

So did the order read, and so it was construed by the officers and soldiers entrusted with its execution. On the other hand, all the bandits, murderers, robbers, thieves, and house burners who had mobbed our people for the five years previous, were now converted into orderly, loyal, patriotic State militia, and mustered into service under pay, or suffered to murder people of every age and sex, and plunder them on their own hook wherever they chose, provided they were considered "Mormons."

While General Clark was mustering his forces for this wholesale murder and treason, Major General D. Lucas and Brigadier General Moses Wilson, who were well known as the old leaders of the former outrages in Jackson County, under this same Boggs—being nearer the scene of action, and wishing to share the plunder and immortalize their names—put themselves at the head of all the old mobbers of Jackson County they could muster, and all those bandits who had more lately infested the counties of Carroll, Davies and Caldwell, and such other militia as they could muster, and marched directly for the City of Far West, where they arrived while General Clark and his forces were several days' journey from the scene of action. The army of Lucas, thus mustered and marched, consisted of some three or four thousand men.

In the meantime the Governor's orders and these military movements were kept an entire secret from the citizens of Caldwell and Davies, who were suffering all this oppression from lawless outrages; even the mail was withheld from Far West. We had only heard that large bodies of armed men were approaching from the south, and we had sent a hundred and fifty men with a flag of truce to make inquiries. While they were absent on this mission an alarm came to town that the whole county to the south was filled with armed men, who were murdering, plundering, and taking peaceful citizens prisoners in their own houses. On the receipt of this intelligence every man flew to arms for the protection of our city.

It was now towards evening, and we had heard nothing from the reconnoitering company who went south in the morning. While we stood in our armor, gazing to the south in anxious suspense, we beheld an army of cavalry with a long train of baggage wagons advancing over the hills, at two miles distance. At first we conjectured it might be our little troop with the flag of truce; but we soon saw that there were thousands of them. Our next thought was that it might be some friendly troops sent for our protection; and then again we thought it might be a concentration of all the bandit forces combined for our destruction.

At all events, there was no time to be lost; for, although our force then present did not exceed five hundred men, yet we did not intend that they should enter the town without giving some account of themselves. We accordingly marched out upon the plains on the south of the city and formed in order of battle. Our line of infantry extended near half a mile. A small company of horses was posted on our right wing on a commanding eminence, and another small company in the rear of our main body, intended as a kind of reserve.

By this time the sun was near setting, and the advance of the unknown army had come within plain view, at less than one mile distant. On seeing our forces presenting a small but formidable front, they came to a halt, and formed along the borders of a stream called Goose Creek.

Both parties sent out a white flag, which met between the armies. Our messenger demanded to know who they were, and what were their intentions? The reply was: "We want three persons out of the city before we massacre the rest!" This was a very alarming and unexpected answer. But they were soon prevailed on to suspend hostilities till morning, by which time we were in hopes to receive some further and more satisfactory information. The enemy, under the command of Major General D. Lucas, of Jackson County mob memory, then commenced their encampment for the night. Our troops continued under arms during the night. The company of a hundred and fifty soon returned from the south, informing us that they had been hemmed in by the enemy during the day, and only escaped by their superior knowledge of the ground.

We also sent an express to Davies County, and by morning were reinforced by quite a number of troops, under the command of Colonel L. White. In the meantime a noted company of banditti, under the command of Cornelius Gillum, who had long infested our borders, and been notorious for their murders and daring robberies, and who painted themselves as Indian warriors, came pouring in from the West to strengthen the camp of the enemy.

Another company of murderers came in from Carroll County, and were taken into the ranks of Lucas, after murdering some eighteen or twenty of our citizens (men, women and children) at Haun's Mill, of which particulars will be given hereafter. Thus both parties were considerably reinforced during the night. The citizens of Far West being determined, if attacked, to defend their homes, wives and children to the last, spent the night in throwing up a temporary breastwork of building timber, logs, rails, floor plank, etc.

In the morning the south side of the city was thus fortified, and also a considerable portion of the east and west sides—the whole line extending a mile and a half.

Chapter 22

October 31, 1838.—In the afternoon we were informed that the Governor had ordered this force against us, with orders to exterminate or
drive every "*Mormon*" from the State. As soon as these facts were ascertained we determined not to resist anything in the shape of authority,
however abused. We had now nothing to do but to submit to be massacred, driven, robbed or plundered, at the option of our persecutors.

Colonel George M. Hinkle, who was at that time the highest officer
of the militia assembled for the defence of Far West, waited on Messrs.
J. Smith, S. Rigdon, Hyrum Smith, L. Wight, George Robinson and
myself, with a request from General Lucas that we would repair to his
camp, with the assurance that as soon as peaceable arrangements could
be entered into we should be released. We had no confidence in the
word of a murderer and robber, but there was no alternative but to put
ourselves into the hands of such monsters, or to have the city attacked,
and men, women and children massacred. We, therefore, commended
ourselves to the Lord, and voluntarily surrendered as sheep into the
hands of wolves. As we approached the camp of the enemy General
Lucas rode out to meet us with a guard of several hundred men.

The haughty general rode up, and, without speaking to us, instantly
ordered his guard to surround us. They did so very abruptly, and we were
marched into camp surrounded by thousands of savage looking beings,
many of whom were dressed and painted like Indian warriors. These all

set up a constant yell, like so many bloodhounds let loose upon their prey, as if they had achieved one of the most miraculous victories that ever graced the annals of the world. If the vision of the infernal regions could suddenly open to the mind, with thousands of malicious fiends, all clamoring, exulting, deriding, blaspheming, mocking, railing, raging and foaming like a troubled sea, then could some idea be formed of the hell which we had entered.

In camp we were placed under a strong guard, and were without shelter during the night, lying on the ground in the open air, in the midst of a great rain. The guards during the whole night kept up a constant tirade of mockery, and the most obscene blackguardism and abuse. They blasphemed God; mocked Jesus Christ; swore the most dreadful oaths; taunted brother Joseph and others; demanded miracles; wanted signs, such as: "Come, Mr. Smith, show us an angel." "Give us one of your revelations." "Show us a miracle." "Come, there is one of your brethren here in camp whom we took prisoner yesterday in his own house, and knocked his brains out with his own rifle, which we found hanging over his fireplace; he lays speechless and dying; speak the word and heal him, and then we will all believe." "Or, if you are Apostles or men of God, deliver yourselves, and then we will be Mormons." Next would be a volley of oaths and blasphemies; then a tumultuous tirade of lewd boastings of having defiled virgins and wives by force, etc., much of which I dare not write; and, indeed, language would fail me to attempt more than a faint description. Thus passed this dreadful night, and before morning several other captives were added to our number, among whom was brother Amasa Lyman.

We were informed that the general officers held a secret council during most of the night, which was dignified by the name of court martial; in which, without a hearing, or, without even being brought before it, we were all sentenced to be shot. The day and hour was also appointed for the execution of this sentence, viz: next morning at 8 o'clock, in the public square at Far West. Of this we were informed by Brigadier-General Doniphan, who was one of the council, but who was so violently opposed to this cool blooded murder that he assured the council that he would revolt and withdraw his whole brigade, and march them back to Clay County as soon as it was light, if they persisted in so dreadful an undertaking. Said he, "It is cold blooded murder, and I wash my hands of it." His firm remonstrance, and that of a few others, so alarmed the haughty murderer and his accomplices that they dare not put the decree in execution.

Thus, through a merciful providence of God our lives were spared through that dreadful night. It was the common talk, and even the boast in the camp, that individuals lay here and there unburied, where they had shot them down for sport. The females they had ravished; the plunder they had taken; the houses they had burned; the horses they had stolen; the fields of grain they had laid waste, were common topics; and were dwelt on for mere amusement, or, as if these deeds were a stepstone to office; and it is a fact that such deeds were so considered.

No pen need undertake to describe our feelings during that terrible night, while there confined—not knowing the fate of our wives and children, or of our fellow Saints, and seeing no way for our lives to be saved except by the miraculous power of God. But, notwithstanding all earthly hopes were gone, still we felt a calmness indescribable. A secret whispering to our inmost soul seemed to say: "Peace, my sons, be of good cheer, your work is not yet done; therefore I will restrain your enemies, that they shall not have power to take your lives."

While thus confined, Wm. E. McLellin, once my fellow laborer in the gospel, but now a *Judas*, with hostile weapon in hand to destroy the Saints, came to me and observed: "Well, Parley, you have now got where you are certain never to escape; how do you feel as to the course you have taken in religion?" I answered, "that I had taken that course which I should take if I had my life to live over again." He seemed thoughtful for a moment, and then replied: "Well—I think, if I were you, I should die as I had lived; at any rate, I see no possibility of escape for you and your friends."

Next morning Gen. Lucas demanded the Caldwell militia to give up their arms, which was done. As soon as the troops who had defended the city were disarmed, it was surrounded by the enemy and all the men detained as prisoners. None were permitted to pass out of the city—although their families were starving for want of sustenance; the mills and provisions being some distance from the city.

The brutal mob were now turned loose to ravage, steal, plunder and murder without restraint. Houses were rifled, women ravished, and goods taken as they pleased. The whole troop, together with their horses, lived on the grain and provisions. While cattle were shot down for mere sport, and sometimes men, women and children fared no better. On the third morning after our imprisonment we were placed in a wagon, in order for removal. Many of the more desperate then crowded around, cocked their rifles, and singling us out presented them to our breasts, and swore they would blow us through. Some guns were snapped, but missed fire, and the rest were in a small degree restrained by the officers, and we still lived.

We were now marched to Far West, under the conduct of the whole army; and while they halted in the public square, we were permitted to go with a guard for a change of linen and to take final leave of our families, in order to depart as prisoners to Jackson County, a distance of sixty miles.

This was the most trying scene of all. I went to my house, being guarded by two or three soldiers; the cold rain was pouring down without, and on entering my little cottage, there lay my wife sick of a fever, with which she had been for some time confined. At her breast was our son Nathan, an infant of three months, and by her side a little girl of five years. On the foot of the same bed lay a woman in travail, who had been driven from her house in the night, and had taken momentary shelter in my hut of ten feet square—my larger house having been torn down. I stepped to the bed; my wife burst into tears; I spoke a few words of comfort, telling her to try to live for my sake and the children's; and expressing a hope that we should meet again though years might separate us. She promised to try to live. I then embraced and kissed the little babes and departed.

Till now I had refrained from weeping; but, to be forced from so helpless a family, who were destitute of provisions and fuel, and deprived almost of shelter in a bleak prairie, with none to assist them, exposed to a lawless banditti who were utter strangers to humanity, and this at the approach of winter, was more than nature could well endure.

I went to Gen. Moses Wilson in tears, and stated the circumstances of my sick, heart-broken and destitute family in terms which would have moved any heart that had a latent spark of humanity yet remaining. But I was only answered with an exultant laugh, and a taunt of reproach by this hardened murderer.

As I returned from my house towards the troops in the square, I halted with the guard at the door of Hyrum Smith, and heard the sobs and groans of his wife, at his parting words. She was then near confinement; and needed more than ever the comfort and consolation of a husband's presence. As we returned to the wagon we saw S. Rigdon taking leave of his wife and daughters, who stood at a little distance, in tears of anguish indescribable. In the wagon sat Joseph Smith, while his aged father and venerable mother came up overwhelmed with tears, and took each of the prisoners by the hand with a silence of grief too great for utterance.

In the meantime, hundreds of the brethren crowded around us, anxious to take a parting look, or a silent shake of the hand; for feelings were too intense to allow of speech. In the midst of these scenes orders were given, and we moved slowly away, under the conduct of Gen. Wilson and his whole brigade. A march of twelve miles brought us to Crooked River, where we camped for the night. Here Gen. Wilson began to treat us more kindly; he became very sociable; conversing very freely on the subject of his former murders and robberies committed against us in Jackson. He did not pretend to deny anything; but spoke upon the whole as freely as if he had been giving the history of other ages or countries, in which his audience had no personal concern. Said he:

"We Jackson County boys know how it is; and, therefore, have not the extremes of hatred and prejudice which characterize the rest of the troops. We know perfectly that from the beginning the Mormons have not been the aggressors at all. As it began in '33 in Jackson County, so it has been ever since. You Mormons were crowded to the last extreme, and compelled to self-defence; and this has been construed into treason, murder and plunder. We mob you without law; the authorities refuse to protect you according to law; you then are compelled to protect yourselves, and we act upon the prejudices of the public, who join our forces, and the whole is legalized, for your destruction and our gain. Is not this a shrewd and cunning policy on our part, gentlemen?

"When we drove you from Jackson County, we burned two hundred and three of your houses; plundered your goods; destroyed your press, type, paper, books, office and all—tarred and feathered old Bishop Partridge, as exemplary an old man as you can find anywhere. We shot down some of your men, and, if any of you returned the fire, we imprisoned you, on your trial for murder, etc. Damn'd shrewdly done, gentlemen; and I came damn'd near kicking the bucket myself; for, on one occasion, while we were tearing down houses, driving families, and destroying and plundering goods, some of you good folks put a ball through my son's body, another through the arm of my clerk, and a third pierced my shirt collar and marked my neck. No blame, gentlemen; we deserved it. And let a set of men serve me as your community have been served, and I'll be damn'd if I would not fight till I died.

"It was repeatedly insinuated, by the other officers and troops, that we should hang you prisoners on the first tree we came to on the way to Independence. But I'll be damn'd if anybody shall hurt you. We just intend to exhibit you in Independence, let the people look at you, and see what a damn'd set of fine fellows you are. And, more particularly, to keep you from that G—d damn'd old bigot of a Gen. Clark and his troops, from down country, who are so stuffed with lies and prejudice that they would shoot you down in a moment."

Such was the tenor of the conversation addressed by Gen. Wilson to his prisoners. Indeed, it was now evident that he was proud of his prey, and felt highly enthusiastic in having the honor of returning in triumph to Independence with his prisoners, whom his superstition had magnified into something more than fellow citizens—something noble or supernatural, and worthy of public exhibition.

As we arose and commenced our march on the morning of the 3d of November, Joseph Smith spoke to me and the other prisoners, in a low, but cheerful and confidential tone; said he: *"Be of good cheer, brethren; the word of the Lord came to me last night that our lives should be given us, and that whatever we may suffer during this captivity, not one of our lives should be taken."* Of this prophecy I testify in the name of the Lord, and, though spoken in secret, its public fulfilment and the miraculous escape of each one of us is too notorious to need my testimony. In the after part of the day we came to the Missouri River, which separated us from Jackson County. Here the brigade was halted and the prisoners taken to a public house, where we were permitted to shave, change our linen, and partake of some refreshment. This done, we were hurried to the ferry and across the river with the utmost haste in advance of the troops. This movement was soon explained to us. The truth was, Gen. Clark had now arrived near the scene of action, and had sent an express to take us from Gen. Wilson and prevent us from going to Jackson County—both armies being competitors for the honor of possessing the wonderful, or, in their estimation, royal prisoners.

Clark and his troops, from a distance, who had not arrived in the city of Far West till after our departure, were desirous of seeing the strange men whom it was said had turned the world upside down and of possessing such a wonderful trophy of victory, or of putting them to death themselves. On the other hand, Wilson and his brigade were determined to exhibit us through the streets of Independence as a visible token of their own achievements. Therefore, when demanded by Gen. Clark's express, they refused to surrender us; and hurried us across the ferry with all possible despatch. Marching about a mile, we encamped for the night in the wilderness, with about fifty troops for our guard—the remainder not crossing the ferry till the next morning.

Some of the neighboring citizens visited us next morning—it being Sunday. One of the ladies came up and very candidly inquired of the troops which of the prisoners the "Mormons" worshipped? One of the guards pointing to Mr. Smith with a significant smile, said, "This is he." The woman, then turning to Mr. Smith, inquired whether he professed to be the Lord and Saviour?

Do not smile, gentle reader, at the ignorance of these poor innocent creatures, who, by the exertions of a corrupt press and pulpit, are kept in ignorance and made to believe in every possible absurdity in relation to the Church of the Saints. Mr. Smith replied, that he professed to be nothing but a man, and a minister of salvation, sent by Jesus Christ to preach the gospel. After expressing some surprise, the lady inquired what was the peculiar nature of the gospel, as held by himself and his Church? At this the visitors and soldiers gathered around, and Mr. Smith preached to them faith in the Lord Jesus Christ, repentance towards God, reformation of life, immersion in water, in the name of Jesus Christ, for remission of sins, and the gift of the Holy Ghost by the laying on of hands.

All seemed surprised, and the lady, in tears, went her way, praising God for the truth, and praying aloud that the Lord would bless and deliver the prisoners.

At ten o'clock the brigade had all crossed the river, and come up with us. We were then marched forward in our carriages, while the troops were formed into a front and rear guard, with quite a martial appearance. As we passed along through the settlements hundreds of men, women and children flocked to see us. General W. often halted the whole brigade to introduce us to the populace, pointing out each of us by name. Many shook us by the hand, and, in the ladies at least, there appeared some feelings of human compassion and sympathy.

In this way we proceeded till we arrived at Independence. It was now past noon, and in the midst of a great rain; but hundreds crowded to witness the procession, and to gaze at us as we were paraded in martial triumph through the principal streets, the bugles sounding a blast of triumphant joy.

Chapter 23

This ceremony being finished, a vacant house was prepared for our reception, into which we were ushered through the crowd of spectators
which thronged every avenue.

The troops were then disbanded. In the meantime we were kept
under a small guard, and were treated with some degree of humanity,
while hundreds flocked to see us day after day. We spent most of our time
in preaching and conversation, explanatory of our doctrines and practice. Much prejudice was removed, and the feelings of the populace
began to be in our favor, notwithstanding their former wickedness and
hatred. In a day or two we were at liberty to walk the streets without a
guard. We were finally removed from our house of confinement to a
hotel, where we boarded at the public table, and lodged on the floor,
with a block of wood for a pillow. We no longer had any guard; we went
out and came in when we pleased—a certain keeper being appointed
merely to watch over us, and look to our wants.

With him we walked out of town to the westward, and visited the
desolate lands of the Saints, and the place which, seven years before, we
had dedicated for the building of a Temple. This was a beautiful rise of
ground, about half a mile west of Independence centre. When we saw it
last it was a noble forest, but our enemies had since robbed it of every
vestige of timber, and it now lay desolate, or clothed with grass and
weeds.

O, how many feelings did this spot awaken in our bosoms! Here we
had often bowed the knee in prayer, in bygone years. Here we had assembled with hundreds of happy Saints in the solemn meeting, and offered our songs, and sacraments, and orisons. But now all was solemn

166

and lonely desolation. Not a vestige remained to mark the spot where stood our former dwellings. They had long since been consumed by fire, or removed and converted to the uses of our enemies.

While at Independence we were once or twice invited to dine with General Wilson and some others, which we did.

While thus sojourning as prisoners at large, I arose one morning when it was very snowy, and passed silently and unmolested out of the hotel, and as no one seemed to notice me, or call me in question, I thought I would try an experiment. I passed on eastward through the town; no one noticed me. I then took into the fields, still unobserved. After travelling a mile I entered a forest; all was gloomy silence, none were near, the heavens were darkened and obscured by falling snow, my track was covered behind me, and I was free. I knew the way to the States eastward very well, and there seemed nothing to prevent my pursuing my way thither; thoughts of freedom beat high in my bosom; wife, children, home, freedom, peace, and a land of law and order, all arose in my mind; I could go to other States, send for my family, make me a home and be happy.

On the other hand, I was a prisoner in a State where all law was at an end. I was liable to be shot down at any time without judge or jury. I was liable to be tried for my life by murderous assassins, who had already broken every oath of office and trampled on every principle of honor or even humanity. Hands already dripping with the blood of aged sires, and of helpless women and children, were reaching out for my destruction. The battle of Crooked River had already been construed into *murder* on the part of the brave patriots who there defended their lives and rescued their fellow citizens from kidnappers and land pirates, while the pirates themselves had been converted into loyal militia.

To go forward was freedom, to go backward was to be sent to General Clark, and be accused of the highest crimes, with murderers for judge, jury and executioners.

"Go free!" whispered the tempter.

"No!" said I, "never, while brother Joseph and his fellows are in the power of the enemy. What a storm of trouble, or even of death, it might subject them to."

I turned on my heel, retraced my steps, and entered the hotel ere they had missed me. As I shook the snow off my clothes the keeper and also brother Joseph inquired where I had been. I replied, just out for a little exercise. A walk for pleasure in such a storm gave rise to some pleasantries on their part, and there the matter ended.

There was one thing which buoyed up our spirits continually during our captivity: it was the remembrance of the word of the Lord to brother Joseph, saying, that our lives should all be given us during this captivity, and not one of them should be lost. I thought of this while in the wilderness vacillating whether to go or stay, and the thought struck me: *"He that will seek to save his life shall lose it; but he that will lose his life for my sake shall find it again, even life eternal."* I could now make sure of my part in the first resurrection, as I had so intensely desired when about eleven years old. But, O, the path of life! How was it beset with trials!

At length, after repeated demands, we were sent to General Clark, at Richmond, Ray County. Generals Lucas and Wilson had tried in vain for some days to get a guard to accompany us. None would volunteer, and when drafted they would not obey orders; for in truth, they wished us to go at liberty. At last a colonel and two or three officers started with us, with their swords and pistols, which were intended more to protect us than to keep us from escaping. On this journey some of us rode in carriages and some on horseback. Sometimes we were sixty or eighty rods in front or rear of our guards, who were drinking hard out of bottles which they carried in their pockets.

At night, having crossed the Missouri River, we put up at a private house. Here our guards all got drunk, and went to bed and to sleep, leaving us their pistols to defend ourselves in case of any attack from without, as we were in a very hostile neighborhood. Next morning we rode a few miles, and were met by an express from General Clark, which consisted of one Colonel Sterling Price and a guard of soldiers. This company immediately surrounded us with poised pieces, in regular military order, as if we had been Bonaparte and staff on the way to St. Helena; thinking, perhaps, that if we should escape, the whole United States and all Europe would be immediately overthrown.

In this manner we were escorted to Richmond, the headquarters of General Clark and his army of three or four thousand men. Here, as usual, we had to endure the gaze of the curious, as if we had been a caravan of animals for exhibition. Troops were paraded to receive us, which, as we approached, opened to the right and left, thus forming a long avenue, through which we passed into a block house, and were immediately put in chains, under a strong guard, who stood over us continually with poised pieces, cocked and primed. Colonel Price continued in the superintendence of the prisoners and the guards.

General Clark at length called to see us. He seemed more haughty, unfeeling, and reserved than even Lucas or Wilson had been when we first entered their camp. We inquired of the general what were his intentions concerning us. I stated to him that we had now been captives for many days, and we knew not wherefore, nor whether we were considered prisoners of war or prisoners of civil process, or *"prisoners of hope."* At the same time remarking, that all was wrapt in mystery, for, as citizens of the United States and of Missouri, in time of peace, we could in nowise be considered as prisoners of war; and, without civil process, we were not holden by civil authority; and as to being "prisoners of hope," there was not much chance to hope, from our present appearances!

He replied that *"we were taken to be tried."*

"Tried? By what authority?"

"By court martial."

"What! Ministers of the gospel tried by court martial! Men who sustain no office in military affairs, and who are not subject by law to military duty; such men to be tried by court martial! And this in time of peace, and in a republic where the constitution guaranteed to every citizen the right of trial by jury?"

"Yes. This is in accordance with the treaty of stipulations entered into at Far West at the time of the surrender, and as agreed to by Colonel Hinkle, your commanding officer."

"Colonel Hinkle, our commanding officer! What had he to do with our civil rights? He was only a colonel of a regiment of the Caldwell County Militia."

"Why! was he not the commanding officer of the fortress of Far West, the headquarters of the *Mormon forces?"*

"We had no *'fortress'* or *'Mormon forces,'* but were part of the State militia."

At this the general seemed surprised, and the conversation ended.

We were astonished above measure at proceedings so utterly ignorant and devoid of all law or justice. Here was a Major-General, selected by the Governor of Missouri, and sent to banish or exterminate a religious society. And then, to crown the whole with inconceivable absurdity, said religious society is converted by this officer and his associates into an independent government, or foreign nation. And last, and equally absurd, the State of Missouri assumed her independence of the Federal Government so far as to *treat* with this imaginary *"Mormon Empire,"* or foreign nation. A colonel of militia, subordinate to the general then in the field, is converted into a foreign minister, an envoy extraordinary, in behalf of the "Mormon Empire," to enter into treaty stipulations with his Missouri majesty's forces, under Generals Lucas, Wilson and Clark!

The City of Far West, the capital of *"Mormonia,"* is the *"Ghent,"* where this treaty of peace is ratified. The standing army of the conquered nation stack their arms, which are carried in triumph to Richmond. Preachers of the gospel are converted into *"noble"* or *"royal prisoners,"* chained to the car of the victorious champions to be led captive as sport for the Philistines, or to be shot or hung at pleasure, while the residue of the inhabitants of the fallen empire—men, women and children—are to have their real estate and all other goods confiscated, and themselves banished the State on pain of death. A few, however, are selected from among these exiles to be imprisoned or executed at the mere dictation of a Nero or a Nicholas.

Was this in America, in the nineteenth century? Were these scenes transacted in a constitutional republic? Yes, verily, and worse,—a tale of horror, of woe, of long years of lawless outrage and tyranny is yet to be told, of which this is a mere stepping stone or entering wedge.

Chapter 24

MASSACRE AT HAUN'S MILL

We here introduce the testimony of Joseph Young, an eye witness of one of the most awful scenes which ever stained the annals of history in any age or country.

"The following is a short history of my travels to the State of Missouri, and of a bloody tragedy enacted at Haun's Mill, on Shoal Creek, October 30, 1838:

"On the 6th of July last I started with my family from Kirtland, Ohio, for Missouri—the county of Caldwell, in the upper part of the State, being the place of my destination. On the 13th of October I crossed the Mississippi at Louisiana, at which place I heard vague reports of the disturbances in the upper country, but nothing that could be relied on.

"I continued my course westward till I crossed Grand River, at a place called Compton's Ferry, where I heard for the first time that if I proceeded any further on my journey I would be in danger of being stopped by a body of armed men.

"I was not willing, however, while treading my native soil and breathing republican air, to abandon my object, which was to locate myself and family in a fine, healthy country, where we could enjoy the society of our friends and connections. Consequently, I prosecuted my journey till I came to Whitney's Mills, situated on Shoal Creek, in the eastern part of Caldwell County. After crossing the creek and going about three miles we met a party of the mob, about forty in number, armed with rifles and mounted on horses, who informed us that we could go no further west, threatening us with instant death if we proceeded any further.

"I asked them the reason of this prohibition, to which they replied that we were 'Mormons,' and that every one who adhered to that religious faith would have to leave the State within ten days, or renounce their religion. Accordingly, they drove us back to the mills above mentioned.

"Here we tarried three days, and on Friday, the 26th, we recrossed the creek, and, following up its banks, we succeeded in eluding the mob for the time being, and gained the residence of a friend in Myers' Settlement. On Sunday, October 28, we arrived at Haun's Mill, where we found a number of our friends collected, who were holding a council and deliberating upon the best course for them to pursue to defend themselves against the mob who were collecting in the neighborhood under the command of Colonel Jennings, of Livingston, and threatening them with house burning and killing.

"The decision of the council was that the neighborhood should put itself in a state of defence. Accordingly about twenty-eight of our men armed themselves, and were in constant readiness for an attack, if any small body of mobbers might come upon them.

"The same evening, for some reason best known to themselves, the mob sent one of their number to enter into a treaty with our friends, which was accepted on the condition of mutual forbearance on both sides, and that each party, as far as their influence extended, should exert themselves to prevent any further hostilities.

"At this time, however, there was another mob collecting on Grand River, at William Mann's, which was threatening us; consequently, we remained under arms on Monday, the 29th, which passed away without molestation from any quarter.

"On Tuesday, the 30th, that bloody tragedy was enacted, the scenes of which I shall never forget.

"More than three fourths of the day had passed in tranquility as smiling as the preceding one. I think there was no individual of our company that was apprised of the sudden and awful fate which hung over our heads like an overwhelming torrent, and which was to change the prospects, the feelings and sympathies of about thirty families.

"The banks of Shoal Creek, on either side, teemed with children sporting and playing, while their mothers were engaged in domestic employments. Fathers or husbands were either on guard about the mills or other property, or employed in gathering crops for winter consumption. The weather was very pleasant, the sun shone clearly, all was tranquil, and no one expressed any apprehension of the awful crisis that was near us, even at our doors.

"It was about 4 o'clock, p.m., while sitting in my cabin with my babe in my arms, and my wife standing by my side, the door being open,

I cast my eyes on the opposite bank of Shoal Creek, and saw a large body of armed men on horses directing their course towards the mills with all possible speed. As they advanced through the scattering trees that bordered the prairie they seemed to form themselves into a three square position, forming a vanguard in front. At this moment, David Evans, seeing the superiority of their numbers (there being two hundred and forty of them, according to their own account), gave a signal and cried for peace. This not being heeded they continued to advance, and their leader, a man named Comstock, fired a gun, which was followed by a solemn pause of about ten or twelve seconds; when all at once they discharged about one hundred rifles, aiming at a blacksmith's shop, into which our friends fled for safety. They then charged up to the shop, the crevices of which, between the logs, were sufficiently large to enable them to aim directly at the bodies of those who had there fled for refuge from the fire of their murderers. There were several families tented in the rear of the shop whose lives were exposed, and, amid showers of bullets, fled to the woods in different directions.

"After standing and gazing at this bloody scene for a few minutes, and finding myself in the uttermost danger, the bullets having reached the house where I was living, I committed my family to the protection of Heaven; and, leaving the house on the opposite side, I took a path which led up the hill, following in the trail of three of my brethren that had fled from the shop.

"While ascending the hill we were discovered by the mob, who immediately fired at us, and continued so to do till we reached the summit. In descending the hill I secreted myself in a thicket of bushes, where I lay till 8 o'clock in the evening. At this time I heard a voice calling my name in an undertone. I immediately left the thicket and went to the house of Benjamin Lewis, where I found my family—who had fled there in safety—and two of my friends, mortally wounded, one of whom died before morning. Here we passed the painful night in deep and awful reflections on the scenes of the preceding evening. After daylight appeared some four or five men, with myself, who had escaped with our lives from this horrid massacre, repaired as soon as possible to the mills to learn the condition of our friends, whose fate we had but too truly anticipated.

"When we arrived at the house of Mr. Haun, we found Mr. Merrick's body lying in the rear of the house; Mr. McBride's in front, literally mangled from head to foot. We were informed by Miss Rebecca Judd, who was an eye witness, that he was shot with his own gun after he had given it up, and then cut to pieces with a corn cutter by a man named Rogers, of Davies County, who keeps a ferry on Grand River, and who has since repeatedly boasted of this act of savage barbarity. Mr. York's body we found in the house. After viewing these corpses we immediately went to the blacksmith's shop, where we found nine of our friends, eight of whom were already dead—the other, Mr. Cox, of Indiana, in the agonies of death, who soon expired.

"We immediately prepared and carried them to the place of interment. This last office of kindness due to the remains of departed friends was not attended with the customary ceremonies nor decency; for we were in jeopardy, every moment expecting to be fired on by the mob, who, we supposed, were lying in ambush, waiting the first opportunity to despatch the remaining few who were providentially preserved from the slaughter of the preceding day. However, we accomplished without molestation this painful task. The place of burial was a vault in the ground, formerly intended for a well, into which we threw the bodies of our friends promiscuously.

"Among the slain I will mention Sardius Smith, son of Warren Smith, about nine years old, who, through fear, had crawled under the bellows in the shop, where he remained till the massacre was over, when he was discovered by one Glaze, of Carroll County, who presented a rifle near his head and literally blew off the upper part of it. Mr. Stanley, of Carroll County, told me afterwards that Glaze boasted of this fiendlike murder and heroic deed all over the country.

"The number killed and mortally wounded in this wanton slaughter was eighteen or nineteen, whose names, as far as I can recollect, were as follows: Thomas McBride, Levi Merrick, Elias Benner, Josiah Fuller, Benjamin Lewis, Alexander Campbell, Warren Smith, Sardius Smith, George Richards, Mr. Napier, Mr. Harmer, Mr. Cox, Mr. Abbott, Mr. York, Wm. Merrick (a boy eight or nine years old), and three or four others whose names I do not recollect, as they were strangers to me.

"Among the wounded who recovered were Isaac Laney, Nathan K. Knight, Mr. Yokum, two brothers by the name of Myers, Tarlton Lewis, Mr. Haun and several others. Miss Mary Stedwell, while fleeing, was shot through the hand, and, fainting, fell over a log, into which they shot upwards of twenty balls.

"To finish their work of destruction, this band of murderers composed of men from Davies, Livingston, Ray, Carroll and Chariton Counties, led by some of the principal men of that section of the upper country (among whom, I am informed, were Mr. Ashby, from Chariton, member of the State Legislature; Col. Jennings, of Livingston County; Thos. O'Bryon, Clerk of Livingston County; Mr. Whitney, Dr. Randall and many others), proceeded to rob the houses, wagons and tents of bedding and clothing; drove off horses and wagons, leaving widows and orphans destitute of the necessaries of life, and even stripped the clothing from the bodies of the slain!

"According to their own account they fired seven rounds in this awful butchery; making upwards of sixteen hundred shots, at a little company of men about thirty in number.

"I hereby certify the above to be a true statement of facts, according to the best of my knowledge.

"JOSEPH YOUNG."

"STATE OF ILLINOIS,
County of Adams.

"I hereby certify that Joseph Young this day came before me, and made oath in due form of law, that the statements contained in the foregoing sheets are true, according to the best of his knowledge and belief. In testimony whereof I have hereunto set my hand, and affixed the seal of the Circuit Court at Quincy, this fourth day of June, in the year of our Lord one thousand eight hundred and thirty-nine.

"C. M. WOODS,
"Clerk of Circuit Court of Adams Co., Ill."

Chapter 25

Speech of Major-General Clark, Delivered at Far West while its Citizens Were Held As Prisoners, November, 1838.

"Gentlemen: You, whose names are not on this list, will now have the privilege of going to your fields to obtain grain for your families—wood, etc. Those that compose the list will go from thence to prison, to be tried, and receive the due demerits of their crimes. But you are now at liberty, all but such as charges may hereafter be preferred against. It now devolves upon you to fulfil the treaty that you have entered into—the leading items of which I now lay before you.

"The first of these items you have already complied with—which is, that you deliver up your leading men to be tried according to law. Second, that you deliver up your arms—this has been attended to. The third is, that you sign over your property to defray the expenses of the war; this you have also done. Another thing yet remains for you to comply with; that is: that you leave the State forthwith; and, whatever your feelings concerning this affair, whatever your innocence, it is nothing to me. General Lucas, who is equal in authority with me, has made this treaty with you. I am determined to see it executed.

"The orders of the Governor to me, were, that you should be exterminated, and not allowed to remain in the State. And had your leaders not been given up, and the treaty complied with before this, you and your families would have been destroyed and your houses in ashes.

"There is a discretionary power resting in my hands, which I shall try to exercise for a season. I did not say that you must go now, but you must not think of stopping here another season, or of putting in crops; for the moment you do the CITIZENS WILL BE UPON YOU. I am determined to see the Governor's orders fulfilled, but shall not come upon you immediately. Do not think that I shall act as I have done any more; but if I have to come again because the treaty which you have made is not complied with, you need not expect any mercy, but extermination; for I am determined that the Governor's order shall be executed.

"As for your leaders, do not think, do not imagine for a moment, do not let it enter your mind that they will be delivered, or that you will see their faces again, for their fate is fixed, their die is cast, their doom is sealed.

"I am sorry, gentlemen, to see so great a number of apparently intelligent men found in the situation that you are. And, oh! that I could invoke the Spirit of the unknown God to rest upon you, and deliver you from that awful chain of superstition, and liberate you from those fetters of fanaticism with which you are bound. I would advise you to scatter abroad and never again organize with bishops, presidents, etc., lest you excite the jealousies of the people, and subject yourselves to the same calamities that have now come upon you.

"You have always been the aggressors; you have brought upon yourselves these difficulties by being disaffected, and not being subject to rule; and my advice is, that you become as other citizens, lest by a recurrence of these events you bring upon yourselves inevitable ruin."

Chapter 26

THE PRISONERS—SECOND INTERVIEW WITH GENERAL CLARK—INQUISITION—
SICKNESS OF ELDER RIGDON—COLONEL PRICE AND GUARDS—THEIR CONDUCT—
REBUKE BY JOSEPH SMITH—TRIAL—SIMILARITY BETWEEN KING HEROD AND GOV-
ERNOR BOGGS—JUDGE AUSTIN A. KING IN OPEN COURT THREATENS A WHOLESALE
EXTERMINATION OF THE "MORMONS"—OTHER PRISONERS OBTAINED BY
STRATAGEM—ADVICE OF GENERAL DONIPHAN, ATTORNEY FOR THE PRISONERS—
DECISION—DISPOSAL OF THE PRISONERS—FLIGHT OF THE CHURCH TO ILLINOIS—
CONDUCT OF THE OUTLAWS—MY FAMILY VISITS ME IN PRISON.

I must not forget to state that when we arrived in Richmond as prisoners there were some fifty others, mostly heads of families, who had been marched from Caldwell on foot (distance 30 miles), and were now penned up in a cold, open, unfinished court house, in which situation they remained for some weeks, while their families were suffering severe privations.

The next morning after our dialogue with General Clark he again entered our prison and informed us that he had concluded to deliver us over to the civil authorities for an examining trial. He was then asked why he did not do away with the unlawful decree of *banishment,* which was first ordered by General Lucas, in compliance with the Governor's order, and which compelled thousands of citizens to leave the State. Or upon what principle the military power aided the civil law against us, while at the same time it caused our families and friends to be murdered, plundered and driven, contrary to all law?

He replied that he approved of all the proceedings of General Lucas, and should not alter them. I make this statement because some writers have commended Clark for his heroic, merciful, and prudent conduct towards our society, and have endeavored to make it appear that Clark was not to be blamed for any of the measures of Lucas.

The Court of Inquiry now commenced, before Judge Austin A. King. This continued from the 11th to 28th of November, and our brethren, some fifty in number, were penned up in the cold, dreary court house. It was a very severe time of snow and winter weather, and we suffered much. During this time Elder Rigdon was taken very sick, from hardship and exposure, and finally lost his reason; but still he was kept in a miserable, noisy and cold room, and compelled to sleep on the floor with a chain and padlock round his ankle, and fastened to six others. Here he endured the constant noise and confusion of an unruly guard, the officer of which was Colonel Sterling Price, since Governor of the State.

These guards were composed generally of the most noisy, foulmouthed, vulgar, disgraceful rabble that ever defiled the earth. While he lay in this situation his son-in-law, George W. Robinson, the only male member of his family, was chained by his side. Thus Mrs. Rigdon and her daughters were left entirely destitute and unprotected. One of his daughters, Mrs. Robinson, a young and delicate female, with her little infant, came down to see her husband, and to comfort and take care of her father in his sickness. When she first entered the room, amid the clank of chains and the rattle of weapons, and cast her eyes on her sick and dejected parent and sorrow worn husband, she was speechless, and only gave vent to her feelings in a flood of tears. This faithful lady, with her little infant, continued by the side of her father till he recovered from his sickness, and till his fevered and disordered mind resumed its wonted powers.

In one of those tedious nights we had lain as if in sleep till the hour of midnight had passed, and our ears and hearts had been pained, while we had listened for hours to the obscene jests, the horrid oaths, the dreadful blasphemies and filthy language of our guards, Colonel Price at their head, as they recounted to each other their deeds of rapine, murder, robbery, etc., which they had committed among the "*Mormons*" while at Far West and vicinity. They even boasted of defiling by force wives, daughters and virgins, and of shooting or dashing out the brains of men, women and children.

I had listened till I became so disgusted, shocked, horrified, and so filled with the spirit of indignant justice that I could scarcely refrain from rising upon my feet and rebuking the guards; but had said nothing to Joseph, or any one else, although I lay next to him and knew he was awake. On a sudden he arose to his feet, and spoke in a voice of thunder, or as the roaring lion, uttering, as near as I can recollect, the following words:

"SILENCE, ye fiends of the infernal pit. In the name of Jesus Christ I rebuke you, and command you to be still; I will not live another minute and bear such language. Cease such talk, or you or I die THIS INSTANT!"

He ceased to speak. He stood erect in terrible majesty. Chained, and without a weapon; calm, unruffled and dignified as an angel, he looked upon the quailing guards, whose weapons were lowered or dropped to the ground; whose knees smote together, and who, shrinking into a corner, or crouching at his feet, begged his pardon, and remained quiet till a change of guards.

I have seen the ministers of justice, clothed in magisterial robes, and criminals arraigned before them, while life was suspended on a breath, in the Courts of England; I have witnessed a Congress in solemn session to give laws to nations; I have tried to conceive of kings, of royal courts, of thrones and crowns; and of emperors assembled to decide the fate of kingdoms; but dignity and majesty have I seen but *once*, as it stood in chains, at midnight, in a dungeon in an obscure village of Missouri.

In this mock Court of Inquiry the Judge could not be prevailed on to examine the conduct of murderers and robbers who had desolated our society, nor would he receive testimony except against us. By the dissenters and apostates who wished to save their own lives and secure their property at the expense of others, and by those who had murdered and plundered us from time to time, he obtained abundance of testimony, much of which was entirely false. Our Church organization was converted by such testimony into a temporal kingdom, which was to fill the whole earth and subdue all other kingdoms.

This Court of Inquisition inquired diligently into our belief of the seventh chapter of Daniel concerning the kingdom of God, which should subdue all other kingdoms and stand forever. And when told that we believed in that prophecy, the Court turned to the clerk and said: *"Write that down; it is a strong point for treason."* Our lawyer observed as follows: "Judge, you had better make the Bible treason." The Court made no reply.

These texts and many others were inquired into with all the eagerness and apparent alarm which characterized a Herod of old in relation to the babe of Bethlehem, the King of the Jews.

The ancient Herod, fearing a rival in the person of Jesus, issued his exterminating order for the murder of all the children of Bethlehem from two years old and under, with a view to hinder the fulfilment of a prophecy which he *himself* believed to be true.

The modern Herod (Boggs), fearing a rival kingdom in *"the people of the Saints of the Most High,"* issued his exterminating order for the murder of the young children of an entire people, and of their mothers as well as fathers, while this Court of Inquisition inquired as diligently into the one prophecy as his predecessor did into the other. These parallel actions go to show a strong belief in the prophecies on the part of the actors in both cases. Both believed, and feared, and trembled; both hardened their hearts against that which their better judgment told them was true. Both were instigated by the devil to cause innocent blood to be shed. And marvellously striking is the parallel in the final result of the actions of each.

The one slew many young children, but failed to destroy the infant King of the Jews.

The other slew many men, women and children, but failed to destroy the Kingdom of God.

The one found a timely refuge in Egypt.

The other in Illinois.

Jesus Christ fulfilled his destiny, and will reign over the Jews, and sit on the throne of his father, David, forever.

The Saints are growing into power amid the strongholds of the mountains of Deseret, and will surely take the Kingdom, and the greatness of the Kingdom, under the whole Heaven.

Who can withstand the Almighty, or frustrate his purposes? Herod died of a loathsome disease, and transmitted to posterity his fame as a tyrant and murderer. And Lilburn W. Boggs is dragging out a remnant of existence in California, with the mark of Cain upon his brow, and the fear of Cain within his heart, lest he that findeth him shall slay him. He is a living stink, and will go down to posterity with the credit of a wholesale murderer.

The Court also inquired diligently into our missionary operations. It was found, on investigation, that the Church had sent missionaries into England and other foreign countries. This, together with our belief in the Bible, was construed into treason against the State of Missouri, while every act of defence was set down as murder, etc. The Judge, in open court, while addressing a witness, proclaimed, that if the members of the Church remained on their lands to put in another crop they should be destroyed indiscriminately, and their bones be left to bleach on the plains without a burial. Yes, reader, the cultivation of lands held by patents issued by the United States land office, and signed by the

President of the Republic, was, by Judge Austin A. King, in open court, pronounced a capital offence, for which a whole community were pre-judged and sentenced to death. While those who should be the instru-ments to execute this sentence were called by the dignified name of citizens, and these *good* citizens afterwards elected that same Judge for Governor of the State.

The Judge inquired of the prisoners if they wished to introduce any witnesses for the defence. A list of names was supplied by the prisoners, when, who should be selected to go to Far West to obtain and bring them before the Court, but the identical bandit, Bogart, and his gang, who were defeated by us in the battle of Crooked River, after they had become famous for kidnapping, plundering and murdering!

Of course, every man in Caldwell would flee from such a gang if they could; but he succeeded in capturing a few of our friends, whose names were on the list, and bringing them before the Court, when, instead of being sworn, they were immediately ordered to prison to take their trial. Others were sent for, and, as far as found, shared the same fate. This manoeuvre occupied several days, during which the Court was still in session, and the fate of the prisoners suspended.

At length the Judge exclaimed to the prisoners: "If you have any witnesses bring them forward; the Court cannot delay forever—it has waited several days already." A member of the Church, named Allen, was just then seen to pass the window. The prisoners requested that he might be introduced and sworn. He was immediately called in and sworn. He began to give his testimony, which went to establish the in-nocence of the prisoners, and to show the murders, robberies, etc., com-mitted by their accusers. But he was suddenly interrupted and cut short by cries of *"Put him out;" "Kick him out;" "G—d d—n him, shoot him;" "Kill him, d—n him, kill him;" "He's a d—d Mormon."*

The Court then ordered the guard to put him out, which was done amid the yells, threats, insults and violence of the mob who thronged in and around the court house. He barely escaped with his life. Mr. Doniphan, attorney for the defence, and since famed as a general in the Mexican war, finally advised the prisoners to offer no defence; "for," said he, "though a legion of angels from the opening heavens should declare your innocence, the Court and populace have decreed your destruc-tion." Our attorney offered no defence, and thus the matter of our trials was finally submitted.

By the decision of this mock Court some twenty or thirty of the ac-cused were dismissed, among whom was Amasa Luman Gibbs, Darwin

Chase, Norman Shearer and myself and themselves and bail both forced to leave the State, thus forfeiting the bail bonds, while Joseph Smith, Hyrum Smith, Sidney Rigdon, Lyman Wight, Caleb Baldwin and Alexander McRay (all heads of families) were committed to the jail of Clay County on the charge of treason; and Morris Phelps, Luman Gibbs, Darwin Chase, Norman Shearer and myself were committed to the jail of Richmond, Ray County, for the alleged crime of murder, said to be committed in the act of dispersing the bandit, Bogart, and his gang.

This done, the civil and military authorities dispersed, and the troubled waters became a little more tranquil.

As our people were compelled by the memorable *"Treaty of Far West"* to leave the State by the following spring, they now commenced moving by hundreds and by thousands to the State of Illinois, where they were received in the most humane and friendly manner by the authorities, and by the citizens in general. In the meantime bands of murderers, thieves and robbers were roaming unrestrained among the unarmed and defenceless citizens, committing all manner of plunder, and driving off cattle, sheep and horses, abusing and insulting women.

My wife and children soon came to me in prison, and spent a portion of the winter in the cold, dark dungeon, where myself and fellow prisoners were frequently insulted and abused by our dastardly guards, who often threatened to shoot us on the spot, and who made murder, robbery and whoredoms with negro slaves their daily boast.

Chapter 27

The State legislature were soon in session; and from this body, so high in responsibility, we had hoped for some redress and protection. Memorials and petitions from those aggrieved, and others, were addressed to the legislature, praying for an investigation of the whole matter, and for redress and protection against the criminal proceedings of the Governor and his troops, in seizing our property, murdering our citizens, kidnapping our leaders and others, and driving us from the State.

Yes, in fact, American citizens petitioned a republican legislature for the privilege of occupying and cultivating their own lands, purchased of the Government of the United States, and for the privilege of dwelling in the houses built by their own hands, on their own real estate. How strange! How incredible, in the nineteenth century! Who can realize it? And yet it must stand on record, and go down to posterity as a fact, a stubborn, undeniable public fact.

The following extract of a petition addressed to the legislature of Missouri, dated Dec. 10, 1838, Far West, Caldwell County, Missouri, and signed by a committee appointed by the citizens, will show for itself the foregoing to be true. It was signed by

EDWARD PARTRIDGE,	JOHN M. BURK,
HEBER C. KIMBALL,	BRIGHAM YOUNG,
JOHN TAYLOR,	ISAAC MORLEY,
THEODORE TURLEY,	GEORGE W. HARRIS,
	JOHN MURDOCK.

It read as follows:

"The last order of Governor Boggs, to drive us from the State or exterminate us, is a thing so novel, unlawful, tyrannical and oppressive that we have been induced to draw up this memorial and present this statement of our case to your honorable body, praying that a law may be passed rescinding the order of the Governor to drive us from the State; and also, giving us the sanction of the Legislature to inherit our lands in peace. * * * In laying our case before your honorable body we say that we are willing, and ever have been, to conform to the Constitution and laws of the United States and of this State.

"We ask, in common with others, the protection of the laws. We ask for the privilege guaranteed to all free citizens of the United States and of this State to be extended to us, that we may be permitted to settle and live where we please, and worship God according to the dictates of our conscience without molestation. And while we ask for ourselves this privilege, we are willing all others should enjoy the same."

If the necessity for such a petition seems strange, how much more strange appears the fact, that sduch petition was denied by the Legislature of a State? And to crown the whole, all investigation was utterly refused; nay more, the Legislature itself became accessory to these crimes, by appropriating two hundred thousand dollars to pay the murderers and robbers for committing these crimes.

This last act of outrage sealed with eternal infamy the character of the State of Missouri. She fell to rise no more. She should be looked upon by her sister States as a star fallen from the American constellation; a ruined and degraded outcast from the family of States. The whole civilized world will detest and abhor her as the most infamous of tyrants. Nay, tyranny itself will blush to hear her deeds mentioned in the annals of history.

The most cruel persecutors of the Christians or Reformers in pagan or papal Rome will start with astonishment from their long slumbers, and, with a mixture of envy and admiration, yield to her the palm. As a State she has acted the part of a pirate, a wholesale murderer and robber. Every department—civil, military, executive and legislative—tramples all law under foot, and plunges into crime and blood.

Many of the State journals have tried to hide the iniquity of the State by throwing a covering of lies over her atrocious deeds. But, can they hide the Governor's cruel order for extermination or banishment? Can they conceal the fact of the disgraceful treaty of the generals with a portion of their own officers and men at Far West? Can they conceal the fact that ten or twelve thousand citizens, of all ages and of both sexes, have been banished from the State without trial or condemnation? Can they conceal the fact that the State Legislature appropriated two hundred thousand dollars to pay the criminals for committing these crimes; and this while the petitions of the sufferers lay on the table before them, praying for investigation, redress and protection? Can they conceal the fact that citizens have been kidnapped and imprisoned for many months, while their families, friends and witnesses have been driven from the State?

Can they conceal the blood of the murdered husbands and fathers, or stifle the cries of widows and orphans?

Nay, the rocks and the mountains may cover them in unknown depths; the awful abyss of the fathomless deep may swallow them up, and still their horrid deeds will stand forth in the broad light of day, for the wondering gaze of angels and of men—they cannot be hid.

Chapter 28

This chapter is an extract from the statement of Hyrum Smith, one of the prisoners, given under oath, before the Municipal Court of the city of Nauvoo, Illinois, in the summer of 1843.

"The next morning after the close of this mock court (held at Richmond, Judge Austin A. King presiding), a large wagon drove up to the door of our prison house, and a blacksmith entered with some chains and handcuffs. He said his orders from the Judge were to handcuff and chain us together. He informed us that the Judge made out a *mittimus* and sentenced us to jail for treason; he also said that the Judge had stated his intention to keep us in jail until all the Mormons were driven from the State; and that the Judge had further stated that if he let us out before the Mormons had left the State there would be another d—d fuss kicked up. I also heard the Judge say myself, while he was sitting in his pretended court, 'that there was no law for us, or any of the Mormons in the State of Missouri; that he had sworn to see then exterminated, and to see the Governor's order executed to the very letter, and he would do so.'

"However, the blacksmith proceeded to put the irons upon us. We were then ordered into the wagon and drove off for Clay County. As we journeyed along the road, we were exhibited to the inhabitants. This public exhibition lasted until we arrived at the town of Liberty, Clay County. There we were thrust into prison again, and locked up; and were held there in confinement for the space of six months.

"Our place of lodging was the square side of hewed white oak logs, and our food was anything but good and decent. Poison was administered to us three or four times. The effect it had upon our systems was, that it vomited us almost to death, and then we would lay some two or three days in a torpid, stupid state, not even caring or wishing for life.

"The poison would inevitably have proved fatal had not the power of Jehovah interposed in our behalf, to save us from their wicked purpose. We were also subjected to the necessity of *eating human flesh!* for the space of five days, or go without food, except a little coffee or a little corn bread. I chose the latter alternative. None of us partook of the flesh except Lyman Wight. We also heard the guard which was placed over us, making sport of us, saying that 'they had fed us upon *Mormon beef.*'

"I have described the appearance of this flesh to several experienced physicians, and they have decided that is was human flesh. We learned afterwards through one of the guards that it was supposed that such acts of cannibalism as feeding us with human flesh would be considered a popular deed. But those concerned, on learning that it would not take, tried to keep it secret; but the fact was noised abroad before they took that precaution.

"While we were incarcerated in prison we petitioned the Supreme Court of the State of Missouri for *habeas corpus* twice, but we were as often refused by Judge Reynolds, who is now Governor of that State.

"We also petitioned one of the county judges for a writ of *habeas corpus.* This was granted in about three weeks afterwards; but we were not permitted to have any trial. We were only taken out of jail, and kept out for a few hours, and then remanded back again. In the course of three or four days after that time Judge Turnham came into the jail in the evening, and said he had permitted Mr. Rigdon to get bail; but said he had to do it in the night, and had also to get away in the night, and unknown to any of the citizens, or they would kill him; for they had sworn to kill him if they could find him. And, as to the rest of us, he dare not let us go for fear of his own life, as well as ours.

"He said it was hard to be confined under such circumstances, for he knew we were innocent men, and the people also knew it; and that it was only persecution and treachery, and the scenes of Jackson County acted over again, for fear we would become too numerous in that upper country. He said, 'the plan was concocted from the Governor down to the lowest judge, and that that wicked Baptist priest, Riley, was riding into town every day to watch the people—stirring up the minds of the people against us all he could—exciting them, and stirring up their religious prejudices against us, for fear they would let us go.'

"Mr. Rigdon, however, got bail and made his escape to Illinois. The jailor, Samuel Tillory, told us also 'that the whole plan was concocted from the Governor down to the lowest judge in that upper country early the previous spring; and that the plan was more fully matured at the time

General Atchison went down to Jefferson County with Generals Wilson, Lucas and Gillum.' This was sometime in September, when the mob was collected at De Witt. He also said that the Governor was now ashamed enough of the whole transaction, and would be glad to set us at liberty if he dared to do it; 'but,' said he, 'you need not be concerned, for the Governor has laid a plan for your release.' He also said that Mr. Birch, the State's Attorney, was appointed to be Circuit Judge in the district including Davies County, and that he (Birch) was instructed to fix the papers so that we would be clear from any encumbrance in a very short time.

"Sometime in April we were taken to Davies County, as they said, to have a trial; but when we arrived at that place, instead of finding a court or a jury, we found another Inquisition; and Birch, who was the District Attorney, the same man who was one of the *court martial* when we were sentenced to death, was now the Circuit Judge of that pretended court, and the Grand Jury that were impanelled were at the massacre at Haun's Mill, and lively actors in that awful, solemn, disgraceful, cold-blooded murder. All the pretence they made of excuse was 'they had done it because the Governor ordered it done.'

"The same jury sat as a jury in the day time, and were over us as a guard by night. They tantalized and boasted over us of their great achievements at Haun's Mill and at other places; telling us how many houses they had burned, and how many sheep, cattle and hogs they had driven off belonging to 'Mormons,' and how many rapes they had committed, etc.

"These fiends of the lower region boasted of these acts of barbarity and tantalized our feelings with them for ten days. We had heard of these acts of cruelty previous to this time; but we were slow to believe that such acts had been perpetrated.

"This Grand Jury constantly celebrated their achievements with grog and glass in hand, like the Indian warriors at the war dances, singing and telling each of their exploits in murdering the 'Mormons,' in plundering their houses, and carrying off their property. All this was done in . . . presence of *Judge* Birch, who had previously said in our hearing: *'That there was no law for the Mormons in the State of Missouri.'*

"After all these ten days of drunkenness we were informed that we were indicted for 'treason! murder! arson! larceny! theft and stealing!!' We asked for a change of venue from that county to Marion County; but they would not grant it. But they gave us a change of venue from Davies to Boone County, and a *mittimus* was made out by the pretended Judge

Birch, without date, name or place. They fitted us out with a two horse wagon and horses, and four men, besides the Sheriff, to be our guard— there were five of us.

"We started from Gallatin, the sun about two hours high, p.m., and went as far as Diahman that evening, and stayed till morning. There we bought two horses of the guard, and paid for one of them in clothing which we had with us, and for the other we gave our note.

"We went down that day as far as Judge Morin's—a distance of some four or five miles. There we stayed until morning, when we started on our journey to Boone County, and travelled about twenty miles. There was bought a jug of whiskey, of which the guard drank freely. While there the Sheriff showed us the *mittimus*, before referred to, without date or signature, and said that Judge Birch told him never to carry us to Boone County, and to show the *mittimus;* and, said he, I shall take a good drink of grog and go to bed, and you may do as you have a mind to. Three others of the guard drank pretty freely of whiskey sweetened with honey; they also went to bed and were soon asleep. The other guard went with us and helped us to saddle our horses. Two of us mounted the horses and the other three started on foot, and thus we took our change of venue for the State of Illinois.

"In the course of nine or ten days we arrived safely in Quincy, Adams County, where we found our families in a state of poverty, although in good health—they having been driven out of the State previously by the murderous militia under the exterminating order of the Executive of Missouri. And now the people of that State, or a portion of them, would be glad to make the people of this State believe that my brother Joseph has committed treason, and this they seek to do for the purpose of keeping up their murderous and hellish persecution. They seem to be unrelenting in thirsting for the blood of innocence, for I do know most positively that my brother Joseph has committed no treason, nor violated one solitary item of law or rule in the State of Missouri.

"But I do know that the Mormon people, *en masse,* were driven out of that State, after being robbed of all they had, and that he barely escaped with his life. And all this in consequence of the exterminating order of Governor Boggs; the same being confirmed by the Legislature of that State.

"And I do know, so does this Court and every rational man who is acquainted with the circumstances, and every man who shall hereafter become acquainted with the particulars thereof, will know that Governor Boggs and Generals Clark, Lucas, Wilson and Gillum, also Austin

A. King, have committed treasonable acts against the citizens of Missouri, and did violate the Constitution of the United States, and also the Constitution and laws of the State of Missouri, and did exile and expel, at the point of the bayonet, some twelve or fourteen thousand inhabitants of the State, and did murder some three or four hundred of men, women and children in cold blood in the most horrid and cruel manner possible. And the whole of it was caused by religious bigotry and persecution, and because the *Mormons* dared to worship Almighty God according to the dictates of their own conscience and agreeably to His Divine Will, as revealed in the Scriptures of eternal truth; and had turned away from following the vain traditions of their fathers and would not worship according to the dogmas and commandments of those men who preach for hire and divine for money, and teach for doctrines the commandments of men, expecting that the Constitution of the United States would have protected them therein.

"But, notwithstanding the *Mormon* people, had purchased upwards of two hundred thousand dollars' worth of land, most of which was entered and paid for at the Land Office of the United States, in the State of Missouri, and although the President of the United States has been made acquainted with these facts and the particulars of our persecutions and oppressions by petitions to him and to Congress, yet they have not even attempted to restore the Saints to their rights, or given any assurance that we may hereafter expect redress from them.

"And I do also know, most positively and assuredly, that my brother, Joseph Smith, Junior, has not been in the State of Missouri since the spring of the year 1839. And further this deponent saith not.

"HYRUM SMITH."

Chapter 29

On the 17th of March, 1839, my wife took leave of the prison with her little children, and, with a broken heart returned to Far West, in order to get passage with some of the brethren for Illinois. She tarried in Far West a month. All the Society had gone from the State, but a few of the poor and widows, and the Committee who tarried behind to assist them in removing. About the middle of April a gang of robbers entered Far West armed, and ordered my wife, and the Committee, and the others to be gone by such a time, or they would murder them. This gang destroyed much furniture and other property.

Thus my wife was driven away according to the Governor's previous order, while I was still detained in a filthy dungeon. My family were conveyed to Quincy, Illinois, distance two hundred and eighty miles, by David W. Rogers, of New York, who is a descendant of the celebrated martyr, John Rogers, of Smithfield celebrity, England.

On the 20th of April, 1839, the last of the Society departed from Far West. Thus had a whole people, variously estimated at from ten to fifteen thousand souls, been driven from houses and lands and reduced to poverty, and had removed to another State during one short winter and part of a spring. The sacrifice of property was immense — including houses, lands, cattle, sheep, hogs, agricultural implements, furniture, household utensils, clothing, money and grain. One of the most flourishing counties in the State and part of several others were reduced to desolation, or inhabited only by marauding gangs of murderers and robbers.

On the 24th of April our cases came before the Grand Jury of the county of Ray; which Grand Jury, the reader is aware, would be naturally composed of our persecutors and their accessories; and at whose head was the same Judge King who had presided in the former mock trial and Inquisition which committed us to prison.

Darwin Chase and Norman Shearer were dismissed, after being imprisoned near six months. This release happened just as Mr. Shearer came to visit his son for the last time before he left the country. He came into the prison and took an affectionate leave of his son, who wept as if his heart would break; but while he yet lingered in town his son was called before the Court, and, together with Mr. Chase, was told that he might go at liberty. The father and son then embraced each other, almost overcome with joy, and departed.

At the same time my brother, Orson Pratt, whom I had not seen for a year, came from Illinois to see me, but was only permitted to visit me for a few moments, and then was ordered to depart.

Mrs. Phelps, who had waited in prison for some days, in hopes that the Court would release her husband, now parted with him, overwhelmed with sorrow and tears, and, with her infant, went away to remove to Illinois.

Thus our families wander in a strange land, without our protection, being robbed of house and home. O Lord! how long?

Our number in prison were now reduced to four—one having been added about the middle of April. His name was King Follett; he was dragged from his distressed family just as they were leaving the State, being charged with robbery, which meant that he was one of a posse who took a keg of powder from a gang of ruffians who were out against the *Mormons.* Thus, of all the *Mormon* prisoners first kidnapped, only two remained in the State—Mr. Gibbs having denied the faith to try and regain his liberty—these were Morris Phelps and myself.

All who were liberated on bail were forced to leave the State, together with those who bailed them, thus forfeiting many thousands of dollars to the coffers of the State.

Is it possible! Have I been recording the history of realities as the scenes transpired in the broad light of the nineteenth century—in the boasted land of liberty—and in the most renowned republic now existing on the globe? Alas! it is too true; would to God it were a dream—a novel, a romance that had no existence save in the wild regions of fancy. But the prison door yet grating on its hinges,—the absence of my wife and little ones,—the gloom of the dungeon where I yet repose,—these and ten thousand other things cause me to think that my almost incredible narrative is no fiction, but an awful reality—a fact more truly distressing than my feeble tongue or pen can find words to set forth.

How often in my sleeping visions I see my beloved wife, or my play-ful children surrounded with the pleasures of home in my sweet little cottage, or walk with them in some pleasant grove or flowery field, as in years past. How often I see myself surrounded with listening thousands, as in bygone years, and join with them in the sacred song and prayer, or address them with the sound of the everlasting gospel. But, alas! I soon awake, and, to my inexpressible grief and sorrow, find myself still in my lonely dungeon.

> O Liberty!
> O sound once delightful to every American ear!
> O sacred privilege of American citizenship!
> Once sacred; now trampled under foot.

When shall I and my injured family and friends again enjoy thy sweets? When shall we repose beneath thy bower, or bask in thy bound-less ocean of felicity? When shall we sit again under our vine and under our fruit trees, and worship our God, with none to molest or make us afraid?

> Awake, O Americans!
> Arise, O sons and daughters of freedom!

Restore a persecuted and injured people to their rights, as citizens of a free republic. Down with tyranny and oppression, and rescue your liberties from the brink of ruin. Redeem your much injured country from the awful stain upon its honor; and let the cries of helpless orphans and the tears of the sorrowing widow cease to ascend up before the Lord for vengeance upon the heads of those who have slain, plundered, impris-oned and driven the Saints. And let the news go forth to the wondering nations that Columbia still is free.

O tell it not in Britain; nor let the sound be heard in Europe that Liberty is fallen; that the free institutions of our once happy country are now destroyed, lest the sons and daughters of Britannia rejoice and laugh us to scorn; lest the children of monarchy triumph and have us in deri-sion.

> O freedom must thy spirit now withdraw
> From earth, returning to its native heaven,
> There to dwell, till, armed with sevenfold vengeance,
> It comes again to earth with King Messiah,
> And all His marshaled hosts, in glory bright,
> To tread the winepress of Almighty God,

And none escape? Ye powers of Heaven, forbid;
Let freedom linger still on shores of time,
And in the breasts of thine afflicted saints,
Let it find a peaceful retirement—
A place of rest, till o'er the troubled earth,
Mercy, justice and eternal truth,
While journeying hand in hand to exalt the humble
And debase the proud; shall find some nation,
Poor, oppressed, afflicted and despised;
Cast out and trodden under foot of tyrants
Proud; the hiss, the byeword, and the scorn of knaves—
And there let freedom's spirit wide prevail,
And grow and flourish 'mid the humble poor—
Exalted and enriched by virtue,
Knowledge, temperance and love; till o'er the earth
Messiah comes to reign; the proud consumed,
No more oppress the poor,
Let freedom's eagle then (forthcoming, like
The dove from Noah's ark) on lofty pinions soar,
And spread its wide domain from end to end,
O'er all the vast expanse of this wide earth;
While freedom's temple rears its lofty spires
Amid the skies, and on its bosom rests
A cloud by day and flaming fire by night!

But stay my spirit, though thou fain would'st soar
On high, 'mid scenes of glory, peace and joy;
From bondage free, and bid thy jail farewell.
Stop!—wait awhile!—let patience have her perfect work.
Return again to suffering scenes, through which
The way to glory lies, and speak of things
Around thee—Thou'rt in prison still!
But spring has now returned; the wintry blasts
Have ceased to howl through prison crevices—
The soft and gentle breezes of the South
Are whistling gaily past, and incense sweet,
On zephyr's wing, with fragrance fills the air,
Wafted from blooming flowerets of the spring;
While round my lonely dungeon oft is heard
Melodious strains, as if the birds of spring,
In anthems sweet, conspired to pity and
Console the drooping spirits there confined.

All things around me show that days, and weeks,
And months have fled, although to me not mark'd
By Sabbaths, and but faintly marked by dim

And sombre rays of light, alternate 'mid
The gloom of overhanging night, which still
Pervades my drear and solitary cell.
Where now those helpless ones I left to mourn?
Have they perished? No. What then! Has some
Elijah call'd and found them in the last
Extreme, and multiplied their meal and oil?
Yes, verily; the Lord has filled the hearts
Of his poor saints with everlasting love,
Which, in proportion to their poverty,
Increased with each increasing want, till all
Reduced unto the widow's mite, and then,
Like her, their living they put in; and thus
O'erflowed the treasury of the Lord with more
Abundant stores than all the wealth of kings.
And thus supported, fed and clothed, and moved
From scenes of sorrow to a land of peace,
They live! and living still, they do rejoice
In tribulation deep—
Well knowing their redemption draweth nigh.

Chapter 30

"***H**on. Sir*—Having been confined in prison near seven months, and the time having arrived when a change of venue can be taken in order for the further prosecution of our trials, and the time when I can speak my mind freely, without endangering the lives or liberties of any but myself, I now take the liberty of seriously objecting to a trial anywhere within the bounds of this State, and of earnestly praying to your honor and to all the authorities, civil and military, that my case may come within the law of BANISHMENT! enacted by Governor Boggs, and so vigorously enforced upon from ten to fifteen thousand of our Society, including my wife and little ones, together with all my witnesses and friends.

"My reasons are obvious, and founded upon notorious facts which are known to you, sir, and to the people in general of this republic, and, therefore, need no proof; some of them are as follows:

"First: I have never received any protection by law, either of my person, property or family, while residing in this State, to which I first emigrated in 1831.

"Secondly: I was driven by force of arms from Jackson County, wounded and bleeding, in 1833, while my house was burned, my crops and provisions robbed from me or destroyed, and my land and improvements kept from me until now, while my family was driven out, without shelter, at the approach of winter.

"Thirdly: These crimes still go unpunished, notwithstanding I made oath before the Hon. Judge Ryland, then acting District Judge, to the foregoing outrages, and afterwards applied in person to his excellency, Daniel Dunklin, then Governor of the State, for redress and protection of myself and friends, and the restoration of more than a thousand of our fellow citizens to our homes.

"Fourthly: My wife and children have now been driven from our house and improvements in Caldwell County, and banished the State on pain of death, together with about ten thousand of our Society, including all my friends and witnesses, and this by the express orders of his excellency, Lilburn W. Boggs, Governor of the State of Missouri, and by the vigorous execution of this order by Generals Lucas and Clark, and followed up by murders, rapes, plunderings, thefts and robberies of the most inhuman character, by a lawless mob who had, from time to time, for more than five years past, trampled upon all law and authority, and upon all the rights of man.

"Fifthly: All these inhuman outrages and crimes go unpunished, and are unnoticed by you, sir, and by all the authorities of the State. Nay, rather, you are one of the very actors. You, yourself, threatened in open court the extermination of the 'Mormons' if they should ever be again guilty of cultivating their lands.

"Sixthly: The Legislature of the State has approved of and sanctioned this act of banishment, with all the crimes connected therewith, by voting an appropriation of two hundred thousand dollars for the payment of troops engaged in this unlawful, unconstitutional and treasonable enterprise.

"In monarchial governments the banishment of criminals after their legal trial and condemnation has been frequently resorted to, but the banishment of innocent women and children from house, and home, and country, to wander in a strange land, unprotected and unprovided for, while their husbands and fathers are retained in dungeons, is an act unknown in the annals of history, except in this single instance, in the nineteenth century, when it has actually transpired in a republican State, where the Constitution guarantees to every man the protection of life, liberty and property, and the right of trial by jury.

"These, sir, are outrages which would put monarchy to the blush, and from which the most despotic tyrants of the dark ages would turn away with shame and disgust. In these proceedings, sir, Missouri has enrolled her name on the list of immortal fame. Her transactions will be handed down the stream of time to the latest posterity, who will read with wonder and astonishment the history of proceedings which are without a parallel in the annals of time.

"Why should the authorities of the State strain at a gnat and swallow a camel?

"Why be so strictly legal as to compel me to pass through all the forms of a slow and pretended legal prosecution (previous to my enlargement), out of a pretence of respect to the laws of the State, which have been openly trampled upon and disregarded towards us from first to last?

"Why not include me in the general wholesale banishment of our Society, that I may support my family, which are now reduced to beggary in a land of strangers?

"But, sir, when the authorities of the State shall redress all these wrongs, shall punish the guilty according to law, and shall restore my family and friends to all our rights, and shall pay all the damages which we, as a people, have sustained, then I shall believe them sincere in their professed zeal for law and justice; *then* shall I be convinced that I can have a fair trial in the State.

"But until *then* I hereby solemnly protest against being tried in this State, with the full and conscientious conviction that I have no just grounds to expect a fair and impartial trial.

"I, therefore, most sincerely pray your honor, and all the authorities in the State, to either banish me without further persecution, or I freely consent to a trial before the Judiciary of the United States.

"With sentiments of consideration and due respect, I have the honor to subscribe myself,

"Your prisoner,
"P. P. PRATT."

Chapter 31

The four following chapters are extracted from the *Millennial Star,* published in Liverpool, England, Numbers 9, 10 and 11, Vol. VIII. I give them in full, with some little revision, although they contain a repetition of some of the things recorded in the foregoing chapters:

At the end of this extraordinary mock trial or inquisition, which lasted over two weeks, I was unchained from Joseph and Hyrum Smith, and the others, and being separated from them, was conducted to a gloomy, dark, cold and filthy dungeon in Richmond, Ray County, where I was doomed to spend the winter and spring, and await a further trial; while they shared a similar fate in a place called Liberty, in Clay County.

When I first entered the dungeon there were some twenty men, mostly heads of families, who had been torn from their families in those awful times, and thrust into prison. It was not only crowded to suffocation, without a chair, stool, bench, bed, furniture or window light, but just then completely filled with smoke by a fire which was lighted in a stove without a pipe, or any conductor for the smoke to pass out, except at the crevices between the timbers, where the winter storm was passing in. When my guard conducted me to the door of this miserable cell it grated on its huge hinges and opened like the pit yawning to receive me; a volume of thick smoke issued forth and seemed to forbid my entrance; but, urged in my rear by bayonets and loaded pistols in the hands of savage beings, I endeavored to enter, but was forced to retreat again outside of the door to breathe for a moment the free air. At this instant several pistols were cocked and presented at my head and breast, with terrible threats and oaths of instant death if I did not go in again. I told them to fire as soon as they pleased, for I must breathe a moment or die in the attempt. After standing a few moments, I again entered the prison, and threw myself down, my face to the floor, to avoid the smoke. Here I remained for some time, partly in a state of insensibility; my heart sickened within me, and a deathlike feeling came over me, from which I did not wholly recover for several days.

I arose, however, as soon as I was able, and began to speak to and recognize my fellow prisoners—most of whom were my neighbors and acquaintances. The door was now locked, bolted and barred, and several guards placed before it. The fire died away, and the smoke gradually cleared away from the dungeon; but the floor formed a hard and cold winter lodging.

In a few days all those in our prison, except five, were released on bail, and themselves and bail banished from the State, with the rest of the Society; thus compelling them to forfeit their bail bonds, which amounted in all to many thousand dollars. The five who remained were Morris Phelps, Darwin Chase, Norman Shearer, Luman Gibbs and myself. Two of these were finally dismissed—being boys scarcely out of their teens. But another was soon added by the name of King Follett.

This made our final number four. One of this number, viz.: Luman Gibbs, denied the faith and turned a traitor to the others; becoming their most inveterate enemy. This was in order to save his life and gain his liberty. However, he was still kept in prison as a spy upon us, lest it should be said that it was wholly a religious persecution; but he was treated very well, and went out to dine with the Sheriff or others, or to spend a day with his wife whenever it pleased him to do so. Our food was of the most unwholesome kind, and scant at that; consisting of bones and remnants of meat, coarse corn bread, and sometimes a little coffee. We generally partook of our meals in a standing position, using our fingers instead of knives, forks or plates. A tin cup served us for our coffee. We were guarded very strictly, both by night and day, by two or three men with loaded pistols.

These consisted of the most unprincipled, profligate villains that could be found anywhere. They would swear, drink, gamble, and sing the most obscene and disgusting songs. They would boast of shooting the *Mormons;* robbing and plundering them; committing rapes, etc. They would also insult every female slave or black woman who might happen to come within hearing, and then boast of their criminal connections with them. The blasphemy; the noisy grumbling; the blackguard chit chat; doleful lullaby and vulgar songs of these guards grating daily upon our ears, seemed like the howls and wailings of the damned, or like wandering spirits and demons hovering around to torment us. What greatly added to our affliction, as if to complete our hell, the old apostate, Gibbs, became very quarrelsome and noisy—not only to us, but with his wife also, who sometimes came into the prison to spend a few days with him. He was a hard faced, ill formed man, of about fifty years of age; full of jealousy, extremely selfish, very weak minded, and withal, a little love cracked; and, I may say, that he seemed not to possess one redeeming quality.

His wife was about the same age, and withal, a coarse, tall, masculine looking woman, and one of whom he had no reason to complain or be jealous. True, she did not love him—for no female could possibly do that; but then no one else would love her, nor was she disposed to court their affections. However, he was jealous of her, and, therefore, abused her; and this kept a constant and noisy strife and wrangling between them whenever she was present.

Whole nights were spent in this way, during which no one in or about the prison slept. After a quarrel of some two or three days and nights between them, he would attempt to regain her love, and a conversation like the following would ensue. Luman, drawing down his face and drawling his words with a loud and doleful tone, commenced as follows:

"Now, Phila, won't you love me? Come; here's my watch, and here's all the money I've got!" Then turning to us, he would exclaim: "Boys, I'll tell you all about it; the fact is, she never did love me; she only married me out of pity—we being members of the Baptist church together in Vermont." Then again addressing his wife: "Come now, Phila; won't you love me? O, that I had been born a rich man! I would give you a dollar a minute to love me."

Phila would then laugh and call him "a silly old fool." Whereupon he would turn away in a rage, and exclaim: "Go along away, you——, you! Nobody wants your love, no how!"

On one occasion they had quarrelled and kept us awake all night, and just at break of day we heard a noise like a scuffle and a slamming against the wall; next followed a woman's voice, half in laugh and half in exultation: "Te-he-he-he, Luman, what's the matter? What's the matter, Luman?" Then a pause, and afterwards a man's voice in a grum, sorry, and rather a whining tone was heard at a distance from the bed, exclaiming: "Now, I swan, Phila, that's tu bad."

The truth of the matter was this: She had braced her back against the wall, and with both her feet placed against his body, had kicked him out of bed, and landed him upon the opposite side of the room.

Such scenes as these and all the folly of the guards served to enhance the misery of imprisonment, and to render our sufferings complete. We tried to keep them quiet, but tried in vain. Neither threats nor persuasion, coaxing nor reasoning had any influence over them. This miserable specimen of humanity was a peculiar favorite of the Sheriff and guards, and other citizens of Richmond. He was considered by them as the only honest, good, deserving man in the prison. They often expressed pity for him, and wished he was at liberty. He, in turn, watched our movements closely, and was ready to betray us on the least show, on our part, of any meditated plan of escape.

Under these painful circumstances we spent a long and dreary winter. Our whole community, who were not in prison, were forced out of the State, with the loss of homes, property, and many lives. They fled by thousands to Illinois.

My wife visited me several times in prison; but at length the period expired that the State authorities had stipulated for every Mormon to be gone, and my wife and children, and a few others who remained behind, were obliged to fly or be exterminated, as bands of armed men were roaming amid the deserted settlement, robbing, plundering, destroying property, and threatening all who remained.

My fellow prisoners, who had been separated from me and sent to the prison at Liberty, had also effected their escape, and had fled to Illinois to join their families. In short, all were gone, except King Follett, Morris Phelps and myself, and the old apostate, who was left to torment us.

Alone in a State which was wholly governed by an open banditti of murderers and robbers, we seemed abandoned to our fate, and doomed to suffer that full weight of vengeance and fury which seemed in reserve for an entire people; but that people were now beyond their reach; all the fury of the storm, therefore, seemed now to beat upon our heads. We were daily threatened with assassination, without the form of a trial; and were repeatedly told that we never should escape alive from the State. Our guards were doubly vigilant, while the Sheriff took every possible precaution. Luman, the apostate, was also in constant watchfulness, and busy in forming plans for escape; then accusing us and pretending to reveal wonderful things to our keepers in regard to our plans; which, in fact, only existed in his lying brain. This increased the severity of our confinement, and seemed to preclude the possibility of escape.

To be tried without friends or witnesses, or even with them, by a set of "Gadianton robbers" and murderers, who could drive out and murder women and children, was but to be condemned and executed; to tarry there and drag out a miserable life, while our wives and children wandered abroad in a land of strangers, without the protection of husbands and fathers, was worse than to die ten thousand deaths.

Under these circumstances, and half way between hope and despair, I spent several days in fasting and prayer, during which one deep and all absorbing inquiry, one only thought, seemed to hold possession of my mind. It seemed to me that if there was a God in Heaven who ever spake to man on earth I would know from him the truth of this one question. It was not how long shall I suffer; it was not when or by what means I should be delivered; but it was simply this: Shall I ever, at any time, however distant it may be, or whatever I may suffer first; shall I ever be free again in this life, and enjoy the society of my dear wife and children, and walk abroad at liberty, dwell in society and preach the gospel, as I have done in bygone years?

Let me be sure of this and I care not what I suffer. To circumnavigate the globe, to traverse the deserts of Arabia, to wander amid the wild scenes of the Rocky Mountains to accomplish so desirable an object, would seem like a mere trifle if I could only be sure at last. After some days of prayer and fasting, and seeking the Lord on the subject, I retired to my bed in my lonely chamber at an early hour, and while the other prisoners and the guard were chatting and beguiling the lonesome hours in the upper apartment of the prison, I lay in silence, seeking and expecting an answer to my prayer, when suddenly I seemed carried away in the spirit, and no longer sensible to outward objects with which I was surrounded. A heaven of peace and calmness pervaded my bosom; a personage from the world of spirits stood before me with a smile of compassion in every look, and pity mingled with the tenderest love and sympathy in every expression of the countenance. A soft hand seemed placed within my own, and a glowing cheek was laid in tenderness and warmth upon mine. A well known voice saluted me, which I readily recognized as that of the wife of my youth, who had for near two years been sweetly sleeping where the wicked cease from troubling and the weary are at rest. I was made to realize that she was sent to commune with me, and answer my question.

Knowing this, I said to her in a most earnest and inquiring tone: Shall I ever be at liberty again in this life and enjoy the society of my family and the Saints, and preach the gospel as I have done? She answered definitely and unhesitatingly: "YES!" I then recollected that I had agreed to be satisfied with the knowledge of *that one* fact, but now I wanted more.

Said I: Can you tell me how, or by what means, or when I shall escape? She replied: "THAT THING IS NOT MADE KNOWN TO ME YET." I instantly felt that I had gone beyond my agreement and my faith in asking this last question, and that I must be contented at present with the answer to the first.

Her gentle spirit then saluted me and withdrew. I came to myself. The doleful noise of the guards, and the wrangling and angry words of the old apostate again grated on my ears, but Heaven and hope were in my soul.

Next morning I related the whole circumstance of my vision to my two fellow prisoners, who rejoiced exceedingly. This may seem to some like an idle dream, or a romance of the imagination; but to me it was, and always will be, a reality, both as it regards what I then experienced and the fulfilment afterwards. * * *

In order to show some pretence of respect for some of the forms of law, Judge Austin A. King now entered our prison and took our testimony, preparatory to a change of venue. I shall never forget this interview. There stood our Judge, face to face with those who, by his cruelty and injustice, had lived a cold half year in a dungeon. He refused to look us in the eye; hung his head and looked like a culprit before his betters about to receive his doom. The looks of guilt and misery portrayed in his countenance during that brief interview bespoke more of misery than we had suffered during our confinement. I actually pitied him in my heart. With an extraordinary effort and a voice scarcely audible, he administered the oaths and withdrew.

By means of this change we were finally to be removed one hundred miles down the country, and confined in the prison at Columbia, Boone County, to await a final trial.

A long, dreary winter and spring had now passed away, and the time drew near for our removal. We looked forward to the change with some degree of hope and expectation, for it could not be for the worse, and might, perhaps, be for the better. At any rate, the journey would give us a chance to leave our dark and loathsome dungeon, and look upon the light of day, the beauties of nature, and to breathe the untainted air.

The morning of the departure at length arrived. Mr. Brown, the Sheriff, entered our prison with a fierce and savage look, and, bidding us hold out our hands, coupled us together in pairs, with irons locked on our wrists, and marched us out; and, amid a throng of people, placed us in a carriage. Accompanied with four other guards on horseback, with loaded pistols, we bid farewell to Richmond.

It was a pleasant morning in early summer, when all the freshness and beauty of spring seemed blended in rich profusion, with the productions peculiar to the season as it advanced towards maturity. The leaves on the trees were full grown, and the forest presented a freshness of beauty and loveliness which reminded me of Paradise. The plains were covered with a coat of green, and the wild flowers of the prairie, blooming in all their variety, sent forth a perfume which mingled with every zephyr, and wafted sweet odors on every breeze. To prisoners who had breathed only a tainted air for half a year the very ground itself seemed to send forth a sweetness which was plainly perceptible to the senses. We enjoyed our ride through that delightful country more than any being could who had never been confined for weary months in a dreary dungeon.

The day at length closed, and we were taken into a house and stretched upon our backs on the floor, all fastened together with wrist and ankle irons in such a manner that we could not turn nor change our position. The doors and windows were then made fast, and the sentinels on duty guarded us by turns until morning. This was our night's rest after forty miles travel.

The next day proved extremely rainy, with heavy thunder; but still we travelled. In the course of the day we came to a stream which was swollen by the rains to that degree that we had to swim over it and stem a swift current. This hindered us for some hours—in crossing over with horses, wagons, baggage, etc.; and as all of us were engaged in this business, our chains were taken off for the time.

When we had crossed over, put on our clothes, and replaced the baggage, saddles, arms, etc., ready for a start, it was night, and we were very weary and hungry, having had no refreshments during the day. The rain was also pouring in torrents, and the night setting in extremely dark. Four miles of wild country, partly covered with forests and underwoods, still lay between us and the nearest house. Through the hurry of the moment, or for some other reason, they neglected to replace our irons, and our limbs were free. The carriage drove through a thick forest during the extreme darkness, and was several times on the eve of upsetting. This caused us to assume a position for saving ourselves by rising upon our feet, ready to jump out in case of the carriage upsetting.

The Sheriff and guards seeing this, rode close on each side, and, cocking their pistols, swore they would shoot us dead if we attempted to leave the carriage, and that if it upset they would shoot us anyhow, for fear we might attempt to escape.

After two days more of rain, hail and travel, we arrived at Columbia, where we were immediately thrust into a gloomy dungeon filled with darkness, filth and cobwebs; the naked floor was our lodging. We had travelled hard, through rain and fatigue, for several days, and on the last day had rode till sundown without refreshment. We were extremely hungry and weary, but received no refreshment, not even a drink of water, till late in the evening, when our new keeper, Mr. John Scott, visited us with some buttermilk and bread; but we were now too much exhausted and too low spirited to eat. We thanked him for his kindness, and sank down exhausted on the floor, where we rested as well as we could till morning. We saw no more of Sheriff Brown or his guards, and will now take final leave of them, merely observing that they made it a point to insult every black woman they met on the way, frequently turning aside with them into the woods and fields. On returning to the company they would boast and glory in their criminal intercourse with them.

After spending one night in our new dungeon we were called on by the Sheriff to come up into a more comfortable apartment, and were treated with some degree of humanity. We were no longer troubled with guards, and even Luman and Phila behaved much better. We had been in our new situation something like a month, when we were visited by some friends from Illinois, from whom we learned the fate of our families and friends.

The wife of Mr. Phelps rode one hundred and sixty miles on horseback, accompanied by her brother, a young man named Clark. They arrived in Columbia and paid us a visit in prison about the 1st of July. My brother Orson also arrived on horseback about the same time. With these friends we had a good visit for some days—they being permitted to stay in the prison with us. They also brought a letter from my wife, by which I learned that she made her escape from Far West to Quincy, Illinois, with her children and some of her goods, by the aid of Mr. David Rogers, of New York. During this journey they were much exposed to hardships and trouble, having to camp by the way, in company with other women and children who were in a like condition. On crossing a swollen stream, Mrs. Pratt had left the carriage to cross on a foot bridge, leaving the children to ride through it. She had just crossed over and turned to look back, to see whether the carriage came through in safety, when she discovered a little girl's bonnet floating down the stream, and, on examination, as the carriage rose the bank, her daughter, a girl of six years old, was missing from the carriage. The next moment she saw her floating down the swift current. She gave the alarm to Mr. Rogers, the driver, who instantly dropped the reins and sprang after her into the stream.

At this instant the horses, being high spirited and active, began to run, and would probably have dashed themselves and the carriage, goods, and the other child to pieces but for the timely interference of a large prong of a tree, which caught the carriage with such a strong hold that all was brought to a stand. In the meantime Mr. Rogers succeeded in rescuing the child and bringing her safe to shore.

She had, as she stated, pitched head foremost out of the carriage into the water. One of the wheels ran over her, and crushed her fast into the mud at the bottom of the stream; but as it rolled over she caught the spokes with her hands, and by this means the same weight that crushed her down brought her to the surface and saved her life. On examination the marks of the wheel were distinctly seen on both her thighs, which were seriously injured and nearly broken.

After a wearisome journey and various toils and dangers, they at length arrived at Quincy, Illinois, where Mrs. Pratt rented a small house, and by the sale of a few books, with the use of her two cows, which some of the brethren had brought from Missouri for her, she was making shift to live from day to day. She still expressed some faint hopes of seeing her husband again in a land of liberty, although at present there was little ground to hope, and she was sometimes nearly in despair.

Such was the news brought us by the arrival of our friends in the prison at Columbia on the 1st of July, 1839, after eight months of weary confinement. Previous to their arrival the Lord had shown me in a vision of the night the manner and means of escape. And, like Pharaoh's dream, the thing had been doubled—that is shown to me on two occasions in the same manner.

Mrs. Phelps had the same thing shown to her in a vision previous to her arrival; my brother, Orson Pratt, also came to us with a firm impression that we were about to be delivered. He even predicted that we should go to Illinois, when he should return there. As we sat pondering upon these things, and comparing our visions and manifestations of the spirit on this subject, my brother Orson opened the Book of Mormon, when the first sentence that caught his eye was the words of Ammon to King Lamoni: "Behold, my brother and my brethren are in prison, in the land of Middoni, and I go to deliver them!" This was indeed a similar instance to ours. Ammon, on that occasion had an own brother in prison, and also brethren in the ministry, and did deliver them. Our case was exactly similar, not in Middoni, but in Missouri. And, what was still more strange, in a book of six hundred pages, this was the only sentence which would have fitted our case.

He now began in earnest to make arrangements for our escape. If there had been no strong bolts and bars to overcome, still there was one serious obstacle which a miracle alone could immediately remove, which was this: I was then very sick and scarcely able to stand on my feet, or to go up and down from the upper room, where we were in the day time, to the dungeon where we slept.

It was the second of July, and our friends could only make an excuse for staying to spend the great national holiday with us (the 4th) before they must leave or excite the suspicions and ill will of the people; and, as that day had been a lucky one for our fathers and our nation, we had determined on that time as the proper one to bid farewell to bondage and gain our liberty. In short, we had determined to make that notable day a jubilee to us, or perish in the attempt. We, therefore, prayed earnestly to the Lord, that if he had determined to favor our plan, he would heal and strengthen me, and give us all courage to act well our part. Through the ministration of the ordinance appointed for healing, I was instantly healed, and from that moment began to feel as strong and fearless as a lion.

Our plan was this: My brother, Orson Pratt, was to wait on the Judge and Attorney, and obtain various papers and arrangements for summoning witnesses from Illinois to attend our trial, which had just been adjourned for some months to come. He was also to procure an order from the Court to take affidavits in Illinois, in case the witnesses should object to come to the State from which they had been banished, in order to attend the trials.

These active preparations on our part to defend our case, together with engaging a lawyer or two, and paying a part of their fees beforehand, served as a sufficient blindfold to cover our real intentions. This done, and the papers all prepared in the hands of my brother, he and Mrs. Phelps and her brother were to stay with us until the 4th, and after celebrating the day with a dinner in the prison (which we obtained leave to do), he and the young Mr. Clark were to take leave with their horses, and also with the horse and saddle on which Mrs. Phelps had ridden, on pretence of taking him home with them to Illinois, while she stayed with her husband a few weeks in the prison; in the meantime engaging her board in the family of the keeper, who occupied part of the building in connection with the prison.

This measure, on the part of Mrs. Phelps, served the double purpose of lulling them into serenity, and also of furnishing a third horse; as there were three of us. These three horses were to be stationed in a thicket, or forest, about half a mile from the prison, and there the two friends were to await, in readiness for us to mount, should we be so fortunate as to reach the thicket alive.

Sundown, on the evening of the fourth, was the moment agreed upon, and if we did not then appear they were to give us up for lost, and make the best of their way to Illinois and inform our friends that we had gone to Paradise in attempting to come to them. The reason for appointing this hour was this: Our door would be opened at sundown to hand in our supper, and we must then make the attempt as our only chance; for it was customary to lock us up in the lower dungeon as soon as the shades of evening began to appear.

This plan all matured, and the arrangements completed with the court and the lawyers, the fourth of July dawned upon us with hope and expectation. While the town and nation were alive with the bustle of preparation for the celebration of the American Jubilee, and while guns were firing and music sounding without, our prison presented a scene of scarcely less life and cheerfulness; for we were also preparing to do proper honors to the day. We had prevailed on the keeper to furnish us with a long pole, on which to suspend a flag, and also some red stripes of cloth. We then tore a shirt in pieces, and took the body of it for the ground work of a flag, forming with the red stripes of cloth an eagle and the word *"Liberty,"* in large letters. This rude flag of red and white was suspended on the pole from the prison window, directly in front of the public square and court house, and composed one of the greatest attractions of the day. Hundreds of the people from the country, as well as villagers who were there at the celebration, would come up and stare at the flag, and reading the motto, would go swearing or laughing away, exclaiming, "Liberty! Liberty! What have the Mormons to do with celebrating *liberty* in a damned old prison?"

In the meantime active preparations were in progress for our public dinner; and with the contributions of our friends who were to partake with us, and a portion served from the public table of the citizens of the town, we had a plentiful supply. And, as we considered it was to be a day of release, we partook of our feast with much cheer, and with thankful as well as social feelings, which I think have been seldom if ever surpassed.

O ye sons of Columbia, at home and abroad! Think back to the fourth of July, 1839; call to mind your feast in honor of national freedom, and ask yourselves the question, whether in all your pomp and show of joy and social glee, you felt anything compared with *our* feelings, or the interest excited during that feast.

Eight months and four days we had been deprived of the sweets of that liberty which a whole nation was then engaged in celebrating; and we felt that:

> Now's the day, and now's the hour,
> To trample on a tyrant's power;
> To burst at once the prison's gloom,
> Or find a martyr'd hero's tomb.

The dinner over, our brethren took a final leave of us and our prison, loaded with love, respects, compliments and messages to our families and friends in Illinois. All these, together with the goodbyes and farewells, were heard and witnessed by the keeper's family, and served the purpose for which they were intended, viz: To lull them into security, and to remove all possible ground of suspicion as to our intentions.

After riding out of town a mile or two in the forest, on the road towards Illinois, they turned off into the thick leaved wilderness, and made their way in secret, as best they could, to the thicket agreed upon, within about half a mile of the prison; where, with horses saddled and bridle reins in hand, they awaited in anxious suspense the slow progress of the setting sun.

Chapter 32

The prison at Columbia was situated in the same square with the court house, being on the north edge of the town. Between it and the wilderness, where our friends held the horses in waiting, there were several fields and fences, say for the distance of half a mile, consisting of meadow and pasture land, and all in full view of the town. The prison consisted of a block house, two stories high, with two rooms below and two above. The keeper and his family occupied one end, and the other was used as the prison—the only entrance being through the lower room of the dwelling part, which was occupied by the family, and then up a steep flight of stairs, at the head of which was a heavy oaken door, ironed, locked and bolted as if to secure a Bonaparte or a Samson. On the inside of this was still another door, which was but slender, with a square hole near the top, of sufficient size to hand in the food and dishes of the prisoners.

The large, heavy door had always to be opened when food, drink, or other articles were handed in; and while open, the inner door served as a temporary guard to prevent prisoners from escaping, and was not always opened on such occasions, the food being handed through the hole in the top of the door, while the door itself remained locked. However, as a fortunate circumstance for us, the coffee pot when filled would not easily slip through the hole in the door, and, rather than spill the coffee and burn his fingers, the keeper would sometimes unlock and open the inner door, in order to set in this huge and obstinate pot; and once in, the door would immediately close, and the key be turned, while the outer door would perhaps stand open till the supper was finished, and the dishes handed out.

Now, our whole chance of escape depended on the question, whether the inner door would be opened that evening, or the coffee pot squeezed in at the hole in the top. Mrs. Phelps and Mrs. Gibbs were in the upper room of the keeper's apartment, near the head of the stairs, and only a log or timber partition between us and them, and several open crevices in the same, so that we could easily communicate with them. One of them was waiting the issue of the great scene about to be enacted with almost breathless interest and feverish anxiety, as on the good or ill success of that moment depended her future hopes through life, while the other was totally ignorant of the whole affair. In a far corner of our prison sat Luman, the old apostate, entirely ignorant of the whole plan, and with no other anxiety than a slight wish for the sun to go down, that he might enjoy his supper and the society of his dear "Phila" in his curtained bed in the upper room, while we were locked in the dungeon below to sleep on an oak floor, amid cobwebs and filth.

The citizens of the town were now some of them gathering in small groups outside of their doors to enjoy the quiet of a summer evening, to smoke a cigar or chat over the merits of the celebration; while others were on horseback, to enjoy an evening's ride or to return to their homes. Bands of music, or rather an occasional beat of the drum, or blast of the bugle, was still to be heard in the distance; while a few soldiers, or rather militia in uniform, were hurrying to and fro. Groups of boys were playing about the square, and last, though not least, our flag was still on high, with "Liberty" and the eagle in bold colors waving to the night breeze. This had so attracted the attention of the little fellows that once and again they begged of us to make them a present of it; but we told them we could not spare it till the next morning—the fact is, we were not willing to surrender our castle before the time, or till we made good our retreat.

As the sun began to decline behind the long range of forest which bounded the western horizon, and the lengthened shadows of the tall trees were thrown over our prison, we called upon the Lord to prosper us and open our way, and then sang aloud the following lines:

Lord, cause their foolish plans to fail,
    And let them faint or die:
Our souls would quit this poor old jail,
    And fly to Illinois—

To join with the embodied Saints,
    Who are with freedom blest:
That only bliss for which we pant,
    With them awhile to rest.

Give joy for grief—give ease for pain,
    Take all our foes away;
But let us find our friends again
    In this eventful day.

These lines were sung several times over, with the spirit and with the understanding also, and very loud and distinct—being heard by the old apostate and his wife, and by the keepers of the prison; but the doctrine of spiritualizing had become so prevalent that neither this, nor the flag of liberty, nor any other Scripture seemed to them to have any literal meaning, till they found too late the true interpretation by the fulfilment.

The sun was now setting, and the footsteps of the old keeper were heard on the stairs—the key turned, the outer door grated on its huge hinges, while at the same moment we sprang upon our feet, hats and coats on (rather an unusual dress for a hot day in July—for, by the bye, my hat proved to be a fur cap, which I wore when first taken in November previous), and stood by the door to act the part of waiters in receiving the dishes and food for supper, and placing them on the table. Dish after dish was handed in through the small aperture in the door, and duly received and placed upon the table by us, with as much grace and as calm countenances as if we thought of nothing else but our suppers. And I will now venture to say that famishing men never watched the movements of a coffee pot with more anxiety than we did on this occasion. At length the other dishes all being handed in, the huge pot made its appearance in the hole in the top of the door, but one of us cried out to the keeper—"Colonel, you will only spill the coffee by attempting to put it through, besides, it burns our fingers; it will be more convenient to unlock and hand it in at the door." With this it was lowered again, and the key turned on the inner door.

In this, as in most other fields of battle, where liberty and life depend on the issue, every one understood the part assigned to him and exactly filled it. Mr. Follett was to give the door a sudden pull, and fling it wide open the moment the key was turned. Mr. Phelps being well skilled in wrestling was to press out foremost, and come in contact with the jailer; I was to follow in the centre, and Mr. Follett, who held the door, was to bring up the rear, while sister Phelps was to pray.

No sooner was the key turned than the door was seized by Mr. Follett with both hands; and with his foot placed against the wall, he soon opened a passage, which was in the same instant filled by Mr. Phelps, and followed by myself and Mr. Follett. The old jailer strode across the way, and stretched out his arms like Bunyan's Apollion, or like the giant Despair in Doubting Castle, but all to no purpose. One or two leaps brought us to the bottom of the stairs, carrying the old gentleman with us headlong, helter skelter, while old Luman sat and laughed in his corner of the prison, and Mrs. Phelps exclaimed, "O Lord God of Israel, thou canst help." Old Mrs. Gibbs looked on in silent amazement, while the jailer's wife acted the part of the giant Despair's wife, Diffidence, and not only assisted in the scuffle, but cried out so loud that the town was soon alarmed. In the meantime we found ourselves in the open air, in front of the prison and in full view of the citizens, who had already commenced to rally, while Mr. Phelps and the jailer still clinched fast hold of each other like two mastiffs. However, in another instant he cleared himself, and we were all three scampering off through the fields towards the thicket.

By this time the town was all in motion. The quietness of the evening was suddenly changed into noise and bustle, and it was soon evident that the thrilling scenes of the great drama of the 4th of July, and of the Columbian celebration of liberty were yet to be enacted. The streets on both sides of the fields where we were running were soon thronged with soldiers in uniform, mounted riflemen, footmen with fence stakes, clubs, or with whatever came to hand, and with boys, dogs, etc., all running, rushing, screaming, swearing, shouting, bawling and looking, while clouds of dust rose behind them. The cattle also partook of the general panic and ran bellowing away, as if to hide from the scene. The fields behind us also presented a similar scene. Fences were leaped or broken down with a crash; men, boys and horses came tumbling over hedge and ditch, rushing with the fury of a whirlwind in the chase; but we kept our course for the thicket, our toes barely touching the ground, while we seemed to leap with the fleetness of a deer, or as the young hart upon the mountains.

Escape from prison

Our friends who had stood waiting in the thicket, had watched the last rays of the sun as they faded away, and had observed the quiet stillness of the evening as it began to steal over the distant village where we were confined; and had listened with almost breathless anxiety for the first sound which was to set all things in commotion, and which would say to them in language not to be misunderstood, that the struggle had commenced. For some moments after the last golden beam had disappeared they listened in vain. The occasional lowing of a cow as she came home from the woodland pasture, impatient for her calf and the milkmaid to ease her of her rich burthen; the mingled sound of human voices in the distance in common conversation, the merry laugh of the young beaux and their sweethearts, the quiet song of the whippoorwill, mingled with the merry notes of the violin, the thrill of the bugle, or the soft and plaintive notes of the flute, stole upon the silence of the evening, and were occasionally interrupted by the clatter of hoofs, as a few of the citizens were retiring from the enjoyments of a public day to their own peaceful homes in the country. These, and the beatings of their anxious and almost bursting hearts, were the only sounds which fell upon their ear, till suddenly they heard a rumbling and confused noise, as of footsteps rushing down the stairs of a prison, then a shrill cry of alarm from Mrs. Diffidence, the giantess, and soon followed by the shouts and rush of men, dogs, horses and prisoners towards the spot where they were located. They then sprang forward to the edge of the fields and ran back again to the horses, and again returned, as if the using of their own limbs would serve to add nimbleness to those of the prisoners, and to quicken their speed.

As soon as the prisoners drew near, they were hailed by their friends, and conducted to the horses. They were breathless and nearly ready to faint; but in a moment they were assisted to mount, and a whip and the reins placed in their hands, while the only words interchanged were—"Fly quickly, they are upon you!" "Which way shall we go?" "Where you can; you are already nearly surrounded." "But what will you do? they will kill you if they cannot catch us." "We will take care of ourselves; fly, fly, I say, instantly." These words were exchanged with the quickness of thought, while we were mounting and reining our horses; in another instant we were all separated from each other, and each one was making the best shift he could for his own individual safety.

I had taken about the third jump with my horse when I encountered a man rushing upon me with a rifle, and, taking aim at my head, he said, "G—d d—n you, stop, or I'll shoot you." He was then only a few paces from me, and others were rushing close in his rear, but I turned my horse quickly in another direction, and rushed with all speed into the thickest of the forest, followed for some minutes by him and his dog; but I soon found myself alone, while I could only hear the sound of distant voices, the rushing of horsemen in every direction, with the barking of dogs. What had become of my companions or our friends, I knew not. I rode on at full speed for a mile or more, when the woods terminated, and no alternative was left for me but to go either to the right or to the left into one of the public highways where I would be every moment exposed to my pursuers, or go over the fence and pass through the open fields to the wilderness beyond, or, on the other hand, to turn back into the heart of the forest, partly towards the town and prison from whence I had escaped. As horses' feet and men's voices were already heard along the highways which lay on each side of me, I determined upon the latter. I, therefore, changed my course, took my back track, and plunged into the depth of the forest. I then dismounted, tied my horse in a thicket, walked some distance from him and climbed a tree—intending to wait in this situation amid the concealment of the thick foliage till the darkness of evening would enable me to proceed with safety. Seating myself in one of its forked branches, and placing my arms in two other similar forks, I was supported from falling, although in a moment after I had ceased my exertions I fainted away. In this situation I remained for some time, without the least power to change my position or help myself; my breath was gone through over exertion, and my mouth and throat parched with a burning thirst, my stomach sickened, and as I began to breathe I was seized with vomiting, and threw up nearly all the food which my stomach contained. I then gradually recovered my strength till I could speak, when I began to call on the Lord, saying, "O Lord, strengthen me this once, deliver me from my persecutors and bring me in safety to a land of liberty, and I will praise thy name and give thee all the glory, and the remnant of my days shall be wholly devoted to thy service; for surely my life is now at stake, and if preserved, it is thy gift, therefore I shall owe it all to thee."

The darkness of evening was now fast setting in, and every moment seemed to increase my safety and security from immediate discovery, although I could still hear the distant sound of tramping horses, and the voices of men and dogs in pursuit, and sometimes so near that I could distinguish some of their words. It was a dark and moonless evening, the sky was only lighted by the glimmer of a few stars partly obscured by the clouds, and the thick foliage of the forest increased the gloom, and served to render the darkness nearly complete. I now came down from the tree and felt my way to the place where I had tied my horse, but as good or ill luck would have it, he had loosed himself and gone, leaving me to my fate. I then groped my way amid the dark shades of the forest to a small stream of warm, muddy water, and, stooping down, partly quenched my thirst. I then made my way to the highway and commenced my journey on foot, carefully watching on either hand lest I should be surprised and taken.

I was an entire stranger to the country—having no guide but the polar star. My road lay nearly northward, and upwards of a hundred miles of a wild country, peopled only by enemies, still lay between me and a State where the principles of freedom yet prevailed in a sufficient degree to insure my safety. If I could make my way through this wilderness of enemies, on foot, after the weakness and debility caused by eight months' confinement, and after the fatigues of my evening's race, and neither inquire the way nor make my appearance at any house for entertainment and refreshment, then I should still have the great Mississippi River to ferry over, and be liable to be discovered and retaken in the act, while in sight of liberty. The thoughts of these dangers, the anxious inquiries of my mind as to what had become of my fellow prisoners and friends, which I had no means of satisfying, and the hopes and expectations of soon meeting my family and friends in a land of liberty, alternately occupied my mind as I slowly pursued my solitary way during that dark and, to me, eventful night.

Chapter 33

At length the morning began to dawn, but it proved to be a cloudy day; no mark was left in the heavens to determine the point of compass, while at the same time my road became every moment more obscure, and finally terminated in a deer path, which wound along among the hills and vales of a dense and entirely unsettled forest, and finally disappeared. It was now broad day. The wild forest extended around far and wide, and no sign of human existence or occupation. I still wandered slowly on, not knowing whether I was every moment travelling nearer to friends, and home, and liberty, or to the place of dreary confinement. The deer and wild turkey occasionally started up before me, and the howl of the wolf was heard in the distance. At length I came to a beautiful clear stream, which seemed to wind through a fine valley. The wild flowers blooming in richest variety sent forth sweet odors, and the birds of the forest were pouring forth in profusion their morning songs.

I now sat down in safety, and took a small biscuit from my pocket which sister Phelps had kindly provided, and which was my only store of food for the journey. With a hearty drink from the crystal stream and this biscuit I made my first breakfast, after my imprisonment, as a free son of Columbia. I recollect that while I sat enjoying this solitary meal, far from friends and home, surrounded with a scenery strange and wild, and without any guide or any knowledge where I should claim the next refreshment, I thought of the sweets of liberty I now enjoyed, and with a thankful and joyous heart I exclaimed aloud, "Thank God for this hour, it is the happiest of my life; I am free, although lost in the wilderness, and if I cannot find myself, thank God nobody else can find me." In this happy valley the reader may leave me to rest awhile if he chooses, while he looks after the fate of the other prisoners and our two friends, and also, Mrs. Phelps and the affairs of the prison; bearing in mind at the same time that he must return again and accompany me through the whole dangers, toils and incidents of my journey to a land of liberty.

At the time we were separated in the heat of the pursuit, Mr. Phelps made his escape much in the same manner as myself. He was at first closely pursued, but at length he out distanced them all, and, once out of their sight, he struck directly into the road, and rode on toward Illinois. He had proceeded a few miles on his way, when he was suddenly surrounded in the darkness of the night by a company of horsemen who were out in pursuit of the prisoners. They immediately hailed him, and cried out, "Say, stranger, G—d damn you, what is your name?" He replied in the same rough and careless manner, "You damned rascals, what is yours?" On finding he could damn as well as themselves, they concluded he could not be a Mormon, while his bold and fearless manner convinced them that he was not a man who was fleeing for his life. They then begged his pardon for the rough manner in which they had accosted him, "Oh, you are one of the real breed. By G—d, no damned Mormon could counterfeit that language, you swear real natteral; hurrah for old Kentuck. But whar mought you live, stranger?" He replied, "just up here; you mout a kno'd me, and then agin you moutn't. I think I've seed you all a heap o' times, but I've been so damned drunk at the fourth of independence, I hardly know myself or anybody else, but hurrah for old Kentuck; and what about the damn'd Mormons?" "What about 'em? egad, you'd a know'd that without axin', if you'd a seed 'em run." "What! they are not out of prison, are they?" "Out of prison! Yes, the damn'd rascals raised a flag of liberty in open day, and burst out, and down stars right in the midst of the public celebration, out rassling the damn'd jailer, and outrunning the whole town in a fair foot race. They reached the timber jist as they war overtaken, but afore we could cotch 'em they mounted their nags, and the way they cleared was a caution to Crockett. We tuk one on 'em, and seed the other two a few feet distant, rushin' their nags at full speed, but we couldn't cotch 'em nor shoot 'em either; I raised my new Kentucky rifle, fresh loaded and primed, with a good percussion, and taking fair aim at one of their heads only a few yards distant, I fired, but the damn'd cap burst, and the powder wouldn't burn." "Well, now, stranger, that's a mighty big story and seems enemost on-

possible. Did you say you cotched one on 'em? Why I'd a tho't you'd a
kilt him on the spot; what have you done with him?" "They tuk him
back to prison, I suppose, but it was only the old one. If it had been one
o' them tother chaps we would a skinn'd 'em as quick as Crockett would
a coon, and then eat 'em alive without leaving a grease spot."

This interview over, the horsemen withdrew and left Phelps to pursue his way in peace. He rode on during the night without further molestation; but when day appeared he found himself in rather an awkward fix
for a traveller, having lost his hat in the race the preceding day; he was,
therefore, bareheaded, besides, his face was somewhat bruised and
scratched in the scuffle; however, he concluded to make the best of it,
and trust to Providence for the issue. Riding up to a farm house to call for
breakfast and to have his horse fed, he began to banter the host to sell
him an old straw hat; "For," said he, "I got such a power of drink last evening at the big doings that I couldn't ride straight, and tumbled off my
horse once or twice, and finally lost my hat." Judging from his manner,
and the dirt and scratches on his face, they readily believed his tale, and
furnished him with an old wide-brimmed, miserable looking hat, which
served as a very good disguise during the remainder of the journey. Himself and horse refreshed, he renewed his journey, and finally arrived in Illinois in safety, having reached the ferry before his pursuers, and before
the news of the escape had spread so far. By his arrival the news soon
spread far and wide that we had made our escape from prison, and that
we might be looked for soon. This news was received with a general joy,
and produced a lively sensation, not only throughout the Society, but
among the public, generally—for all parties had looked upon us as martyrs, doomed to suffer the vengeance of a set of blood-thirsty outlaws and
murderers. My brother, O. Pratt, and the young Mr. Clark, who furnished us with the horses, must now be looked after.

When we parted in the thicket, as has been before described, they
had only time to flee a few paces, when they found themselves completely surrounded on every hand, and no possibility left them of escape
by running; they, therefore, dropped down into a small ravine which
had been made by the water during some former freshet, and there lay as
close to the earth as a young quail when its nest is disturbed. The enemy
passed close by them a number of times, and so very near that they dared
not to make the least motion—not even to look up to see whether they
were discovered.

At length night came on; the pursuers retired, and they arose and
pursued their journey on foot, and arrived safely in Illinois soon after the

arrival of Mr. Phelps. My brother immediately repaired to the residence of my wife and children, who were waiting his return in anxious suspense, in hopes to hear some news from me, whom they considered still in prison—not having as yet heard any news of the escape. As he entered the door Mrs. P. raised her anxious and sorrowful eyes, and eagerly inquired:

"Have you seen my husband?"

"I have."

"Is he yet alive?"

"Yes."

"Is he well?"

"He is."

"O, thank God for that! Is there any prospect that he will ever get free and return alive?"

"Well, I hope so; for the last time I saw him he was astride a horse in the woods, and headed towards home on a gallop."

I shall not attempt to describe her feelings at that moment, as the reader can best imagine them; but suffice it to say, after her first transports were over he sat down and related to her the whole affair which had transpired up to the time he last saw me. She was now full of hope and expectation—although mingled with fear and anxiety indescribable. If I eluded the pursuit of my enemies and arrived in safety it was now time to look for my arrival; but if, on the other hand, I was taken back and chained down in a dungeon; or if I was shot down and left without a burial to be a prey to wolves and turkey buzzards,—Oh, dreadful thought! Oh, horrible suspense! Oh, the hope, joy, sorrow, anguish, misery, happiness, frenzy, and feelings undefined which agitate and distract the bosom of a wife and mother at such a moment! If man—hardhearted, unfeeling man—could read the heart of a woman on such an occasion, he would never more drive, imprison or kill his fellow man.

She soon set about preparing for the reception of her husband, in case he should arrive, faint and exhausted with hunger and fatigue. The table was spread, and food placed upon it; the house was illuminated through the night, during which her anxious and beating heart would not suffer her for one moment to sleep. She watched during the entire night, and on several occasions opened the door and looked abroad; but still the morning dawned and he came not. Surely, thought she, he is slain or again confined in a dungeon, loaded with chains, and kept for a sure prey to glut the vengeance of a furious mob who have been disappointed of the rest of their victims.

The excitement now became general; friends crowded in to inquire the news and to sympathize with her, and to endeavor, if possible to keep up her hopes. They argued that the same God who had delivered him from prison, and strengthened him in the chase, and the same God who prevented the powder from taking fire when the deadly rifle was aimed at him, would also stand by him, and bring him safely to his friends and home. This, in some measure, still kept her spirits from sinking in despair.

Armed men were now despatched in various directions along the river, and into Missouri, to endeavor, if possible, to meet with him and protect him home. Another day and night at length passed away in the same suspense, no tidings having been heard from him nor from any of those who had gone in search. The pursuers, however, were known to be at the ferry on the other side of the river, watching his arrival. The same precaution was taken by them at all the public ferries for some distance up and down the river.

The suspense and anguish of her aching bosom now became intolerable; in vain they continued to assure her that he would be preserved and return in safety. She could plainly see that, while they sought to comfort her with hope, they themselves were half in doubt and beginning to despair of his deliverance. Another long day passed and another night set in, and still no news—except that the ferries on the Missouri side were all strictly guarded, and the entire people on the lookout to take him dead or alive. She had now kept her table spread both day and night, and had watched for three entire nights without sleep. "He cannot be alive and free," exclaimed she, "or I know he would fly to meet the fond welcome of his wife and children, and relieve their aching hearts."

We must now return with our readers to the prison at Columbia, and take a glance at the scenes which followed our departure, and learn the fate of Mr. Follett and Mrs. Phelps. As soon as the prisoners had cleared from the jailer, and were fairly under way, Mrs. Phelps, who was still an inmate of the dwelling, became the particular object of their spite and rage. The old jailer and his wife commenced to rail and curse her as the author of all the mischief. They threatened her with instant death, and finally turned her out of doors in the dusk of the evening, and in the midst of a mob who had gathered in great numbers around the prison and raging like so many tigers disappointed of their prey. Being a stranger and without money, friends, or acquaintances in the place, she knew not where to go or what to do. She finally sat down in the open air in the midst of the mob, by whom she was assailed, cursed, insulted, threatened, and abused in the most unfeeling manner for some time. But she still remained on the spot, and scarcely noticed the slang and abuse of the raging rabble, so intent was she upon the issue of the race—not knowing from one moment to the other whether her husband would be shot down, or whether he would be taken and brought back in triumph.

At length, after a watchful glance towards the wilderness, she heard the shout of triumph amidst the hosts of the enemy, and next was re-echoed from crowd to crowd, amid vollies of oaths, curses and exulting laughs, "We've catched one of the damn'd Mormons and we'll roast him alive over a slow fire, damn him." They now rallied around her in great numbers, exulting and threatening, and boasting that they had taken her husband and would kill him on the spot. While they were thus abusing her she saw another crowd coming and a prisoner in the midst, on whom they were venting their rage, as if he would be torn to pieces. As they approached nearer it proved to be Mr. Follet, on Mrs. Phelps' horse and side-saddle. He had been surrounded, overpowered and taken at the time we were each separated from the other. He was finally rescued from the mob, and thrust alive into the lower dungeon and chained down to the floor. He remained in this doleful situation for a few days, till the wrath of the multitude had time to cool a little, and then he was unchained by the Sheriff and again brought into the upper apartment and treated with some degree of kindness.

They now laughed with him about his adventure, praised him for his bravery, and called him a good fellow. The truth of the matter was, they had no great desire to take the lives of any but those whom they had considered leaders; and since they had discovered that Mr. Follett and Mr. Phelps were not considered religious leaders among our Society, they were in no great danger, except they should happen to be killed in the heat of excitement or passion.

We now leave him in his lonesome prison, with no other society than the old apostate, Luman, and his dear Phila, while we get Sister Phelps out of the trouble she was in. After the fate of the prisoners seemed determined, she sank down exhausted on a block of wood in the open air amid the surrounding darkness. Here she was still mocked and insulted by the unfeeling rabble, till a certain young man, more feeling than the others, declared that he was not accustomed to see a female treated thus in America, and that if she had no home his father and mother would receive her kindly and give her protection under their roof till she could return to Illinois. He then went home, and in a few minutes returned with his mother, by whom she was kindly invited to their dwelling. On arriving there she was treated in the kindest manner for about two weeks, during which time her horse was kept from her and rode in search of the prisoners. They finally restored her horse and saddle to her, and she rode home in peace, where she eventually met her husband, and rejoiced that she had been, in some measure, the means of his deliverance.

And here I might as well inform the anxious reader of the final liberation of the two remaining prisoners. Mr. Follett remained in confinement for several months, and finally was dismissed and sent home to Illinois, where he met his family, who had been expelled from the State of Missouri, in common with others, during his confinement. And, last of all, the old apostate came out by fair acquittal. And should any of our readers have the curiosity to see the charming couple, whose singular courtship and history run through and make a principal thread of our narrative, they will call at the little town of Augusta, a few miles from Fort Madison, Iowa Territory, and inquire for "Luman and Phila," who were living there in quiet at the last accounts.

Chapter 34

I suppose by this time the reader has either forgotten the circumstances in which he took leave of myself, or else is somewhat weary with the winding of the narrative and impatient for it to come to a close. The only apology I have to offer for the many digressions and wanderings through which he has been led is, that I consider it impolite and disrespectful to get myself out of a bad place until I have first seen my friends all safely out. True, I did not strictly observe this rule of good breeding in the escape itself; therefore it becomes me to take the more care to observe it now, when there is no danger, excepting that of being deserted by some of my readers before I am safely out. However, if you still wish to accompany me in all the windings of my wearisome and dangerous adventure we will now turn to the happy valley, where you recollect leaving me on the morning of the fifth of July in the act of breakfasting on a small biscuit, while, to all appearances, I was lost to myself and to all mankind.

After resting a few minutes I arose and travelled onward, without any way to determine the course I was travelling. After some miles, I came to a house in the woods, and ventured to inquire of the woman the way to Columbia, and what course it lay from there. By this means I learned that I was fourteen miles distant from the prison in a northerly direction. I then took a course directly opposite to her directions, and soon found myself among settlements, and in a kind of road, but very indirect and winding among fields and woods, or in the language of that county, among "clarens" and "timber." I paid but little respect to the road, but rather wandered around among the forests, and made my course as well as I could without being seen.

At last the clouds thickened and it began to rain. In the meantime I had again plunged into the depths of an unknown forest, and lost all idea of the true point of the compass. The air now became dense with thick clouds and mist, and the rain was pouring in torrents. At first I thought that rather than expose myself by another inquiry, I would sit down at the bottom of a large oak and wait patiently for the clouds to break away, so that I could see the sun, and thus determine my course, as to travel in uncertainty would exhaust my strength for naught. I accordingly sat down; but after waiting for a length of time, I found there was no prospect of seeing the sun, moon, or stars for some days to come. In the meantime I was becoming wet and cold, lame and stiff jointed from the effects of my exertions the night previous. I was also aware that hunger would soon be preying upon me, as I already felt very much in need of refreshment. I, therefore, arose and wandered on till I saw another house in the distance. I there ventured another inquiry, by which I was enabled to make my way through the windings of the forest, and finally to enter upon a vast prairie or untimbered plain without inhabitants. Through this plain there was a direct road to a place called Paris, which was now some twenty miles distant and directly on my way. Here I could travel in solitude, and have no difficulty in finding my way either by night or day; and should I chance to meet a traveller in pursuit, I could see him for some miles distant in the day time, and have time to leave the road and hide myself in the grass before he could be near me.

It was now drawing towards evening, and the rain was still pouring in torrents, while the wind blew almost to a tempest. I was weary and exhausted with fatigue and hunger, and chilled and benumbed with the rain and wind which had drenched me for some hours. It had been my intention to travel through the night, but I now saw it was impossible. I would be obliged to rest my weary limbs somewhere; and to sit or lie down without shelter in such a tempest, and benumbed as I then was, would be death; or at least it would be what I could not endure; and to lodge at any house would expose me to be discovered and taken by my pursuers. As night approached I hesitated for some time whether to continue to brave the tempest and to pass the night in the rain, or to run the risk of being taken by turning off the road and going a mile or two through the wet grass to a settlement which was in sight, in the borders of the wilderness, on the left of my road. At last I was compelled by the severity of the storm to choose the latter. I accordingly made for a house;

but how was I to account for being a traveller, and on foot—as nearly all men in that country travel on horseback? However, my ingenuity soon prepared me a way to account for this suspicious circumstance.

As I drew near the house the owner stood in the door looking out upon the tempest and watching my approach—it being rather strange to see a person from the open plain amid such a tempest. As I drew near, all wet and dripping, I cried out very sociably, saying: "Sir, can you entertain a drowning man here this terrible night?" The answer was, "I reckon we mout: come in, stranger, you seem in a mighty bad fix." I hobbled in as well as I could, being very lame with walking, as well as benumbed with the storm; and without giving time for any more inquiry, I began to complain of the fatigue of walking, and how it had lamed me; at the same time observing that my horse had played a very bad trick with me; he had got away from me and strayed into the timber, where I could not find him. "Ah," said he, "how did you happen to lose him?" "Why," said I, "I am from Indiana, and have been out in your wild woods back here looking for land. I had been in the habit of letting my horse bait a little occasionally, as he never seemed inclined to leave till, last evening, he of a sudden wandered out of my sight in the woods, and dark coming on, I could not track him, and finally lost him; and, what is worse, he carried off my clothing and all the fixings I had with me, even to my shooting irons and ammunition. I shall now have to go clear to Paris on foot, and then remain there a few days till I can advertise him and obtain him again."

"Oh!" exclaimed he, "it's a pity you should have such a heap of trouble. Where did you stay last night?" I replied "the devil himself could hardly answer that; for in hunting my horse I got benighted, and lost myself instead of finding him; however, I made my way out to the first cottage I could find, and took up with very curious fare, I assure you." "What part of Indiana are you from?" continued he. "From near Terre Haute," replied I. "What is the price of land in that country now?" he inquired. I replied that it had risen very much since the completion of the great national road; "indeed," said I, "as a specimen of the rise of property, I could now take twenty-five dollars per acre for my little place in the backwoods, which a few years ago only cost me three dollars and seventy-five cents, so I thought I would just mount my nag and ride west here, and take a look in Illinois and Missouri, and if I could suit myself I would go home and sell out, and come out here and purchase." "Well," said he, "I reckon you must do a heap better here than there, as we've a smart chance of land here that's very cheap, besides," continued he, "we can make corn here so easy; and then, agin, there's a power of range for cattle and horses." In this kind of conversation the evening passed off very sociably. After eating a hearty supper I retired to bed.

In the morning I awoke much refreshed, and found the storm had subsided, and the sun shining in his strength. I tarried to breakfast, which consisted of a good cup of coffee and a fowl, with some corn bread or "dodger." After breakfast I vented my spite once more, with angry and impatient words about my poor horse; grumbled sorely at being so lame, and regretted very much at having to go on foot all the way to Paris; "and," said I, "I get so hungry and faint in walking over these lonesome plains, where the houses are a dozen miles apart, I believe, with your leave, I'll just pocket the remainder of the dodger and chicken." "O, yes," said the good woman, "take it and welcome. You mout want it, and then agin you mout not; and although its coarse fare, yet we've seen a heap o' times in this new country that we couldn't get as good." I thanked her, and then settled my bill with her husband, and making her a present of a quarter of a dollar, I took leave, and soon found my way back to the road I had left the evening before. On arriving at the road I found a fresh horse track had been made since the rain, and immediately concluded one of my pursuers had passed in pursuit, which I afterwards learned to be the fact.

I would here remark that some persons will perhaps be disposed to censure me for saying that which was not strictly true in all its points, in order to avoid discovery, and make good my escape. But I can say, from the bottom of my heart, that I feel perfectly justified in so doing, not only because it accomplished a good object, and seemed according to wisdom, but we have numerous instances in Scripture where God's prophets and people acted in a similar way for a similar end. For in- stance, the New Testament justifies Rahab, and even commends her, and includes her in the sum of the faithful, because she hid the spies under the flax and deceived their pursuers by stating that they had left the city and fled to the mountains; and thus she became an accomplice, or an aider and abettor of the people and purposes of God. David also, who was the Lord's anointed, and a man after his own heart, dissembled a number of times to save his life. At one time he deceived the national priest, and thus obtained both bread and armor, under pretense of being on the king's errand, while he was in fact an outlaw, then in the act of fleeing for his life from that same Saul. And Jesus himself mentions this to the Jews, and justifies it. At another time he feigned himself insane, by figuring on the wall and letting his spittle drizzle down on his beard, in order to escape the Philistine judges. Oh, yes, says one, but he was the Lord's anointed, and, therefore, had a right to save his life at all hazards to fulfil God's purposes. To this I reply, that I am also God's anointed, and have a greater reason for living and a more worthy object to accomplish than he had. That may be, says the objector, but who believes it? I answer, one hundred people believe me in the days of my trouble and humility where one believed David. And well they may; for I have a greater work to accomplish than he ever had. But the world may blame unjustly. I care not a straw for their judgment. I have one only that I serve, and him only do I fear. The hypocrite who censures me may yet be placed under similar circumstances, and then judge ye how he would act.

But, to drop the argument and resume the history; I now pursued my way until I entered upon a public road called the Louisiana road, as it was connected with a ferry on the Mississippi at a place called by that name. I had traveled that road before, and I was not a little rejoiced to find myself on ground I was so well acquainted with that I could travel by night without any danger of missing my way. I was now in a part of the State which was comparatively thickly inhabited, and, therefore, considered it unsafe to proceed in the daytime, as the news of our escape must by this time have spread far and wide. I, therefore, spent the day either in concealment among the thickets, or in slowly progressing on my journey with much caution and many deviations from the road, in order to shun plantations and houses; but at night I pursued my way with all the strength I had.

On the third or fourth day after my escape from prison I found myself in the neighborhood of a settlement where I had formed some acquaintances years before, and where once lived a small branch of the Church, but they had all moved West, and, as I supposed, were driven out of the State with the others. But I recollected a family by the name of Ivy, who would still be living on the road, and who had been members, but were now dissenters. I was now very hungry and wanted a friend, but was in doubt whether they would befriend or betray me, as they had once been my friends, and not only so, but their near kindred had suffered in the general persecution, and had shared the common banishment. I hesitated, prayed, and at length came to the conclusion that I would venture past their door in open day, and if no one discovered or recognized me I would take it as a Providence, and conclude it was wisdom in God, as I would not be safe with them; but if, on the other hand, I was saluted by them, then I would think it a sign which Providence had given me as a witness that I could trust to them. I accordingly walked past their dwelling on Sunday evening, about two hours before sundown. As I got nearly past, the little children who were playing in the front door yard discovered me and cried out with surprise and joy, "there is brother Pratt!" At this a young man came running out to me, who proved to be one of my acquaintances, who was still a member of the Church, and who had been driven from the upper country; but, instead of going to Illinois with the rest, he had come back and settled in his old neighborhood. I asked him where Mr. Ivy, the man of the house, was. He replied that he and his wife had gone to a neighbor's, two or three miles distant, on a visit; "and," continued he, "I also am here on a visit at the same time, and by this means I have very unexpectedly met with you; and I am very glad, for the news has just reached here that the prisoners had escaped, and that they burst a cap at one, and took another and carried him back to prison. The other two have not been found." This was the first news I had heard either of myself or the others. I then requested him to go and charge the children strictly not to mention that they had seen me, and then come with me into the woods.

He did so. I then told him I was very hungry, faint and weary; and not only so, but so lame I could hardly move; besides, my feet were blistered, skinned and bloody. He said that his brother, who was also a member, and had been driven with him from the upper country, lived in an obscure place in the woods, some two miles distant, and that his brother's wife and children were as true and genuine Mormons as ever lived. He then took me on his horse and conducted me through a pathless wild for two miles, and, coming in sight of his brother's house, I dismounted and hid myself in a deep valley, whose sides were nearly perpendicular and formed of craggy rock, while he went to reconnoitre the house, and to get something ready for me to eat. He soon returned, informing me that his brother was out, and would not be in till dark; but the family wished very much that I would come in, as the children would hold their tongues, and it was thought to be perfectly safe. I declined, however, for the present, and he brought me out some bread, milk and cream, on which I refreshed myself till they prepared a more substantial supper.

As evening came on, being pressed to come in, I finally consented.

On entering, I was received with joy by the family, and sat down to sup-per. One of their neighbors, a young man, soon came in and seemed de-termined to tarry till the arrival of the man of the house, as he had some errand with him. This embarrassed me very much, for I was fearful that he would arrive and salute me as an old acquaintance, and call my name in the presence of the young man. But the little children (bless their souls) took good care for that matter, they watched very narrowly for the arrival of their papa, and when they saw him they whispered to him that brother P. was there, and, being just out of prison, he must not know him till Mr. —— had gone.

The man came in, and I looked up with a vacant stare, or rather with a strange and distant air, and inquired if he was the man of the house? He nodded coolly in the affirmative. I then inquired of him if he had seen any stray "nags" in his neighborhood? I then went on to de-scribe my horse which had strayed from me, and observed that I was out in search of him, and, being weary and hungry, I had stopped to get some refreshment with him. He said I was welcome to his house, and to such fare as he had; but he had not seen any nags, except what was owned in the neighborhood.

The young man soon did his errand and withdrew. We then shook each other by the hand most heartily, and, with a burst of joy and smiles, inquired after each other's welfare. I told him I was well nigh exhausted and worn out, and, withal, very lame, but still I had some hopes of mak-ing my escape out of the State, and of living to see my friends once more in a land of liberty. I then begged of him to exchange with me, and take my fur cap and give me a hat in its stead, which he did, and then saddled his horse with a side saddle, as the young man who was in had just bor-rowed the other saddle, and, placing me on horseback, he ran before me and by my side on foot, to take me on my journey. In this way we trav-elled till twelve o'clock at night, when I dismounted, and he bid me farewell, in order to reach his home again before the neighbors would arise and find him missing.

He had given me directions which would lead to the Mississippi River much nearer than the Louisiana ferry, and also more in the direct course towards my family, who resided at Quincy, and, besides all these advantages, the route was more obscure, and, therefore, safer for me. I now pursued my course the remainder of the night with renewed courage and strength, although so very lame, foot sore, and so much exhausted

that, in lying down to refresh myself, I could not again rise and put myself in motion short of extraordinary and repeated exertion, sometimes
having to crawl on my hands and knees till I could get sufficiently lim-
bered to arise and walk, and frequently staggering and falling in the attempt.

At length the day began to dawn, and I must soon be under the
necessity of hiding in the thickets, or making deviations from the road,
in order to avoid discovery in passing the settlements. I, therefore,
wished to push my way with all speed while it was yet too early for people
to be stirring; but sleep now completely overpowered me. As I was walking along the road I could scarcely open my eyes for a moment to look my
way for a few rods ahead, and they would then close in sleep in spite of
all my powers. I would then proceed a few paces in my sleep till I stumbled, or till I had need to take another look at the road before me; then
I would open my eyes and take one glance, and the lids would fall again
as powerless as if I had no life. In this way I walked on, alternately sleeping and waking, till, I presume, I had more than fifty naps without ceasing to walk; and each time I opened my eyes and came to my senses I
firmly resolved to keep them open and run no further risk; but while this
resolution was still passing in my mind sleep would again steal over me,
not exactly unawares, for I realized it each time, but had no power to
prevent it.

At length the twilight gave place to the full blaze of the morning;
the sons of the earth were again in motion; I therefore retired, like the
owl, to the thicket, and took a morning rest. When I awoke the sun was
high in the heavens, and, feeling somewhat refreshed, I arose from the
ground and wandered slow and solitary amid the wilds of oak, interspersed with hazel and underwood—sometimes stopping to pick and eat
a few unripe blackberries, and sometimes resting beneath the shade of a
spreading tree.

I had now great hopes of having to pass but one more night in the
land of enemies, as I could easily reach a small town in the course of the
day, which was then only two or three miles distant; and then, if I could
by any means get on to the right track before night, I would only have
about eight or ten miles' travel for the whole night, which would bring
me to a small town on the Mississippi. I wandered on amid the wilds, but
at length about half a mile of open plain or prairie intervened between
me and the town. To pass this in a public road, in open day, would be
running a great venture, and to wait for the cover of darkness would
perhaps keep me wandering another night, for the want of being started

in the right road from the town before me to the landing on the river. I, therefore, concluded to venture across the plain, along the public highway, in the day time, and should I be discovered I would sell my life as dear as possible sooner than be taken back to prison. I, therefore, walked boldly on. I had proceeded about to the middle of the plain, when, on a sudden turn of the road, two men appeared on horseback, each with a rifle on his shoulder. They were then too near for me to retreat, or to make any other shift than to meet them. As soon as they discovered me they both halted as if surprised, and one said to the other, "there he is now." They then rode on towards me, and I expected every moment that they would hail and attempt to stop me. In such a case I felt determined to seize one of their rifles, and overpower or frighten them, or die in the struggle.

I at length passed between them in the middle of the road, and looked as calm and unconcerned as if I hardly knew they were there. Either from this circumstance or some other, unaccountable to me, they never spoke to me at all, but rode on, and I saw them no more. I soon passed the plain, and made my way into a small thicket of trees which lay adjoining the little town. I then crept up near the court house, which occupied a public square in the centre, and endeavored, without being discovered or noticed by any person, to ascertain as well as I could, by my own judgment, which of all the roads would seem to lead off towards the river. After reconnoitering the town and the various bearings of the roads, I retreated back into the wilderness, with the satisfaction that I had not yet been discovered by the citizens; I had also the satisfaction of seeing the highlands and the hilly, broken country which evidently bordered on the Mississippi. The river, therefore, could be but a few miles distant, and as it was yet several hours to sundown I concluded that I could take my course, and, without any particular regard to roads, reach some spot on the river that evening, as nothing was to be so much dreaded as a public ferry—for there I knew my enemies would set their traps.

I immediately took my course, and after wandering for an hour or two, with great fatigue, among thickets of brush, briars and vines almost impassable, I at length descended a steep decline of perhaps two hundred feet, and then came down to what is called in that country the "river bottom," covered with the growth of thick forest, and appearing in some places somewhat swampy and gloomy; but still I pushed on with all speed, supposing I was not many miles from the river Mississippi. After travelling for some distance in this disagreeable and swampy wild, what was my surprise and disappointment, when on a sudden I came to a dark, deep, and muddy looking river, some forty rods wide, and rolling with a swift and turbulent current. This surely could not be the Mississippi; and yet it was something that intervened between me and that great river, and seemed to present an impassable barrier. I then heaved a deep sigh, and feeling exhausted and almost discouraged, I exclaimed to myself half aloud, how long shall I wander and find no rest? It does seem as though an enchanted ground lay between me and liberty. I turned round, and with the little strength that then remained I made my way back to the town. When I arrived again in sight of the town the sun was setting, and another wearisome night was approaching, in which I must reach the river, or I would probably be exhausted with hunger and fatigue, so as to be entirely disabled.

I now resolved to venture boldly into a public highway, and to ascertain the right road before it would be too dark to find my way or choose my course. There would not only be danger of exposure by inquiring, but although I knew there was a little town on the Mississippi, near the place I was then in, yet I had never heard the name of it; and to appear like a stranger who did not know the country, and yet be on foot and without a parcel or valise, or anything which travellers are accustomed to carry, and withal a beard near a week old, together with sweat and dirt over my clothes from lying and tumbling on the ground, would altogether make me seem like a very suspicious character; but yet I must venture an inquiry, which I determined to do the first providential opportunity which occurred. I walked along the edge of the town and struck into a public highway which seemed to lead the right course. I had not travelled far when I came to a branch of the same river which I had encountered in the swampy bottom. On one side of the road a mill was situated on its bank, and on the other side a dwelling house. Several persons were about the mill, and it was not yet dark.

I was now determined to pass by boldly, and if any one passed near me to speak to them and inquire the way, and then pass on so quick that they would have no time to have suspicion or to question me. Just as I was passing between the house and the mill, I said, "Good evening, sir. How do you cross this river?" He replied, "that the teams and horsemen ford it, but a footman may chance to cross it on the mill dam, yonder." Said I, "is this the right road to—to—what the plague is it you call that little town yonder—your nearest landing on the river—what is its name; I can seldom think of it?" "Oh, Saverton—Saverton," replied he. "Oh, yes; Saverton," I repeated. "Yes," said he, "this is the direct road to it."

I replied, "Thank you, sir. How far is it?" "Nine miles," said he. By this time I was some distance past him, and in another moment I was balancing my clumsy and worn out body on the edge of the dam, while the waters were roaring and foaming beneath me.

I got safely over, and now pursued my way with increasing hope and certainty. However, I had not gone to exceed half a mile before I came to another fork of the river, larger and swifter than the one I had just crossed, and, withal, neither dam nor bridge. I soon forded boldly into it, determined either to sink, swim, or ford it. It proved to be about a yard deep, with a strong current, and several yards wide; but I forded it in safety, and still pursued my way. After wandering for a mile or two along the bottom lands, I ascended a high bluff of several hundred feet, and thus entered upon the high, rocky and unsettled wilds which intervened between the bed of the river and the great Mississippi.

It was now dark, and I was fairly under way for my night's journey, which at most could not exceed seven or eight miles, and feeling extremely exhausted and also at leisure, I stepped aside from the road and laid me down at the foot of a tree, with a block of wood for a pillow, where I intended to sleep for an hour or two. It was a wild scene in which to slumber; no human abode was near, no voice or sound stole upon the stillness of the evening. The stars shone forth in unwonted splendor in the heavens, while wild and grassy hills, and rocky steeps pierced with deep vales and chasms, extended far and wide on all sides, as if reposing in eternal and undisturbed quiet and loneliness. Ah! thought I, as I lay in silent meditation and contemplated the scene, here is peace, here is rest, here is a solitude of grand and sacred repose, scarcely polluted by the bloodthirsty dwellers upon the degraded earth. And were it not for the ties of wife, children, and duties which bind me to society, how gladly would I seek a lone cavern or some unknown retreat amid these romantic wilds, and never more feel the ills and suffer the evils which now distract and disturb the peace of a poor, miserable world. As I had finished these meditations and was about to fall asleep I turned to my side and made a slight movement in adjusting my wooden pillow, when I heard the well known rattle of a rattle snake (eez, eez, eez,) close by my side, as if disturbed in his repose, or as if I had more than my portion of the bed. I then recollected the old proverb, that "travelling makes strange bedfellows," and also the Scripture which says, "If two lie together there is heat, but how can one be warm alone?" Said I, "old friend, I'll not argue with you as my first mother did with your venerable ancestor, and rather than quarrel or keep you awake, we will part." With this, I arose and very condescendingly sought out another bed, where I was so fortunate as to remain in undisturbed possession till the chill of the night air admonished me to be again on the move.

I then arose, and, after much exertion, became at length able to use my limbs, and thus continued my journey. Early dawn found me standing on a height which overlooks the little village of Saverton and the broad river, which was the only barrier between me and safety from my enemies. As the rays of the morning began to expand with increasing light, the dark outlines of the wooded bottoms of Illinois were distinctly visible. I had now seen with my eyes the land of peace, and a land which contained family, friends, and all that was dear to me; but oh, if I should be intercepted at the ferry, and thus lose at once my labor and my hope! I now knelt down and prayed fervently to God for deliverance, and thanked Him for the past, and for His mercy and providence which had preserved me thus far.

I then descended from the height and entered the town, the people yet being wrapt in repose. I examined the shore and soon convinced myself that no public ferry was kept there. I was extremely glad to learn this fact—being fully aware that by this time all the ferries would be watched. I next tried to find some road or path up the river bank, so as to pass along and obtain the use of some chance canoe, but this was impossible. Huge rocks and mountainous steeps, with alternate ditches or patches of mire, rendered it impossible, even for a footman, to pass up the bank of the river. I then made my way down along the sandy beach which lay before the town, and just as the people were beginning to stir, I left the town and continued down along the river for some five miles, sometimes climbing steep and rocky spires of the bluffs, and sometimes wading through mire and marsh.

At length I came to a dwelling on the banks of the river, and saw several canoes lying in the water before it. I entered the house and inquired of the lady whether I could get a passage over the river in a canoe. She replied that her husband sometimes set people across, but owing to the swift current, and a large island several miles in length, which lay in the middle of the river, it was a tedious job, for which he never charged less than a dollar; but, however, he was very busy in the harvest field, about a mile distant, and owing to the hurry of the harvest, she did not think he could be prevailed on to do it at any price. I was now ready to faint from extreme heat, and exertion, and hunger, and to walk another mile and back upon an uncertainty was altogether out of the question, to say nothing of the danger of the exposure to which it would subject me.

I cast my eyes towards the canoes and they looked very tempting, and I know not but I might have been tempted to charter one without the leave of the owner, but just then I saw a boy of ten or twelve years of age playing about the water. I asked him if he was accustomed to paddling a canoe. He replied, yes. I then offered him a good price if he would set me across the river. He refused to do this, saying that his parents would whip him for so doing. "But," said he, "I will set you over on to yon big island, which is one mile from here; you can then walk a mile or two through the woods and come to the opposite shore of it, and then shout and make signs to the people on the Illinois shore, who will come across their half of the river and take you from the island." He observed that people had often crossed over in this way. I hardly believed him, but still I thought an uninhabited island was preferable to staying another minute in Missouri.

The boy soon set me over and left me on the shore of the island, pointing out my course as well as he could. I paid him well, and then commenced my overland journey, among nettles, flies, mosquitoes and heat. I was soon entangled in thickets of hazel, thorn and grape vines, which made my progress very slow, as well as extremely laborious and difficult. These, however, were soon intersected with sloughs of mire and water, which could only be crossed with the utmost difficulty, by picking my way on old logs and wood, and sometimes wading in mire and water. After crossing several of these I at length came to one much larger, which I judged was navigable for a steamboat, and I now found, to my inexpressible horror and disappointment, that he had deceived me. I had now no alternative left but to make my way back through the same difficulties I had just passed, and to the shore where he had just left me, and then I should have no other chance but to call and make signs to the Missouri shore, which I had just left with so much joy, and, as I hoped, forever. This was at length accomplished, and I had the inexpressible joy of seeing my sign answered by the same boy, who soon came paddling to me. As soon as his canoe touched the island I bounded into it, and said to him with a determined tone and manner, "you have deceived me, my boy, so now you have to go to the opposite shore if you never went before, and I will then pay you another dollar, which will pay you, even if your parents chasten you for going." We now headed up the current, and, after a painful and laborious exertion of an hour or two, we doubled the cape at the head of the island, and shot off across the river at a rapid rate.

We soon landed in the woods in a low bottom, with no signs of inhabitants, although while crossing I had seen some houses on the shore a mile or two below. I now paid the boy his dollar, and he pushed off and commenced his way back exceedingly well pleased. I immediately stepped a few paces into the woods, and, kneeling down, kissed the ground as a land of liberty, and then poured out my soul in thanks to God. I then arose and made my way down the river for some two miles through woods and swamps, and finally came to a house. I entered it, determined to call for something to eat; no one was in but a little boy, but he said his mother would be in in two or three minutes. I asked him for some milk, and he gave me a vessel which was full, probably containing between one and two quarts. I intended only to taste of it to keep me from fainting, and then wait till the woman came, and ask her leave to drink the remainder, as it was all she had; but once to my famishing mouth it never ceased to decrease till it was all swallowed; I now felt somewhat abashed and mortified at what I had done, but concluded money would pay all damages. Hearing the footsteps of the woman at the door, I was fixing my mouth for an awkward apology, when I heard a sudden scream; on looking up, Mrs. Sabery Granger stood before me, with both hands lifted up in an ecstacy of amazement. I said to her, "be not afraid—handle me and see, for a spirit hath not flesh and bones as you see me have." She exclaimed, "why, good Lord, is that you? Why all the world is hunting you—both friends and enemies; they had almost given you up." She then flew around, scolded the children, talked to the ducks and chickens to keep out of the house and out of the garden, and not stray off. She washed my feet, gave me some clean stockings, got me some dinner, told me a thousand things about our friends, asked five hundred questions, laughed, cried and again scolded the children and chickens.

This over and dinner eaten, she on with her bonnet and accompanied me to her husband, who was clearing a small spot of land near by. (I had forgotten to say that this woman had been one of our nearest neighbors in Ohio for several years.) Her husband now dropped his work, and accompanied me as a guide for five miles across a wet, low, untimbered bottom, covered mostly with high grass and stagnant water, and entirely destitute of shade or refreshment of any kind. The air was now extremely sultry, and the sun poured in scorching beams, while we could get no water to drink, nor any rest or retreat for a moment. To sit down in the tall grass under these scorching rays, without a breath of wind, would be overwhelming.

I had not proceeded more than a mile or two before I became so weak and faint that I could hardly speak or stand, and parched with a burning thirst. I was upon the point of lying down in the hot and stagnant water, but he took me by the arm and partly supported me, and drew me along for some distance, exhorting and begging of me to try my utmost to hold up a little longer. In this way I finally reached the upland and the shade of a fence, within about half a mile of a settlement of the Saints and other citizens, which extended along the bluff. I dropped down under the shade of this fence, and fainted entirely away; the man ran to the house of a Brother Brown and got some cool spring water and a little camphor, and was returning with it. Sister Brown, who had never seen me, came running before him to my relief; while they were yet distant I had partly come to, and feeling a dreadful faintness at my stomach, and a raging thirst which knew no bounds, I made an effort to arise and run towards them, at the same time making signs for them to hasten; I staggered a few paces like a drunken man, and again fell to the earth. This singular appearance, and my dirty clothes and long beard so frightened the woman that, instead of hurrying, she halted till the man came up with her, and then she exclaimed, "It cannot be Elder Pratt, of whom I have heard so much—it must be some old drunkard." But the man assured her it was me, and they then came on together. They bathed my temples and wrists in cold water and camphor, and finally gave me a spoonful or two at a time to drink. In about half an hour I was so far revived as to be able to arise and be led to the house. I then shaved and washed myself, and borrowed a change of linen, and got into a comfortable bed.

Next morning I felt quite refreshed, and, after resting through the day, I was so far recruited as to be able to mount a horse at evening and ride towards Quincy, which was still twenty-five miles distant. Brother Brown furnished me a good horse and saddle, and himself another, and we started for Quincy in high spirits just as the sun was setting. We rode on at a brisk rate, and arrived in Quincy at about two o'clock the next morning. Riding up to the dwelling which (from the partial recollection

of Mr. Brown, as well as from the fact of my two Missouri cows lying before it quietly chewing their cud) we judged was my wife's residence, we
dismounted and gave a gentle knock at the door. She had watched for
four successive nights and most of the fifth, and had now just lain down
and given up all for lost. On hearing the knock she sprang from bed and
opened the door, and in another instant I had clasped her in my arms.

Chapter 35

Opinions of the Press

EXTRACTS FROM THE "COLUMBIA PATRIOT"—"BANNER OF LIBERTY"—"BOONE'S LICK DEMOCRAT"—"SATURDAY NEWS"—"MISSOURI REPUBLICAN"—"NEW YORK SUN"—"QUINCY ARGUS"—MINUTES OF A PUBLIC MEETING IN QUINCY—"NEW YORK COMMERCIAL ADVERTISER"—PUBLIC MEETING IN NEW YORK—CLOSING REMARKS.

Extract of a letter from A. W. Turner, member of the Legislature of Missouri, dated City of Jefferson, November 31st, 1838, originally published in the *Columbia* (Missouri) *Patriot:*

"The Mormon war is the most exciting subject before the Legislature or the community; it involves an inquiry the most critical of any ever presented to the Legislature of this country; one in which the rights of a portion of the free citizens of the State is concerned, on the one side, and the rights of another portion of the same citizens on the other. Upon the decision of this subject the character of the State is suspended. If, upon full investigation, it is found (and reported by the committee to the Legislature) that the Mormons are not the aggressors, and that some of them have been murdered, others driven from the State by military force, and others imprisoned by order of the Executive, then our character will be established as the most lawless invaders of religious and civil rights."

Will the public believe that, with the foregoing view of the subject, the Legislature avoided an investigation?

The following is from a Missouri paper, printed in Callaway County, entitled *The Banner of Liberty:*

"The Governor of Missouri has negotiated a State loan with the Bank of Missouri, of three hundred and forty thousand dollars. Of this sum, two hundred thousand dollars are to go towards paying the expense of the troops called out to *drive the Mormons from the State.*"

The following is taken from the *Boone's Lick Democrat,* a Missouri paper, under date of January 9, 1839:

"A letter under date of the 29th of November, 1838, has been written by Michael Arthur, of Clay County, to the delegation from that county in the General Assembly now in session, from which the following is an extract: 'Humanity to an injured people prompts me at present to address you this.

"'You were aware of the treatment to some extent before you left home, received by that unfortunate race of beings called Mormons, from devils in the form of human beings; inhabiting Davies, Livingston and part of Ray Counties.

"'Not being satisfied with a relinquishment of their rights, as citizens and human beings, in the treaty forced upon them by General Lucas, of giving up their arms and throwing themselves upon the mercy of the State and their fellow citizens generally (hoping thereby to gain protection of their lives and property); they are now receiving treatment from those demons which makes humanity shudder, and the cold chills run over any man not entirely destitute of humanity.

"'These demons are now strolling up and down Caldwell County in small companies armed, insulting the women in any and every way, and plundering the Mormons of all the means of sustenance (scanty as it was) left them, driving off their cattle, horses, hogs, etc., and rifling their houses and farms of everything thereon; taking beds, bedding, wardrobes, and such things as they see they want—leaving the Mormons in a starving and naked condition. These are facts I have from authority that cannot be questioned, and can be maintained and substantiated at any time.'"

The following appeared in the St. Louis (Mo.) *Saturday News.* The reader may draw his own contrast between the two statements:

"THE MORMONS—That self-afflicted class of people who has chosen the fancy name of Mormons has elicited some sympathy and well intended compassion from some of our charitable citizens, and two meetings have been called to devise means of relieving their present wants. Although many of the Mormons deserve hanging, as an atonement for their criminal proceedings and corrupt intentions, they are truly objects of charity.

"But if this intrinsically vagrant race (the Mormons) would relieve themselves from the humiliating necessity of asking charity, they should mind their own business, * * * abandon abolition, and apply themselves to hard labor, as those do who are actively engaged in attempting their relief.

"No attempt should be made to retain a single Mormon within the boundaries of Missouri. A colonization society might find advantageous employment in sending them all off to Botany Bay."

The following resolves were adopted at a public meeting of the people of Davies County, Missouri, and published in one of the journals of the State:

"1st. *Resolved,* That we esteem the laws of our country our great bulwark, and the only safe refuge to protect us in this and every other emergency.

"2d. *Resolved,* That we highly approve of the course of the Executive in placing Gen. Clark in command of the forces ordered out AGAINST THE MORMONS, and that his orders to EXTERMINATE AND DRIVE THEM FROM THE STATE was dictated by the imperious duty of his office as Governor of the State."

The following is from the *Missouri Republican,* published at St. Louis:

"To show our readers the amount of injury which is now inflicted on the character of our State, and which there is no means of repelling (the Legislature having refused to inquire into the matter), we copy the following from the proceedings of a public meeting held in Quincy, Illinois, as published in the *Quincy Whig* of the 2d. inst:

"'Mr. Sidney Rigdon rose and read the memorial which his people had presented to the Legislature of Missouri, and other documents, going to show the absence of all law and justice in the course the Missouri authorities had pursued toward them, from Governor Boggs down to the lowest grade of officers.'"

"After another had addressed the meeting the same account says: 'Mr. Rigdon again took the floor, and in a very eloquent and impressive manner related the trials, sufferings and persecutions which his people have met with at the hands of the people of Missouri. We saw the tears standing in the eyes of many of his people while he was recounting their history of woe and sorrow, and, in fact, the gentleman himself was so agitated at different periods of his address that his feelings would hardly allow him to proceed.'

"We are satisfied that his address will have a lasting and good effect, sustained, as it was, by the public documents which he produced.

"We will not attempt to follow him through the cold blooded murder, by the mob of Missouri, of Mormon men and children, the violation of females, the destroying of property, the burning of houses, etc.

"In vain may the press in Missouri protest against these representations. In vain may we declare that Rigdon and his followers were doing injustice, misrepresenting and slandering our people, their institutions and officers, etc., the public abroad will judge us by the course of our Legislature. We have made our bed and must lie down on it.

"A friend, residing in Lafayette County, a few days since called our attention to reports in circulation in New York seriously affecting the character of the State, growing out of this subject, and requesting us to contradict them. Most cheerfully would we undertake the task, but we know it is hopeless."

The following is from the New York *Sun*. After giving some extracts from St. Louis papers, showing the outrages of the people of Missouri against the Mormons, the editor proceeds thus:

"That Captain Bogart must be very much like a blackguard and a coward, if he is not a decided candidate for both titles. He was one of those who started the horrible stories of the 'cutting up of Missourians, fifty at a hatch, by the Mormons.' Probably he ran away from his company, and imagined the horrible stories he carried. The shooting down of a flag staff bearing a flag of truce is characteristic of the bravery of a coward, when backed by 3,000 men against 700.

"They must have a primitive mode of administering justice in Missouri. These Mormons are as much citizens as the others, and yet, without trial, upon the *ex parte* testimony of the persons who had provoked the Mormons to retaliation, the Governor issues orders, if we understand the case, for the expulsion of the Mormons from the State of Missouri.

"The Emperor of Russia, the Shah of Persia, or the Sultan of Turkey could not embrace in his own person more legislative, judicial and executive power than is here assumed. Legislative, in the enactment and promulgation of an edict of banishment. Judicial—extra judicial—in sentencing them to banishment under it. Executive, in summoning the force of the State to put in force his own judgment upon his own edict. Well done, Governor Boggs!

"We are sorry to hear of the massacre of the Mormons by the armed mob; however, this violence, being the natural promptings of infuriated men, is positively less culpable than the cool ignorance and impudent, illegal assumption of the Governor of Missouri."

From the *Quincy* (Ill.) *Argus*, March 16, 1839:

"We give in today's paper the details of the recent bloody tragedy acted in Missouri—the details of a scene of terror and blood unparalleled in the annals of modern, and, under the circumstances of the case, in ancient history; a tragedy of so deep, and fearful, and absorbing interest that the very life blood of the heart is chilled at the simple contemplation. We are prompted to ask ourselves if it be really *true* that we are living in an enlightened, a humane and civilized age, in an age and quarter of the world boasting of its progress in everything good and great, honorable, virtuous and high minded; in a country, of which, as American citizens, we could ask whether we are living under a Constitution and laws, or have not rather returned to the ruthless times of the stern Atilla—to the times of the fiery Hun—when the sword and flame ravaged the fair fields of Italy and Europe, and the darkest passions held full revel in all the revolting scenes of unchecked brutality and unbridled desire?

"We have no language sufficiently strong for the expression of our indignation and shame at the recent transaction in a sister State, and that State *Missouri*, a State of which we had long been proud, alike for her men and history, but now so *fallen*, that we could wish her star stricken out from the bright constellation of the Union. We say we know of no language sufficiently strong for the expression of our shame and abhorrence of her recent conduct. She has written her own character in letters of blood, and stained it by acts of merciless cruelty and brutality that the waters of ages cannot efface. It will be observed that an organized mob, aided by many of the civil and military officers of Missouri, with Governor Boggs at their head, have been the prominent actors in this business, incited too, it appears, against the Mormons by political hatred, and by the additional motives of plunder and revenge. They have but too well put in execution their threats of extermination and expulsion, and fully wreaked their vengeance on a body of industrious and enterprising men, who had never wronged or wished to wrong them, but, on the contrary, had ever comported themselves as good and honest citizens, living under the laws and having the same rights with themselves, to *the sacred immunities of life, liberty and property.*"

"PUBLIC MEETING:

"Wednesday, Feb. 27, 1839. 6 P.M.

"The members of the Democratic Association, and the citizens of Quincy generally, assembled in the court house, to take into consideration the state and condition of the people called 'The Latter-day Saints,' and organized the meeting by appointing Gen. Leach, chairman, and James D. Morgan, secretary.

"Mr. Whitney, from the committee appointed at a former meeting, submitted the following report:

"The select committee, to whom the subject was referred, of inquiring into and reporting the situation of the persons who have recently arrived from Missouri; and whether their circumstances are such that they would need the aid of the citizens of Quincy and its vicinity, to be guided by what they might deem the principles of an expanded benevolence, have attended to the duties assigned them, and have concluded on the following

REPORT:

"The committee believe that their duties at this time and on this occasion, are all included within the limits of an expanded benevolence and humanity, and which are guided by that charity which 'never faileth.' From the facts already disclosed, independent of the statement furnished by the committee, they feel it their duty to recommend to this association that they adopt the following resolutions:

"*Resolved,* That the strangers recently arrived here from the State of Missouri, known by the name of The Latter-day Saints, are entitled to our sympathy and kindest regard; and that we recommend to the citizens of Quincy to extend to them all the kindness in their power to bestow, as to persons who are in affliction. * * *

"*Resolved,* That the committee last aforesaid be instructed to use their utmost endeavors to obtain employment for all these people who are able and willing to labor; and also to afford them all needful, suitable and proper encouragement. * * *

"All of which is submitted.

"J. W. WHITNEY, *Chairman.*

QUINCY, *February 27, 1839.*

"Mr. Rigdon then made a statement of the wrongs received by the Mormons from a portion of the people of Missouri, and of their present suffering condition.

"On motion of Mr. Bushnell, the report and resolutions were laid upon the table till tomorrow evening.

"On motion of Mr. Bushnell, the meeting adjourned to meet at this place on tomorrow evening at seven o'clock."

"Thursday evening, Feb. 28.

"Met, pursuant to adjournment.

"The meeting was called to order by the chairman.

"On motion of Mr. Morris, a committee of three was appointed to take up a collection; Messrs. J. T. Holmes, Whitney and Morris were appointed.

"The committee subsequently reported that $48.25 cents had been collected.

"On motion the amount was paid over to the committee on behalf of the Mormons.

"On motion of Mr. Holmes, a committee of three, consisting of S. Holmes, Bushnell and Morris, was appointed to draw up subscription papers and circulate them among the citizens, for the purpose of receiving contributions in clothing and provisions.

"On motion, six were added to that committee.

"On motion of J. T. Holmes, J. D. Morgan was appointed a committee to wait on the Quincy Grays, for the purpose of receiving subscriptions.

"Mr. Morgan subsequently reported that $20 had been subscribed by that company.

"The following resolutions were then offered by J. T. Holmes:

"Resolved, That we regard the rights of conscience as natural and inalienable, and the most sacred guaranteed by the Constitution of our free Government.

"Resolved, That we regard the acts of all mobs as flagrant violations of law, and those who compose them individually responsible, both to the laws of God and man, for every depredation committed upon the property, rights, or life of any citizen.

"Resolved, That the inhabitants upon the western frontier of the State of Missouri, in their late persecutions of the class of people denominated Mormons, have violated the sacred rights of conscience, and every law of justice and humanity.

"Resolved, That the Governor of Missouri in refusing protection to this class of people, when pressed upon by a heartless mob, and turning upon them a band of unprincipled militia, with orders encouraging their

extermination, has brought a lasting disgrace upon the State over which he presides.

"The resolutions were supported in a spirited manner by Messrs. Holmes, Morris and Whitney.

"On motion, the resolutions were adopted.

"On motion, the meeting then adjourned.

"SAMUEL LEACH, *Chairman.*

"J. D. MORGAN, *Secretary.*"

From the New York *Commercial Advertiser.*

"MEETING IN BEHALF OF THE MORMONS

"Last evening, pursuant to public notice, a large meeting assembled at National Hall, to listen to the recital of the wrongs and sufferings of the Mormons, and to devise means for the relief of their women and children.

"The meeting was organized by placing Mr. Charles King in the chair, and Mr. Marcus Spring as Secretary. The Chairman having briefly stated the object of the meeting, and read the circular letter signed by Governor Carlin, of Illinois; Senator Young, from that State, and other residents, vouching for the trustworthiness of Mr. Green, who is deputed by this people to make their case known to the country, the Chairman introduced Mr. Green to the meeting.

"Mr. Green proceeded to give a plain, unadorned, and, as is believed, unexaggerated narrative of the settlement of the Mormons in Missouri, of the constant outrages to which they were subjected, and the series of persecutions which were only ended by their forcible expulsion from the State; and the surrender, without compensation, of the lands and houses they had acquired by their own money, or built with their own hands.

"Mr. Green was himself an actor and witness in many of the scenes he described, and he related them without any attempt at ornament or appeal to passion.

"When Mr. Green took his seat, Joseph Blunt, Esq., addressed the meeting with ability and great effect, and offered the resolutions that will be found below. He was eloquently followed and seconded by Hiram Ketchum, Esq. The resolutions were further supported by several speakers, among whom were Dr. D. M. Reese and W. L. Stone, Esq.; when the question was taken on them separately, and they were carried almost without a dissenting voice.

"Upon a suggestion from the Chair, that as the wants of the sufferers were urgent, good might arise from some immediate contributions—a mechanic in his working jacket stood up, saying that having often witnessed the good effects of example on such occasions, he proposed, although, as he added, the sum he could give was humble, if nine others would do likewise, to give five dollars, and immediately walked up to the table and deposited the money. The challenge was accepted by several others, and a sum exceeding fifty dollars was collected on the spot.

"The meeting then adjourned, it being understood that, the committee named to receive and distribute contributions would at once enter upon their duties.

"*Resolved,* That as Americans, we have heard with shame and indignation the narrative given by Mr. Green of the persecutions, sufferings and lawless violence of which a body of American citizens have been the subjects and the victims, for no other apparent cause than that without hinderance to others, or violation of any law of the land, they had acted upon the right guaranteed them by the Constitution of the United States of a free exercise of religion.

"*Resolved,* That, without meaning to express any opinion whatever, as to the religious views or practices of the Mormons as a sect, we condemn and desire to bear our testimony against mob law, lynch law and all other forms of outrage and violence where an excited populace becomes at once jury, judge and executioner.

"*Resolved,* That the Mormons, as wronged, persecuted, exiled and defrauded Americans, are entitled to the sympathy and support of their countrymen; and that especially in behalf of the women and children, driven from their homes at the point of the bayonet, we appeal to the known benevolence of our fellow citizens at large for pecuniary aid.

"*Resolved,* That the Chairman and Secretary be a committee, with power to add to their numbers, to obtain subscriptions in aid of the women and children of the Mormons; such subscriptions to be applied after due investigation by the committee themselves.

"*Resolved,* That these resolutions be signed by the Chairman and Secretary, and published in the newspapers.

"CHARLES KING, *Chairman.*

"MARCUS SPRING, *Secretary.*"

From the foregoing numerous extracts the public can see that my horrible tale of woe is not a fiction; but an awful reality. I might fill a volume with similar quotations from the public journals of every part of the Union, but I forbear, with the full conviction that the foregoing are

sufficient to show that an impartial public, who stand entirely unconnected with our Society, as religionists, bear out my narrative in its
awful tale of woe and suffering; and I now submit the subject to the
perusal of all people, willing to meet my statements in the foregoing at
the bar of Him who knows all secret things, and who judges righteously.

Chapter 36

Being once more at liberty, and in the enjoyment of the society of family and friends, I spent a few days in rest and refreshment, and in receiving the congratulations of my friends and fellow citizens. My house was thronged from day to day, not only with my old acquaintances and fellow exiles, but with strangers of every sect and party, all anxious to see a martyr, as it were, who had been so wonderfully and miraculously delivered from bondage and death in their most terrible forms.

After a few days spent in this way, we removed to Nauvoo, a new town, about fifty miles above Quincy. Here lived President Joseph Smith and many of the refugees who had survived the storm of persecution in Missouri. It had been already appointed as a gathering place for the scattered Saints, and many families were on the ground, living in the open air, or under the shade of trees, tents, wagons, etc, while others occupied a few old buildings, which they had purchased or rented. Others, again, were living in some old log buildings on the opposite side of the Mississippi, at a place called Montrose, and which had formerly served the purpose of barracks for soldiers.

The hardships and exposures consequent on the persecutions, caused a general sickness. Here and there, and in every place, a majority of the people were prostrated with malignant fevers, agues, etc.

When we first arrived we lived in the open air, without any other shelter whatever. Here I met brother Joseph Smith, from whom I had been separated since the close of the mock trial in Richmond the year previous. Neither of us could refrain from tears as we embraced each other once more as free men. We felt like shouting hosannah in the highest, and giving glory to that God who had delivered us in fulfilment of His word to His servant Joseph the previous autumn, when we were being carried into captivity in Jackson County, Missouri. He blessed me with a warmth of sympathy and brotherly kindness which I shall never forget. Here also I met with Hyrum Smith and many others of my fellow prisoners with a glow of mutual joy and satisfaction which language will never reveal. Father and Mother Smith, the parents of our Prophet and President, were also overwhelmed with tears of joy and congratulation; they wept like children as they took me by the hand; but, O, how different from the tears of bitter sorrow which were pouring down their cheeks as they gave us the parting hand in Far West, and saw us dragged away by fiends in human form.

After the gush of feelings consequent on our happy meeting had subsided, I accompanied Joseph Smith over the Mississippi in a skiff to visit some friends in Montrose. Here many were lying sick and at the point of death. Among these was my old friend and fellow servant, Elijah Fordham, who had been with me in that extraordinary work in New York City in 1837. He was now in the last stage of a deadly fever. He lay prostrate and nearly speechless, with his feet poulticed; his eyes were sunk in their sockets; his flesh was gone; the paleness of death was upon him; and he was hardly to be distinguished from a corpse. His wife was weeping over him, and preparing clothes for his burial.

Brother Joseph took him by the hand, and in a voice and energy which would seemingly have raised the dead, he cried: "BROTHER FORDHAM, IN THE NAME OF JESUS CHRIST, ARISE AND WALK." It was a voice which could be heard from house to house and nearly through the neighborhood. It was like the roaring of a lion, or the heavy thunderbolt. Brother Fordham leaped from his dying bed in an instant, shook the poultices and bandages from his feet, put on his clothes so quick that none got a chance to assist him, and taking a cup of tea and a little refreshment, he walked with us from house to house visiting other sick beds, and joining in prayer and ministrations for them, while the people followed us, and with joy and amazement gave glory to God. Several more were called up in a similar manner and were healed.

Brother Joseph, while in the Spirit, rebuked the Elders who would continue to lay hands on the sick from day to day without the power to heal them. Said he: "It is time that such things ended. *Let the Elders either obtain the power of God to heal the sick or let them cease to minister the forms without the power.*"

City of Nauvoo, Illinois

Nauvoo and the temple, from a daguerreotype, 1846

After these things I joined with brother Kimball in purchasing some land in the contemplated city of Nauvoo, which was then a wilderness, and both of us went to work together with our own hands to build us a log house each. After toiling a few days in this manner I sold out my improvement and prepared for a mission to England, as our quorum were now appointed to visit that country.

On the 29th of August, 1839, I took leave of my friends in Nauvoo and started for a foreign land. I was accompanied by my wife and three children (having obtained my son Parley from his nurse, Mrs. Allen), and Elders Orson Pratt and Hiram Clark. We journeyed in our own private carriage, drawn by two horses. Our route lay through the wild and but partially inhabited countries of Illinois, Indiana and Michigan, for about five hundred and eighty miles, to Detroit, the capital of the State of Michigan, situated at the head of Lake Erie.

The first day we rode seventeen miles through a beautiful plain, or prairie. Our route was a most delightful one.

On all sides, as we turned our eyes, we beheld a boundless field of grass and flowers, with here and there a small grove of timber; the landscape was level or diversified with gentle swells; the surface smooth as a garden; the soil extremely rich; and, although there was no road marked by art, yet our carriage rolled as smoothly and easily as if it had been on a railway. Most of this delightful prairie was without inhabitants, and could, probably, have been purchased for one dollar and a quarter per acre.

It is well calculated for the purposes of agriculture, producing in richest profusion, when cultivated, almost every kind of grain and grass, and every vegetable suited for the climate.

After travelling seventeen miles through this delightful scenery, we arrived in Carthage, a flourishing village. Here we stopped for the night with a member of our Society, who received us kindly; and at evening preached in a large court room to an attentive audience. Next day we rode some twenty-five miles through a similar country, and at evening arrived at a fine village called Macomb. Here we were kindly entertained over Sabbath by a brother Miller. We preached in the court house.

My brother Orson and brother Clark went still ahead about thirty miles, where they preached on Sunday. On Monday morning we started and rode thirty miles through a delightful country.

Sometimes we were in the midst of flourishing farms and villas, and sometimes the wild deer would startle from their grazing at our approach, and go bounding over the wild expanse till lost in the distance.

In the evening we arrived at the house of my brother, Wm. Pratt, where we found brothers Orson Pratt and Clark. We preached at a neighboring house, which was crowded by an attentive congregation. Next morning we rode eight miles to Canton, and found some Saints who persuaded us to stay till morning. We consented; and in the evening preached to the people who crowded the house and yard, and who seemed very anxious to hear more.

Continuing our journey we came next day to Peoria, thirty miles; a flourishing town on the Illinois River. Here we tarried with one of the members of the Church, and were kindly entertained. Next day made thirty miles, and, providentially, stopped for the night at the house of the only member of our Society in that region. When he learned who we were he welcomed us, and finally prevailed upon us to stay two or three days, after which we blessed him and his household and departed.

We then journeyed about thirty-three miles every day for four weeks, and at length found ourselves within part of a day's journey of Detroit. Here we found several small branches of the Church; and being worn down with our journey, we tarried with them six days, during which we ministered the gospel. Brother O. Pratt, in particular, preached in several towns to large and attentive audiences. Taking leave of the brethren, we rode to Detroit, where I found my brother Anson Pratt and family; whom I had not seen for many years, and also my aged father and mother, who were now living with him. My father was now about seventy years of age, and was on his death bed with a heavy fever. We tarried with them two weeks; during which I preached in the City Hall at Detroit, and superintended some printing and publishing matters.

While here we sold our horses and carriage, and at length took leave of our kindred and a last farewell of our sick father, and took passage on a steamboat down Lake Erie to Buffalo; distance three hundred miles.

Previous to our departure from Detroit brothers O. Pratt and Clark took leave of us, and passed down the lake into Ohio; intending to meet us again at New York.

After landing safe in Buffalo, we took the Erie Canal and railroad to Albany—distance three hundred and fifty miles; thence to New York by steamer down the Hudson River—distance one hundred and fifty miles. Here we arrived in safety after a journey of about one thousand four hundred miles. We were received by the Saints in New York almost as one of the old saints risen from the dead. I had been absent nearly two years, during which time I had lain eight months in prison. Brother Adison Everett, a High Priest of the Church in that city and one of the first members I had baptized there, related to me that the Church in that city were assembled in prayer for me on the evening of the 4th of July previous, that I might be delivered from prison and from my enemies in Missouri. When, on a sudden, the spirit of prophecy fell on him, and he arose and declared to the Church that they might cease their prayers on that subject; "For," said he, *"on this moment brother Parley goes at liberty."*

We found the Church in New York strong in the faith, and rejoicing in the truth. They had become numerous in the city and in several parts of the country around.

In this city I resided with my family some six months, during which I preached most of the time in the city, and also superintended the printing and publishing of several of our books. I also performed occasional missions in the country; I visited Long Island, New Jersey, Philadelphia and the City of Washington. In this latter place I published an address in a printed circular to each member of Congress, and to the President of the United States and his Cabinet, setting forth our principles in plainness, and bearing testimony of the truth; while, at the same time, our petitions for redress were pending before them—President Joseph Smith and others having visited them in person, with an earnest appeal for investigation and redress of our grievances in Missouri. In Philadelphia I had the happiness of once more meeting with President Smith, and of spending several days with him and others, and with the Saints in that city and vicinity.

During these interviews he taught me many great and glorious principles concerning God and the heavenly order of eternity. It was at this time that I received from him the first idea of eternal family organization, and the eternal union of the sexes in those inexpressibly endearing relationships which none but the highly intellectual, the refined and pure in heart, know how to prize, and which are at the very foundation of everything worthy to be called happiness.

Till then I had learned to esteem kindred affections and sympathies as appertaining solely to this transitory state, as something from which the heart must be entirely weaned, in order to be fitted for its heavenly state.

It was Joseph Smith who taught me how to prize the endearing relationships of father and mother, husband and wife; of brother and sister, son and daughter.

It was from him that I learned that the wife of my bosom might be secured to me for time and all eternity; and that the refined sympathies and affections which endeared us to each other emanated from the fountain of divine eternal love. It was from him that I learned that we might cultivate these affections, and grow and increase in the same to all eternity; while the result of our endless union would be an offspring as numerous as the stars of heaven, or the sands of the sea shore.

It was from him that I learned the true dignity and destiny of a son of God, clothed with an eternal priesthood, as the patriarch and sovereign of his countless offspring. It was from him that I learned that the highest dignity of womanhood was, to stand as a queen and priestess to her husband, and to reign for ever and ever as the queen mother of her numerous and still increasing offspring.

I had loved before, but I knew not why. But now I loved—with a pureness—an intensity of elevated, exalted feeling, which would lift my soul from the transitory things of this grovelling sphere and expand it as the ocean. I felt that God was my heavenly Father indeed; that Jesus was my brother, and that the wife of my bosom was an immortal, eternal companion; a kind ministering angel, given to me as a comfort, and a crown of glory for ever and ever. In short, I could now love with the spirit and with the understanding also.

Yet, at that time, my dearly beloved brother, Joseph Smith, had barely touched a single key; had merely lifted a corner of the veil and given me a single glance into eternity.

While visiting with brother Joseph in Philadelphia, a very large church was opened for him to preach in, and about three thousand people assembled to hear him. Brother Rigdon spoke first, and dwelt on the Gospel, illustrating his doctrine by the Bible. When he was through, brother Joseph arose like a lion about to roar; and being full of the Holy Ghost, spoke in great power, bearing testimony of the visions he had seen, the ministering of angels which he had enjoyed; and how he had found the plates of the Book of Mormon, and translated them by the gift and power of God. He commenced by saying: "If nobody else had the courage to testify of so glorious a message from Heaven, and of the finding of so glorious a record, he felt to do it in justice to the people, and leave the event with God."

The entire congregation were astounded; electrified, as it were, and overwhelmed with the sense of the truth and power by which he spoke, and the wonders which he related. A lasting impression was made; many souls were gathered into the fold. And I bear witness, that he, by his faithful and powerful testimony, cleared his garments of their blood. Multitudes were baptized in Philadelphia and in the regions around; while, at the same time, branches were springing up in Pennsylvania, in Jersey, and in various directions.

Among the Elders who were instrumental in doing a good work in those regions, I would make honorable mention of Benjamin Winchester, of Philadelphia, since fallen from the faith; and Lorenzo Barnes, who labored and did a great work in Chester County, Penn., and afterwards laid down his life while on a mission in England.

Soon after my arrival in New York City, Elders O. Pratt and Clark, who left us at Detroit, arrived, having performed a mission through some parts of Ohio and New York. Elders Turley, John Taylor, and Wilford Woodruff, had also arrived from the West on their way to England.

Brother Clark and two Elders soon sailed for Liverpool. Brothers Taylor, Woodruff, and Turley, sailed a few weeks afterwards. Brother O. Pratt labored in the country around New York with good success.

Elders Brigham Young, Heber C. Kimball, George A. Smith, and R. Hedlock, also arrived in New York City late in the winter, after performing a long and important journey and mission through the States of Illinois, Indiana, Ohio, and New York.

Finding ourselves together once more, after all our trials and sufferings, we rejoiced exceedingly and praised God for all His mercies to us. During the few days that we were together in New York we held many precious meetings in which the Saints were filled with joy, and the people more and more convinced of the truth of our message. Near forty persons were baptized and added to the Church in that city during the few days of our brethren's stay there.

We held a general Conference, in the "Columbian Hall," previous to our departure, in which the following song, composed by myself, was written expressly for that occasion and sung by those present:

> When shall we all meet again?
> When shall we our rest obtain?
> When our pilgrimage be o'er—
> Parting sighs be known no more;
> When Mount Zion we regain,
> There may we all meet again.
>
> We to foreign climes repair;
> Truth, the message which we bear;
> Truth, which angels oft have borne;

Truth to comfort those who morn.
Truth eternal will remain,
On its rock we'll meet again.

Now the bright and morning star
Spreads its glorious light afar,
Kindles up the rising dawn
Of that bright Millennial morn;
When the Saints shall rise and reign,
Then may we all meet again.

When the sons of Israel come,
When they build Jerusalem;
When the house of God is reared,
And Messiah's way prepared;
When from Heaven he comes to reign,
In the clouds we'll meet again.

When the earth is cleansed by fire;
When the wicked's hopes expire;
When in cold oblivion's shade,
Proud oppressors all are laid;
Long will Zion's Mount remain,
There we all may meet again.

On the 9th of March, 1840, we embarked on board the ship "Patrick Henry," for Liverpool, England. We were accompanied to the water by my family, and by scores of the congregation, of both sexes. We bade them farewell amid many tears, and taking a little boat were soon on board ship—which lay at anchor a short distance from the shore.

From there we could still see the crowd of our friends on the shore, while a wave of their hats and handkerchiefs in the air bid us a last adieu. At twelve o'clock we were under way, being towed by a steamer for some distance until the sails were all unfurled before a fair breeze. The steamer now bade us farewell with three cheers, and we found ourselves fairly under way on the broad expanse of ocean. The sun was soon setting behind a distant promontory, which looked like a dark cloud on the bosom of the ocean: while to the north the distant shores of Long Island were still in view.

Next morning we found ourselves tossing upon a rough sea before the wind with no land in sight. We had a rough passage of twenty-eight days, and on the sixth of April landed in Liverpool, England. Brother

Kimball had been there before; but it was the first time that the other brethren and myself had set our feet on the shores of the old world.

We soon found brother Taylor, who had raised the standard of truth in Liverpool, and had already baptized about thirty. From him we learned that all those who had sailed before us had arrived in safety, and had commenced their missions in various parts with good success. We soon called a general Conference in Preston, where we were enabled to rejoice together with most of our brethren in the ministry.

Thus, through the mercy of God, we have been enabled to fulfil His commands thus far, and have accomplished a journey of five thousand miles under circumstances which would have discouraged any except such as were upheld by the arm of Jehovah.

When we take into consideration the persecution, imprisonment, and banishment, together with the robbing and plundering which has been inflicted upon our people in the West, and the consequent sickness, poverty, and distress to which ourselves, families and friends were reduced, previous to our undertaking this mission—when we consider that it has been opposed by persecution, sword, flame, dungeons, chains, sickness, hunger, thirst, poverty, by death and hell, by men and devils, and all the combined powers of darkness—it would have been no marvel, if, like Paul, we had failed to accomplish the mission at present, and had addressed an epistle to the Church in England, saying, "We would have come unto you once and again, but Satan hindered us."

But this could not take place with us, as it did with Paul, because our mission to Europe was by express command of the Almighty, and therefore it had to be accomplished in spite of men and devils.

One might suppose, from the opposition that it met with, that Satan was aware that if once accomplished, it would result in the ultimate overthrow of his kingdom, and the enlargement of the kingdom of God—which may God grant for Christ's sake.

Chapter 37

GENERAL CONFERENCE AT PRESTON, ENGLAND—PUBLISHING COMMITTEE—
EDITORIAL APPOINTMENT—FIRST NUMBER OF THE "MILLENNIAL STAR" ISSUED—
MY OWN MINISTRY IN MANCHESTER AND VICINITY—NEW HYMN BOOK—ACTION
OF CONGRESS ON THE MISSOURI TRAGEDIES.

On the 15th of April, 1840, a general conference was convened in the "Temperance Hall," Preston, Lancashire, in which thirty-three branches of the Church were represented, including a total of near two thousand members.

In this conference, Elders Brigham Young, Heber C. Kimball and myself were appointed a publishing committee for the Church. I was also appointed editor and publisher of a monthly periodical, to be called the *Millennial Star*.

While the residue of the committee travelled in the ministry, I repaired to Manchester and commenced preparing to fulfil my new appointments.

The first number of the *Star* was issued in May. The following hymn was written by myself expressly for the introduction of this periodical, and originally appeared on its cover:

> The morning breaks, the shadows flee;
>   Lo! Zion's standard is unfurled!
> The dawning of a brighter day
>   Majestic rises on the world.
> The clouds of error disappear
>   Before the rays of truth divine;
> The glory, bursting from afar,
>   Wide o'er the nations soon will shine.
> The Gentile fulness now comes in,
>   And Israel's blessings are at hand;
> Lo! Judah's remnant, cleans'd from sin,
>   Shall in their promised Canaan stand.
> Jehovah speaks! Let earth give ear,
>   And Gentile nations turn and live!

His mighty arm is making bare,
   His covenant people to receive,
Angels from heaven, and truth from earth
   Have met, and both have record borne;
Thus Zion's light is bursting forth,
   To bring her ransomed children home.

While engaged in editing and publishing the *Star* I also preached the gospel continually to vast congregations in and about Manchester, and the spirit of joy, and faith and gladness was greatly increased, and the number of the Saints was multiplied. I also assisted my brethren in selecting, compiling and publishing a hymn book. In this work was contained nearly fifty of my original hymns and songs, composed expressly for the book, and most of them written during the press of duties which then crowded upon me.

In the third number of the *Star*, page 65, is published the final action of the Congress of the United States, on the subject of the outrages committed by the State of Missouri, upon the Church of the Saints. It reads as follows:

"TWENTY-SIXTH CONGRESS, FIRST SESSION

"In Senate of the United States, March 4, 1840. Submitted, laid on the table, and ordered to be printed.

"Mr. Wall made the following report:

"The Committee on the Judiciary, to whom was referred the Memorial of a Delegation of the Latter-day Saints, report:

"The petition of the memorialists sets forth, in substance, that a portion of their sect commenced a settlement in the County of Jackson, in the State of Missouri, in the summer of 1831; that they bought lands, built houses, erected churches and established their homes, and engaged in all the various occupations of life; that they were expelled from that county in 1833 by a mob, under circumstances of great outrage, cruelty and oppression, and against all law, and without any offence committed on their part; and to the destruction of property to the amount of one hundred and twenty thousand dollars; that the society thus expelled amounted to about twelve thousand souls; that no compensation was ever made for the destruction of their property in Jackson County; that after their expulsion from Jackson, they settled in Clay County, on the opposite side of the Missouri River, where they purchased lands, and entered others at the land office, where they resided peaceably for three years, engaged in cultivation and other useful and active employments, when the mob again threatened their peace, lives and property, and they became alarmed, and finally made a treaty with the citizens of Clay County, that they should purchase their lands, and the Saints should remove, which was complied with on their part, and the Saints removed to the County of Caldwell, where they took up their abode, and reestablished their settlement, not without having pecuniary losses and other inconveniences; that the citizens of Clay County never paid them for their lands, except for a small part.

"They remained in Caldwell from 1836 until the fall of 1838; and, during that time, had acquired by purchase from the Government, the settlers and pre-emptionists, almost all the lands in the County of Caldwell, and a portion of the lands in Davies and Carroll Counties— the former county being almost entirely settled by the Saints, and they were rapidly filling up the two latter counties.

"Those counties, where the Saints first commenced their settlements, were for the most part wild and uncultivated, and they had converted them into large and well improved farms, well stocked.

"Lands had risen in value to ten, and even twenty-five dollars per acre; and those counties were rapidly advancing in cultivation and wealth.

"That in August, 1838, a riot commenced, growing out of an attempt of a Saint to vote, which resulted in creating great excitement, and the perpetration of many scenes of lawless outrage, which are set forth in the petition. That they were finally compelled to fly from those counties, and on the 11th of October, 1838, they sought safety by that means, with their families, leaving many of their effects behind. That they had previously applied to the constituted authorities of Missouri for protection, but in vain.

"They allege that they were pursued by the mob, that conflicts ensued, deaths occurred on each side; and, finally, a force was organized under the authority of the Governor of the State of Missouri, with orders to drive the Saints from the State, or to exterminate them. The Saints thereupon determined to make no further resistance; but to submit themselves to the authorities of the State. Several of the Saints were arrested and imprisoned, on a charge of treason against the State; and the rest, amounting to about fifteen thousand souls, fled into other States; principally in Illinois, where they now reside.

"The petition is drawn up at great length, and sets forth with feeling and eloquence the wrongs of which they complain; justifies their own conduct, and aggravates that of those whom they call their persecutors;

and concludes by saying that they see no redress, unless it is obtained of the Congress of the United States, to whom they make their solemn, last appeal, as American citizens, as Christians, and as men; to which decision they say they will submit.

"The committee have examined the case presented by the petition, and heard the views urged by their agent with care and attention; and, after full consideration, unanimously concur in the opinion, that the case presented for their investigation, is not such a one as will justify or authorize any interposition by this Government.

"The wrongs complained of are not alleged to have been committed by any of the officers of the United States, or under the authority of its Government, in any manner whatever. The allegations in the petition relate to the acts of the citizens, and inhabitants, and authorities of the State of Missouri, of which State the petitioners were, at the time, citizens or inhabitants. The grievances complained of in the petition are alleged to have been done within the territory of the State of Missouri. The committee, under these circumstances, have not considered themselves justified in enquiring into the truth or falsehood of the facts charged in the petition. If they are true, the petitioners must seek relief in the courts of judicature of the State of Missouri; or of the United States, which has the appropriate jurisdiction to administer full and adequate redress for the wrongs complained of; and, doubtless, will do so fairly and impartially; or the petitioners may, if they see proper, apply to the justice and magnanimity of the State of Missouri; an appeal which the committee feel justified in believing will never be made in vain by the injured or oppressed. It can never be presumed that a State either wants the power, or lacks the disposition, to redress the wrongs of its own citizens, committed within her own territory; whether they proceed from the lawless acts of her officers, or any other persons.

"The committee therefore report, that they recommend the passage of the following resolution:

"*Resolved,* That the Committee on the Judiciary be discharged from the further consideration of the memorial in this case; and that the memorialists have leave to withdraw the papers which accompany their memorial."

The action of the general Government on this momentous subject, establishes the precedent that there is no power in the Government to carry out the principles of its own Constitution. Fifteen thousand citizens of the United States can be murdered, robbed, plundered, driven from their lands, or disinherited, while the Constitution guarantees to them liberty and protection, *and yet there is no power to protect or reinstate them.* Congress only mocks them by referring them to their murderers for redress. It seems almost superfluous to say that the Saints appealed to a higher tribunal—even the throne of God, where the case is yet pending; and that the Congress of the United States are charged with being accessory to these highest crimes known to the laws of God and man. They hold in fellowship this guilty partner—Missouri—after knowing her to be a wholesale murderer and land pirate.

As the case is yet pending before the court of Heaven, we will drop the subject and proceed with our own history.

Chapter 38

On the 6th of July, 1840, a General Conference was convened at Manchester, in the "Carpenter's Hall," a building which would seat near five thousand people.

There were present of the Twelve Apostles: Brigham Young, H. C. Kimball, Wilford Woodruff, John Taylor, Willard Richards, George A. Smith, and myself. Of other officers: High Priests, 5; Elders, 19; Priests, 15; Teachers, 11; and Deacons, 3.

At this Conference Parley P. Pratt was unanimously chosen President; and William Clayton, Clerk.

Two thousand seven hundred and sixty-seven members were represented, including 254 officers.

The publishing committee had just completed the new Hymn Book, which was presented to the Conference, and accepted by them by unanimous vote.

Three persons were then ordained to the high Priesthood, viz.: Thomas Kington, Alfred Cordon and Thomas Smith; also John Albertson, John Blezord, William Berry, John Sanders, John Parkinson, James Worsley, and John Allen were ordained Elders; seven individuals were ordained to the lesser Priesthood.

Many Elders were also selected and appointed to labor in the ministry in various parts. There was a variety of business transacted, and much instruction given by Brigham Young and others, after which, Conference was adjourned to the 6th of October, at the same place.

During this Conference I received a letter from my family in New York, informing me that they were dangerously ill of scarlet fever. I, therefore, by advice of the other members of the quorum, concluded to cross the ocean once more and bring them to England, where I was likely to remain for several years rather in a stationary position as an editor and publisher. I accordingly repaired immediately to Liverpool and embarked for New York. I was thirty-seven days confined on this dreary passage, without any friends or associates who cared for me or the cause of truth.

I then landed in New York, found my wife and children recovered from their sickness, for which I felt truly thankful. They were agreeably surprised at seeing me so soon and so unexpectedly, and so were the Saints in that city and vicinity. After several joyful meetings among them, I went to the State of Maine on a visit with my wife and children to her parents and kindred. They lived in Bethel, Oxford County, about sixty miles from Portland, the seaport where we landed. The day before our arrival my wife's sister, a Mrs. Bean, prophesied to her husband that Brother Pratt and family would arrive there the next evening, and she actually changed the bedding and prepared the best room for our reception, as if she had received notice of our coming. At this her husband and friends laughed in derision; "for," said they, "our brother-in-law is in England and his family in New York; how, then, will he be here tonight?" But she still persisted, and made ready the room and all things for our reception, assuring them that I would arrive that night with my family.

Night came, the deep shades of evening gathered around, a dark and gloomy night set in, and still no signs of us. They still laughed her to scorn for her superstition, and she still persisted in her anticipations of our momentary arrival. At length, as they were about to retire to rest, we knocked at the door and were joyfully received—it being the first time that any of my wife's kindred there had seen my face.

Mrs. Bean had a dream a few days previous to our arrival, in which she dreamed that I came to her and gave her a key to the Bible. As she related the dream to me, I presented her with my "Voice of Warning." It seemed to her and her husband as they read it as if it was indeed a key to the doctrine and prophecies of the Holy Scriptures. They rejoiced with exceeding joy, and promised to be baptized, and to gather to Nauvoo if God would only open their way to sell their farm.

My father-in-law, Aaron Frost, and household, and all our kindred and many others in that region, received me with joy and hospitality, and I preached several times in their churches.

I finally took leave of them and returned to New York, accompanied by my wife's sister, Olive Frost, a young lady of some twenty years of age, who accompanied us to England to help us in the family.

We soon embarked, and after a long and tedious passage we arrived again in England in October, 1840. My family then consisted of my wife and wife's sister, and my wife's daughter, Mary Ann Stearns, and my sons, Parley and Nathan.

I now again resumed the editorial duties in Manchester, and assisted in the publishing department and in the presidency of the Manchester Conference, and the general Presidency of the work in that country. The *Star* had, during my absence, been edited and published by Elders Young and Richards.

My brother-in-law, Samuel Bean, soon sold out, according to his desires, and started with his family to remove to Nauvoo.

He arrived in Portland, ready to embark, when he heard some lying tales about the "*Mormons,*" as is usual, and being darkened in mind he turned back and bought a farm in Maine, and soon afterwards died without ever obeying the Gospel or gathering with the Saints. His wife and children were left as a widow and orphans to drag out a lonely existence on a farm which was not saleable, and without means to gather with the Saints, and without opportunity to obey the Gospel—a solemn warning to all persons not to delay or neglect a strict and punctual obedience to their convictions.

On the 6th of October, a general Conference convened at Manchester, according to adjournment.

I had hoped to land from America in time to attend it, but was disappointed by contrary winds.

The following members of my quorum were present, viz: Brigham Young, Orson Pratt, Wilford Woodruff, John Taylor, Willard Richards, H. C. Kimball and G. A. Smith; other officers, viz.: High Priests, 5; Elders, 19; Priests, 28; Teachers, 4; and Deacons, 2.

In this Conference, Elder Orson Pratt was called to the chair, and Elder George Walker chosen clerk.

A general representation showed a great increase since the July Conference, and a spread of the work into many parts.

Many ordinations took place; much instruction was given; and many additional missionaries were sent out.

In a few days after this Conference, I landed in safety with my family, and again repaired to Manchester, and resumed the editorial duties; and, in connection with Elder Young, superintended the publishing department.

The October number of the *Star* contains much cheering news of the spread of the work in various parts of the United States, England, Scotland and Isle of Man, and an interesting account of Elder Orson Hyde's appointment on a mission to Jerusalem, in connection with Elder John E. Page.

May the Almighty speed His work, and bless the believers with signs following, and with grace and wisdom to escape all the judgments which await the wicked, and to stand before the coming of the Son of Man; for Christ's sake. Amen.

Thus closed the year 1840 with us and our labors. An eventful year it had been to us, and to the Church of the Saints. It was the first mission of the Twelve modern Apostles, as a quorum, to a foreign country. It had been undertaken under circumstances which would have deterred men of a less holy and sacred calling and responsibility. It had overcome chains and dungeons, and gloomy cells, and perils of robbers and of death. It had triumphed over poverty and sickness, and perils by sea and land. And it had triumphed and been crowned with a success unparalleled, even by the history of the ancient Apostles.

It was the hand of God that performed it, and to his name be ascribed honor and majesty, and power and glory, forever and ever. Amen.

Chapter 39

On the 19th of January, 1841, I visited Bolton for the first time; found
an interesting Society there consisting of about one hundred and thirty
members, including some small branches in the vicinity. They appeared
to be dwelling together in truth and love, and zealously united in the
cause of God and godliness. Their presiding officer is an aged minister by
the name of Crooks, formerly of Stockport; through whose labors the
Society there has grown from a small handful to its present flourishing
condition. The meetings are crowded to excess, and scores of people are
pressing forward and uniting with the Church by repentance and baptism. The Holy Ghost is poured out into their souls, and its fruits are
manifested in their gifts and blessings.

On Wednesday evening, the 20th, I attended one of their meetings,
and had the privilege of addressing a full and attentive audience. The
subject was confined to a few scriptural observations, in which the precepts and promises of Christ were clearly set forth, as contained in the
written word of the New Testament. These were contrasted with the systems of Christianity as they now exist, and the difference was so manifest that the people saw clearly that the religion of Christ was *one thing*,
and modern sectarianism another. This so exasperated some craftsmen
who were present, viz.: a Mr. James Pendlebury, professedly a Primitive
Methodist preacher, and Mr. Thomas Balsham, of the New Connection, that they could no longer hold their peace. For while the sermon
was proceeding, the said Pendlebury arose and began speaking so loud
that the speaker paused and requested the interruption to cease; but was
not heeded, for the intruder with stentorian voice continued to cry out,

saying: "This is a new doctrine, and we cannot believe it without miracles; here is a blind man, heal him; here is a blind man, heal him! You
have preached a new doctrine—a new doctrine, sir, and we want the
proof—we want the proof!" By this time the house was all confusion,
everyone endeavoring to act as moderator. We endeavored from the pulpit to command silence, and expressed our surprise that the New Testament doctrine should be a new doctrine; but we found that it was a new
doctrine to him, as was manifest in his behavior. Indeed, the doctrines
of common law and civilization were to him equally as strange and new
as the doctrine of Christ, for he still continued to disturb the meeting.
The Saints commenced singing, and finally closed the meeting. But
while this was proceeding the riot grew more and more violent, till at
length a form was broken, and some other damage done. While the civil
part of the people were retiring from the room they were variously insulted by him and his comrades, some crying out, "He hath a devil,"
some challenging to debate, and some calling for a miracle. At length a
policeman arrived and took this brave champion into custody, and his
associate, T. Balsham.

These were handcuffed, marched away, and finally held to bail.
Next morning they had a warrant served on them for a breach of the
peace, and were brought before James Arrowsmith, Esq., Mayor, and
five magistrates. An able plea was made by Attorney John Taylor, Esq.,
and a laborious attempt on the part of the prisoners to justify themselves
by the introduction of several witnesses belonging to several different orders of Methodists, whose testimony was more calculated to throw a false
coloring over our doctrine than anything else. At length Pendlebury was
found guilty of a breach of the peace, had to pay for the form and make
good the damages and costs of suit; and was bound in the penal sum of
ten pounds to keep the peace for six months.

It is to be hoped that these prompt measures will put a stop to similar
disturbances in our public worship, and also prove a warning to other
priests not to turn infidels against the doctrines of the New Testament,
and then use such vile measures against the truth.

Since this affair we have heard verbally from Bolton, that many are
embracing the truth and coming to the waters of baptism. May the Lord
shed forth His Spirit upon the people of Bolton, and cause a great work
to be done among them.

During February, about two hundred and forty of the Saints embarked at Liverpool for America, intending to settle with the Saints at
Nauvoo.

An edition of the Book of Mormon, consisting of 5,000 copies, was issued by us at Liverpool during this month.

On the 6th of April, 1841, the Council of the Twelve assembled at Manchester, in the "Carpenter's Hall," for the first time to transact business as a quorum, in the presence of the Church in a foreign land, being the first day of the twelfth year of the rise of the Church of Jesus Christ of Latter-day Saints.

Nine of the quorum were present, viz.: Brigham Young, Heber C. Kimball, Orson Hyde, Parley P. Pratt, Orson Pratt, Wilford Woodruff, Willard Richards, John Taylor, and George A. Smith.

President Young having called the house to order and organized the Conference, then opened by prayer. Elder Thomas Ward was then chosen Clerk. The President then made some introductory remarks relative to the organization of the Church in the house of the Lord in America; in reference to the different quorums; in their respective orders and authorities in the Church.

The representations of the Churches and Conferences throughout the kingdom were then called for. The total numbers of which were as follows: 5,814 members; 136 Elders; 303 Priests; 169 Teachers; and 68 Deacons, besides about 800 souls who had emigrated to America during the year, who were not included in this representation. * * *

Eleven persons were chosen and ordained to the High Priesthood during this Conference, and twelve persons were ordained Elders.

Several new Conferences were also organized, and Presidents were appointed for each Conference in the kingdom.

The names of the several Conferences, with their respective Presidents, were as follows: Manchester, P. P. Pratt; Edinburgh, G. D. Watt; Liverpool, J. Greenhouse; London, Lorenzo Snow; Macclesfield, J. Galley; Staffordshire, A. Cordon; Birmingham, J. Riley; Glasgow, J. McAuley; Gadfield Elm, Thomas Richardson; Preston, P. Melling; Brampton, J. Sanders; Garmay, Levi Richards; Clitheroe, Thomas Ward; Froomes Hill, William Kay.

The business of the Conference being accomplished, several appropriate discourses were delivered by different members of the quorum in relation to the duties of the officers in their respective callings, and in relation to the duties and privileges of the members, also on the prosperity of the work in general. * * *

Elders Young and Miller then sang the hymn, "Adieu, my dear brethren," etc., and President Young blessed the congregation and dismissed them.

This Conference closed the mission of the Twelve for the present in England, and as they were about to take their departure for America, all save myself, an epistle was addressed by them to the Saints in the British Isles. It was written by my own hand, under the direction of the President of the quorum, and signed by each of the nine members present in that country. It was dated at Manchester, April 15, 1841.*

In the month of September, 1841, Brother Amos Fielding and myself chartered a large new ship called the "Tyrean," Captain Jackson, master, for New Orleans. On which we sent two hundred and seven passengers of our Society bound for Nauvoo.

Our chartered ship, the "Tyrean," sailed with two hundred and seven passengers on the morning of the 21st of September. On going out of the dock the previous day, many hundreds crowded around to witness a ship load of the sons and daughters of Zion depart from their native shore for the promised land. They moved slowly out into the river, singing:

> Lovely native land, farewell!
> Glad I leave thee—Glad I leave thee—
> Far in distant lands to dwell.

Next morning they weighed anchor about ten o'clock, and hoisted sail before a fair wind; moving away under the flag of liberty—the American Stars and Stripes.

The emigrants were all on deck, and in good spirits; and as our little boat came off with three hearty cheers, they were singing the favorite hymn:

> How firm a foundation, ye Saints of the Lord,
> Is laid for your faith in His excellent word!

The last lines which we heard, as their voices were lost in the distance, were as follows:

> When through the deep waters I call thee to go,
> The rivers of sorrow shall not thee o'erflow.

Hats and handkerchiefs were still waving in view as a last token of farewell. Soon all was a dim speck upon the ocean; a few moments more

---

*See *Millennial Star*, April, 1841.

and they vanished from view in the wide expanse and lost in the distance. May God speed them onward in their course, and land them safely in their destined port.

The *Star* for October, 1841, contains several other communications of interest; giving cheering accounts of the spread of the work in various places, but we will not record them here.

The November number opens with an editorial on "The Philosophy of the Resurrection," from which we extract the following:

The mysterious works of God in the formation, progress, changes, and final destiny of creation, are all wonderful and miraculous in one sense. The formation of the natural body in embryo, or even of a plant or flower, is as much a miracle as the creation or reorganization of a world or the resurrection of the body. Each effect has its cause, and each cause its effect; and the light, spirit or truth which proceeds from Deity is the law of life and motion; the great governing principle of the whole machinery of the universe, whether natural or spiritual, temporal or eternal. It is the cause of causes; the main spring of nature's time piece. By it we live; in it we move and have a being.

Let man be placed upon a lofty eminence surrounded with the original elements of uncreated worlds; let him contemplate the confused and chaotic mass of unorganized existence; let him hear the voice of truth and power as its first sentence rolls in majesty of wisdom from the lips of Deity; let him behold the first movement of chaos as it begins to come to order.

Let him contemplate its various workings till the heavens and earth, and man and beast, and plant and flower startle into conscious being in all the beauty of joyous existence; let him observe every minute particular of its progress through time in all its various changes; let him contemplate the changing seasons as they roll in hours and days, and months, and years; let his thoughts reach to the starry heavens and view them in all their motions and revolutions; the sun in its daily course; the planets in their annual revolutions; the blazing comet as it moves afar in the wilds of ether, and returns from its journey of a hundred or a thousand years; let him return to earth and view the vegetable kingdom as it blooms and ripens and falls again to decay in the revolving seasons; the time-worn oak of a thousand years, as it braves the tempest, or the modest flower whose life is but a day; let him view the animal creation in all its variety, as it appears and passes in turn from the stage of action; let him contemplate man from his infant formation through all the changes

of his various life till he returns to dust; let him view the laborious revolutions of the groaning earth and its various inhabitants through all
their temporal career, till wearied Nature sinks to rest, and, worn by
slowly rolling years, the earth itself shall die; and lastly, let him contemplate all Nature regenerated, renewed, and starting into being,
while death itself shall conquered be and immortality alone endure.

The vision ended. Man! what hast thou seen?

Nothing out of the ordinary course; all I beheld was Nature moving
in perfect accordance with the law of its existence; not one single devia-
tion or shadow of turning from the immutable laws of truth.

But hast thou seen no miracle?

Yes, it was all miraculous; it was all achieved by the law of light,
which was the immediate power of God; but it was all upon the most natural, easy, simple and plain principles of Nature in its varied order, and
which to call the most miraculous I know not, whether it was the creation of a world, the blossoming of a flower, the hatching of a butterfly,
or the resurrection of the body, and the making of new heavens and a
new earth. All these were so many displays of the power of God.

All these were miraculous.

All these were natural.

All these were spiritual.

All these were adapted to the simplest capacity, aided by the Spirit
of God. All these were too sublime for an archangel to comprehend by
his own capacity, without the spirit of revelation.

On Sunday, October 17, 1841, the Manchester Conference convened at the "Carpenter's Hall." Twelve branches were represented,
consisting of one thousand, five hundred and eight-one members, with
appropriate officers. Many were called to the ministry, and ordained to
their respective offices. Instructions were given in relation to the duties
of the officers, members, etc., and they were particularly exhorted to
abstain from intoxicating drinks, together with tobacco, snuff and all
other evil habits.

After the ordinations, the Saints present partook of the Lord's Supper, and sung and rejoiced together. Several interesting and useful addresses were delivered at evening, and the meeting concluded with a
spirit of joy and satisfaction. The number of officers present at this conference was about one hundred, and members not far from one
thousand.

Some hundreds had emigrated from this conference, and still it numbered near one thousand, five hundred members, all of whom had been gathered in about two years, and that from an obscure beginning in a small basement in Oldham Road, being the first place where the fulness of the Gospel was preached within the bounds of what now comprises the Manchester Conference.

On the 8th of November we sent out the ship "Chaos," with about one hundred and seventy passengers of the Saints.

Cheerfulness and satisfaction seemed to pervade every heart as they bid farewell to their native shores, and set sail for the land of promise.

Several interesting communications were received during the month of November, from various parts of the country, the purport of which was that the sick were healed, the lame walked, the old men dreamed dreams, the young men saw visions, and the Lord's servants and handmaidens spake in tongues and prophesied, while the Lord was showing wonders in heaven above, and signs in the earth beneath— blood, fire and vapor of smoke.

In the meantime, the wicked rage, and the people imagine a vain thing; the priests take counsel together against the Lord and against His anointed ones. The most artful falsehoods ever inspired by Satan continue to flood the country, both from the press and pulpit, and reiterated by those who profess to be followers of Jesus. We went on a short mission to the Isle of Man of late, and after preaching to vast multitudes the plain truth of the Scriptures, they would mock and make light of the Bible, and everything quoted from it.

The priests too were busy in church and chapel, in lying against the Saints, and perverting the written Word, and thus inspiring the people with violence, hatred and every cruel work; yet we found the Saints rejoicing in the truth, and the honest in heart disposed to inquire into it.

We have just returned from a visit to Middlewich and Norwich. In the former place we had a very candid hearing in the magistrate's room, which was filled. In the latter place many hundreds of people assembled at our meeting house, among which were a large number of "Association Methodists" and other professors, with one Thompson at their head, who came possessed of the devil to make disturbance. These made all manner of noises, such as whooping, shouting, laughing, whistling, mocking, etc. They openly hissed and mocked the written Word of Jesus Christ and His Apostles, and made such a noise as to finally break up the meeting; after which they began to rush among the people, and to bellow like bulls, and to run over, and knock down, and trample under foot all who came in their way. We narrowly escaped, but finally got out of their midst. Mr. Thompson then addressed them, justifying and applauding their conduct. The lights were at length extinguished, and the room cleared, but not until some persons were wounded, and some forms broken.

Chapter 40

The following appointment for a General Conference for the British Isles appeared in the March number of the *Star:*

"The several Conferences of the Church of Jesus Christ of Latter-day Saints, in the United Kingdom of Great Britain, are hereby informed that a General Conference will be held in Manchester, to commence on Sunday, the 15th day of May next, and to continue for several days, or until all the business is completed.

"Each Conference is requested to appoint one or more delegates to represent them in the General Conference, and to assist in such business as may be necessary for the general welfare and prosperity of the cause of truth. It is very desirable that a full representation should be made of all the Conferences, branches, and members of this realm.

"P. P. Pratt, *President.*
"Thomas Ward, *Clerk.*"

In the *Star* for March, 1842, the following editorial introduces an extract of a letter from Elder Hyde in Jerusalem:

"We have lately received two lengthy and highly interesting letters from Elder Orson Hyde, dated at Trieste, January 1 and 18, containing a sketch of his voyages and travels in the East; his visit to Jerusalem; a description of ancient Zion; the Pool of Siloam, and many other places famous in Holy Writ; with several illustrations of the manners and customs of the East as applicable to Scripture texts; and several conversations held between himself and some of the Jewish missionaries, etc., in Jerusalem; together with a masterly description of a terrible tempest and thunder storm at sea, with a variety of miscellaneous reflections and remarks, all written in an easy, elegant and masterly style; partaking of the

---

*See *Millennial Star*, October 1842.

eloquent and sublime, and breathing a tone of that deep feeling, tenderness and affection so characteristic of his mission and the spirit of his holy and sacred office.

"Elder Hyde has, by the grace of God, been the first proclaimer of the fulness of the gospel both on the Continent and in far off Asia, among the nations of the East. In Germany, Turkey, Egypt and Jerusalem he has reared, as it were, the ensign of the Latter-day glory, and sounded the trump of truth; calling upon the people of those regions to awake from their thousand years slumber and to make ready for their returning Lord.

"In his travels he has suffered much, and has been exposed to toils and dangers; to hunger, pestilence and war. He has been in perils by land and sea, in perils among robbers, in perils among heathens, Turks, Arabs and Egyptians; but out of all these things the Lord has delivered him, and has restored him in safety to the shores of Europe, where he is tarrying for a little season for the purpose of publishing the truth in the German language—having already published it in French and English in the various countries of the East. And we humbly trust that his labors will be a lasting blessing to Jew and Gentile."

Being about to return to America, I published in the October number of the *Star*, 1842, my Farewell Address, from which I here give a few extracts:

FAREWELL ADDRESS TO OUR READERS AND PATRONS

Brethren and Friends:—As I am about to take leave of the STAR, and give it to the management of others, I feel it necessary to make a few remarks suited to the occasion.

This publication was undertaken two years and six months since. Since that time I have labored diligently, as far as a pressure of other duties would admit, to render it a useful and interesting periodical. I have published the principles of the Latter-day Saints, together with a choice selection of the most interesting items of news in relation to the progress of these principles among men.

I have also endeavored at all times to defend the cause of truth, and to ward off the arrows of envy and slander which have been hurled at the children of light by the strong arm of thousands who speak evil of things they understand not.

I feel great satisfaction in a review of my editorial course; I feel my conscience clear, and a secret whispering within, that I have done my duty faithfully before God.

I also feel to rejoice in the success which has attended the efforts of the servants of God in this country in the publication of truth. At the commencement of the STAR, the Saints in Europe numbered less than two thousand, they now number near ten thousand, besides thousands who have emigrated to a distant land. This, surely, is a great triumph of the truth, when we take into consideration the prejudice and opposition which we have had to encounter. Surely the STAR has stood forth as a beacon on a hill, as a lonely lamp amid surrounding darkness, to light the weary pilgrim on his toilsome journey, and to kindle up the dawn of a day of glory when the effulgent beams of the sun of righteousness shall shine forth as the morning, and dispel the misty vapors which, like a gloomy cloud, have for ages hovered over the pathway of mortals.

Dear Brethren and Sisters—Though I now take leave of the editorial department, and withdraw from the shores of Europe, yet I have the satisfaction of leaving the STAR to shine among you in its full glory, being conducted by one who has a willing heart and a ready pen, and one who, I hope, will be so aided by his patrons and by Divine favor as to be able to conduct it with effect, till its feeble rays shall be lost amid the effulgence of the rising morn.

I now return my sincere thanks to all our agents and patrons, and to all who have in any way contributed to our assistance in this great and good work; and I pray that the blessings of God may rest upon them and upon the thousands who may hereafter peruse this work.

I must now take leave of you for a season, as duty calls me home. I have labored among you in the ministry between two and three years, and for the last eighteen months (since the departure of the rest of the Twelve) I have had the more particular Presidency of the Church in Europe, and as one of old said, "in some measure the care of all the churches."

In this highly responsible trust I have endeavored so to serve you in all things, both temporal and spiritual, and to go in and out among you in the fear of God, exercising judgment, mercy, and charity according to the ability which God has given me. I have endeavored to teach the ignorant, to reclaim the transgressor, and to warn the wicked; to comfort the feeble-minded, to bind up the broken hearted, and to administer to the poor.

I recommend and appoint Elder Thomas Ward as my successor in the office of the General Presidency of the Church in Europe, in connection with Elders Lorenzo Snow and Hiram Clark. To these persons I commit the care and government of the Church in this country for the present, trusting that they will conduct and counsel in all things according to the mind of the Spirit, and according to the counsel which shall be given them from Nauvoo, from time to time, by the quorum of the Twelve, or the first Presidency.

On taking leave of you for a season I take this opportunity to assure you before God, to whom we are all accountable, *that the fulness of the gospel is true, that the Book of Mormon is true, and that the everlasting covenant is true, and will stand when heaven and earth shall pass away.*

I now take a pleasing farewell of the Saints, with a firm conviction that I have labored diligently and done my duty thus far, and I have nothing to regret but my own weaknesses and imperfections, which I trust you will all be willing to forgive, and that God will forgive also.

Please remember me in your prayers, and may the Lord Almighty bless you all, and preserve us faithful to the end, that we may meet again with joy. Amen.

Chapter 41

Between the middle of September and my own embarkation in October, I chartered three vessels for New Orleans, and filled them with the emigrating Saints, viz:

The "Sidney," with one hundred and eighty souls; the "Medford," with two hundred and fourteen souls; and the "Henry," with one hundred and fifty-seven.

I next chartered the "Emerald," on which I placed about two hundred and fifty passengers, including myself and family.

Having finished my present mission in England and taken an affectionate leave of the Saints and friends there, I embarked on the "Emerald," and sailed on the 29th of October. We had a tedious passage of ten weeks, and some difficulties, murmurings and rebellions; but the Saints on board were called together, and chastened and reproved sharply, which brought them to repentance. We then humbled ourselves and called on the Lord, and he sent a fair wind, and brought us into port in time to save us from starvation.

We landed in New Orleans early in January, 1843. Here I chartered a steamer called the "Goddess of Liberty," and took passage with the company for St. Louis. Running up the river for about a week, I landed with my family in Chester, Illinois—eighty miles below St. Louis. The company continued on to St. Louis. My reason for landing here was, that I would not venture into Missouri after the abuses I had experienced there in former times.

Here I wrote the following historical letter, which appeared in the *Star* of April 1, 1843.

CHESTER, STATE OF ILLINOIS,
January 21, 1843.

DEAR BROTHER WARD—I take this opportunity of communicating a few items of news which may be of use to your readers. I arrived here two weeks since with my family. We are all well, except my eldest daughter, Olivia, who has the whooping cough. We are living here a few weeks, waiting for the river to open for Nauvoo. We are comfortably situated, a few yards from the landing, in a stone house in a small village, eighty miles below St. Louis, and three hundred from Nauvoo. Provisions are cheaper than ever; Indian corn is 20 cents per bushel; wheat, 40 cents; flour 3½ dollars per barrel; oats, 15 cents per bushel; pork and beef, from 2 to 3 cents per lb.; butter, 10 cents; sugar, 5 cents; chickens, 8 cents each. Cows, from 8 to 10 and 12 dollars per head; good horses, from 25 to 50 dollars; land, from 1¼ to 4 dollars per acre.

We were ten weeks on the "Emerald," and one in coming up the river. The weather was very fine until the day before we landed, when it became extremely cold and snowy; but after a week of severe weather, it became suddenly warm and pleasant, and it remains so yet—all ice and snow have disappeared, and the weather is like May.

I have not heard from Nauvoo, except by the public prints. From these I learn that brother Joseph Smith gave himself up to the authorities of Illinois, agreeably to the Governor's writ of last fall to attempt to deliver him to the State of Missouri. He was brought by *habeas corpus* before the Judge of the Supreme Court of the United States, and after a trial at Springfield, the seat of Government for Illinois, he was honorably discharged—the Judge deciding that he must not be delivered to the Missouri authorities, according to the demand of the Governors of the two States. Thus, one more malicious lawsuit has terminated in which the rulers have been disappointed and bloodthirsty men have lost their prey—the prophet of the Lord having found protection under the wings of the eagle.

Brother William Smith, Joseph's brother, is a member of the Legislature of Illinois, which is now in session. They have introduced two bills for the purpose of taking away all our Nauvoo charters, but they have both been lost without becoming a law, and the charters still stand good. The first was a bill for the repealing of all city charters in the State (for the avowed object of getting rid of Nauvoo), this bill was lost by a majority of one. Next a bill was introduced to repeal the Nauvoo charter alone. This was too barefaced to be countenanced, and was lost by an overwhelming majority; but not until some warm debating on Mormonism had occupied the house for some time. The fact is, it grieves the enemies of the Saints very much to see them enjoying political privileges in common with others, and every exertion is made to hinder the progress of a people and of principles which they consider as already becoming too formidable to be easily trampled under foot.

I have now been here two weeks, and have minded my own affairs as a private man, in no way seeking to be public, or even to be known. I have spent my time in providing for my family, getting wood for fire, bringing water, etc., together with reading papers, educating my children, etc., and have not mentioned "Mormonism," or any other "ism," or principle, till it was first mentioned to me. Mrs. Pratt and I attended a Presbyterian meeting last Sabbath, and listened in silence to a dry sermon.

But after all my endeavors to be quiet, it is noised abroad, through all parts of the town and surrounding country for twenty-five miles, that a "Mormon" is here. All parties are on tiptoe to hear him preach; the citizens have sent the postmaster to me with a request to hear me, and have opened their chapel for to-morrow, where we heard the Presbyterian last Sabbath. I have consented, and commence my public ministry to-morrow. In the meantime I have lent and sold several books, "Voice of Warning," "Book of Mormon," etc., and these are having the desired effect. The people here were greatly prejudiced against something called "Mormonism;" they knew not what, having never read or heard any of the Saints; indeed they had not the most distant idea of our holding to Christianity in any shape.

Yesterday a brother called here, from twenty-five miles in the country; he had heard of my coming and came to see me. He is a rich farmer, possessing two hundred acres of land well improved. He informed me of a small branch of the Church in his neighborhood, and made an appointment for me to go to George Town (sixteen miles distant), on Monday next, and another to his own house, nine miles further, for Tuesday evening, so you see I am getting into business fast. This man brought me two Nauvoo *Wasps*, the latest of which was printed January 7th. From these I learned that all was peace, industry and prosperity there; a fine hard winter had set in so early that none of our ships' companies which had sailed this season had been able to get up the river to

Nauvoo; they are scattered from New Orleans to St. Louis, and are waiting to swarm Nauvoo in the spring. From the weather, I judge that the river is about opening that far; it is now open above St. Louis.

No one landed here with me but sister Mary Aspen, and my family. Sister A. is with us now, she is well and much pleased with the country; most of our passengers went to St. Louis.

January 26th—Last Sunday, preached twice to an attentive audience. Monday, walked sixteen miles; preached in George Town; good attention. Tuesday, rode ten miles; preached twice among the Saints. Wednesday, baptized two young men; held confirmation meeting, then rode twenty-five miles to this place.

The river is now open, and is twelve feet higher than it was last week, the weather is like May. I start for Nauvoo on horseback to-morrow, my family will follow in two weeks by water. I shall write again soon.

Yours truly, in Christ,

P. P. PRATT.

January 27th, 1843, I started for Nauvoo on horseback, and after a ride of some eight days I arrived there in safety—a distance of some two hundred and eighty miles.

I was astonished to see so large a city all created during my absence, and I felt to rejoice. I visited my brothers Orson and William and their families, by whom I was hospitably entertained. I also visited President Smith and family, who received me with the usual welcome and "*God bless you, Bro. Parley.*"

While on this visit to Nauvoo I was invited to Shockoquon, a small town up the river, a few miles above Nauvoo, in company with President Smith, Elder O. Hyde and others. We started February 15th; stayed over night at a Mr. Russel's. On the next day we dined at McQueen's Mills; visited Shockoquon and returned to the said mills at evening. Here President Smith spoke for about two hours. The crowded congregation seemed deeply interested—most of them being strangers to "*Mormonism.*"

After a few days I returned to my family in Chester County on horseback. The weather being extremely cold the Mississippi did not open till very late in the spring.

I at length sent my family per steamer to St. Louis, and stopped at a hotel myself on the opposite side of the river, in Illinois Town. In this situation we still had to remain for several days awaiting the opening of the river above.

A small steamer arrived, commanded by Captain Dan Jones, and was finally chartered for Nauvoo, and filled with Saints, including my family. I passed by land to Alton, and there went on board.

Captain Jones was a good and kind hearted Welshman, and was much interested in the fulness of the gospel. He soon joined the Church, and was finally ordained and appointed a mission to Wales, where he preached the fulness of the gospel and gathered thousands into the Church.

April 12th we landed in Nauvoo, and were kindly welcomed by President Smith and scores of others, who came down to the wharf to meet us.

My time, from my arrival until the last of the year, was spent in the ministry, and in building, travelling, etc.

Chapter 42

MISCELLANEOUS WRITINGS—MISSION TO THE EAST—IMPRESSIONS OF THE SPIRIT—MARTYRDOM OF JOSEPH AND HYRUM SMITH—SPIRIT OF EXULTATION—RETURN TO NAUVOO—SIDNEY RIGDON DISFELLOWSHIPPED.

January 1, 1844.

In the opening of this year I completed a number of miscellaneous works, some of which were published in pamphlet form. Among these were *"An Appeal to the State of New York,"*—*"Immortality of the Body,"*—*"Fountain of Knowledge,"*—*"Intelligence and Affection,"* and *"The Angel of the Prairies."* This last work was a curious and extraordinary composition, in the similitude of a dream. It was designed as a reproof of the corruptions and degeneracy of our Government, in suffering mobs to murder, plunder, rob and drive their fellow citizens with impunity, etc. It also suggested some reforms. It was read in the presence of President Joseph Smith and a General Council, and was highly applauded; but never appeared in print.

In the spring I went to Boston as a missionary, and on business. I proclaimed the gospel, as usual, while on this journey, on steamers on the lakes and rivers; in the cities of the Atlantic, and in whatever village or neighborhood I had opportunity. Visiting North Bridge, a short distance from Boston, and having a day's leisure, I wrote a dialogue entitled *"Joe Smith and the Devil,"* which was afterwards published in the *New York Herald*, and in various papers in America and Europe. It was finally published and republished in pamphlet form, and had a wide circulation; few persons knowing or mistrusting who was the author.

President B. Young, and most of the members of the quorum of the Twelve, were then on a mission through the Eastern States, as well as myself. While on this mission, on the 27th of June, 1844, a mob murdered the Prophet Joseph Smith, and his brother Hyrum, in a jail at Carthage, Illinois, while Governor Ford had pledged the faith of the State for their protection.

Carthage Jail, Illinois, where the Prophet Joseph Smith and his brother Hyrum were martyred in 1844

A day or two previous to this circumstance I had been constrained by the Spirit to start prematurely for home, without knowing why or wherefore; and on the same afternoon I was passing on a canal boat near Utica, New York, on my way to Nauvoo. My brother, William Pratt, being then on a mission in the same State (New York), happened, providentially, to take passage on the same boat. As we conversed together on the deck, a strange and solemn awe came over me, as if the powers of hell were let loose. I was so overwhelmed with sorrow I could hardly speak; and after pacing the deck for some time in silence, I turned to my brother William and exclaimed—"Brother William, this is a dark hour; the powers of darkness seem to triumph, and the spirit of murder is abroad in the land; and it controls the hearts of the American people, and a vast majority of them sanction the killing of the innocent. My brother, let us keep silence and not open our mouths. If you have any pamphlets or books on the fulness of the gospel lock them up; show them not, neither open your mouth to the people; let us observe an entire and solemn silence, for this is a dark day, and the hour of triumph for the powers of darkness. O, how sensible I am of the spirit of murder which seems to pervade the whole land." This was June 27, 1844, in the afternoon, and as near as I can judge, it was the same hour that the Carthage mob were shedding the blood of Joseph and Hyrum Smith, and John Taylor, near one thousand miles distant. My brother bid me farewell somewhere in Western New York, he being on his way to a conference in that quarter, and passing on to Buffalo I took steamer for Chicago, Illinois.

The steamer touched at a landing in Wisconsin, some fifty or sixty miles from Chicago, and here some new passengers came on board and brought the news of the martyrdom of Joseph and Hyrum Smith. Great excitement prevailed on board, there being a general spirit of exultation and triumph at this glorious news, as it was called, much the same as is generally shown on the first receipt of the news of a great national victory in time of war.

Many passengers now gathered about me and tauntingly inquired what the Mormons would do now, seeing their Prophet and leader was killed.

To these taunts and questions I replied, that they would continue their mission and spread the work he had restored, in all the world. Observing that nearly all the prophets and Apostles who were before him had been killed, and also the Saviour of the world, and yet their death did not alter the truth nor hinder its final triumph.

At this reply many of them seemed astonished, and some inquired who would succeed him, and remarked to me: "Perhaps you will be the man who will now seek to be leader of the Mormons in his stead—who are you, sir?" I replied: "I am a MAN, sir; and a MAN never triumphs and exults in the ruin of his country and the murder of the innocent." This was said in the energy of my soul, and by constraint of the Spirit, and a powerful and peculiar accent was thrown upon the word MAN each time it occurred in the sentence. This served as a sufficient rebuke, and all were silent.

Landing in Chicago I found great excitement, and the press had issued extras announcing the triumph of the murderous mob in killing the Smiths.

I now hastened on to Peoria, and, staying over night, started next day on foot across the country to Nauvoo—distance 105 miles.

During the two or three days I spent in travelling between Chicago and Peoria I felt so weighed down with sorrow and the powers of darkness that it was painful for me to converse or speak to any one, or even to try to eat or sleep. I really felt that if it had been my own family who had died, and our beloved Prophet been spared alive, I could have borne it, and the blow would have fallen on me with far less weight. I had loved Joseph with a warmth of affection indescribable for about fourteen years. I had associated with him in private and in public, in travels and at home, in joy and sorrow, in honor and dishonor, in adversity of every kind. With him I had lain in dungeons and in chains; and with him I had triumphed over all our foes in Missouri, and found deliverance for ourselves and people in Nauvoo, where we had reared a great city. But now he was gone to the invisible world, and we and the Church of the Saints were left to mourn in sorrow and without the presence of our beloved founder and Prophet.

As I walked along over the plains of Illinois, lonely and solitary, I reflected as follows: I am now drawing near to the beloved city; in a day or two I shall be there. How shall I meet the sorrowing widows and orphans? How shall I meet the aged and widowed mother of these two martyrs? How shall I meet an entire community bowed down with grief and sorrow unutterable? What shall I say? or how console and advise twenty-five thousand people who will throng about me in tears, and in the absence of my President and the older members of the now presiding council, will ask counsel at my hands? Shall I tell them to fly to the wilderness and deserts? Or, shall I tell them to stay at home and take care of themselves, and continue to build the Temple? With these reflections and inquiries, I walked onward, weighed down as it were unto death. When I could endure it no longer, I cried out aloud, saying: O Lord! in the name of Jesus Christ I pray Thee, show me what these things mean, and what I shall say to Thy people? On a sudden the Spirit of God came upon me, and filled my heart with joy and gladness indescribable; and while the spirit of revelation glowed in my bosom with as visible a warmth and gladness as if it were fire. The Spirit said unto me: "Lift up your head and rejoice; for behold! it is well with my servants Joseph and Hyrum. My servant Joseph still holds the keys of my kingdom in this dispensation, and he shall stand in due time on the earth, in the flesh, and fulfil that to which he is appointed. Go and say unto my people in Nauvoo, that they shall continue to pursue their daily duties and take care of themselves, and make no movement in Church government to reorganize or alter anything until the return of the remainder of the Quorum of the Twelve. But exhort them that they continue to build the House of the Lord which I have commanded them to build in Nauvoo."

This information caused my bosom to burn with joy and gladness, and I was comforted above measure; all my sorrow seemed in a moment to be lifted as a burthen from my back.

The change was so sudden I hardly dared to believe my senses; I, therefore, prayed the Lord to repeat to me the same things the second time; if, indeed, I might be sure of their truth, and might really tell the Saints to stay in Nauvoo, and continue to build the Temple.

As I prayed thus, the same spirit burned in my bosom, and the Spirit of the Lord repeated to me the same message again. I then went on my way rejoicing, and soon arrived in Nauvoo, and delivered this message both to the people and friends individually, and in the great congregation. In confirmation that the message was right, I found them already renewing their labors on the Temple, under the direction of John Taylor and Willard Richards, who were members of our quorum, and were in jail with the prophets when they were murdered—Taylor being wounded with four bullets, and Richards escaping uninjured.

We then, being the only members of the quorum now present in Nauvoo, united in daily councils at Bro. Taylor's, who was confined by his wounds, and counseled for the good of the Church. We were enabled to baffle all the designs of aspiring men, such as Rigdon and others (who strove to reorganize and lead the Church, or divide them), and to keep the Church in a measure of union, peace and quiet till the return of President Young and the other members of the quorum.

Elder Rigdon arrived from Pittsburgh soon after my arrival, and with the aid of Elder Marks, local President of the Nauvoo Stake, and others, attempted to worm himself in as President of the whole Church. A public meeting was actually called and appointed for that purpose; the call being made and the day appointed by President Marks on the public stand. President W. Richards was present when this appointment was announced.

On being informed of this untimely and underhanded attempt, I called upon Elder Rigdon to meet with us—that is, the three of the Twelve then in the city, at the house of brother Taylor, who was still confined with his wounds, and there we expostulated with him, and showed our reasons for being opposed to such a course.

I finally told him that no such meeting should be held, nor any such business attempted in the absence of the general authorities of the Church. And that, if any such meeting was attempted, I should be there and oppose it, and show my reasons, and then dismiss the congregation and take my hat and walk away. He finally assured us that no business of the kind should be attempted, and that the meeting should only be the usual prayer meeting. We likewise forbade President Marks from attempting any general business till the return of the general authorities.

About this time, President Marks joined with the widow of the martyred Joseph and some others, in a council in the upper room of brother Joseph's house, to try to nominate and appoint a trustee in trust for the whole Church. I entered this council and heard Mrs. Emma Smith plead in relation to this matter, the great importance and absolute necessity of immediate action on this subject, as delay would endanger much property of a public and private character, and perhaps cause a loss of scores of thousands. I arose and protested against any action of the kind, telling them plainly that the appointment of a trustee in trust was the business of the whole Church, through its general authorities, and not the business of the local authorities of any one stake of the Church, and that, therefore, it could not be done till the remainder of the quorum returned. To this it was replied that by this delay much property would be lost. I again repeated that dollars and cents were no consideration with me, when principle was at stake, and if thousands or even millions were lost, let them go. We could not and would not suffer the authorities and principles of the Church to be trampled under foot, for the sake of pecuniary interest. The council finally broke up without accomplishing anything.

At length the day for Mr. Rigdon's great meeting arrived, when the remainder of the quorum, or a majority, with President Young at their head, arrived in time to be present. Mr. Rigdon was frustrated in his ambitious schemes, and with his adherents, including President Marks, soon left the place, being disfellowshipped by the Church.

President Brigham Young was unanimously chosen and upheld in the Presidency of the whole Church; the keys of which he held by virtue of his apostleship, being the senior and President of the highest quorum of the Church then living in the flesh.

October 6th.—The half yearly Conference was held at Nauvoo, which I attended.

Parley P. Pratt's home in Nauvoo, Illinois

Orson Pratt's home on
bank of Mississippi
River at Nauvoo

Chapter 43

December 2d.

Having been appointed by the President and others of the Twelve to go East, and take charge of churches in the Atlantic States, I this day bade farewell to home, family and the City of Saints and started on this journey. I rode to Quincy; stayed over night at brother Haywood's, and next morning took boat and soon arrived in St. Louis. I was accompanied by Elders E. T. Benson and P. Brown, who were sent to assist me in this eastern mission. Nothing worthy of note transpired on the passage. We arrived in New York towards the close of the year. I appointed brother Benson to take charge of Boston and vicinity, and brother Brown to the charge of Philadelphia and vicinity.

January 1st, 1845.—I sent forth a proclamation in a New York paper, called the *Prophet*, edited and published by Samuel Brannan, and professedly devoted to the interests of the Church of the Saints. *

As we gradually became acquainted with circumstances pertaining to the Church in these parts, we found that Elders William Smith, G. J. Adams, S. Brannan and others, had been corrupting the Saints by introducing among them all manner of false doctrine and immoral practices, by which many of them had stumbled and been seduced from virtue and truth. While many others, seeing their iniquity, had turned away from the Church and joined various dissenting parties. We, therefore, in accordance with the instructions of the Holy Spirit in President Young before we left home, directed William Smith and G. J. Adams to return to Nauvoo, where, in process of time, they were cut off from the Church.

---

*See *Millennial Star*, No. 10, Vol. 5, page 149.

We also warned brother Brannan and others to repent speedily of all such evil practices or we would withdraw fellowship from them. They promised faithfully to repent and lead a new life, and therefore we bore with them. We also taught the Church to beware of all impure and wicked doctrines and practices, and not to receive any Elder or minister who sought to seduce them by any false teachings. With these exertions and the continual labors of Elders Benson, Brown, Grant and many others, with myself, we succeeded in setting in order the churches and reestablishing pure gospel principles. There were, however, many who would not believe us, nor hearken to our advice, but continued in their abominations and dissensions. Elder Brannan was at length disfellowshipped at Nauvoo, as appeared in the official organ of the Church there. On seeing this notice I called his attention to it, and urged him to repair immediately to the authorities there; acknowledge and frankly repent of his faults, and seek restoration to his standing. He did this, and returned in full fellowship. But, as it finally proved, this was only to disgrace himself and the cause still more in a wider and more responsible career in California, where he, under our instruction, soon after repaired with a colony of Saints in the ship "Brooklyn." He was a corrupt and wicked man, and had the Church and myself been less long suffering and merciful, it would have saved the Church much loss, and, perhaps, saved some souls which were corrupted in California, and led astray and plundered by him. I have always regretted having taken any measures to have him restored to fellowship after he was published in Nauvoo as cut off from the Church. However, if I erred, it was on the side of mercy.

I devoted the winter in the presidency of the eastern churches, to writing for the *Prophet* and in visiting the churches in Boston, Lowell, Philadelphia, Long Island and various other places, and preaching the gospel among them.

The following pieces from my pen are found in the above periodical, under their appropriate dates and titles: "Materiality;" "New Proverbs."

I continued writing for this periodical in New York, which had, however, changed its name, and was now published as the *New York Messenger*. From my numerous editorials and communications in that paper, I select the following as worthy of record: "Heaven."

July 20th, 1845, I published an address to those under my charge.

Soon after the publication of the foregoing, I took leave of the Saints and friends in the Eastern States, and returned to Nauvoo by way of the Erie Canal and the lakes, journeying from Chicago to Nauvoo by land, by private conveyance, accompanied by a few of the Saints from

Hannahette Sniveley Pratt,
wife of Parley P. Pratt

Alma Pratt, son

Lucy Pratt Russell, daughter

Henriette Pratt Russell, daughter

Children of Parley P. and Hanahette Sniveley

Mary Wood Pratt, *wife*

Helaman Pratt, *son*

Mary Pratt Young, *daughter*

Mathoni W. Pratt, *son*

Helaman Pratt, *son*

Cornelia Pratt Driggs, *daughter*

Children of Parley P. and Mary Wood

the East. We arrived in Nauvoo sometime in August. I found my family mostly in health, and was rejoiced to meet them.

From the time of my arrival home until the end of the year, I was engaged in the cares of my family, in finishing my house, and in my official duties.

In autumn the mobs re-commenced their murders, robbings, house and grain burnings, and driving families away from their lands and homes in the borders of our county, and elsewhere.

The Sheriff of the County called out several *posses* and dispersed them, killing some and arresting others.

This bold and energetic execution of the sworn duties of Sheriff Backenstos did not seem to be quite congenial to the spirit of the Governor and citizens of the State of Illinois—they being to a great extent in favor of mob violence, murder, plunder and house burning. Therefore, Sheriff Backenstos was arrested to answer to the charge of murder, and another Sheriff was imposed on the county, unlawfully, entirely independent of the ballot box. Backenstos, however, was afterwards discharged by the Court, who justified his killing some of the mob, pronouncing it an official act in perfect conformity with his duties as an officer. The Governor sent troops to our county, on pretence of aiding the law, but, in reality, to aid the mob to escape justice and carry out their expressed resolutions of driving every member of the Saints, and their families, from the State. General Hardin and Major Warren, who had the command of this expedition, joined their advice with Judge S. A. Douglass and others, some of them citizens of Quincy, and meeting with President Young and our other leaders in council, advised and urged us strongly to yield to the mob, and abandon our houses, farms, cities, villages and Temple to this wholesale banditti, who were engaged against us, and sell them for what we could get, and remove out of the country. But very little of the real estate was ever sold.

To these extravagant counsels we finally yielded assent, and agreed to move West in the spring, and to advise others of our Society so to do, as fast as we could sell.

We continued, however, our work on the Temple, a portion of which was finished and dedicated.

"It was the first specimen of a new order of architecture, introduced by President Joseph Smith, and was the most beautiful building in the Western States, erected at a cost of a million dollars. The mob subsequently set fire to it, the light of which was visible for thirty miles."

As winter approached, President Young, myself, the quorum, and many others were daily engaged in the Temple, administering in the holy ordinances of Endowment, to many hundreds of people. Thus closed the year 1845.

January 1st, A.D. 1846, I continued to minister in the Temple night and day, with my President and the rest of the Twelve, until early in February.

Soon after these things the ministrations in the Temple ceased; and President Young, with the rest of the quorum and many others, bade farewell to their homes in the beloved city of Nauvoo, and crossed the Mississippi River, with their families and such teams and wagons as they could get. They formed an encampment on Sugar Creek, in the State of Iowa.

February 14th, I crossed the river with my family and teams, and encamped not far from the Sugar Creek encampment, taking possession of a vacant log house, on account of the extreme cold. This encampment was about seven miles from Nauvoo. In leaving home at this inclement season, I left a good house, lot and out buildings, worth about seven thousand dollars, and several lots and houses of less value, besides a farm in the country worth near two thousand. But I was much in debt. I, therefore, left Mr. Bickford as my agent, authorized to sell the property, settle up my business, and take care of such of my family or friends as might be left in his care, including my aged mother, and the father, mother and sister of my wife. I was intending, when things were settled, to place the surplus, if any, at the disposal of the Church or its agents, in aid of the removal of such as were not able to remove without assistance.

While we lay encamped, some one hundred and twenty miles west of Nauvoo, President Young coming up with the main body of the camps, formed an encampment a few miles in the rear, and sent for me and the members of the Twelve, who were with me, and George Miller, to meet with the council at his camp. His letter censured us on account of some of our moves, and as heavy rains had swollen the small streams which intervened between the two encampments (so that they could only be passed by swimming), and myself being sick on account of exposure in the storms, we did not immediately attend the council, as requested. However, we found means to cross after a little delay, and were proceeding to his camp when an express met us with another letter from the President, censuring us still more severely.

We hastened on and met in council. The President then reproved

Three pictures of Belinda Marden Pratt

Nephi Pratt, son

Belinda Pratt Musser, daughter

Lehi Pratt, son

*Isabella Eleanor Pratt Robison
(Birdie), daughter, about 56
years of age*

*Isabella Eleanor Pratt,
as a child*

*Isabella Eleanor Pratt,
age 16*

*Isabella Eleanor Pratt Robison
(Birdie), about 40 years of age*

Children of Parley P. and Belinda Marden Pratt

and chastened us severely for several things, among which was our drawing off from the council and main body of the camp and going ahead. He
said there was manifestly a spirit of dissension and of insubordination
manifested in our movements. I could not realize this at the time, and
protested that in my own heart, so far as I was concerned, I had no such
motive; that I had been actuated by the purest motives, merely seeking
to sustain the teams and people, and to make what progress we could
with that end in view. However, the sequel soon proved that it was the
true Spirit which reproved and chastened us. For Bishop Miller, who was
a leading and active member of our camp, has since left us and gone his
own way, having refused to be led by the counsels of the Presidency, and
removed to Texas. And here I would observe that, although my own
motives were pure, so far as I could know my own heart, yet I thank God
for this timely chastisement; I profited by it, and it caused me to be more
watchful and careful ever after.

All things being harmonized and put in order, the camps moved on.
Arriving at a place on a branch of Grand River we encamped for a while,
having travelled much in the midst of great and continued rains, mud
and mire. Here we enclosed and planted a public farm of many hundred
acres and commenced settlement, for the good of some who were to tarry
and of those who should follow us from Nauvoo. We called the place
"Garden Grove." It is in Iowa, perhaps one hundred and fifty miles from
Nauvoo. After assisting to fence this farm and build some log houses, I
was dispatched ahead by the Presidency with a small company to try to
find another location. Crossing this branch of Grand River, I now
steered through the vast and fertile prairies and groves without a track or
anything but a compass to guide me—the country being entirely wild
and without inhabitants. Our course was west, a little north. We crossed
small streams daily, which, on account of deep beds and miry banks, as
well as on account of their being swollen by the rains, we had to bridge.
After journeying thus for several days, and while lying encamped on a
small stream which we had bridged, I took my horse and rode ahead
some three miles in search of one of the main forks of Grand River,
which we had expected to find for some time. Riding about three or four
miles through beautiful prairies, I came suddenly to some round and
sloping hills, grassy and crowned with beautiful groves of timber; while
alternate open groves and forests seemed blended in all the beauty and
harmony of an English park. While beneath and beyond, on the west,
rolled a main branch of Grand River, with its rich bottoms of alternate
forest and prairie. As I approached this lovely scenery several deer and

wolves, being startled at the sight of me, abandoned the place and bounded away till lost from my sight amid the groves.

Being pleased and excited at the varied beauty before me, I cried out, "this is *Mount Pisgah.*" I returned to my camp, with the report of having found the long sought river, and we soon moved on and encamped under the shade of these beautiful groves. It was now late in May, and we halted here to await the arrival of the President and council. In a few days they arrived and formed a general encampment here, and finally formed a settlement, and surveyed and enclosed another farm of several thousand acres. This became a town and resting place for the Saints for years, and is now known on the map of Iowa as a village and post-office named "*Pisgah.*"

June 1. We crossed the river, and, travelling one mile, encamped; next day we travelled nine miles, and the third day twenty miles.

Passing on from day to day, we at length came to a large river which could not be forded, called the Nishnabotna. Here was the home of the Pottowatamie Indians who were very friendly and civil to us.

We tarried here some days and built a large bridge, over which the camps were enabled to cross.

In July we arrived at the Missouri River, near Council Bluffs. There we encamped for several weeks; opened a trade with upper Missouri, exchanging wagons, horses, harness and various articles of furniture, cash, etc., for provisions, oxen, cows, etc.

In the meantime we built a ferry boat, fixed landings, made dugways, etc., and commenced ferrying over the Missouri. The ferry ran night and day for a long time, and still could not complete the crossing of the camps till late in the season.

While we tarried here I returned on the road as far as Pisgah—being sent on a mission to the camps and settlements in the rear—distance, in going and returning, two hundred miles. In this journey I came near drowning, in attempting to swim a branch of the Nishnabotna on horseback. My horse refused to swim, reared on his hind feet to try to touch bottom, and caused me to slide off behind him in the middle of a very strong current with all my clothes on, including hat, coat and boots, and a large parcel under my arm. The parcel contained letters and important documents. I, therefore, clung to it and to my hat also, and stemming the current with the other hand, swam to shore, a distance of several rods. Passing on a mile or two, I came to a camp of the Saints and dried my letters and clothing. As I returned from this mission I met President Young and others, who were going down to Pisgah and to intermediate

Photo not
available

Sarah Huston Pratt, wife

Julia Pratt Gardner, daughter

Teancum Pratt, son

Sarah Pratt King, daughter

Three of the children of Parley P. Pratt and Sarah Huston Pratt

Ann Agatha Walker Pratt, wife

Agatha Pratt Ridges, daughter

Agatha Pratt Ridges, as a girl

Malona Pratt Eldredge, daughter

Moroni Pratt, son

Evelyn Pratt Woods, daughter

Children of Parley P. Pratt and Ann Agatha Walker

camps to try to raise five hundred men, who had just been called for by the United States as recruits for the Mexican war. These troops were soon raised by the united exertions of President Young and Council, and were mustered into service by Lieutenant-Colonel Allen, and called the Mormon Battalion.

This is that famous battalion which marched through more than two thousand miles of a trackless waste on foot, and helped to take and maintain California—some of the members of which first discovered the gold mines of that country, and thus turned the world the other side up.

The lateness of the season, the poverty of the people, and, above all, the taking away of five hundred of our best men, finally compelled us to abandon any further progress westward till the return of another spring. The camps, therefore, began to prepare for winter.

The place for winter quarters was finally selected on the west bank of the Missouri River, in what is since known as the territory of Nebraska. This was a beautiful town site. The land sloping up from the immediate banks of the river sufficiently high to be secure from high water, and then stretching away in an unbroken plain to the hills, which swelled up at less than half a mile distant in beautiful rounded grassy points, or in rising benches, one above another.

Vast quantities of hay was cut and secured, and some seven hundred log cabins and one hundred and fifty dugouts (cabins half under ground) were built in the course of the autumn and winter. Other large settlements were also formed on the other side of the river, and back into the country.

President Young also caused the erection of a good flouring mill on a small stream which here entered the river.

This city, which is was known by the name of Winter Quarters, is now (1856) called Florence, and is becoming a thriving place in Nebraska.

While the camps lay in these parts, and soon after I had, with my teams and family, crossed the Missouri, Presidents Orson Hyde, John Taylor and myself were appointed a mission to England. The reason for this mission under the present distressing circumstances was this: Elder R. Hedlock, who was then presiding in England, was in transgression, and was engaged in a wild scheme of financiering, by which he obtained vast sums of money from the Church in a kind of joint stock organization, which professedly had for its object the emigration of the Saints to America, while in reality the money was squandered by himself and others in any and every way but to do good. Our mission was for the purpose of breaking up this scheme of fraud, and displacing him and regulating all the affairs of the Church in the British Isles.

July 31.—I bid a solemn farewell to my family and friends, then dwelling in tents and wagons on the west side of the Missouri River, and started for England. I met Elders Hyde and Taylor as agreed upon, and we took passage down the river in an open scow, or flat boat, in company with a family of Presbyterian missionaries who had been residing on the Loupe fork of the Platte River, among the Pawnee Indians, and who were now bound for St. Joseph, Missouri. We floated or pulled the oars for some days, tying up and sleeping on shore at night. Arriving at St. Joseph, the missionaries landed and sold the boat to us. We then continued down the river to Leavenworth, where we found the Mormon Battalion, who were just receiving money for clothing, etc., preparatory to their long march thence to California.

We visited with them a day to two, and they contributed several hundred dollars to aid us on our mission to England.

They also made up a purse of between five and six thousand dollars for their families and friends at the Bluffs, and furnishing me a horse, it was finally agreed by my two brethren that I should return to the Bluffs with this money. Accordingly, I took leave of Elders Hyde and Taylor and the brethren of the battalion, and started on horseback for the camp of the Saints. I rode with all speed, and in less than three days reached home—distance one hundred and seventy miles. Unexpected as this visit was, a member of my family had been warned in a dream, and had predicted my arrival and the day, and my family were actually looking for me all that day.

I delivered the money to President Young and Council, with the list of subscribers, and of the persons for whom it was sent, and again prepared for my departure. Obtaining a light buggy, I harnessed my horse before it, and started for Chicago, Illinois, by land—distance five hundred and fifty miles. I performed this journey in safety in eleven days, averaging fifty miles per day. Arriving in Chicago towards evening, I immediately sold my horse and buggy, and then took steamer the same evening across Lake Michigan, thence by railroad to Boston; thence to New York, where I arrived a day or two sooner than the day agreed upon. I was hindered a little, being at a loss for funds to pay my passage; but one Elder Badlam kindly assisted me, and I soon embarked in the cabin of a splendid ship, and set sail for Liverpool. On this same ship was Franklin D. and Samuel Richards, and M. Martin, on a mission to the same country.

Photo not
available

Phoebe Soper Pratt, wife

Phoebe Pratt Holdaway,
daughter

Wife and child of Parley P. Pratt

Elizabeth Brotherton Pratt, wife

Eleanor J. Pratt, wife

Photo not
available

Martha Monks, wife

Photo not
available

Keziah Downes, wife

Wives of Parley P. Pratt

We had a long passage, and arrived in Liverpool October 14, in good health and spirits.

We found Elders Hyde and Taylor there all well, and were kindly received and entertained by the Saints.

A General Conference was convened in Manchester October 17; an account of which will be found in the *Star,* No. 7, Vol 8.

In this Conference it was agreed that President Hyde should edit the *Star,* and attend to all business in the publishing office at Liverpool, while President Taylor and myself should visit the different conferences in the British Isles. We, therefore, published our appointments beforehand in the *Star,* and so commenced our winter's mission. I will not detain the reader with a detail of our journeyings, visits and meetings in pursuance of this arrangement; but, suffice it to say, we travelled from conference to conference by railway, coaches, steamers, etc., visiting nearly all the principal towns in England and Scotland. We were everywhere received and treated with the utmost hospitality, and with demonstrations of joy and gladness not soon to be forgotten. The Saints and others convened from far and near at the sessions of our several conferences, and vast crowds of strangers, as well as Saints, listened to us. Public feasts, tea parties, public dinners and all kinds of demonstrations of joy and welcome greeted us as we visited from place to place. So that our sojourn was more like a triumphal procession than like a dreary pilgrimage. We preached the gospel, set in order the churches, directed the labors of the Elders, comforted the Saints, and reproved and corrected the abuses introduced by President Hedlock and others in relation to the joint stock companies, etc.

Hedlock fled at our approach, leaving many debts unpaid, and finally lived incog. in London with a vile woman—he being severed from the Church.

It was during my travels in England on this mission that I wrote the following letter in blank verse to my family, whom I had left at Council Bluffs, on the Missouri River. It was published in England at the time, on a beautiful sheet with a handsome border, and designed to be put in a frame as a household ornament; and is frequently seen to this day (1856) as a memorial in the parlors of the Saints on both sides of the Atlantic.

May it be handed down to posterity as a monument of suffering and self-denial of women and children for the gospel's sake.

Chapter 44

An Apostle of the Church of Jesus Christ, of Latter-day Saints

WAS IN THE ISLAND OF GREAT BRITAIN FOR THE GOSPEL'S SAKE; AND BEING IN THE SPIRIT ON THE 24TH OF NOVEMBER, 1846, ADDRESSED THE FOLLOWING WORDS OF COMFORT TO HIS DEARLY BELOVED WIFE AND FAMILY, DWELLING IN TENTS, IN THE CAMP OF ISRAEL, AT COUNCIL BLUFFS, MISSOURI TERRITORY, NORTH AMERICA; WHERE THEY AND TWENTY THOUSAND OTHERS WERE BANISHED BY THE CIVILIZED CHRISTIANS OF THE UNITED STATES FOR THE WORD OF GOD AND THE TESTIMONY OF JESUS:

MY DEAREST WIFE,

> Thy kindly soul and all
> Thine acts of love to him, thy chosen head,
> Are treasured deep in memory's archives.
> And when, amid the busy throng of towns,
> I pass unheeded, or wander lonely
> In some country lane, or gravelled highway,
> Lined with hawthorn hedge—or turn aside
> From the busy walks of men in meadows green,—
> Or wander 'mid the solitary grove
> At twilight hour, where silence reigns, and the
> Fading tints of autumn tell of time's flight,
> And the low murmur of the whispering breeze
> Steals o'er the senses like a funeral dirge,—
> Or flying swift o'er country hedge and ditch
> In flaming chariot; while hills and vales—
> And towns, and villas, farms, plains, and woods
> Are swiftly whirled behind—or musing in
> The midnight hour in lonely solitude
> Upon my bed—'Tis then I think of thee.
> Sweet thoughts steal gently o'er the memory;
> And my spirit wanders o'er the wide sea
> And far away o'er Alleghany's heights,
> And down the broad Ohio, from its source
> To where it mingles its limpid waters

316

With the dark waves of Missouri's current;
And onward still, with lightning speed it flies,
Till towns and cities all are left behind;
And the last trace of Gentile dwelling fades
From view, and disappears in the far east.
    At length the long sought vision bursts to view
And stays my spirit in its onward flight.
    Towering bluffs; deep indented vales; wide spread
Prairies; boundless plains and beauteous groves
Expand to view; all clad in green, and deck'd
In summer's richest livery of flowers;
Or with the grey tints of fading autumn
Crown'd—emblem of Nature's dissolution.
    There one eternal silence seems to reign,
And slumb'ring Nature rests in solitude.
    There peace prevails; the Sabbath rules the year;
And, in its own primeval innocence,
Uncursed by man's polluted touch, the earth
Seems resting in sacred, sublime repose.
    No Gentile tyrant sways his sceptre there;
No pris'ners groan in solitary cells.
    There freedom dwells; no superstitious creed
Enslaves the mind of man; no Christian mobs
To drive him from his home or shed his blood.
    O sacred solitude, divinely blest—
Zion's retreat; where dwell the great and good.
    There, with delight my spirit lingers still,
And would prolong the heavenly vision.
    I love thee, for thyself, O land of Zion!
The beauty of thy landscape, thy flowers,
Thy boundless immensity of green fields,
Mingling with the wide expanse of Heaven's
Blue arch; thy star-bespangled firmament
Have charms for me.
                    The mellow moonlight
Gently stealing o'er thy sacred forests;
The fading tints of twilight painted on
Your evening sky; the soft and plaintive voice
Of the autumnal cricket, as he sings
The funeral knell of expiring insects,
Or sounds a requiem to the closing year—
    All these steal o'er my senses with delight,
And wake the memory to scenes afar:
    They whisper to the lonely exile,
And tell of youth, and friends, and native clime.
    Yet not for these charms alone I love thee;

Nor yet for peace, or freedom sweet, or rest,
Or sacred Sabbath of sublime repose.
    All these, though dear to me, are worthless toys,
Mere baubles, compared to that precious *gem*
Which yet remains to beautify my verse,
And swell the music of my joyous theme.
    There dwell my family, my bosom friends,
The precious lambs of my Redeemer, my
Best of Heaven's gifts to man, my germs of
Life and immortality, my hope of Heaven,
My principality on earth began,
My kingdom in embryo, big with thrones
Of endless power and wide dominion.
    Ye kindred spirits from worlds celestial!
Offsprings of Deity; Sons and daughters
Of eternity; Ye nobles of Heaven
Whose dwellings were of old among the Gods
In everlasting mansions, and who stood
In the councils of the High and lofty
One, ere chaos sprang to order, or the
Foundations of the everlasting hills
Were laid: Why came ye to this world of woe?
Why this disguise? This painful sojourn in
A land of death?
    Why wander far from Heaven's eternal fold,
And from the bosom of your Father there?
Had *He* no love? No fond affection for
His own, that you are banished thus, and left
As exiles wandering in some dreary waste?
And if thus fallen, and forsaken quite,
Like evil spirits thrust from Heaven, to
Return no more; why that latent spark of
Heaven's pure love still glowing in your breast?
Why does your bosom swell with hope and joy,
And fire celestial kindle in your eye?
    O heavenly gift! The key of knowledge
Restored to man, the mystery unfolds
Of God's elect—their final destiny.
    You are here because your Father loved you;
Because in Heaven ye kept your first estate,
And firm remained when angels did rebel,
And Lucifer drew a third of Heaven's host
From God; and with them sunk in dark despair.
    You are here for further proof and trial;
For a second estate; which if ye keep
As ye did the first, will purify your souls,

Pioneers en route to the valleys of the Rocky Mountains

Buffalo hunt on the prairies

And fit you for a Heaven celestial.
    You came to the earth to be born of flesh,
To fashion and perfect your earthly house,
To *live,* to *love,* to suffer and to die,
To *rise* and *reign* in immortality.
To form your kindred ties with kindred souls,
To blend your sympathies by mutual acts
Of kindly charity—
                    To love and serve
Each other in ten thousand nameless ways;
And thus give exercise to mutual love,
And qualify yourselves for union endless
In that world of bliss.
O ye beings of noble birth! ye lambs
Of celestial origin, to Zion bound!
I know ye now; and knowing, can but love.

    O my Father in Heaven! Thine they were,
And Thou gavest them to me—Precious gifts!
Endear'd by long acquaintance in the heavens,
By the soul's best affections on the earth,
By mutual love and sympathy of soul,
By all the kindred ties which twine around
The heart in sacred, inexpressible
Delight—Made nigh by a Savior's blood—
Seal'd by the Holy Ghost, and secur'd
By the spirit and power of Elijah—
By which the hearts of the fathers are turn'd
To the children: Enliven'd by the hope
Of endless union in that world of life
Where all is pure—

                    Thrones, principalities,
Powers, majesty, might and dominion,
As a mutual reward! Who can but love?

    O precious kindred! my loveliest, best!
Are motives wanting still to prompt my love,
And kindle my soul's affection to its
Highest, purest flame? sweet memory dwells
On all the past—Your sufferings with me;
Your sacrifices for the Gospel's sake.

    For *me* and truth you gladly left your home,
Your native clime, your father, mother, friends,
And kindred dear, and wandered far away
O'er mountain, seas, and continents. The wide
Expanse of ocean—its waves and tempests
Could not quench your love, or cool your courage—
    Towering mountains rose before you; rivers

Intervened to check you on your journey—
       Wide lakes, gloomy forests, and desert plains
Forbid your further progress, but in vain.
       Truth was the prize you sought; and love impell'd
You onward. These overcome, a host
Of fiends assailed you next, with lying tongues
To flatter, frown, to pity or deceive;
To coax, or drive you from your chosen course.
       When slander, rage, and lies, and pity fail'd,
Then came the deadly strife! The fire consum'd;
The sword devour'd; Widows and orphans mourn'd;
Hell's artillery bellow'd; Martyrs bled;
The world exulted; Devils hugely grinn'd;
Heaven wept; saints prayed; Justice stood aghast;
Mercy, retiring, dropped a tear of blood;
Angels startling, half drew their glittering swords;
And the Gods, in solemn council decreed
A just VENGEANCE!
       Amid these awful scenes ye firmly stood
For truth, and him you loved; And leaving house
And home again behind, in poverty
Ye fled; and pitch'd your humble tent amid
The storms of winter: And wandering o'er the
Wide, unsheltered plain, ye braved the tempest
Many a weary month without a murmur—
       Without a *murmur*! Nay more—Ye smiling
Stood, amid the awful storms, and hail'd the
Tempest welcome. The solitary wilds
Reverb'rated with freedom's joyful songs,
While there you fondly pressed your infant to
Your bosom, smil'd on your lord, receiv'd his
Smile in turn, and realized your freedom.
Supremely blest with heaven's approving smile,
With peace and friendship, liberty and love;
And with the daily presence of your lord,
Whose best affection sweeten'd every care;
Ye still were happy in your low estate,
Nor sighed for more.
       One only sacrifice remained for us
To make, to further test our depth of love
For God and truth; t'was all that Heaven could ask.
       Will you, my lambs, be left *alone*, to spend
Another winter in this dreary wild,
While him *you love* shall wander far away
Beyond the sea, for truth and Zion's sake?
       Your pulse beat quick; your bosom heav'd a sigh;

Your heart swell'd with emotion; a big tear
Gush'd forth, and stole in silence down your cheek;
While your spirit said: *"If I must, I will!"*
　　The Recording Angel smil'd; Heaven approv'd,
And said: *"It is enough,"* record the same,
And with it Our decree: They are Elect!
Eternal life is theirs: They shall be ONE,
WHILE ENDLESS AGES ROLL!

PARLEY P. PRATT.

Chapter 45

Early in January, 1847, having completed our mission in the British Isles, Brother John Taylor and myself went to Liverpool, preparatory to our return, with a few of the Saints, who were accompanying us as emigrants. Here we soon made arrangements for passage to New Orleans, chartering the second cabin of a large new ship, called "America."

We bid adieu to our warm hearted and affectionate friends in England, and embarked on this ship. Our company consisted of fourteen persons in all, composed of returning Elders and a few families or individuals who were emigrating with us. We were very comfortable in our own little cabin, where we had our own provisions, and set our own table, hiring the ship's cook to do our cooking. We sailed January 19th, but we soon met a gale of wind, which was directly contrary to us. This gale continued for nine days, without any cessation or abatement, during which time we were beating in a land-locked channel between Ireland and England, without gaining fifty miles on our course, being in imminent danger of being cast away on a lee shore. During all this time our Captain lay sick in his berth with a fever on the brain, and much of the time in a state of mental derangement. We frequently watched with him, and in his rational moments he would converse a little. He said his family lived in America, and he much wished to get to them, but was very positive he should never see them more, having been for many days oppressed with a sure and certain presentiment that he should never reach America alive. We, in reply, allowed that presentiments of that kind were possible, and sometimes true, and to be depended on, but not always. And Brother Taylor and myself assured him, as men of God, that his present presentiment was false, and that both him and his vessel would reach America in safety. This we assured him over and over again, from day to day. After nine days of severe struggle with the wind and waves, the mate and supercargo becoming discouraged, and the men worn out, they counselled with us and concluded to put back into the port of Liverpool, which was accordingly done after some difficulty and delay. Here the Captain, who was still dangerously ill, went on shore, and under proper medical aid, recovered, and afterwards landed in America per steamer, where he reached his family in safety. Our mate was sworn in captain, and we again put to sea, after visiting our friends on shore, and recruiting our stock of provisions. On taking this second farewell of our friends in the British Isles I sent forth through the columns of the *Star* the following farewell address:

TO THE SAINTS IN GREAT BRITAIN

Beloved Brethren—Having been so crowded with business and care on my late departure from your shores for my home in the distant wilds of western America, I had no time to say *farewell,* or to leave my blessing with you in a formal manner as a whole, although expressed frequently in our farewell meetings. I have, therefore, providentially returned to your midst, after nine days of seafaring life, in order to take a fair start, and to say farewell through the medium of the *Star.*

I feel the most perfect satisfaction with the manner of our reception and entertainment among you as men of God. I also feel that we have, as far as time would permit, accomplished the work for which we came, and that the utmost success and prosperity has attended our labors. The Church universally has manifested a spirit of confidence and obedience to the instructions we had to impart, and the measures we were sent to propose for their prosperity and deliverance, both temporally and spiritually.

We have also been received and entertained in the most kind and hospitable manner in every place we have been permitted to visit. We have been lodged, fed, comforted and cheered as if we had been angels of glad tidings, and we feel the utmost satisfaction in expressing our most grateful thanks for all the kindness and assistance rendered unto us while in your midst; and, in the name of Jesus Christ, and by authority of the Holy Priesthood and Apostleship vested in us, we bless the congregations of the Saints throughout this land, with all the officers and members thereof, with the blessings of time and eternity in all their fulness. We also bless the Queen, ministers, magistrates, and people of this realm, while they continue to administer equal justice for the protection of every subject, without respect of persons; and we pray that Heaven's choicest blessings may rest upon the Saints, and upon all that fear God and work righteousness in this land. Ye sons and daughters of Zion, be of good cheer; for God will deliver you in due time, and gather in one the children of God. Pray for us and for the camp of the Saints in the wilderness. Farewell.

P. P. PRATT.

LIVERPOOL, *January 29, 1847.*

Elder Hyde did not sail with us, but stayed a few days longer to complete the business in the office. Soon after we set sail Elder Joseph Cain, returning missionary, was married on board to Miss Elizabeth Whittaker. It was a fine affair, and we had a good dinner on the occasion. The wind was now fair continually, and we were only thirty-five days in coming to anchor off the port of New Orleans—having sailed some seven or eight thousand miles. Here we were delayed a day or two by a dense fog, but as the weather cleared, a tug steamer soon got hold of us, and took us into port.

Here, as soon as we could get clear of the custom house, we took a steamer, and, in about six days, arrived in St. Louis.

Here I left Brother Taylor to pass up the Missouri River on a steamer, with the company and baggage, while I took a horse and rode through the northwestern portion of Missouri, and into Iowa, by land. I went *incog.* for fear of my old enemies in that State.

I struck the wagon trail we had made the year before, near Garden Grove, and tarried there with the Saints one day. It was then quite a flourishing place—the farms which I helped to open and enclose the previous year having yielded abundance of provisions, and other farms having been opened.

Being a little refreshed I passed on to "Mount Pisgah," where I found another flourishing settlement of the Saints, and stayed over night. Thence I passed on to the Missouri River, finding Saints to entertain me every night. In making the journey from St. Louis to Missouri River, near Winter Quarters, I had probably travelled near four hundred and fifty miles on horseback. I crossed over the ferry at noon of a fine April day, and came suddenly upon my friends and family. This was April 8, 1847. I found my family all alive, and dwelling in a log cabin. They had, however, suffered much from cold, hunger and sickness. They had oftentimes lived for several days on a little corn meal, ground on a handmill, with no other food. One of the family was then lying very sick with the scurvy—a disease which had been very prevalent in camp during the winter, and of which many had died. I found, on inquiry, that the winter

Native homes in Utah

An old Indian who saw the Mormon pioneers enter the Salt Lake Valley

had been very severe, the snow deep, and, consequently, that all my
horses (four in number) were lost, and I afterwards ascertained that out
of twelve cows I had but seven left, and out of some twelve or fourteen
oxen only four or five were spared.

President Young and Council, with a company of pioneers, were
then encamped on the Elk Horn River, twenty miles west, ready to start
for the mountains. Some of them, however, returned to Winter Quarters on business, and I had an interview with them. I then gave a relation
of our European mission, and delivered to them an account of four
hundred and sixty-nine sovereigns in gold, collected in England as tithing, which had crossed the sea in my charge, and was then in charge of
Elder Taylor on the Missouri River, and might be expected soon. This
small sum proved a very acceptable and timely relief in aiding the Presidency to relieve some of the distress, and to fit out as pioneers for the
mountains.

The President and Council seemed well pleased with our mission
and management. They expressed an earnest wish for me to accompany
them on the pioneer trip to the mountains; but my circumstances
seemed to forbid, and they did not press the matter.

After a few days' rest I began to prepare for journeying to the mountains with my family. My wagons were overhauled and put in order, tires
reset, chains repaired, yokes and bows arranged in order, wagon bows
made or mended, etc., etc. This occupied most of my time till June.

Early in June I loaded my goods and family into my wagons, and, obtaining a few more cattle, started for the Rocky Mountains; or rather for
the Elk Horn River, where we expected to form a rendezvous, and establish a ferry, and wait the arrival of others, and the organization of companies for the purpose of mutual safety in travelling.

Arriving at Elk Horn River with a small company, we made a ferry
of a raft of dry cotton-wood timber, and rafted over our own company of
about fifty wagons. We then organized for herding and grazing purposes,
and continued to aid others in crossing and organizing until five hundred
and sixty-six wagons were finally crossed and organized ready for a
march. In the final organization of this vast company Father Isaac Morley and Bishop Whitney assisted, or rather took the oversight—being a
committee appointed for that purpose by the Presidency before they left.
As Brother Taylor and myself were present, we were appointed and invited to take a general superintendency of this emigration.

The organization consisted of companies of tens, fifties and hundreds, with a captain over each, and the whole presided over by a president and two counselors, a marshal, etc. President John Young was called to preside—having been nominated by the Presidency before their departure. John Van Cott was appointed marshal.

Thus organized, this large company moved on up the Platte about the Fourth of July. There were some difficulties and jealousies during the first few days, on account of some misunderstanding and insubordination in the order of travel. This at length became so far developed that it was found necessary to call a general halt on the Platte River, and hold a council of the principal officers, in which things were amicably adjusted and the camp moved on.

Arriving at the Loupe Fork of Platte River, we continued up it quite a distance above the trail the pioneers had made, as we could not ford the river in their track. We at length found a ford, and with some difficulty on account of quicksands, forded the river and made our way over to the Main Platte, re-entering the pioneer trail. As we passed up the Platte on this trail the companies in front had frequently to halt and build bridges, etc. On one occasion Peregrine Sessions, who was captain of our company of fifty, and myself found two horses which had probably strayed from some former travellers, and which, after several unsuccessful attempts by different parties, Brother Taylor succeeded in driving into camp, and he and I captured them. We were at the time ahead of the company, following up a stream to try and find a ford. This was a very timely providence to me, as I had lost all my horses the previous winter, and was now pioneering for the company without any horse, and on foot.

After journeying for several hundred miles up the Platte, we at length met two messengers from the pioneers under President Young, from Salt Lake Valley. These were P. Rockwell and E. T. Benson; who had been sent out to try to find us and report our progress and circumstances. Having visited all the camps, they returned to the valley, or rather to where they met the President and pioneers, on their way back to Winter Quarters on the Missouri. I accompanied them back nearly one day's ride on the way, and then bid them God speed, and returned to my own camp. Soon after this our fifty met the President and company of pioneers and camped with them one day.

A council was called, in which I was highly censured and chastened by President Young and others. This arose in part from some defect in the organization under my superintendence at the Elk Horn, and in part from other misunderstandings on the road. I was charged with neglecting to observe the order of organization entered into under the superintendence of the President before he left the camps at Winter Quarters; and of variously interfering with previous arrangements. In short, I was severely reproved and chastened. I no doubt deserved this chastisement; and I humbled myself, acknowledged my faults and errors, and asked forgiveness. I was frankly forgiven, and, bidding each other farewell, each company passed on their way. This school of experience made me more humble and careful in future, and I think it was the means of making me a wiser and better man ever after.

After bidding farewell to the President and pioneers, and to my own brother, Orson Pratt, who was one of them, we continued our journey; and after many toils, vexations and trials, such as breaking wagons, losing cattle, upsetting, etc., we arrived in the Valley of Great Salt Lake late in September, 1847. Here we found a fort commenced and partly built by the pioneers, consisting of an enclosure of a block of ten acres with a wall, or in part of buildings of adobes or logs. We also found a city laid out and a public square dedicated for a Temple of God. We found also much ground planted in late crops, which, however, did not mature, being planted late in July; although there were obtained for seed a few small potatoes, from the size of a pea upward to that of half an inch in diameter. These being sound and planted another year produced some very fine potatoes, and, finally, contributed mainly in seeding the territory with that almost indispensable article of food.

After we had arrived on the ground of Great Salt Lake City we pitched our tents by the side of a spring of water; and, after resting a little, I devoted my time chiefly to building temporary houses, putting in crops, and obtaining fuel from the mountains.

Having repented of our sins and renewed our covenants, President John Taylor and myself administered the ordinances of baptism, etc., to each other and to our families, according to the example set by the President and pioneers who had done the same on entering the valley.

These solemnities took place with us and most of our families, November 28, 1847.

Some time in December, having finished sowing wheat and rye, I started, in company with a Brother Higby and others, for Utah Lake with a boat and fish net. We travelled some thirty miles with our boat, etc., on an ox wagon, while some of us rode on horseback. This distance brought us to the foot of Utah Lake, a beautiful sheet of fresh water, some thirty-six miles long by fifteen broad. Here we launched our boat and tried our net, being probably the first boat and net ever used on this sheet of water in modern times.

We sailed up and down the lake shore on its western side for many miles, but had only poor success in fishing. We, however, caught a few samples of mountain trout and other fish.

After exploring the lake and valley for a day or two the company returned home, and a Brother Summers and myself struck westward from the foot of the lake on horseback, on an exploring tour. On this tour we discovered and partly explored Cedar Valley, and there crossed over the west mountain range and discovered a valley beyond; passing through which we crossed a range of hills northward, and entered Tooele Valley. Passing still northward, we camped one night on a bold mountain stream, and the next day we came to the southern extreme of Great Salt Lake, and passing round between it and the west mountain we journeyed in an eastern course, and, crossing the Jordan, arrived in Salt Lake City—having devoted nearly one week to our fishing, hunting and exploring expedition. During all this time we had fine weather and warm days; but the night we arrived home was a cold one, with a severe snow storm. And thus closed the year 1847.

Four pictures of Orson Pratt

Chapter 46

January 1st, 1848.

The opening of the year found us and the community generally in good, comfortable, temporary log or adobe cabins, which were built in a way to enclose the square commenced by the pioneers, and a portion of two other blocks of the city plot. Here life was as sweet and the holidays as merry as in the Christian palaces and mansions of those who had driven us to the mountains.

In February we again commenced to plough for spring crops, while I had the happiness to behold the tender blade of my wheat and rye clothing a few acres with a beautiful green, pleasingly contrasted with the gray, wild, wormwood and other traits of our dreary solitude; while similar pleasing sights stretched away in the distance, marking the bounds of agriculture as possessed by my neighbors.

March 25th—My oldest son Parley celebrated his birthday with a family party—being then eleven years of age.

After dinner, in presence of the assembled family, I related the circumstances of his being a promised child, with an account of his birth, his history, and the death of his mother. I reminded him that he was my first born—my heir, both to estate and Priesthood. I exhorted him to prepare to walk in my footsteps, and to do good and serve God and his fellow men by a well ordered life, and by laying hold of knowledge and a good education. I rehearsed to him my own sufferings, and the sufferings of my family, and of the Church while in the States—telling him of the murder of our prophets and Saints, and how we had been driven to the mountains, robbed and plundered of a very large amount of property and possessions. The day was spent most pleasantly and profitably by all.

I continued my farming operations, and also attended to my ministry in the Church. Devoting my Sabbaths and leisure hours to comforting and encouraging the Saints, and urging them to faith and persevering industry in trying to produce a first harvest in a desert one thousand miles from the nearest place which had matured a crop in modern times.

We had to struggle against great difficulties in trying to mature a first crop. We had not only the difficulties and inexperience incidental to an unknown and untried climate, but also swarms of insects equal to the locusts of Egypt, and also a terrible drought, while we were entirely inexperienced in the art of irrigation; still we struggled on, trusting in God.

During this spring and summer my family and myself, in common with many of the camp, suffered much for want of food. This was the more severe on me and my family because we had lost nearly all our cows, and the few which were spared to us were dry, and, therefore, we had no milk to help out our provisions. I had ploughed and subdued land to the amount of near forty acres, and had cultivated the same in grain and vegetables. In this labor every woman and child in my family, so far as they were of sufficient age and strength, had joined to help me, and had toiled incessantly in the field, suffering every hardship which human nature could well endure. Myself and some of them were compelled to go with bare feet for several months, reserving our Indian moccasins for extra occasions. We toiled hard and lived on a few greens and on thistle and other roots. We had sometimes a little flour and some cheese, and sometimes we were able to procure from our neighbors a little sour skimmed milk or buttermilk.

In this way we lived and raised our first crop in these valleys. And how great was our joy in partaking of the first fruits of our industry.

On the 10th of August we held a public feast under a bowery in the center of our fort. This was called a harvest feast; we partook freely of a rich variety of bread, beef, butter, cheese, cakes, pastry, green corn, melons, and almost every variety of vegetable. Large sheaves of wheat, rye, barley, oats and other productions were hoisted on poles for public exhibition, and there was prayer and thanksgiving, congratulations, songs, speeches, music, dancing, smiling faces and merry hearts. In short, it was a great day with the people of these valleys, and long to be remembered by those who had suffered and waited anxiously for the results of a first effort to redeem the interior deserts of America, and to make her hitherto unknown solitudes "blossom as the rose."

During this autumn our little colony was reinforced by the arrival of President Young and family, accompanied with large trains of emigrants, amounting in all to several thousands. Under his wise counsels city lots were given out, and people began to build on them and vacate the forts. I obtained some lots south of the Temple square, and built a temporary adobe house, where I soon removed with most of my family. Here, in our new habitation, we spent the remainder of the year.

January 1st, 1849—Our city now began to take form and shape, and to be dotted here and there with neat little cottages, or small temporary buildings, composed of adobes or logs. The roofs were generally of poles or timbers covered with earth. Saw mills were now in operation, and a few boards were obtained for floors, doors, etc. Our happy new year passed off merrily, and we were probably as happy a people as could be found on the earth.

February 12th—I met in council with the First Presidency and members of the Twelve, in which certain vacancies in our quorum were filled. We were then instructed to assist in reorganizing the different quorums here, and in establishing righteousness. We accordingly met with the Presidency almost daily, and proceeded to organize and ordain the Presidency of the High Priests quorum, the Presidency of the Stake at Salt Lake City, with its High Council, and to divide the city and county into wards and ordain a bishop over each. In these and similar duties, and in meeting with my quorum and teaching and preaching in the several branches of the Church my time was chiefly spent until spring.

March 15th—I was appointed by a General Convention as one of a committee of ten to draft a constitution for the Provisional State of Deseret.

March 18th—The committee reported, and the Convention unanimously adopted the constitution.

I devoted the fore part of the summer to farming; but, my crop failing, I commenced in July to work a road up the rugged canyon of Big Canyon Creek. I had the previous year explored the canyon for that purpose, and also a beautiful park, * and passes from Salt Lake City to Weber River eastward, in a more southern and less rugged route than the pioneer entrance to the valley. Emigrants now came pouring in from the States on their way to California to seek gold. Money and gold dust was plenty, and merchandise of almost every description came pouring into our city in great plenty.

I soon so far completed my road as to be able to obtain a large amount of fuel and timber. In November I ceased operations in the canyon and broke up my mountain camp and returned to the city.

---

*Since called Parley's Park.

Pony Express station in Parley's Canyon. The first toll road in Parley's Canyon, southeast of Salt Lake City, was built by Parley P. Pratt and was used during the gold rush of 1849.

I now received a commission from the Governor and Legislative Assembly of the State of Deseret to raise fifty men, with the necessary teams and outfit, and go at their head on an exploring tour to the southward.

This company was soon raised, armed, equipped, and ready for a march into the dreary and almost unknown regions of Southern Utah.

I will here give the list of names composing the company, and also a short summary of the report that I gave in to the Legislative Assembly on our return.

PARLEY P. PRATT, *President.*
W. W. PHELPS, D. FULMER, *Counselors.*
ROBERT L. CAMPBELL, *Clerk.*

February 7th, 1850.

FIRST TEN

Isaac C. Haight, *Captain.*
Parley P. Pratt,
William Wadsworth,
Rufus Allen,
Chauncey West,
Dan. Jones,
Hial K. Gay,
George B. Mabson,
Samuel Gould,
Wm. P. Vance.

SECOND TEN

Joseph Matthews, *Captain.*
John Brown,
Nathan Tanner,
Sterling G. Driggs,
Homer Duncan,
Wm. Matthews,
Schuyler Jennings,
John H. Bankhead,
John D. Holiday,
Robert M. Smith.

THIRD TEN

Joseph Horn, *Captain.*
Wm. Brown,

George Nebiker,
Benjamin F. Stewart,
Alexander Wright,
James Farrer,
Henry Heath,
Seth B. Tanner,
Alexander Lemon,
David Fulmer.

FOURTH TEN

Ephraim Green, *Captain.*
Wm. W. Phelps,
Charles Hopkins,
Sidney Willis,
Andrew Blodgett,
Wm. Henry,
Peter Dustin,
Thomas Ricks,
Robert Campbell,
Isaac H. Brown.

FIFTH TEN

Josiah Arnold, *Captain.*
Jonathan Packer,
Christopher Williams,
Stephen Taylor,
Isaac B. Hatch,
John C. Armstrong,
Dimick B. Huntington.

Our company had 12 wagons; 1 carriage; 24 yokes of cattle; 7 beeves; number of horses and mules, 38.

Average in flour, 150 lbs. to each man; besides crackers, bread and meal. One brass field piece; firearms; ammunition in proportion.

At Captain John Brown's, on Cotton Wood, 23d of November, 1849, at 2 P.M., a meeting of the company for exploring the south was convened. Called to order by P. P. Pratt, who gave instructions relative to the necessity of peace, order and good feelings being preserved during this expedition. Supported in this by W. W. Phelps and David Fulmer.

Voted, that Parley P. Pratt be President of the company. That W. W. Phelps and David Fulmer be his Counselors; carried unanimously.

Voted, That John Brown be Captain of Fifty; carried unanimously.

Voted, That W. W. Phelps act as Topographical Engineer; carried unanimously.

Voted, That Ephraim Green be Chief Gunner; carried unanimously.

During our exploring expedition we encountered severe weather, deep snows, and many hardships and toils incident to such an undertaking. We explored the best portions of the country south from Great Salt Lake City to the mouth of Santa Clara, on the Rio Virgin, which is a principal branch of the Rio Colorado. Our distance in going and returning was (counting the direct traveled route as afterward opened), between seven or eight hundred miles. In much of this distance we made the first track; and even the portion which had before been penetrated by wagons was so completely snowed under that we seldom found the trail.

It was during these toils, and perils, and amid the snows of these regions, that I composed the song, beginning, "O, come, come away, from northern blasts retiring," which became a favorite with the singers in camp, and seemed to beguile the tedious winter evenings around our camp fires.

I here give a few extracts from my journal while on our return trip:

January 21st—Having been on our homeward journey for some twenty days, and it snowing severely, we remained in camp. This day I was taken very sick of a bilious attack, and was confined to my bed. We held a council, and finding that our provisions would only sustain half of our company till spring, and traveling with the wagons was impossible, we decided upon leaving half the company to winter there with the wagons and cattle, and the other half, with some of the strongest mules and horses, should attempt to reach Provo—the southern frontier—distance upwards of one hundred miles. The company that remained were mostly young men without families. My counselor, David Fulmer, being placed in command.

It was in a country of shrub cedars, which would afford some shelter for the animals, and richly clothed in bunch grass, and some portions of the hill sides where the snow had blown off being nearly bare, the cattle could live.

January 22d—In the morning I was still sick, but about noon bid farewell to those who stayed, mounted a mule, and, with upwards of twenty men and animals, we commenced our wallowing in the snow. We made about nine miles, and camped in a cedar thicket. Being unable longer to sit on my mule, or stand on my feet, the snow was shoveled away, some blankets spread, and I lay down. I had not eaten one mouthful for a day or two, but vomited many times very severely.

Wednesday, 23d—I was better, and we again started, the snow being from three to four feet deep on a level. The men went ahead on foot, the entire company, men and animals, making but one track. The person breaking the track would tire out in a few moments, and, giving place to another, would fall into the rear. This day we made nine or ten miles, and camped in a mountain pass, thirteen miles south of the Sevier River.

Thursday, 24th—It was long after night when we wallowed into camp, waist deep in snow; and, shoveling away the snow, we made fires, spread our blankets, and sank down to rest, being entirely exhausted— our animals either tied to cedar bushes without food, or wallowing up the hills in search of bare spots of bunch grass.

Friday, 25th—We were obliged to leave several of our animals which gave out. We passed through Round Valley, made about ten miles, camped on the heights, some four miles south of the Sevier. It was still snowing; our animals found some bunch grass on the hill sides.

Saturday, 26th—In the morning we found ourselves so completely buried in snow that no one could distinguish the place where we lay. Some one rising, began shoveling the others out. This being found too tedious a business, I raised my voice like a trumpet, and commanded them to arise; when all at once there was a shaking among the snow piles, the graves were opened, and all came forth! We called this Resurrection Camp. Passing on, we forded the Sevier, and camped on the heights, six or seven miles north of the same, the snow this day being much less.

Sunday, 27th—Our provisions being nearly exhausted, Chauncey West and myself volunteered to take some of the strongest animals and try to penetrate to Provo, which was still some fifty miles distant, in order to send back provisions to the remainder, who were to follow slowly.

We started at daylight, breaking the way on foot, and leading the mules in our track, and sometimes riding them. Traveled all day, averaging about knee deep in snow. Camped at eleven at night on Summit Creek, extremely hungry and feet badly frozen. We built a small fire, it being the coldest night we had ever experienced, and after trying in vain to thaw out our frozen shoes, stockings and the bottoms of our drawers and pants, we rolled ourselves in our blankets, and lay trembling with cold a few hours.

Monday, 28th—Arose long before day; bit a few mouthfuls off the last black frozen biscuit remaining. Saddled up our animals, and, after another laborious day, living on a piece of biscuit not so large as our fist, we entered Provo at dark; raised a *posse* of men and animals, with provisions, and sent back same night.

These picked up one of our men, whose name was Taylor, who had wandered off ahead of the rest, and had reached within some eight miles of Provo. They found him sunk down in the snow, in a helpless condition, his horse standing by him, and both nearly frozen to death. He lived, but in a measure lost the use of his limbs.

This relief company met those we had left behind somewhere in the southern end of Utah Valley, some twenty miles from Provo. They were entirely out of food and very faint and weary. They were plentifully supplied and safely conducted to the settlement.

I rested a day or two in Provo and then started again for home. After riding thirty-six miles on a mule, I took supper with a friend in Cottonwood, and, leaving the mule, started at sundown and walked the other ten miles which brought me once more to my home. This was about the first of February, 1850.

The company we had left with the wagons and oxen wintered themselves and cattle very well, and finally arrived home in safety in March following.

After my return from my southern exploring expedition I re-entered the Legislature and continued my duties as a member of that body until its annual adjournment.

Some time in this month I again commenced work on my road in

Big Canyon Creek, and in getting out timber and wood from the same. I continued this operation during the remainder of the season—obtaining much building and fencing timber and a large quantity of poles. In July I had so far completed the road as to open it for the California emigration. The amount of toll taken this first season was about one thousand five hundred dollars.

The following winter, being re-elected to the Legislative Assembly of the State of Deseret, I devoted much of the time in the duties thereof. I also continued in the duties of my Priesthood. And, lest any time should run to waste, I filled up the interstices not otherwise occupied, in the study of the Spanish language.

During this winter I was called by the First Presidency and set apart to take charge of a General Mission to the Pacific. I composed a song, which was sung before the congregation in the Tabernacle, on the occasion of our departure on this mission, commencing "Holy, happy, pure and free," etc.

I now close this chapter of my history by saying that my life up to this date has been an eventful one, somewhat hurried and laborious; and, if "variety is the spice of life," I think it may truly be called a spicy one—which circumstance will account for the imperfect sketch I have written of it.

Chapter 47

START ON MY PACIFIC MISSION—SKETCH OF THE JOURNEY—ATTACKED BY IN-DIANS—CROSSING THE DESERT—ARRIVAL AT LOS ANGELES.

I left Great Salt Lake City for the Pacific, on a mission to its islands and coasts, being commissioned and set apart for that work by the First Presidency of the Church of Jesus Christ of Latter-day Saints.

Passing through various settlements, and visiting the brethren, I arrived at Fort Utah, and assisted the Presidency to organize a stake of Zion, with its High Council and other officers, and to ordain and set them apart.

Friday, 21st—I took leave of my friends and pursued my journey on horseback, twenty-eight miles to Peteetneet, where I overtook my teams, and spent Saturday in organizing the company with which we journeyed. Their outfit consisted of about one hundred and fifty wagons. Most of the company were emigrating with C. C. Rich and A. Lyman to Southern California.

My own party of missionaries consisted of the following Elders, viz.: John Murdock, Rufus Allen, Wm. Perkins, S. Woodbury, F. H. Hammond, P. B. Wood, Mr. Hopkins and Morris Miner.

Mr. Perkins, Mr. Woodbury, Mr. Hammond and Mr. Hopkins were accompanied by a wife each, as well as myself.

Monday, 24th—We commenced our journey from Peteetneet organized in companies of tens, fifties and one hundred—fifty journeying together.

Our fifty, commanded by Captain Seely, traveled six miles to Summit Creek.

Tuesday, 25th—I took a walk in the morning about three miles and ascended a beautiful height, which afforded a fair view (with a telescope) of the head of Utah Lake and the valley of Salt Creek, which enters the lake through an extensive meadow at the head of the lake, forming at its junction a beautiful harbor and a convenient beach of sand.

The depth of water not known, but its deep blue color intimated sufficient depth for small crafts.

About two miles west of an encampment on Summit Creek I discovered a beautiful and inexhaustible stone quarry of blue lime, which, both for building and lime, will be very useful and convenient to the settlement which will soon grow up on that beautiful site.

Returning to camp, we journeyed eleven miles to Willow Creek—the country being rich in grass, and watered by Salt Creek, a stream of one and a half rods wide, and several large springs running north into Utah Lake.

Friday, 28th—I ascended a ridge of mountains, and obtained a view of an extensive country to the west, composed of desert plains, hills, and confused fragments of broken mountain chains, without fertility or anything to redeem or enliven this landscape except the windings of the Sevier River and narrow, grassy bottoms. And even this scene soon loses itself amid the black and barren hills of the dreary waste.

This day we passed through about ten miles of waste country, with some grassy spots and cedar groves, and encamped on the Sevier River.

Saturday, 29th—We passed the ford, three feet deep and one hundred and fifty feet wide—a smooth and sluggish current—and encamped on its southern bank.

The weather bad, with squalls of snow and cold winds. The hills afford some scattered bunch grass, which is very good.

Monday, 31st—We traveled thirteen miles through a pass where the hills were very rich in grass and fuel, and full of fine stone quarries. This pass was five miles from the river.

Thence through a valley rich in grass and soil, beautiful and extensive, and abundantly supplied with fuel on its borders, but destitute of living streams, although the melting snows of its bordering mountains supply some streams which run a short distance at certain seasons of the year, and then sink.

April 1st—Camp divided for convenience of travel, and General Rich and myself, with twenty-three wagons, traveled thirteen miles, and encamped at a beautiful spring brook, among grassy hills, interspersed with cedar, like an orchard.

Our road to-day led through a pass in the mountains by a gradual ascent for about three miles, and then down very gradually for ten miles among hills, plains and little vales, more rich in bunch grass and cedar fuel, and more varied and beautiful than any other country I ever beheld. Every high hill, every dell, every vale or nook seemed richly coated with a living green of rich grass, and set about with cedars from twelve to twenty-five feet high, like an old orchard.

Its northern bounds, limited by a rocky and barren range of high mountains through which we had passed.

Its eastern limit was a snowy and timbered range, which divides between the valley where we were and the Sevier River, which heads in the south, near the rim of the Great Basin, in a beautiful salmon trout lake, surrounded with lofty pines and cedars, and runs in a northerly direction, till it sweeps round to the west and southwest, and forms a lake which is in view from our camp, and appears like a silver mirror at some thirty or forty miles distance.

I arose in the morning, and with my large telescope viewed from an eminence the vast country before me.

On the east the high mountain chains at several miles distance appears snowy and timbered, and pierced with gorges accessible for roads to be made to the timber; and giving rise to several streams which meander through this vast valley on our south and west, and enter the lakes or sinks in their own rich alluvials.

To our southwest and northwest the view is almost boundless; consisting of a vast valley interspersed with fertile meadows, desert spots, known by their darker hues; lakes, rivulets, distinguished by the yellow meadow grasses and red willow streaks; and hills here and there dotted with cedars, and the whole bounded, in the vast and dim distance, by dark mountains not very high. Beyond which, at the distance of perhaps a hundred miles, appear other and more lofty peaks white with snow, and looking up like distant white clouds on the horizon.

Here are resources for farming, stock raising, fuel, etc., in sight of our present encampment, probably more than sufficient to sustain the present population of Rhode Island; and yet, not a domestic animal, except those of the passing traveller, or a human being, save the occasional savage in his wanderings, occupies any portion of this wide domain.

Crossing several streams in the same large valley, all bordered by rich lands, we at length left the valley and journeyed two miles over a hilly country, well supplied with cedar and shrub pines for fuel, and bunch grass for feed, but not well watered.

Thence a few miles over a worthless country to the Beaver River.

This is a large stream, swift and clear, running in several branches through a large and fertile bottom; the soil of which appears rich, but highly impregnated with saleratus, and the table lands, which surround it, barren or nearly destitute of pasturage.

However, I think the place worthy of settlement, and, probably, containing eight or ten thousand acres of land which may be watered and cultivated.

Leaving this place, we passed another long stretch of upland, destitute of all resources, except grass and fuel, which were abundant in places.

We were at length met by G. A. Smith and others, from Little Salt Lake settlement; and accompanied by them, we all arrived on Red Creek, in the same valley. Here the camp found water and grass to refresh themselves after so wearisome a journey.

April 10th.—Same evening I arrived in the fort, accompanied by the citizens, who came out to meet us. I found the inhabitants all well, and the settlement in a truly flourishing condition. Hundreds of acres of grain had been sown, gardens planted, etc., and the farming land nearly enclosed; together with a most substantial saw mill, and many houses of wood and of sun dried brick, built and in progress. Building materials consisting of timber of the finest quality, viz: pine, fir and cedar, together with good building stone and brick, were scattered in profusion in every direction.

Water ditches were flowing for mills and irrigation purposes in many directions.

Mechanics' shops were in operation; such as joiners, carpenters, millwrights, coopers, blacksmiths, shoemakers, etc.

All this was the work of two or three months, in winter and early spring; not to mention a large enclosure of pickets in the centre of the fort—a council house of hewn timber, and a bastion of the same material.

The number of men composing the settlement and performing all this work, did not exceed one hundred and twenty all told, including old men, boys and Indian servants, just being tamed and initiated into the first rudiments of industry.

All the camps moved from Red Creek and encamped near the fort, where we tarried a few days.

April 12th.—Celebrated my birthday by a feast jointly provided by us and G. A. Smith, at his house. Ten or twelve persons sat down to a sumptuous repast.

April 14th.—We removed to Summit Creek—distance seven miles. Here we tarried one week, in course of which the rear camp, headed by Amasa Lyman, arrived in good condition.

Sunday, 20th.—All met in a general assembly, to worship God and to edify one another; being joined by the people from the fort, we had a good time. The Spirit was poured out upon us. G. A. Smith and others spake with power in the Spirit and testimony of Jesus; rebuking iniquity, worldly mindedness, unbelief, profanity, and all manner of iniquity, and exhorting the people to obey the servants of the Lord in all righteousness.

As the meeting was about to close P. B. Lewis, who lived in this settlement, was set apart by prayer, prophecy and the laying on of hands of the four Apostles present, as one of the Pacific missionaries. He had already moved into camp with his wife and teams, etc., to accompany us. We travelled eight miles to a stream called Coal Creek. Encamped and built a bridge across the deep and narrow channel, about four feet wide, and tarried here next day for the remainder of our company, some of whom had failed to obtain their animals the day before.

This encampment was about ten miles below the crossing of the same stream on the old road. I had, however, looked out a new route, which would save some eight or ten miles.

This stream forms a rich meadow bottom, of about fifteen miles long and two broad.

Abundance of cedar fuel and rich pasturage is found on the table lands which border this bottom; and iron ore abounds a few miles to the southwest, not to mention a large cottonwood grove in the upper part of the meadow, and a canyon opening into the mountains, from which the stream issues. Taken all together, this place combines materials for a large settlement.

Wednesday, 23d—We travelled twenty miles without water, over hills and plains, and among forests of cedar, and encamped after dark at a spring, having regained the old road a few miles before encamping.

While the cattle were feeding I ascended an eminence, and, with my telescope, viewed the largest valley I had ever seen in the great basin. It might have been seventy miles from south to north, and thirty miles from east to west.

Some signs of water and rich and fertile spots appeared in the dim distance; but, generally speaking, it was a cheerless monotony, without water, and clothed in the leaden hue of the desert.

We travelled several miles over a fine table land, on east of said valley, which still stretched away some thirty miles to the west, and was finally bounded by a low range of mountains on its south and west, and these again were backed by a still higher range and white with snow. Their lofty peaks, at fifty or sixty miles distance, peeping up from behind the nearer hills like distant clouds on the far off horizon.

After passing a few miles of very hilly road we came down upon a small stream, which heads in numerous spring meadows near the rim of the basin, on the divide between it and the Colorado. Here we camped to rest on Saturday and Sunday.

This little mountain paradise was, by the present road, three hundred and eleven miles from the Great Salt Lake City, and was altogether the most beautiful place in all the route. Some thousand or fifteen hundred acres of bottom, or meadow lands, were spread out before us like a green carpet richly clothed with a variety of grasses, and possessing a soil both black, rich and quick—being a mixture of sand, gravel and clayey loam, and the decayed visitations of ages. It was everywhere moistened with springs, and would produce potatoes, vegetables and the smaller grains in abundance without watering.

The surrounding hills were not abrupt, but rounded off, presenting a variety of beauteous landscapes, and everywhere richly clothed with the choicest kind of bunch grass, and bordered in their higher eminences with cedar and nut pine sufficient for fuel.

Afar off, behind the hills in the east, could be seen from the eminence high, snowy mountains, black in places with tall timber, plainly distinguishable with the telescope, probably from ten to twenty miles distance.

May 13th—We encamped at a large spring, usually called the Vegas—having travelled nearly two hundred miles since the foregoing was written. The country through which we have passed is a worthless desert, consisting of mountains of naked rock and barren plains, with the exception of here and there a small stream, with feed sufficient for our cattle.

The longest distance without water is about fifty miles, which we passed on Saturday and Sunday last, and arrived here safe and without much suffering. We have as yet lost no cattle through hunger, thirst, or fatigue. Two cows were stolen from us by the Indians on the Rio Virgin.

The place where we now are is about two hundred and fifty miles from the coast settlements on the Pacific. It is well watered, abundance of grass, and would admit of a small settlement—say one or two hundred families—has a good soil, good water and fuel, but no building timber.

The same remarks would apply to the last stream, fifty-three miles from this, called the Muddy. The Indians already raise wheat and corn there.

Wednesday, 21st—We encamped at a place called Resting Springs, where we arrived on the 19th after dark.

This is a fine place for rest and recruiting animals—being a meadow of rich grass and sufficiently extensive to sustain thousands of cattle. The water is sufficient for all travelling purposes, although the stream is small.

Since leaving the Vegas we have travelled seventy-five miles through a most horrible desert, consisting of mountain ridges and plains of naked rock, or sand and gravel, and sometimes clay, destitute of soil or fertility, except a few small springs and patches of grass.

Attack by Indians

The weather, contrary to our expectations, has been universally cool since we left the Muddy; thick vests, and sometimes coats, have been worn in the noon of a sunny day, and the sun has been sought rather than the shade. The nights have all been cool, and some of them as cold in the middle or latter part of May as the nights usually are in March and April in Great Salt Lake City.

Twenty miles from the Vegas, our camp was assailed in the evening, about ten o'clock, by a shower of arrows from the savage mountain robbers; some of which passed near men's heads and all fell promiscuously among men, women, children and cattle, but did no injury. Our men mustered and returned the fire without effect.

Afterwards, in the same place, a savage, single handed, made his way among the cattle, in open day, while they were under the care of armed herdsmen and shot an ox and a mule; one was wounded in the hip, and the other in the leg; but they are both doing well.

Friday, 23d.—Provided with water and hay we travelled on fourteen miles. Road heavy, up hill and sandy; day hot. Arrived at Salt Spring gold mines towards evening; water brackish; but answered for stock and use.

After resting for a few hours we started on in the evening and travelled all night, with the exception of short intervals of rest. The hot day and heavy road had so harassed the cattle that we made but little progress.

Next morning we continued to travel, finding no grass nor water. The road was up hill for ten or twelve miles, and rough; the day rather cool.

Long before night our hay and water were consumed, and the camp in a suffering condition. Some cattle had given out entirely; and fifteen or twenty miles still intervened between us and water, and without grass sufficient to feed a goat. Six or eight miles of the way was still up hill. This was the most trying time of all.

At dark, about fourteen miles from water, *our ten* was behind, and my two wagons were the rear of all; and some of my oxen had already failed. We still rolled slowly, resting every few minutes. We soon found the different portions of the camp ahead, halted, and lost in slumber— every man and beast, by common consent, sunk in profound slumber, and probably dreaming of water and feed ahead.

We, viz., *our ten*, with some exceptions, slipped quietly past them, and resting often and a few minutes at a time continued to roll. The night was cool, and a miraculous strength seemed to inspire the cattle.

At sunrise next morning we arrived at the Bitter Springs; the water of which was about as palatable as a dose of salts.

The other camps followed us in, and by ten o'clock all were in, except three oxen left by the way, and two wagons with their loads, left twenty miles back.

Men and animals were so exhausted that, after digging and improving the water, and a general watering, it was ten hours or more before the cattle were driven to what little feed there was, a mile or two distant.

I rode back ten miles and carried water and feed to two animals, and tried in vain to drive them in.

In this desert we had travelled, without much intermission, two days and two nights; during which we had no feed nor water, excepting that which we carried with us, and the Salt Springs, and the Bitter Springs, and a little dry feed to refresh upon after this toil—women and children, young and old, and old men walked on foot day and night.

It was certainly the hardest time I ever saw; but we cried unto God, and in the name of Jesus Christ asked Him to strengthen us and our teams, and He did so in a miraculous manner, and we were saved from the horrors of the desert.

Wednesday, 28th.—We arrived on the Mohave River in the evening, in an exhausted condition; having travelled thirty-one miles without water or much rest. The day had been warm and some two or three cattle gave out, and were left by the way.

At this camp we found plenty of water, timber, soil and grass. Those appointed to the Pacific mission (with the exception of brother Hopkins, who said he should not fill the mission), now took leave of brother Rich and company, and travelled twelve miles up the Mohave, and encamped in a pleasant place, with water, feed and fuel.

June 1st.—Rested Sunday. At two o'clock had a prayer meeting in the shade of some trees. All the members of the mission offered themselves in prayer, acknowledging their faults and imperfections; seeking the remission of the same; renewing their covenants with God and with each other; and giving thanks to Him for deliverance from the perils of the desert, and praying that God would graciously open the way for the further prosecution of the appointed mission. All seemed renewed in spirits, faith and union, and felt blessed of the Lord.

Passing on our journey over one hundred miles we came to a fine farm, which had wheat and other grain, gardens, and even bearing fruit trees, etc. We also found a member of our Society by the name of Crisman, who, with his family resided on the place. We were kindly received, and after resting a few days, obtained a team, and brother Wood went to Los Angeles, thirty miles, to obtain supplies to send back. We sent a load of supplies to the companies on the Mohave River, and then moved our camp to brother Crisman's, where we arrived at noon, and were received with welcome; and all rejoiced that our desert and toilsome journey was at an end. Having rested the last week, every man who was with me as a fellow missionary accompanied me to the lone hills, about one mile from camp, where in solitude we joined in prayer with all the energy we possessed; praying in turn, and asking our Father in Heaven, in the name of Jesus Christ, to open our way, to guide us in wisdom in our duties, to give us the gift of the Holy Ghost, and to supply us with means to proceed on our journey in His own way, and in His own time.

We also remembered our families before the Lord, and all the authorities and interests of the kingdom of God.

Selling some of our cattle and one wagon, we journeyed seventeen miles and encamped on a small stream near some hills of wild oats, which served us for feed. We also pulled several bundles to fill our beds, and to take with us to Los Angeles, where we arrived in the evening of the 16th of June.

Several Americans called on us, conversed in a friendly manner, and seemed much interested in the Mormon settlement about to be made. More particularly as to the additional security this population would afford to the peace and order of a distracted country.

Chapter 48

Los Angeles is a fertile, well watered, and delightful valley of vineyards and orchards, with a fine old Spanish town—a mixture of American, European, Spanish and Indian population—and has been cultivated for eighty years.

Thursday, 19th.—I attended the Catholic celebration of Corpus Christi, and witnessed perhaps five hundred people of all ages, sexes and colors, the Indian blood prevailing—three priests at their head—performing the various ceremonies. The ladies in the finest dresses I ever beheld in any country, consisting of silks and satins of various figures and extreme costliness; white muslin, cambric, etc., made in full dresses, together with costly silk and satin shawls worn over the head and enclosing the shoulders, bosom and waist, leaving only the face in view; while all other portions of their persons were buried beneath the rich and ample folds of costly apparel.

In these costly robes every female knelt or sat on the filthy floor of earth in the old church for hours! No seats, carpets, or spreads of any kind; while various images were exhibited in turn, and were worshipped in humble postures, and with low chants, amid the discharges of cannon and crackers, the beating of drums, and the tinkling of bells.

Clouds of incense rose before each image, and perhaps one hundred candles were burning at midday. All the men were also dressed in their best, and knelt in a devout manner, or stood in a reverent posture with hats off.

Not one changed place, or was seen to leave the church, although the services lasted for hours, without one seat or other convenience whereon to rest.

This ended, all formed in procession and moved around the public square, beneath the beautiful arches richly decorated, and the walk lined on each side with green branches.

At proper distances were placed images amid costly decorations, before which all fell upon their knees, and remained for a length of time prostrated in the thick dust with all their finery, chanting hymns, praying and worshipping, while crackers were discharged in profusion. Even all the spectators must stand in the broiling sun in the roads uncovered, or give great offense.

In a few days brother Wood returned from the rear camps where he and brother Allen had been with provisions. Reported all well and prosperous. Brothers Lyman and Rich also paid us a visit, and some others.

Brothers Hammond, Perkins, Wood and Murdock with their baggage, etc., started for the landing at San Pedro. The remainder tarried to complete their sales.

Sunday, 29th.—I preached in the court house in Los Angeles to some forty attentive persons, mostly American gentlemen.

Monday, 30th.—I sold my last wagon and moved down to the Port at San Pedro. Found that portion of the brethren well who went down before, and camped with them on the beach.

July 7th.—We embarked on board the steamship Ohio, and set sail for San Francisco, at 4 o'clock P. M.

After four days' rather rough passage, we arrived in San Francisco on the 11th inst. at eleven o'clock, A. M. Found some good brethren who rendered us assistance in various ways. Rented a house the same day, and all moved into it together.

Brothers Lyman and Rich arrived per steamer Goliah. We visited and received visits.

Sunday, 20th.—I preached at eleven A. M. in a large room, a goodly number of persons out to hear, and good attention. Next morning we repaired to the water and baptized eight persons, and the same evening met at the house of Brother Wimmer and organized a branch of the Church, confirming the above persons.

I was chosen president of this branch, and Philo B. Wood, clerk. The remainder of the week devoted to writing and instructing inquirers who called.

I wrote the following letter to Elder Addison Pratt, Society Isles:

SAN FRANCISCO, *July 26, 1851.*

DEAR BROTHER PRATT: My long contemplated mission to the Pacific has at length become a reality. I am here, having left home in

March last. Eight of us are here, and will go to the Sandwich Islands and elsewhere as the way opens and the Spirit directs. Brother P. B. Lewis and wife would have sailed for your islands with letters, etc., but brothers Clark and Thompkins having arrived, we concluded to send no more laborers to that part of the vineyard at present.

I hold the presidency of all the islands and coasts of the Pacific, under the direction of the First Presidency of the Church—to open the door to every nation and tongue, as fast as the way is prepared and the Lord directs, for the preaching of the gospel of salvation.

As president of that part of the vineyard you will preach the gospel to every people as fast as possible. Send men to the Friendly Isles, or to any other groups where the way may be open, and as circumstances will permit, as you are led by the Holy Ghost. If you need more laborers send to me at this place. I am well known here, and making some progress. Also make your report to me from time to time, and ask such counsel as you may need.

Elder Philip B. Lewis will sail for the Sandwich Islands, accompanied by his wife, brother Hammond and wife, and brother Woodbury and wife. He will have the presidency of those islands. It would be well if you would correspond with him.

The work is prospering wonderfully in Deseret, England, Wales, Scotland, Switzerland, Italy, Denmark, Sweden, Norway, etc. Several young men are with me who will go to Chili and Peru in due time. Bishop Murdock will also go soon to the English Colonies in New Zealand, Van Dieman's Land, or New Holland, if the Lord will.

Our instructions to the Elders abroad, everywhere, are to seek the Spirit and gift of the Holy Ghost, by humble prayer and faith and good works. Also, to take no part in government matters, except to uphold and obey the authorities and laws of every nation where they may labor, and teach others to do so.

The laws of the country we are in will govern us in all things consistent with liberty of conscience, freedom of speech, etc.

With sentiments of love and good will I subscribe myself,

Your brother in the gospel,

PARLEY P. PRATT.

SAN FRANCISCO, *July 26, 1851.*

To His Majesty KING KAMEHAMEHA *and the People of the Sandwich Isles.* GREETING:

I beg leave to introduce to the favorable notice of your Majesty and subjects, and to commend to your protection, hospitality and kind consideration the following persons, who go out as missionaries and residents to your country:

Elders P. B. Lewis, Francis A. Hammond and Stillman Woodbury, with their wives.

These persons are from Great Salt Lake City, Utah Territory, U. S., and have been selected by the Presidency of the Church of Jesus Christ of Latter-day Saints to fulfil a mission to the Pacific.

Mr. Hammond is a former resident and artisan of your kingdom, and we trust is favorably known to your Majesty and some of his fellow citizens. We can confidently recommend these gentlemen as men of good character, and men who bring good news, peace and good will to man.

With sentiments of high consideration and esteem for your Majesty and the people of your realm, I have the honor to subscribe myself,

Your humble servant and the friend of man,

P. P. PRATT,
President of the Pacific Mission of the
Church of Jesus Christ of Latter-day Saints.

I here give a few extracts from a letter to President Brigham Young:

SAN FRANCISCO, *August 28, 1851.*

PRESIDENT YOUNG.

Dear Brother: I am well, or rather so as to be able to perform my daily duties, although not in good health.

I arrived in this place some time in July, together with those who accompanied me on the mission. * * * If the Presidency wishes to make any communication on any subject, letters addressed to me at San Francisco, California, will be forwarded to me to Chili, or elsewhere, as I shall not leave this place without appointing an agent to receive and forward all papers and communications.

The Sandwich Islands are at peace, and enjoy a free government. We have sent to those islands three additional missionaries who sailed on the sixth day of August for the Port of Honolulu. P. B. Lewis is appointed to preside over that mission.

* * * Since I have arrived here I have been diligent in the duties of my calling every hour, and have called upon God for His Spirit to help me with all the energy I possessed, and without ceasing. The result is,

the Spirit of the Lord God has been upon me continually, in such light, and joy, and testimony as I have seldom experienced.

Brothers A. Lyman and C. C. Rich have been here with me some of the time; we have called together the old members and others, and preached repentance and reformation of life. We have re-baptized many of them, and have re-organized the Church. Several new members are being added—some of whom are young people of the old members, and others are strangers from different countries. We are upwards of fifty members in number. We have preaching twice a day on Sundays in a large theatre in the centre of the city, and prayer meetings on Sunday and Thursday evenings. Strangers give good attention. The members feel well, and are full of faith and the good Spirit, and the Spirit is poured out till our hearts are full.

I expect to leave this country soon for South America, unless I should be able to go to New York, *via* the Isthmus, to get some books printed.

I am studying Spanish with all diligence, and will, I trust, master it in the course of a few months.

Now, my dear brethren of the Presidency, accept this manifestation of my remembrance, good wishes and determinations, and rest assured you are always upheld by my prayers and good wishes. I want your prayers—your continued confidence, and your good wishes and fellowship. I want the Spirit of God and His angels to be with me; and I fear not earth, nor hell, nor men, nor devils, nor death. I desire power to do good continually, and to bring about the restoration of His people. I glory in my calling. I would not exchange it for any other position or calling on this earth.

I hope to come home by and by and see you all, and see the preparations for the ordinances and powers of Heaven in your midst in state of forwardness; such as peace, union and diligence can alone produce. So farewell.

With my best wishes and prayers,

Your brother and laborer in the truth,

P. P. PRATT.

During my stay in San Francisco I wrote a proclamation of the gospel addressed to the people of the coasts and islands of the Pacific, which was afterwards published by Elder Wandell in Australia. I also commenced the book entitled *Key to Theology*. At a public meeting of the Saints, Elder George K. Wimmer was unanimously chosen and set apart

to preside over the San Francisco branch—myself being honorably discharged from the duties of the same, with a view of a mission to Chili.

I then spoke of my duties to other parts of the Pacific; was honorably
discharged from the presidency of the branch with a vote of thanks, and
a sum of money, amounting in all to fourteen hundred and ten dollars,
was then and afterwards subscribed to assist me on my mission.

Sept. 5.—I sailed for Valparaiso, Chili, on board the bark Henry
Kelsey. After a tedious and disagreeable passage of sixty-four days, ar-
rived safe in Valparaiso, Nov. 8th, accompanied by my wife and Elder
Rufus Allen, all in tolerable health.

Found the country in a state of civil war, and most kinds of business
at a dead stand—men's hearts failing them for fear.

I then finished the following letter which I had commenced on the
sea:

SHIP "HENRY KELSEY," PACIFIC OCEAN,
Lat. 24 N., Lon. 115 W.,
Sept. 15, 1851.

Dear Family:—Here we are on the deep, bound for Chili, S. A.—
self, Phebe and R. Allen. We sailed from San Francisco on the 5th inst.
Have had fine weather, excepting three days, in which we were be-
calmed; and have sailed more than eleven hundred miles. We are now
running before the wind seven miles an hour. We have all been sea sick,
and have not yet recovered in full. We are the only passengers, and have
the cabin to ourselves, except at meals. We study Spanish every day. It
is a beautiful language, and wonderfully adapted to the simplicity of the
Lamanites. I hope to master it during the passage and a few months' residence among the Chilians.

We pay sixty dollars for passage in the cabin, and found. We expect
to be two months in going.

Well, dear ones, six months have passed, and their events been recorded in the records of eternity since we parted; all this time I have had
not one lisp from you. Oh, how lonesome! Just imagine the monotony!
Sky and sea! Sea and sky! Night and day! Day and night! Infinitude of
space! Boundless waste! Emblem of eternal silence! Eternal banishment!
Eternal loneliness, where the voice of the bridegroom and of the bride
are not heard. Where the holy music of children's voices, in joyous mer-
riment, falls not on the ear; where no changing or varied landscape re-
lieves the eye; where no vegetation, or leafy bower, or sweet blooming
flower cheers the senses; where no birds tune their soft notes of praise to
announce the dawn, or sound the requiem of the closing day.

Even the fierce and ravenous beast of the desert (which, in his native solitude, announces with doleful and prolonged howls the midnight hour, or wakes the weary traveller at early dawn, and gives the signal for another day of thirst, and toil, and suffering) is lacking here.

On this boundless waste of waters there is seldom anything to break the monotony of eternal silence, or, rather, of the roar of the waves as they break in increasing foam upon each other, or against the vessel's side.

Thanks for that promise, *"There shall be no more sea."* Thanks for the hope that all the elements of nature will one day be adapted to the enjoyment or occupation of intellectual life, or social and sympathetic existence.

Just imagine sundown, twilight, the shades of evening, the curtains of the solitary night gathering in silent gloom and lone melancholy around a father who loves his home and its inmates; his fireside and the family altar! Behold him standing leaning over the vessel's side as it glides over the waters of the lone and boundless Pacific, gazing for hours in succession into the bosom of its dark abyss, or watching its white foam and sparkling spray! What are his thoughts? Can you divine them? Behold, he prays! For what does he pray? For every wife, for every child, for every near and dear friend he has on earth, he prays most earnestly! most fervently! He calls each by name over and over again, before the altar of remembrance. And when this is done for all on earth, he remembers those in Heaven; calls their names; communes with them in spirit; wonders how they are doing; whether they think of him. He calls to mind their acts and sufferings in life, their death, and the grave where sleeps their precious dust.

This done, he prays for Zion, Jerusalem, Judah, Israel, the Church, the Holy Priesthood, the resurrection of the just, the kingdom and coming of Messiah, the end of war, and sin, and death, and wrong, and oppression, and sorrow, and mourning, and tears; and for earth, and Heaven, and God, angels and men, to be joined forever in the bonds of eternal peace, and love and truth.

This done, he commends himself, the vessel and his all on board to God, and to the guardianship of his good angel. Amen. Walks the deck a few minutes, examines the sails, the speed of the vessel, the course of the wind, and then retires to rest to dream of home.

October 5th.—Coast of Peru, S. A., lat. 3 deg. 30 m. S. A month has passed on the ocean; much head wind, some calms, and more or less sea-sickness has attended us by turns until the present. We have not been able to read, write, or study much, therefore the time has passed off very tediously indeed.

We have a miser for a captain, who thinks more of a sixpence than he does of our lives or even of his own. He will not suffer the steward to cook potatoes, bread, pies, puddings or any other wholesome food, but keeps us on hard, mouldy bread, full of bugs and worms, and on salt beef and pork—the pork being rotten. He has flour, potatoes and good pork, but will not allow it to be used; thus you will readily perceive that we are truly in unpleasant circumstances.

Last evening we came near a shipwreck, having run near the land without knowing it, and it fell calm. The ship became unmanageable, and was drifting on to the shore, but we cast anchor and awaited the light of morning, when we got under weigh with much labor, and stood again to sea.

FRENCH HOTEL, *Valparaiso, Chili, S. A.,*
November 9th.

Dear Friends:—After a most disagreeable and tedious passage of sixty-four days we have at length arrived in port, in tolerable health. We landed yesterday at noon, and took lodgings and board at a French Hotel, where we have a great variety of good eating, and a front parlor to ourselves—price four dollars per day for three of us. The proprietor speaks French, the clerk French, with a little English, the landlady German, the waiter Spanish, and ourselves English, with a little Spanish.

So you see we have a little Babel of our own, independently of Nimrod or the great tower.

We find the country in the midst of revolution and civil war. Two persons and their adherents fighting for power and rule. Business is dull, living high, and doubt and uncertainty characterizing every transaction in the various business departments.

On Sunday we attended a meeting in a very large building. We saw thousands of both sexes, and of all classes and ages, throng the place, bow down on their knees and worship certain images and paintings with much apparent devotion. No instructions were given in any language, no music, no voice or sound, except a low, plaintive voice in the far end of the room, not addressed to the people, neither sufficiently loud or distinct to be understood by them.

The worshippers were dressed in a variety of degrees of neatness or of its opposite. Some of them wore very costly apparel, and others were very neatly clad. All seemed full of zeal and devotion. All bowed down on their knees in silent, solemn attitudes. All their faces seemed disfigured with a painful and awe-sticken solemnity. All made certain signs and motions, while they said nothing audible, and the impression of a strange observer would be that the image, to which every eye was turned with long and supplicating gaze and imploring look, had no ears to hear, but was deeply versed in the science of physiognomy, and also acquainted with the deaf and dumb alphabet.

On inquiry, we were informed that this kind of worship prevailed throughout Spanish America and various other countries, and that it is called by the dignified name of Christianity, and that it is very ancient.

From all which circumstances I infer that it must have been instituted soon after the Church of Jesus Christ became extinct in the Roman world, and, by some unaccountable blunder, borrowed its name from those institutions, which it does not even resemble in the least in any one feature save the name.

Sunday, November 16th. Dear friends:—During the past week we have rented a house, purchased furniture and commenced housekeeping. We devote almost our entire time to the Spanish language.

Our house is in the rear of a block of buildings which fronts a large and beautiful street, called Victoria street. It opens into a large yard, surrounded with high walls and with other buildings, and filled with beautiful trees, such as orange, fig, peach, pear, etc., together with pinks and a variety of other flowers and shrubs. Its walks and pavements are neatly swept, and the houses around it occupied with widows, orphans, etc., of a good class of Spanish or Chilanoes, and their kind and sociable young people and little children.

We divide our time between reading and studying our Spanish lessons, and chatting, visiting, reading Spanish, hearing them read, and playing with the little ones, etc., all of which pleases them much, and causes us to advance in the language with a rapidity which is almost astonishing to ourselves and to them. Truly Providence has ordered our footsteps and cast our lot in pleasant circumstances, when we were strangers in a strange land, and among a people of a strange tongue. Truly He has opened our way to learn that tongue, and we can learn it if we are diligent.

Rents are high here, provisions and fuel dear. Strawberries, oranges, lemons, etc., are in market, as well as green peas, and other vegetables, and melons. It is, in fact, a state of advanced spring or early summer. The peaches, pears and figs are perhaps one-third their size on the trees, while the flowers are in full bloom.

NOVEMBER IN CHILI

'Tis the spring of the year, all the fountains are full,
    All nature is pregnant with life and with love;
A chorus of voices ascend from each pool,
    A myriad of songsters enliven the grove.
To her nest in the Andes, the condor retires,
    The winds from Magellan no longer prevail,
And Sol, with the north breeze returning, inspires
    New life on the zephyr, and love on the gale.
The forest is clad in its robes of fresh green—
    Where the dove sings an anthem, his mate to decoy.
The orchard is dressed as a holiday queen,
    And the rosebud is bursting with fulness of joy.
The orange, the olive, the fig and the vine
    Are clothed as in Eden, with innocent bloom;
The earth is an altar of incense divine,
    Exhales a sweet odor of richest perfume.

The young of the flock bound exulting away
    While their dams nip the blade, 'mid the dewdrops of morn,
And groups of young children are sportive and gay;
    Yet my heart, 'mid this gladness, is sad and forlorn.
I sigh for the storms of November to come,
    The frost, and the snow-drifted plain I would see;
The bleak, wintry blasts of my own mountain home,
    And the storm-beaten glacier are dearer to me.
The chime of the sleigh-bell again I would hear,
    The low moaning tempest in harmony roll—
It would speak of my country and kindred so dear;
    Oh! this would be music indeed to my soul.
    With sentiments of the most endearing affection,
        I remain yours, &c.,

                                                 P. P. PRATT.

Chapter 49

We have continued to reside in Valparaiso, and to study Spanish diligently until this day. We make much progress, being already able to understand in part that which we read in the Spanish Scriptures, and in the daily papers, as well as in history. We have also gathered much general information of the countries of Spanish America, their manners, customs, laws, constitutions, institutions—civil, religious, &c.

Revolutions have been in progress more or less in nearly all Spanish America during the past year.

In Chili the present revolution has ended with the loss of many thousand lives, and without success.

In Buenos Ayres it still rages, and a great battle is soon expected between the combined armies of Brazil and Montevideo on the one part, and Buenos Ayres on the other—the two armies amounting to near twenty-five thousand men each, as reported.

Priestcraft reigns triumphant in all these countries, as by law established; and by law paid and supported—by marriages and christening fees, forgiving sins, etc.

In Chili the charges are as follows: Twenty-five dollars for a marriage, and one dollar for christening. For forgiveness of sins there are various prices to suit the circumstances of the customers.

We departed from Valparaiso in a cart drawn by oxen, and arrived on the morning of the twenty-fifth at Quillota—a small town situated in a beautiful and fertile valley on a river thirty-six miles from Valparaiso.

Here we have hired a house and live with a widow and two daughters, young ladies of fifteen and seventeen; they are very sociable, and much pleased with us. They can read Spanish, and they take every possible pains to teach us the language. They are very frank and friendly, and seem a much void of guile as little children.

I read to them in the Spanish Testament, which pleases them much, as they have never read it.

The people in this town seem to be a neat, plain, loving and sociable people; very friendly, frank, and easy to become acquainted with. They are mostly white, intelligent, and good looking; very plain and simple in dress and manners. The houses are mostly neat and comely, and are situated on a line with the mud walls which separate the streets from the gardens and vineyards.

The houses are built of sun dried brick, plastered and whitewashed outside and inside; with brick floors and tiled roofs. Many of them, however, have no floors except the earth, and but few of them have glass windows. The streets are straight, and cross at right angles. A clear, cool stream runs in the center of each street, and vast rows of tall stately poplars, as well as fruit trees and vines adorn the entire vale, both in town and country.

A mountain or round hill, perhaps 500 feet in height, rises in the midst of the town, and is surrounded on all sides by the level of the fertile, well watered and well cultivated plain. This hill is near our residence, easy of access, and commands a view of the whole valley with its farms, orchards, vineyards, towns, streets, river and water ditches, fertile as Eden and stretching away till lost in the dim distance; or bounded by lofty hills and mountain chains, whose lower swells are checked with fences and houses, and covered with flocks and herds, while their bosoms are rugged with rocky precipices, and checkered by dark ravines, or mantled with clouds; while the rugged summits repose in solemn grandeur on the bosom of the clear blue sky, unobscured by clouds or any of the gloomy shadows of the lower world.

The land of this valley is extremely fertile, and easily irrigated by small canals from the river.

The whole taken in at one view from the summit of the center hill, presents one of the most beautiful scenes I ever beheld in the old or new world.

On the top of this mountain is a place for retirement and prayer, which I intend to use every evening about sunset or twilight. Figs, plums, pears, peaches, apples, oranges, grapes, and, indeed, most kinds of fruit are very plentiful here. A quarter of a dollar will purchase enough for three of us to eat in one day. The figs and plums are sweet as honey, and will melt in the mouth. There is not much need of other food. The grapes, peaches and apples are not generally ripe yet.

Having dwelt in Quillota one month we returned to Valparaiso, and on the 2d of March embarked on board the ship "Dracut" for San Francisco; weighed anchor on the 5th of March, and sailed out of port with a light breeze.

The following is the copy of a letter written to President Young during the voyage from Chili to San Francisco:

SHIP "DRACUT," PACIFIC OCEAN, lat. 18.
March 13, 1852.

PRESIDENT YOUNG.

Dear Brother—We are well. Elder Rufus Allen, myself and wife, sailed from San Francisco, September 5, 1851, for Chili, S. A., and arrived in Valparaiso, November 8—passage sixty-three days. From that time to the present has been devoted to the study of the Spanish language and the laws, constitutions, geography, history, character, religion, manners, customs, revolution, and events of Chili and Peru in particular, and of Spanish America in general.

By intense application I soon became able to read with a degree of understanding and interest in that language. I have already read through the Spanish Testament; while, in the same language, I have copied in writing many of its most important passages, and have read them over perhaps twenty times—committing some of them to memory.

I have also read a small work, on Natural History of Chili, near three times through, in which are many curious and important facts in relation to the wars with that brave and patriotic *nation of freemen called the Arraucanians.* These have maintained their liberty and independence unimpaired for 300 years against the combined powers of old Spain and of all her colonies, sustaining a defensive war, with but little cessation, for near 200 years, without firearms or other modern means of defense. Some of their history I hope to translate and publish hereafter.

I have also read the Spanish school geography of Chili, and some other works, while a constant perusal of their newspapers, and those of Peru and Buenos Ayres, have given me a general insight into their governments, laws, politics, religion, revolutions, hopes, feelings and prospects.

The civil wars, and my own pecuniary circumstances, but more particularly the want of language, prevented my travelling much in the country, or even visiting the Arraucanians. I, however, visited a small town in the interior, forty miles, and lived there one month.

On the second day of March we embarked on this ship bound for San Francisco, without a sufficiency of the language to turn the keys of the Gospel as yet to these nations. We staid till all our means were exhausted and sought and prayed diligently for our way to open; but we could neither speak the language sufficiently to preach the Gospel nor find any way to earn our living, so we found it necessary to return to California while we still study the language on board.

We have one fine young man in the cabin who is very useful to us. He is a native Chilian, reads and converses fluently in Spanish, is conversant with the Scriptures, which we read together and converse upon. He has borrowed the Spanish Bible of me and is reading it by course. I have told him of our doctrine, baptism, Church persecution, settlement in the mountains, and of the Book of Mormon. Also of the evils of adultery, drunkenness, gambling, and other sins, and the wickedness of the Catholic abominations. He has taken the whole in good part, and talks of going to the mountains with us. What is very remarkable for a Chilian, he neither smokes nor drinks. He has some means, and is going to California to make more. We pray much in secret that God will open his heart and give him to us for a help in the ministry.

The Chilians are a mixed race of Spanish and Indian blood—say four-fifths Indian—consequently coarse features, black hair and eyes, low foreheads, high cheek bones, broad faces, and in most cases copper color in its various shades and degrees, whilst a few are white and even fair and beautiful. In general they are ignorant and devoted Catholics. Probably more than one-half of them can neither read nor write. Their knowledge of arts and industry is extremely limited. In manners they are simple, frank, and extremely sociable and apparently affectionate, but subject to a small low meanness in their dealings, and to trifling thefts. There are, however, many honorable exceptions to those faults or evil habits.

The Bible is not in general use among them, being prohibited by their religion; but I found many who had read it, and all, so far as I tried the experiment, seemed willing to hear it read. Some said they could understand it better when I read it than when it was read by their own natives. I spoke freely to many against their priestcraft and errors; showed them the true mode of baptism, etc., which very seldom gave offense.

They frequently told me of the abominations of their priests, and how they administered all the ordinances for money, at so much per head. The constitution establishes the Roman Catholic religion, supports it out of the treasury, and prohibits all others. There is, notwithstanding this prohibition, a Church of England and an American Congregational Church in Valparaiso.

The latter I visited and conversed with the minister. He said there was no difficulty in landing religious books or papers and circulating the same, although the press is not free to print or publish any religion but the Catholic. He had imported and distributed Bibles in Spanish, and had placed them for sale in the book stores. Foreign books are landed *free of duty.*

The revolution which raged so violently this season in Chili professed to be in favor of universal suffrage, and of absolute liberty of conscience, of speech, and of the press. The masses, so far as I am able to judge, are warm revolutionists, but they don't like to fight. The revolution cost some 5,000 lives, and ended in a general amnesty, without any alteration of the Government. But the people are sanguine in their hopes—they think to accomplish their liberties in a few years.

In the provinces of Buenos Ayres a long civil war has raged, which is now about terminating in favor of the more liberal party, aided by Brazil.

Peru is tranquil. The public prints of Lima, its capital, have interested me much—they are in Spanish, and I have spent days in their perusal. The Government of Peru is much influenced by England and the United States. Its constitution guarantees liberty of the press, of speech, and of worship. But it seems to have remained a *dead letter* on these points till the present year, in which the Congress Peruana has made a special law to carry out these general principles of liberty, making special provision for the liberty of other worship, and for Protestants to officiate in the holy *sacraments of matrimony and of burial,* which is a step ahead of even Protestant England (where all must go to the National Church for these things).

Peru has also made a special treaty with Great Britain, in which all these liberties are guaranteed to British subjects there. These liberal measures have alarmed "His Holiness," the Pope of Rome, to such an extent that he has issued his letter of disfellowship of the Government Peruana, in which he denounces all these liberal measures as *anti-Catholic, un-Christian and heretical.*

This official document, in the hands of the Archbishop of Peru and of his clergy, was brought to bear with considerable power against the liberal proceedings of the Government; but, in the meantime, a very learned and talented man (I suppose a clergyman), called Dr. Vigel, and many other writers come out against the Pope in the columns of the public prints. They denounce him in no measured terms as a usurper of more power than Peter of old, who, they say, meddled not with governments, wealth, or any other thing, but to preach the Gospel and catch fish.

They boldly inquire of "His Holiness" "where's Peter's salary! crown! title! palace, etc.? where his dictations of political government?" They then inform him that Peru is a free and independent sovereignty, and will not be dictated to by any foreign power whatsoever. They refer "*His Holiness*" to Simon Magus, who wished to purchase the gift of God with money. Remind him and the public how much it has cost certain other governments to purchase remission of sins for similar offenses, and inquire how much poor erring Peru will have to pay to His Holiness for the remission of the great sins she has committed in giving her citizens the liberty to worship as they please; and to *marry, die and be buried* in such manner as seemeth to them good.

Such writings have a wide circulation in Peru, and are popular, but are also opposed by lengthy replies and defenses on the part of the more orthodox clergy. All these things go to show that the press, as well as the mind, is beginning to exert its freedom in the countries where, for three centuries, all intellect has slept, and all freedom of thought been *crushed—buried*—under the incubus of the horrid institutions of the great Mother of Abominations.

Should Peru sustain her liberties, a field is opened in the heart of Spanish America, and in the largest, best informed and most influential city and nation of South America, for the Bible, the Book of Mormon, and the fulness of the Gospel to be introduced.

Four-fifths, or perhaps nine-tenths of the vast population of Peru, as well as of most other countries of Spanish America, are of the *blood of Lehi*. 'Tis true they are degraded. Civilization is at a low ebb; and modesty and virtue, in the sense they are understood among the more polished nations, may hardly exist among them, even in idea. Yet Jesus came not to call the righteous but sinners to repentance. The whole need no physicians, but those who are sick.

New Granada has also revolutionized in favor of the same great principles of liberty; while the revolution in Northern Mexico, and other movements of a like nature in other parts, all go to show that a door is opening more wide than can be filled very soon *in the Spanish language*, unless God shall raise up (as in England) thousands of native teachers of the fulness of the Gospel.

I had much desire to go to Peru at this time; but an empty purse and imperfect tongue, which has only barely begun to stammer in that language, together with the want of books or the means to print them, with other circumstances, all combined to cause me to wait a little till I could study the language more fully; while, in the meantime, I return to where I can communicate more fully with the Church at home, with the various missions on the islands and with my family, for whom I must do something as speedily as possible, if God will open my way.

I feel as though the Book of Mormon and some cheap publications should be translated into Spanish and printed, and then the key be turned to these nations while a living Priesthood is accompanied by something for them to read—even those writings which have the promises of God, the prayers and faith of the ancients, and the power and Spirit of God to work with them in restoring the house of Israel.

It is in my heart to translate the Book of Mormon and some other works, and to print the same in Spanish as soon as I have the language sufficiently perfect. As printing is very expensive in all parts of the Pacific, it may be wisdom to go to England and get some printing, and, perhaps, some stereotyping done; and also, to bring out two or three Elders from there with *English passports, etc.*, to assist in Spanish America.

As these contemplated labors would be, under the blessing of God, a furtherance of the great work of laying the foundation for the restoration of unnumbered millions of the house of Israel and of Joseph—even of many nations extending over a large and important portion of the earth—I feel to labor with patience, and to take time to prepare the way before me and before those who will, in due time, be sent unto them in power; knowing that God, who has said certain things, will cause those things to be performed in due time.

If before half these things are accomplished I should return to the valley and sit in council with you and my brethren, or even do the translation *there,* I hope I shall not be counted a slothful servant; for I assure you that I do all in my power, with all diligence, and with all the prayer of faith I possess; and my earnest desire is to be counted worthy to labor for the restoration of Israel until it be accomplished.

I study the language all day and think of it, and even dream and talk it aloud in my sleep, in which I sometimes learn more than in the day. But it is no small work to become familiar with the entire grammar, words and style of a language, so as to write for publication.

If the Twelve Apostles will divide the European languages between them, and each become thoroughly versed in one, so as to translate the fulness of the Gospel and turn the keys of the same, it will be one great step towards the consummation; for a host of fellow laborers would soon be raised up in each to cooperate with them, and these languages command the influence and keys of communication with most of the nations, tribes and languages of the earth. I trust and hope, also, that they will soon be introduced into our University, and among the Elders of Israel, in preference to the dead languages, or of those of less consequence.

PACIFIC OCEAN, lat. 3° N.
March 27, 1852.

Dear Brother—We have now sailed for twenty-three days and made nearly half the passage. We are well, and the wind is generally fair, but now and then a calm. Brother Allen and myself still study the language with diligence, and still talk with the Chilian, who is also reading diligently in our Spanish Bible.

The "Book of Mormon," "Voice of Warning," etc., have been the rounds, and been read by the captain and mates; but they will not believe in them, nor in the testimony of men or angels. However, there is one intelligent, sober young man, who is interested much.

April 29th, lat. 27° N.—Fifty-five days have passed like a dreary imprisonment to us, with but little to eat. We live on a little poor, hard bread, probably baked some two or three years ago, and some beans, and very poor damaged salt beef and pork. We have no flour, potatoes, sugar, molasses, rice, or other comforts, although we pay a good price for cabin passage.

We have not had one day of good sailing in a month; it is either calms or light head winds. We seldom sail more than from thirty to fifty miles in twenty-four hours. We are hungry, and weary, and lonesome, and disconsolate. But, after praying much for a fair wind and speed, we find our prayers are not answered, and we have given it up, and have asked our Heavenly Father to give us patience and reconciliation to His will.

We are now some eight or nine hundred miles from port, and our provisions (poor as they are) must fail us soon. But live or die we trust in God and try to serve Him.

There is no one on board who fears God or regards man, as far as we know, except one of the sailors and ourselves. The most horrid blasphemies resound in our ears every day in the cabin and on deck, from captain and mate together, with gambling and blackguardism.

We are shunned and hated because of our testimony, and because our example is a reproof. But we mind our own business, and study language and the Scriptures every day.

The young man of which I speak is a Mr. Howard, from the United States, who is well educated, and has read our books with much interest during the passage, and has requested to be baptized and join the Church as soon as we land. He is not accustomed to a seafaring life, and wishes to go to the mountains with us. He has been brought up at school and in clerking. I think his calling is to preach the Gospel, but I have not yet even hinted this to him.

Brethren, I want to see you all with a desire above all other times of my life. I feel as though I wanted to sit down with you and seek the powers and gifts of God and the powers of Heaven, even that which shall be shed forth for the restoration of the house of Israel.

Oh, when will the time come? When shall the veil be rent and the full powers of the apostleship be permitted to be exercised on the earth? It must be before long or no flesh be saved—for the powers of darkness prevail abroad to that degree that it can even be felt physically.

There are none who know the Lord; none who seek after the truth; none who appreciate it when found; none who incline to cease from sin. I had like to have said to be found abroad in the earth. To find one is like lighting a candle and searching diligently for food among the dungeons of darkness, death and famine.

Adieu till we land.

Your brother,

P. P. PRATT.

Chapter 50

After a long and tedious passage of seventy-nine days we landed in San Francisco on the 21st of May, having suffered severely for the last forty days for the want of proper food.

After resting and recuperating for a few days, my time was again devoted to the ministry in the Church at San Francisco and San Jose, and in visiting, studying language, writing to the other missionaries, and in the preparations for our homeward journey, until near the end of July; and I would here add, that, through the kindness of my brethren and friends, near twelve hundred dollars in money, mules and a wagon was contributed to assist me in my mission and for my journey home, being given at various times after my arrival from Chili.

I found the Saints in the above named places possessed of some faith and kindness, benevolence and charity. They were also endeavoring to serve the Lord, and to set good examples of life, and they met often to worship and edify each other and as many as came to their meetings. Many attended their meetings and listened with interest, and some were baptized and added to the Church.

I urged the principles of the gathering with all the energy of the gift of God within me, but seemingly almost in vain. The world and the gain thereof seemed to have a strong hold and influence over them. After a trial for months, I only obtained three men to go with me, for Deseret, besides Brother Allen. These were Wm. Follett, Thomas Dual and Elisha Hyatt; with these I started on the steamer "Sea Bird" about the last of July.

We landed in St. Pedro after three days, and on the 14th day of August we arrived all safe in San Barnardino, where we were kindly received by Brother Amasa Lyman and the Saints in general, whom we found well and prosperous. We camped near Sister Rich's, and were entertained by them very hospitably.

Sunday, 15th.—Met with the Saints for worship and preached to them. It was a meeting full of interest, well attended by both sexes; good singing, good instruction, the sacrament, and in the afternoon a Sabbath school.

Their meeting house is large and commodious, and is used for school purposes every day.

August 20th.—Brother C. C. Rich arrived in good health from Salt Lake City with seventeen men, making their journey in twenty-two days without loss or accident, having six wagons. Reports well of the grass and water. Tells of much rain on the desert and in Deseret. Brings good news of all things there, and letters from my family, who were all alive and well.

Sunday, 22d.—Had a joyful meeting with Brother Amasa Lyman, C. C. Rich and the Church. After meeting we three of the Twelve met and appointed certain young men to study the Spanish language, with a view to a mission hereafter, and Brother Stout to teach a class in Spanish, in this place, to consist of such young men.

September 4th.—Attended a harvest feast in the bowery, or meeting house. The entire people made this feast, and assembled to enjoy it. The room was richly and tastefully ornamented and set off with evergreens, specimens of grains, vegetables, etc.

Meeting opened by prayer and singing, and a few remarks from myself and others, after which the entire day and evening was spent in feasting, dancing and speaking.

Every variety almost which the earth produced, or skill could prepare, was spread out in profusion and partaken of by all—citizens, strangers, Spaniards or Indians—with that freedom and good order which is characteristic of the Saints.

The dances were conducted with decorum and propriety. Old and young, married and single, grandsire and child, all mingling in the dance so far as they chose, without a jarring spirit to mar their peace.

With an address from A. Lyman, a few words from C. C. Rich and myself, and benediction, we closed, about nine P.M., one of the most interesting assemblies of the Saints in this place.

Tuesday, 14th.—All being ready, we took leave of the Saints in San Barnardino, and commenced our journey at nine o'clock, A.M.

Brothers Rich and Lyman, with several other friends, accompanied us a few miles, and ox teams and teamsters accompanied us for three days, to haul us over the Cajon Pass, where we took leave of them, and at evening organized our company as follows:—P. P. Pratt and wife, Rufus Allen, William Follett, Clark Ames, Samuel Gould, Andrew Calhoun and wife, Elisha Hyatt, wife and child, Thomas Dual, John Hyatt, John Green, George Clark. John Green was appointed captain of the guard. In all, eleven men, four women and one child.

We were soon joined by five Spaniards, who had near forty animals, mostly horses, who accompanied us for some hundreds of miles, and joined us in guarding, etc. Their animals being poor and unshod, we left them on the Rio Virgin. We met a company of twenty-four emigrants near the Salt Spring.

On the Muddy our camp was thronged with near sixty Indians, in a state of nudity, bringing with them green corn, melons, and dressed skins for sale, or exchange for clothing. They were all good natured and glad to see us; some of them accompanied us twenty-five miles, held our horses, guns, etc., and assisted us up the hills.

After twenty days we all arrived in safety at Santa Clara, about one hundred miles from the settlement in Iron County.

October 7th.—All arrived in safety in the settlement in Iron County, Utah, and were kindly received and entertained by the Saints.

I called on Sister Robinson in the twilight of evening, and asked for the dinner which I had spoken for one and a half years before. We were kindly received by her and others.

We tarried three days in Parowan Fort and preached to the Saints.

Taking leave of the Saints we resumed our journey. Nothing worthy of note transpired during the rest of the journey, which was two hundred and fifty miles, mostly among the settlements, where we were kindly entertained.

On the 18th, near midnight, I arrived home. I found my family in usual health.

On my arrival home I found my wife, Mary Ann Frost, and my two children, Olivia and Moroni, who had arrived from Maine, where they had been for several years. The two children were glad to see me, but their mother had for several years been alienated from me. I, however, supported her until the following spring, when she applied for and obtained a bill of divorce; after which, with the two children, she removed to Utah County.

I spent the remainder of the autumn in the ministry, and in overseeing and assisting in farming, fencing, etc.

I was also chosen a member of the Legislative Council, to which I devoted forty days, commencing in December, 1852. Occupied with these duties, and with the study of Spanish, the year 1852 was brought to a close.

January, 1853.—This month was mostly occupied in the legislative councils.

April 6th.—I attended a General Conference, on which occasion the corner stones of the Salt Lake Temple were laid by the First Presidency, Twelve and others. "The Temple Block is forty rods square, the lines running north and south, east and west, and contains ten acres. The center of the Temple is one hundred and fifty-six feet six inches due west from the center of the east line of the block. The length of said house, east and west, is one hundred and eighty-six and a half feet, including towers, and the width ninety-nine feet. On the east end there are three towers, as also on the west. Draw a line north and south, one hundred and eighteen and a half feet, through the center of the towers, and you have the north and south extent of ground plan, including pedestal."

I devoted the remainder of the season to the ministry, and to farming, building, etc., not wholly neglecting the study of Spanish.

At the August election I was returned to the Legislative Council by unanimous vote, and in December following I attended its session till the end of the year.

January, 1854.—Still in legislative session, which adjourned the latter part of this month.

The remainder of the winter was spent in the ministry; in the active duties of a Regent of the University of Deseret (being one of a Committee on the Deseret Alphabet and a New System of Orthography); in teaching a class in the Spanish language; in ministering in the ordinances of the endowments in the house of the Lord; and in studying, writing, etc.

At a General Conference, held on the 6th day of April, I was appointed to a second mission to California. Donations were contributed to aid me in said mission.

May 5th.—I took leave of my family and friends in Salt Lake City and started on my second mission to California.

Brother Thurston, a young man who had a mission to the isles, accompanied me. We had a small wagon, drawn by two mules.

At Provo we joined Governor Young and train on their trip south, and travelled with them as far as Cedar City. At Parowan we were joined by Elders Silas Smith and Brother West, who had also been selected by the conference as missionaries to the islands.

At this place Brother Young gave me the parting hand and blessed me; and also Brother Kimball rose up and blessed me, and, as he gave me the parting hand, promised many good things. He said I should be blest, and my posterity forever.

Here we parted—Brother Young and company on their return, while I and my company proceeded on our Pacific Mission.

Near Cedar City we were joined by other missionaries, and our company now consisted of twenty-four men and one woman.

Nothing of particular note occurred on our journey, and on June 9th we arrived safely and in good health and spirits at San Barnardino, and were kindly entertained by Elders C. C. Rich and A. Lyman.

After resting a few days I here left the main company and started with Brother J. W. Stewart in a carriage for the port of San Pedro—distance, eighty-five miles. The road was good, and we camped out two nights and arrived on the 14th, and were kindly received by Messrs. Alexander & Co., who kept the warehouse.

Here I unexpectedly met with a company of Saints from Australia, under the direction of Elder William Hyde, and we mutually rejoiced in meeting friends.

I set sail on the steamer "Southerner" for San Francisco on June 24th, and had kind treatment and passage free in cabin. We had head winds and were driven back three times, being five days longer than usual on the passage, arriving there on the 2d of July in safety. In a few days I went to San Jose Valley, and at Brother Cheeney's I found my wife Elizabeth, in very poor health—she having come on business a few months previous. We rested a few days at Brother Cheeney's and were kindly entertained.

We then returned to San Francisco, and about the 10th of July the other missionaries arrived from San Barnardino. I met Brothers Tanner and McBride, who had been on a mission to the Sandwich isles and had returned. Brother Tanner had purchased a vessel in order to transport the Elders both ways and to emigrate the Saints; but we could not pay for it and fit it for sea, notwithstanding I ran in debt to help him, so we had to sell it at a great loss.

We now commenced holding meetings, circulating books, tracts, and in every way we could, to notify and warn the people.

I devoted the time I could spare from the ministry to writing my history and for the press.

*The First Presidency and the Twelve Apostles of The Church
of Jesus Christ of Latter-day Saints*

Some time in August, Elders George Q. Cannon, J. Hawkins, Bigler and Farran, of the Island Mission, landed, and Brother Cannon assisted me some forty days in copying my autobiography.

About the last of August the following was published in a weekly paper, called the *Chronicle*, of San Francisco:

A PROPHET IS AMONG US

Mr. Parley P. Pratt, of Salt Lake notoriety, is among us, and we knew it not. He has just addressed a letter to Mr. J. S. Hittell, whose "proposed course of lectures *against* Christianity" appears to have caught the Prophet's attention.

As Mr. Pratt's letter, which is written on the blank leaf of a printed Latter-day Saint's circular, is curious and characteristic, we give a copy of it. We also give a copy of the circular itself. To enable the reader to understand Mr. Pratt's allusions in the letter, he had better first glance over Mr. Hittell's advertisement in another column. One would scarely have thought that Mr. Pratt could seriously expect to make converts to his faith in this "desperately wicked" California—the very hell on earth of the "Mormons." But so it seems to be. We give him and his cause all the publicity we can, by publishing his circular gratuitously.

SAN FRANCISCO, *September 1st*, 1854.

MR. JNO. S. HITTELL.

Sir—What do you mean by the term "Christianity?" If you mean the system taught by Christ and His Apostles, as recorded in the "New Testament," you need give yourself or the public no uneasiness, for no such system has troubled the earth for the last thousand years at least, so far as we have any knowledge, except in the single instance of its restoration in the United States by the Prophet Joseph Smith; and even this has been misnamed "Mormonism," and driven to the mountains of Utah.

In short, this Christianity of the New Testament is a system of visions, angels, revelations, prophesyings, gifts, miracles, etc. Such a system you can never oppose—it speaks and acts for itself; its votaries know what they experience, see, hear and feel.

As to the modern systems—the forms without power, they are not worth opposing; they are dying of themselves before the power and intelligence of truth made manifest by "Mormonism."

I am happy to subscribe myself

The friend of truth and man,

PARLEY P. PRATT.

CIRCULAR

Repent! ye people of California. *For know, assuredly, the Kingdom of God* has come *nigh unto you.*

Mr. Pratt, missionary from Salt Lake, will impart instruction on the fulness of the Gospel to individuals, families, or congregations who may desire it.

Having authority of Jesus Christ he will also baptize by immersion in water for remission of sins, and administer the gift of the Holy Spirit by the laying on of hands to all penitent believers in Christ who will covenant to cease from sin, and serve God with all their hearts.

Mr. Pratt will accept, with pleasure, any invitations from his fellow citizens to preach in their houses, halls or churches, without respect to party or sect.

When not otherwise engaged, he will hold public meetings at his residence on each Sunday, at the usual hours; also, prayer meetings on Thursdays, at two P. M.

The following appeared in the *Christian Advocate* of San Francisco, September 22:

CASE OF DEFAMATION

P. P. Pratt, an Apostle of "Mormonism," takes us to task in no measured terms for our unregenerate temerity, in daring to quote from the *Richmond Despatch* Dr. Ferris's account of the "Mormon" community at Salt Lake. To have a man possessed of divine authority, and capable of raising the dead, threaten us so, is truly awful. Men have pursued us with bludgeons and revolvers before, but this thing of being sent straight down to the bottom of the bad place, is a sprinkle more terrific than carnal weapons.

We are half inclined to repent, as much as we can, without doubting a word of Dr. Ferris's description.

Our readers will rejoice to know, from an apostle of Joe Smithism, that all lyings, and deceivings, and priestcrafts and *whoredoms* shall be done away. Here is the letter:

Woe to you, priests, editors, hypocrites! You love to publish lies to destroy the innocent. You condemn the just, and he doth not resist you.

Read your *Christian Advocate* of September 15, headed "The Mormons," and *tremble;* for God will not suffer such lies to be published with impunity. "For," thus saith the Lord: "all lyings, and deceivings, and priestcrafts and whoredoms shall be done away, and whosoever will not repent and come unto my beloved Son, will I cut off from among the people, and I will execute vengeance and fury upon them, even as upon the heathen, such as have not heard."

Now, Messrs. Heath, Taylor, Blain and Philips, you know in your own hearts that you have published lies enough about the "Mormons" to sink you and those who patronize your publications to the lowest hell with murderers.

You know the people of Salt Lake to be an innocent community, therefore, repent quickly, or your damnation is sealed, and your hands will be found dripping with innocent blood.   Yours etc.,

P. P. PRATT

A few more such will cause us to retire to private life.—[Eds.

A CHALLENGE

Editor's Chronicle:—I perceive by the tone of the press that politicians, moralists and religionists are in trouble about Utah and Polygamy. "War!" "war!" "blood!" and "destruction" to the poor heathen Mormons! But, thanks to the pious Methodists, the Mormons are going to be converted first. Missionaries are going to be sent to them.

It is the right of the President of the United States to appoint a Governor, and to send troops to Utah. The citizens of that territory know this, and have no objections. But suppose a Governor and troops went there to interfere with the rights and liberties of the people and trample on the laws, why then, of course, the aggressors, in common with all others are amenable to the civil courts, and are liable to fine, imprisonment or execution, according to their crimes. Even if they only threaten, they might be bound over to keep the peace. The courts of Utah have never yet been found remiss in the execution of the laws.

What is the particular crime alleged against the Governor and citizens of Utah, for which they are threatened with destruction or conversion?

We will be told it is Polygamy. Well, "sin," says the Apostle, "is the transgression of law." We should greatly prefer conversion to murder, and here permit me to suggest a plan for a wholesale conversion, without a drop of blood or even the trouble of a journey to Utah.

I am here in California as an official member and representative of the Church in Utah, for which I can produce credentials. I am willing to meet a convention of the ablest lawyers and clergy to be found in our country, and I hereby pledge my honor that I will publicly renounce Polygamy, and that the church I represent will do the same, on the following conditions, viz:

The Old and New Testaments, the Constitution and laws of the United States, and the laws of Utah Territory shall be their standard; and if in all this wide range one item of law can be found wherein God, angels, men, prophets, apostles, the Son of God or the Holy Spirit have made plurality of wives a *crime*, a *transgression of law* or an *immorality*, then, on these conditons, we will renounce Polygamy. But till this is done we shall hold the law of God on the subject of matrimony, including a plurality of wives, as a most sacred institution, binding on our own consciences, in the free exercise of which we claim the protection so freely and fully guaranteed by the constitution of our common country.

If editors in general throughout the country will please publish this, it may tend to investigation and enlightenment, either of the "poor, ignorant Mormons," or of those who think them so far out of the way.

P. P. PRATT.

SANTA CLARA, *November 22d*, 1854.

December 6th.—I returned to San Francisco, and on the second evening attended a discussion at the Mercantile Library Association, on the subject of Governor Young, the Utah Mormons and the general government. Spoke several times, and was appointed to make the opening speech in one week from that time on the same subject, and to be answered by Rev. Mr. Briggs.

FROM THE DAILY "ALTA CALIFORNIA"

Mr. Parley P. Pratt, for whom we have considerable respect as a man and as a teacher, coupled with as much admiration of his talent as the doctrines which he employs to defend it will admit of, Mr. Parley P. Pratt appears to have walked into the temples of our money changers in this city, and fairly put to flight all reason and philosophy by the boldness of his attack upon the Christian Church.

Our readers will remember Mr. Pratt as the self-confessed Apostle of Polygamic Mormonism in California, and his last exploit was to draw upon him the fire of a room full of debaters in the San Francisco Mercantile Library Association, and then commenced a bombardment of the citadel of their reason, and silenced or rendered useless every gun! For several weeks Mr. Pratt has been wheeling and charging his squadron of polygamic arguments in full sight of all our church doors and lecture rooms, and even advanced in person to the foot of our pulpits to proclaim himself the defender of a new faith, flinging the glove even into the minister's desk.

Up to the present time, we believe, no David has gone forth against this Philistine to meet him on either point of law, morality or religion, which he declares himself ready to engage an enemy upon.

We naturally ask, why is this? In a city with so many well supported churches and able divines, can no one be found to match this champion of the Mormons? Or are the abhorrence and contempt of such doctrines, and scorn of their advocates so great as to stifle the power of expression among our worthy controversialists? Either of these causes, we consider fallacious and bad. Passion should play no part in the impulses of Christian minds, and we much doubt the propriety of condemning a doctrine because of its low origin, or despising argument because it may not present a respectable exterior. Missionaries are sent to the heathen; and why should discussion be denied heathenistic doctrines when they are brought to our own very doors?

We have very worthy and respectable street preachers in San Francisco, and we do not see how a religious discussion with a Mormon would profane the walls of any one of our churches, or taint the reputation of any of our ministers of the gospel.

Mr. Pratt seems to have the best of the law on his side so far as the situation of the Salt Lake people is concerned; under our territorial regulations there really appears to be no law to prevent Polygamy.

December 9th.—Returned to Santa Clara by steamer and stage, and found all well.

Sunday, 10th.—Preached twice to an attentive and somewhat numerous audience in a large and commodious hall. Visited and wrote history the four following days, and instructed such as sought me.

Friday, 15th.—Repaired again to San Francisco in company with some five of my friends, and at evening attended the discussion. The place was crowded, and God gave me His Spirit, and truth triumphed.

Chapter 51

On the Subject of the Expediency of the Reappointment of His Excellency Governor Young, of Utah.

My friend, Mr. Briggs, in the fulness of his charity as a "peacemaker," the other evening kindly, gently, and in a Christian-like manner merely suggested a few pious ideas concerning myself; such as theft, robbery, murder, etc., being considered no crime by me and the "Mormons," provided these crimes were committed on the Gentiles, and in favor of the Church treasury, etc.

This puts me in mind of the good, peaceable Quaker who said to a poor dog which he wanted killed, "I will not kill thee, but I will give thee a bad name." So he cried, "Mad dog! Mad dog!" And on hearing this cry the people soon despatched the poor animal.

Perhaps my friend thinks to get the Mormons killed off in the same pious and Christian-like manner. Even should he succeed in his peaceful, pious purposes, it would not be the first time that the blood of martyrs has stained our soil through the influence of such Christian benevolence.

I am truly sorry to see so worthy a fellow citizen—so pious a man— one so full of charity and benevolence—so uninformed, so utterly at fault on the most familiar subjects of Bible history and morality, or of right and wrong, as to insinuate that there is no difference between Polygamy and adultery; between a house full of wives and children and a house full of harlots.

He takes Polygamy, adultery, theft and murder, and compounds them all together as crime! And then seems to infer that a man would steal, commit adultery, etc., simply from the fact that he has a house full of wives and children! And even my good friend, the learned and candid

383

Mr. Hittell, although very just in the main drift of his argument, the other evening seemed to recognize no very clear distinction between Polygamy and adultery, or between a man having his own wife or wives, or robbing a neighbor of his wife.

Sir, in justice to myself and the cause I represent, and in charity to those whose judgments are so warped by tradition and custom; whose otherwise keen perceptions are so blunted by Roman superstitions and Puritan littleness, I must call the attention of these gentlemen to the recognized standard of all Christian nations—"The law and Testimony"—and give them a lesson on the first principles of right and wrong, or of virtues and vices, according to the laws of God and nature.

I will state the question direct, as inferred or inquired, by my friend the "peace maker." What is the difference between a house full of wives and children or a house of "ill fame," or of "harlots?"

Sir, I will tell you. The one leads to *life* and the other to *death*—I mean literally—or, in plainer language, one rightly conducted, under the blessings and law of God, multiplies, preserves and trains our species in the highest order of physical, moral and intellectual endowment; fills the world with cities; gives rise to nations; and has given to the world its principal rulers, kings, prophets, apostles, and, finally, its Messiah, and is the lineage and order through and in which all nations shall be blessed.

The other perverts the order of nature; prostitutes the most holy principles and affections to the vilest of purposes; checks the reproduction of our species; spreads disease and death as a sweeping pestilence through the world; degenerates the race; and if it fills the world at all, fills it with a mean, grovelling, sickly, puny, lustful, deformed and miserable race of beings, whose misfortune is that they were born at all.

Such were the people of the flood; the people of Sodom and the Canaanites, who were so far degenerated that the Lord in mercy interfered, and doomed them to utter destruction, that nations and races so degenerate should no longer propagate their species: and then, by his own holy laws of marriage, repeopled those same countries with a better race.

As polygamists Abraham and Jacob were the friends of God; were worthy to converse with Him, and to receive His blessing on themselves and their wives and children; worthy of associating with angels from Heaven, and of being filled with the holy and pure spirit of prophecy and of revelation; while, for their sakes, kings were reproved, saying, "touch not mine own anointed, and do my prophets no harm."

As a polygamist Jacob gave twelve tribes to the world instead of two, which was the number born by his first intended, his beloved Rachel. While, on the other hand, his sons visited a whole city with the sword, because its *ruler* had seduced their sister Dinah.

As a polygamist Moses beheld the face of God, and was filled with His glory to that degree that his face shone like that of an angel.

As an adulterist, a prince of Israel, named Ziniri, was killed in the very act by Phineas the priest, the grandson of Aaron; which act of justice so pleased the Lord that he stayed the plague which was consuming the camp on account of their whoredoms.

The law of God regulating and sanctioning Polygamy was thundered from Mount Sinai in awful majesty, from the mouth of the God of Israel, although it had existed before, and also among the eternal and unchangeable principles of morality, virtue and purity.

While, on the other hand, the same God, in a voice of thunder, proclaimed, "Thou shalt not commit adultery, nor covet thy neighbor's wife, or anything that is thy neighbor's."

As a bigamist, Elkanah, who had two wives, became the father of Samuel, the Prophet; he being a child of promise, obtained by the fervent prayer of Hannah, his mother, in the Holy Temple, and by her vows devoted to the service of the Temple from his childhood. While, on the other hand, had he been a child of whoredoms, instead of a child of bigamy, he would have been excluded from the house of the Lord, and his children after him, for ten generations.

The first revelation ever given to this child of bigamy rebuked the priests, the sons of Eli, *Hophni* and *Phineas*, for their whoredoms and other sins, and revealed their dooms. In fulfilment of his words these two fornicators fell in battle while bearing the very Ark of God.

As a polygamist, David, the anointed King and Prophet of Israel, was called a man after God's own heart; and God Himself expressly declares, by the mouth of Nathan the Prophet, that he *gave him his wives*.

While, as an adulterer with the wife of Uriah, and the murderer of her husband, he is reproved by the word of the Lord; and, although he sorely repented, yet the child of his adultery died; and his punishment was, that the sword should not depart from his house; that his wives should be taken from him and given to another; and his own salvation was suspended for ages—the Apostle Peter himself declaring, in his day, that the patriarch, David, had not yet ascended into Heaven.

As polygamists, Abraham, Isaac and Jacob are approved and commended by Jesus Christ, who expressly declares that, "many shall come from the east, and from the west, and from the north, and from the south; and shall set down with Abraham, Isaac and Jacob in the Kingdom of God." While, at the same time, he declares that, "those wicked and adulterous persons, who, in that age, considered themselves the children of the kingdom, should be thrust out." I sincerely hope my mistaken friends here will learn, ere that eventful day, to distinguish between a house of Polygamy and a crowd of adulterers; but they might by mistake consider the kingdom of God a house of ill fame, and go with the wrong crowd.

Sir, the Apostle Paul sets forth Abraham, the polygamist, as the father of the faithful; worthy of all imitation, as heir of the eternal covenants and promises; in whose seed all nations shall be blessed. He shows, most clearly, that the gospel introduces us into the family of polygamists; makes us children of Abraham, and heirs to the same covenants.

On the other hand, this same Apostle declares that adulterers and fornicators shall not inherit the kingdom of God.

Again, sir, John the Revelator describes the eternal Jerusalem of Heaven, the Royal City of our God, as peopled and governed by the great family of polygamists; which, in its lineage, includes Jesus and the holy prophets and apostles of all ages. The pearly gates are embellished with the names of twelve polygamists, the sons of four women by one man.

While, on the other hand, this same John expressly declares, that the place for all liars, sorcerers, whoremongers and adulterers is outside; and that there shall in no wise enter into the city anything that defileth or maketh a lie.

Now to come to Utah. There, sir, the law of God is *honored;* by it we determine what is virtue and what is vice. Here, sir, if nowhere else in Christendom, our virtuous wives and children, given us by the law of God, are our *glory;* our *crown of rejoicing;* our *kingdom in embryo,* big with thrones of power and immortality. There, sir, the local administration carries out the principles of the glorious Constitution and laws of our common country—even to the protection of prophets and apostles, who have dared to restore the Laws of God, and to organize and regulate their household by the same. And—

Sir, I have yet to learn by what constitutional or moral right a local State sovereignty makes a crime of that which, rightly conducted, never has been recognized as a crime by God, or angels, prophets or apostles, or even by the Saviour of the world.

I have yet to learn by what right a State of this Union dooms a man to prison for a conscientious act, in embracing the everlasting covenant, made with Abraham and the fathers; while, at the same time, a fornicator, who by the law of God, is worthy of *death*, runs at large, or, at most, pays a fine for his damnable deeds of seduction, and then is at liberty to repeat them, while his purse will hold out to pay the repeated fines and damages.

I have yet to learn that a State has the constitutional right to deprive a Mormon, a Jew, or even a Mahomedan or Pagan of his most sacred rights of conscience in regard to marriage relations or family ties; while they are regulated by the recognized laws of the Bible, or of most civilized nations of ancient and modern times.

Now, sir, let me say that, on account of the corrupt institutions, and the prevalence of whoredoms in modern Christendom, the *race is degenerated*; the cities and nations are corrupted till earth groans; the heavens weep; the sun will, ere long, veil his face in shame; the moon be arrayed in crimson blushes; the starry heavens tremble; the planets be thrown from their orbits, and tremble for very anguish; while plagues, earthquakes, storms and tempests sweep the earth, and famine and the sword devour the wicked; while fire consumes the mystic Babel, the great whore of all the earth.

Then will prevail the kingdom of our God, and the power of his Christ; "and the saints shall possess the kingdom and the greatness of the kingdom under the whole heaven," while the meek inherit the earth; and the house of Israel, under the new and everlasting covenant of eternal matrimony, blossom and bear fruit, and fill the face of the world with cities.

Men, brethren and fathers: It is for the hope of Israel the eternal laws, promises and covenants of God made to the fathers, that myself and the "Mormons" are called in question.

We believe the prophets, sir, and, therefore, expect the wreck of nations; the casting down of thrones; the crash of states, and the winding up of all mere human institutions; while a new dynasty, as a universal Theocracy, shall succeed and stand forever.

The nucleus of this kingdom, sir, is formed; this grain of mustard seed is planted and has sprung up, and is beginning to grow and flourish in the heart of our country, under the fostering care and constitutional guarantee of the very best human government now existing on this earth.

Sir, God raised up the United States and influenced her constitutional institutions for the very purpose of shielding and protecting the Church in the wilderness, and all men in their liberties, and of throwing a guard around His embryo kingdom till He should come, whose right it is to reign and subdue all enemies under his feet.

His kingdom, sir, when organized, in the United States, is a constitutional kingdom of God. It has the perfect liberty and right, guaranteed by our institutions, to organize itself under the administration of prophets and apostles, and to receive the ministrations of angels, and of visions and revelations from Heaven.

Sir, one of the strongest reasons I urge for the reappointment of Governor Young is, that as a polygamist, civilian and an ecclesiastic, he has given the strongest proof of his skill in the science of government, whether of *Family, Church or State.*

Sunday, 17.—Met with the Saints twice, and preached to them, and were truly blessed; and partook of the ordinance of bread and wine, in remembrance of our Lord. Next day I repaired to Oakland and met the Lyceum, and made arrangements for discussing polygamy on the next evening; and, according to appointment (Tuesday, 19), met the Lyceum and a large assembly of both sexes, and discussed the law of marriages till eleven o'clock at night. Truth was triumphant, and my adversaries confounded.

On the last of the month we convened a General Conference at Santa Clara, of two days, during which five branches were represented—in all about one hundred and twenty members. We had a joyful time, much good teaching, and many out to hear.

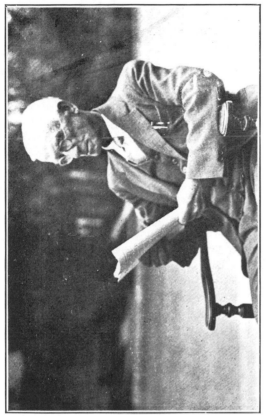

*Mathoni Wood Pratt, who died in 1937, the last survivor
of Parley P. Pratt's children*

Chapter 52

February 24th.

I sat for a large likeness, taken in daguerreotype, as a keepsake for my family, being forty-seven years ten months and twelve days old. I presented this to my son Parley, to be handed down from generation to generation, as long as it will last.

In March a Council was held at my office, and it was concluded to remove the Conference of the 6th of April next from Santa Clara to San Francisco, where I also moved my wife and made my home during the remainder of my mission.

April 12th. —This is my birthday. I am forty-eight years old. I wrote letters for home to-day and sent a set of books, viz: "Book of Mormon," "Doctrine and Covenants," "Hymn Book," "Voice of Warning," "Harp of Zion," etc., to each of my wives and to Parley, Olivia and Moroni, my elder children; also, books to my younger children, Alma, Nephi, Helaman, Julia, Lucy, Agatha, Belinda and Abinadi, Cornelia and Malona, and small presents and candies for the little ones, Phebe, Hannahette, Mary, Lehi and Moroni W., all as a birthday present or memorial.

In May I received a letter from President Young counselling me to return home this coming summer.

June 8th. —The sad news reached us to-day of brother Silas Beckwith being murdered and buried. This Beckwith was one of the Mormon Battalion in the Mexican war, and was, at the time of his death, a worthy member and teacher in the San Juan branch.

I visited his widow and orphans, and spent some hours in the house of mourning. On my second visit I gained and wrote down the following statements pertaining to the history of Joseph Smith:

Mrs. Eunice Corinthia Beckwith, formerly Mrs. Lawn (whose

father's name was Joshua Twitchell), was the widow of John Lawn, captain of a company of Illinois Militia, of McDonough County, who guarded Joseph and Hyrum Smith in Carthage Jail until the morning of the day they were martyred, when himself and company were disbanded by order of Governor Ford, and started for home, leaving the prisoners in the hands of the Carthage Greys.

On taking leave of the prisoners he gave his hand, received Joseph's blessing, and heard him say most solemnly: "Farewell, Captain Lawn; when you and your men leave me my life guard is gone." Previous to this, however, Joseph had read to him the fifty-fifth Psalm, and told him to remember that chapter and read it to his friends when he arrived home. One of the Carthage Greys also read in reply the sixty-first Psalm.

Captain Lawn and his troops had marched about twelve miles towards home when the news reached them of the martyrdom! At this he exclaimed: "O that I had known of this massacre, so soon to transpire! I would have remained, and, when the first ball was fired at the Smiths, I would have fired the second through the body of the villain who fired it or died in the attempt."

A man named Townsend, living in Iowa, near Fort Madison, was one of the mob who assaulted and forced in the jail door. The pistol discharged by Joseph Smith wounded him in the arm, near the shoulder, and it continued to rot without healing until it was taken off, and even then it would not heal.

About six months after he was shot Mrs. Lawn saw his arm and dressed it. He was then gradually rotting and dying with the wound. He stayed over night with Mrs. Lawn's father, and groaned through the night without sleeping. He asked the old gentleman what he thought of Joseph Smith being a Prophet? He replied that he did not know. "Well," said Townsend, *I know he was a Prophet of God!* And, oh, that I had stayed at home and minded my own business, and then I would not have lost my life and been tormented with a guilty conscience, and with this dreadful wound, which *none can heal!*" He died two or three months afterwards, having literally rotted alive!

James Head, of McComb, was also one of the murderers at the Carthage Jail; he was heard by Captain Lawn and others to boast of it afterwards, and Captain Lawn drew a pistol and chased him; but he ran away. He was always gloomy and troubled from the time he helped to murder the Smiths, and frequently declared that he saw the two martyrs always before him! He had no peace.

A colonel of the Missouri mob, who helped to drive, plunder and murder the Mormons, died in the hospital at Sacramento, 1849. Beckwith had the care of him; he was eaten with worms—a large black headed kind of maggot—which passed through him by myriads, seemingly a half pint at a time! Before he died these maggots were crawling out of his mouth and nose! He literally rotted alive! Even the flesh on his legs burst open and fell from the bones! They gathered up the rotten mass in a blanket and buried him, without awaiting a coffin!

A Mr. _____, one of Missouri mob, died in the same hospital about the same time, and under the care of Mr. Beckwith. His face and jaw on one side literally rotted, and half of his face actually fell off! One eye rotted out, and half of his nose, mouth and jaw fell from the bones! The doctor scraped the bones, and unlocked and took out his jaw from the joint round to the centre of the chin. The rot and maggots continued to eat till they ate through the large or jugular vein of his neck, and he bled to death! He, as well as Townsend, stank so previous to their death that they had to be placed in rooms by themselves, and it was almost impossible to endure their presence, and the flies could not be kept from blowing them while alive!

Wm. T. Head, an officer in Captain Lawn's company, and tarrying in Carthage, testified that he saw a certain man raise a large knife to strike off the head of Joseph, when, all at once, and in the midst of a clear day, with no cloud in sight, "a terrible clap of thunder rolled heavily, and forked lightnings flashed in the face of the murderers, and perfectly paralyzed a number of them.

"The ruffian, who had raised his knife and had sworn with a dreadful oath to take the head off Joseph, stood perfectly paralyzed, his arm uplifted with the knife suspended in air, and could not move a limb. His comrades carried him off, and all fled in terror from the scene."

These particulars, and many others, were related to me by brother Beckwith previous to his death, and afterwards by his widow and father-in-law, and others who were conversant with them, and are believed to be correct.

At a General Conference, held June 16—being the eve of my departure—it was the unanimous voice of the meeting to give me a letter of commendation and fellowship from the Conference to the Presidency of the Church in Utah. Elder J. Crosby was set apart as President of the San Francisco Conference, under my hands and others.

I gave them a few words of farewell and blessing, and returned them my sincere thanks for their many marks of kindness and hospitality to me and my wife while we sojourned with them; and I shall long remember the many brethren who have generously assisted me with means whereby I am enabled to pursue my journey home.

While on this mission I have been diligent in preaching, teaching, baptizing, visiting and ministering to the sick, and writing for the press. I feel the Saints have rejoiced under my teachings, and a goodly number have been added to the Church.

June 20th.—I took leave of the Saints and friends at San Francisco and started at noon, with my team, for my home in Utah; crossed the ferry at Oakland ten miles on a steamer, and drove twenty-five miles and stopped after sundown at brother Naile's, near San Jose. After resting a few days, and all being ready, we started from Dr. McIntyre's at nine o'clock A. M., with a company composed of seven men, two women and one child, five wagons and sixteen animals. I thanked God that, after thirteen months and a few days' absence, I was now ready to return to my home in the peaceful valley of the Great Salt Lake.

August 18th.—After a long and wearisome journey of some eight hundred miles we arrived safely home, and rejoiced to find all well.

Sunday, 19th.—I met the great congregation twice in the Tabernacle and bowery; heard Orson Pratt and President B. Young preach, and spoke a few words myself. In the evening met with the Quorum of the Twelve for prayer, as usual.

On Monday I visited my wife Sarah and her two children, Julia and Teancum, who resided on my farm; and, from this date until the Conference of October 6th, my time was engaged in the care and labors of my family, and other duties, although I attended Sabbath meetings, and sometimes preached.

The Conference appointed my brother Orson, and brother Woodruff, and myself, with upwards of twenty others, to a home mission in Utah Territory.

After Conference I spent my time mostly in the House of the Lord, in administering in the endowments, until the 20th of October.

October 15th, Monday.—Agreeable to instructions from President Young I called a meeting of a few of the Twelve, and others concerned in the mission, and divided the territory into missionary districts, and assigned to each his labor, appointing Conferences, or general meetings in each district.

Saturday, 20th.—Commenced my home mission by riding seventeen miles to attend a general meeting in company with O. Pratt, W. Woodruff and others, at Farmington, Davis County. Good attendance and spirited preaching on this day three times. Tarried at sister Haight's.

Sunday, 21st.—At half past eight o'clock, A. M., held a council of the missionaries of the district, and appointed the next quarterly meeting for the districts, to be held in Bishop Stoker's ward on the 18th of November next, and the second to be held December 15th, at ten o'clock, in Bishop Kay's ward.

This day we held three meetings, which were well attended, and greatly blessed with the spirit and power of God.

Monday, 22d.—Returned home and found all well.

November 1st.—Started with my carriage, accompanied by my wife Belinda and child, my brother Orson Pratt and W. Woodruff, and arrived at Ogden on the following day at eleven o'clock, A. M., and put up at President Farr's. Preached in the meeting house three times. The night following a dreadful wind arose, which did some damage. After travelling and preaching through the northern settlements nearly two weeks to large assemblies, who listened with good attention, we returned home and found all well.

Saturday, 17th.—Rode ten miles in my carriage with my wife Mary, and brethren O. Pratt and W. Woodruff, to P. Sessions', and met with the Saints in a Quarterly Conference.

Sunday, 18th.—Met a crowd out of doors, on the south side of the school-house, at Bishop Stoker's. I preached in the forenoon, and brothers Joseph Young and Erastus Snow in the afternoon. Many were out and the good spirit prevailed.

Next morning returned home and found all well.

December 3d.—Bid farewell to my family and started in my carriage with Agatha, my wife, and O. Pratt and W. W. Phelps as passengers, for the city of Fillmore, to attend the Legislative Assembly.

Friday, 7th.—Arrived at Fillmore at 1 P.M. in a heavy snow storm. Put up with brother Bridges.

Sunday, 9th.—Attended meeting twice. Preached in the morning and listened to O. Pratt in the afternoon.

Monday, 10th.—Attended the council of the Legislature and witnessed the organization, and was unanimously elected chaplain of the council. Accepted and was sworn, and entered upon my duties, being charged by the President, Hon. H. C. Kimball, to instruct and exhort the members and others in their duties. I prepared an address on the laws of marriage and morals, which was delivered to the council on the twenty-first. This was so favorably received that the Governor and President called for the reading of it before the joint session. It was accordingly read by the clerk on the thirty-first of December. On motion, it was unanimously voted to have it printed in the *Deseret News;* and, on motion, a vote of thanks was carried unanimously.

January 1st, 1856.

Wrote a letter to the *New York Herald,* and, in the evening, attended a dance in the Legislative Hall. It was a fine party, where old and young engaged in the dance till near midnight.

From this time till the adjournment of the Legislative Assembly nothing worthy of record transpired.

THE STANDARD OF ZION

O, Saints, have you seen, o'er yon mountain's proud height,
  The day star of promise so brilliantly beaming?
Its rays shall illumine the world with its light,
  And the ensign of Zion, exultingly streaming,
All nations invite to walk in its light,
And join to maintain the proud standard of right—
    The Standard of Zion, O long may it wave
    O'er the land of the free and the home of the brave!

Our motto is peace, and the triumph of right;
  And we joyfully hail the Millennial dawning,
When man can emerge from a long dreary night
  And bask in the sunbeams of Zion's bright morning.
The white flag so rare, still floating in air,
Proclaims 'mid the mountains that peace is still there.
    Let the Standard of Zion eternally wave
    O'er the land of the free and the home of the brave.

Though earth and its treasures should melt in the fire—
  The planets be riven with the trumpets' loud thunder,
The sunlight of Heaven wax dim and expire,
  And the veil of eternity parted asunder,
Yet firm and unshaken the truth shall remain,
And the heirs of the Priesthood forever shall reign,
    And the Standard of Zion eternally wave
    O'er the land of the free and the home of the brave.

FILLMORE COUNCIL CHAMBER, *January 8, 1856.*

Tuesday, 15th.—I attended a festival of the Legislature in the State House, where all were treated to abundance of oysters, fruits, wines, etc., by the Hon. Secretary Babbitt.

Friday, 18th.—The Legislature adjourned and all started for home.

We travelled about forty-five miles—some of the distance in about eight inches of snow—and camped at night in a point of cedars. The cold was extreme, but we emptied our carriage and kept a constant fire in the stove. Sat up through the night, as there was not room for all to lie down, and thus we passed the night.

19th.—Rode twenty miles to breakfast; arrived in Nephi about ten o'clock, nearly frozen; but a good breakfast and three hours' rest revived us, and we started again at 1 P.M. and rode to Payson, a distance of twenty-five miles, and were kindly received by brother Donich.

20th.—Started at ten A.M. Rode to Provo and dined at brother Stewart's. Rode ten miles more, and were entertained by Bishop Walker, of Pleasant Grove.

21st.—Rode thirty-five miles and dined at the Bishop's, Unionville, and arrived home at sundown; found all my family in tolerable health except my little daughter Isabel, who had been sick with a fever and cold on the lungs. I ministered to her and she speedily recovered.

Friday, 25th.—Spent the day with my family, and in a meeting with a chartered company, called the Deseret Road and Express Company, of which I was a member.

Saturday, 26th.—and from thence to February 14th was spent with my family, and in preaching occasionally in the Tabernacle and in the different wards in the city. Also in the office of juryman on the Grand Jury of the United States Court.

Tuesday, March 4th.—Attended at the President's office in the duty as a Regent of the University.

Next day attended at the President's office as a Committee of the Regency in raising school books.

Thursday, 6th.—Myself and family fasted and attended meeting in the Fourteenth ward school-house, and at evening visited at brother Southworth's, and attended another meeting in the ward.

Having been elected a delegate of Salt Lake County to a Convention called by the people of the Territory of Utah, to form a Constitution for the State of Deseret, I attended the daily sessions of the Convention for ten days, ending March 27, 1856. My time, after the adjournment of said Convention, was devoted to laboring on the farm, garden, and administering in the various duties of my calling, writing history, etc., until the Annual Conference, which convened April 6th and closed on the 8th. This Conference was held under a bowery adjoining the Tabernacle, and was attended by six or eight thousand people. At this Conference several hundred persons were called to go on missions to the

View of Salt Lake City, looking southeast

United States, England, Australia, the Sandwich Islands and other parts of the earth. The Presidency enjoined upon me the duty of setting apart and ordaining those who were called for their several missions, in which I was assisted by the rest of the Twelve and some of the Presidents of Seventies.

About this period, or immediately after Conference, I was taken sick with a fever and came nigh unto death, which sickness continued about two weeks.

May 26th.—Accompanied by Elder Gates I started on a mission of preaching, visiting and instructing the Saints in the southern part of the Territory; during which tour we held meetings at Union Fort, American Fork, Pleasant Grove, Provo, Payson, Summit, Nephi, Fillmore, Beaver, Paragonah, Parowan, Cedar City and Harmony.

On my return to Salt Lake City called and preached at the different towns and settlements on the route, arriving home June 27, 1856.

While at home my time was occupied in attending meetings, instructing and speaking words of comfort and encouragement to the Saints, and writing my history, assisted by my wife Kezia, as copyist.

Chapter 53

During the summer, after my return from the South, I performed several home missions or preaching tours through Davis, Weber and Box Elder Counties, and in September received an appointment to take a mission to the States, for which I received the following letter of appointment:

UTAH TERRITORY, PRESIDENT'S OFFICE,
GREAT SALT LAKE CITY, *Sept. 10, 1856.*

ELDER PARLEY P. PRATT.

Dear Brother—As you are about to leave on your mission to the States, we feel to give you a word of counsel for your guidance.

We expect that your principal occupation will be to travel and preach the gospel in different places, as you shall be led by the spirit of the Lord.

We are informed that there is quite a large number of Saints in the southwestern part of Virginia, which it is our wish you shall visit and instruct in the principles of the gospel.

Owing to the extra duties of delegate being placed upon brother John Taylor, it is suggested that you also aid him in writing for *The Mormon,* and such other duties as may devolve upon you by the united counsel of brethren now in charge on that mission.

As you are expected to return the ensuing season, we do not consider that it would be wisdom for you to have the burden of the mission to rest upon you, but rather that you should aid the brethren for the brief period which you will remain with them.

If brother Snow should be able to resume *The Luminary,* we should be pleased to have you assist him also in writing for that publication.

We believe that, by thus devoting your time during the ensuing winter, you will render the brethren now upon that mission effective aid, and be a comfort and consolation to the brethren and Saints who shall have the pleasure of your ministerial administrations, and be blest

with your society in this your short visit to the Saints in the States; and
that the Lord will bless you abundantly with His spirit, and enable you to
perform your mission with honor and satisfaction to yourself, and His divine acceptance, is the prayer of

   Your brethren in the Gospel of Christ,

                              BRIGHAM YOUNG,
                              HEBER C. KIMBALL,
                              J. M. GRANT,
                    First Presidency of the Church of Jesus
                          Christ of Latter-day Saints.

   After receiving the foregoing appointment my time was employed
chiefly in settling up my business and preparing for the journey eastward.

   September 7, 1856.—I preached my farewell discourse in the Tabernacle, in which I bore testimony to the Book of Mormon and of the calling of Joseph Smith, and of his Presidency and Apostleship. At noon,
the same day, gave instructions and strict charge to my son, Parley P.,
concerning my business, and the duties that would devolve upon him in
my absence.

   At 5 P.M. met with my quorum in prayer, in which President Young
and others laid their hands upon my head and set me apart for my mission to the States—confirming and sealing upon my head all the keys
and powers of the eternal priesthood, so far as they were held upon the
earth—"and that I should always be numbered among those that were
faithful to the priesthood, both in this life, in the world of spirits and in
the resurrection."

   September 11.—Bid farewell to my family and friends and started on
my eastern mission in company with several Elders and friends, who
were going to the States. We met, on the journey across the plains, several companies, chiefly from Europe. Some of them were companies
traveling with ox teams, and several hand cart companies. The first
hand cart company we met was near Green River, which consisted of
two hundred and thirty men, women and children. These had crossed
the plains from Iowa City—some 1,200 miles—the women as well as
men drawing hand carts and the children walking. They had travelled
twenty miles a day and sometimes more. Their faces were much sun-
burnt and their lips parched; but cheerfulness reigned in every heart, and
joy seemed to beam on every countenance. The company gathered
around us and I tried to address them, observing that this was a new era
in American as well as Church history; but my utterance was choked,

and I had to make the third trial before I could overcome my emotions. We passed on, nothing worthy of note occurring until we arrived at Fort Kearney.

October 17.—We arrived at Fort Kearney; here the death of A. W. Babbitt, and others with him, was confirmed. The commanding officer of the fort came to me and said he had an account of Babbitt's death from the Indians themselves; and that he had obtained his papers and accounts, which he would deliver to Babbitt's wife, if she would come. We pursued our long and wearisome journey through Iowa and Illinois. On the way we saw Nauvoo and the ruins of the Temple in the distance. This called up reflections which I will not attempt to describe. I thought of the Temple and city in their glory; of the twenty thousand Saints once busy there; of the vast congregations once assembled there in prayer and praise; of the martyred Prophets and Saints; of the wholesale murder and plunder perpetrated by ruthless mobs. I thought of my once happy but now fallen country. I greatly desired relief by tears, but tears would not come to my relief. I felt too deeply; but I felt some relief in assuring myself that at last justice would triumph and righteousness reign.

November 18.—We landed in St. Louis after a long and toilsome journey of over two months. Here I remained, attending public meetings with the Saints; visiting, instructing, writing history, and writing for *The Mormon,* then published by Elder John Taylor in New York; visiting and preaching at several places in Missouri and Illinois, until the 16th of December, when I left St. Louis for New York—travelling by railroad. I stopped at Cincinnati, where I arrived at 4 A.M. on the 17th. Here I found some Saints, who took me and my baggage, and extended to me the hospitality of their homes. I remained in Cincinnati, preaching, conversing with the Saints and others, writing correspondence for *The Mormon,* history, etc., until the 22d, when I took leave of the Saints and started by railway for Philadelphia, where I arrived on the 24th—meeting there President John Taylor and other brethren, who kindly greeted me. Here I remained preaching, visiting, conversing, writing history, corresponding with *The Mormons,* etc., until the 31st, when I took the 10 A.M. train for New York, where I safely landed the same day—thus closing another year of my changeful, varied and eventful life. It leaves me among strangers, and yet in my own native State—a pilgrim and almost a stranger in the very city where, twenty years ago, I labored, toiled, prayed, preached, wrote and published the message of eternal truth.

Oh, how darkness prevails! How ignorant, blind and impenetrable are the minds of men! My Father in Heaven, Thy will be done. As a blank of another year of my life is about to commence to be filled up, I will close the volume of the book I have been writing, commending myself to God and the guardianship of his angels; asking, in the name of Jesus Christ, that my sins and follies, up to this date, may be blotted out, and that my labors and records may be accepted; then I will retire to rest with a conscience void of offense, and with a calm and resigned confidence in my Heavenly Father. If I am privileged to awake in the morning of a new year, I will commence a new book or volume of my life.

January 1st, 1857.—Thank God for a new year and for the preservation of my life and health. Spent the day in visiting with President Taylor and others, and at 5 P.M. repaired to the Latter-day Saints' Hall, where I met with some four hundred persons, mostly members of the Church, in a public party.

Judge Appleby called the meeting to order; I opened by prayer. President Taylor made a few remarks, after which there were songs, recitations, speeches, and amusements of various kinds, refreshments, etc., which lasted till eleven o'clock, after which I addressed them, bearing testimony of the restoration of the priesthood and gospel by Joseph Smith; was followed by Presidents Smith and Taylor. While in this party we received news of the safe landing of two hundred and twenty Saints from Europe on the "Columbia." My time was occupied in visiting the Saints, meeting in Council with the brethren, writing, etc., until the 5th, when I met in the evening with brothers Taylor, Smith, Snow and Appleby in Council at brother Taylor's residence. After opening by prayer I was chosen to preside, and brother Appleby acted as clerk. Brother Snow made a statement in relation to the financial condition of the emigration under his agency. We agreed to make this a matter of prayer, and to solicit and influence means into that channel as far as possible. At 7 P.M. brother Taylor having furnished an upper room in his residence, the before-named persons, five in number, met in a room for prayer, in which we humbled ourselves and called on the Lord for remission of our sins and the light of the Spirit of God to guide us in our several duties. We also asked for means, and for our way to be opened up to enable us in all things to magnify our callings; dedicating ourselves renewedly to the service of God. After this we continued in council until a late hour.

January 6th.—I visited Mr. George W. Pratt, No. 89 Gold street, on the subject of genealogy—he being the son of Zadoc Pratt, ex-Member of Congress, and descended from the same parentage as myself, our progenitors being among the early settlers of the New England Colonies. I conversed with him very agreeably for half an hour, and learned that he was in correspondence with brother Orson, in Liverpool, on the subject of our ancestry in England.

January 7th—I was in council all day at brother Taylor's residence with the brethren of the Twelve. We resolved to concentrate our energies this year in forming settlements on or near the Platte River, on the route of our emigration, according to the instructions of President Young. We voted that *The Mormon* be continued, and that it is not expedient for brother Snow to resuscitate the *Luminary* at present. Next day bid farewell to the brethren, and took the train for Trenton, N. J. Here I was kindly received by brother Hurdley and family, where I remained for two days, the weather being very cold.

Saturday, 10th.—Joseph Asay came with a carriage and conveyed me about four miles into the country to his house. This day I completed a communication for *The Mormon* on spiritual communication in modern times.

Sunday, 11th.—Preached to a small congregation in a school house, and returned with brother Asay and spent the evening in instruction—several of the Saints from Trenton being there. Spent the time writing, visiting and conversation with the friends here until the 14th, when I took leave of my kind friends in Trenton; taking the cars for Tacony, where I arrived at noon, went to sister Conrad's, where I was received with every conceivable kindness. After dinner preached to them and read the revelation on marriage. God blessed me to open their understandings, teaching things of the kingdom. Here I wrote a communication for *The Mormon* called the "Looking-glass;" conversed with and instructed the family on many things.

Saturday, 17th.—Returned to Philadelphia and stayed at brother Harmer's; received this evening letters from home, dated November 4th, at which time several of my family were sick. I invoked the blessing of God upon them that they might be healed and comforted.

Sunday, 18th.—Though the wind was very high and extremely cold, attended with a severe snow storm, I repaired to meeting and preached to a few in the morning, and at night attended meeting again in our own hall, the Spirit of God being among the Saints in the meeting.

Monday, 19th.—Still being very snowy, cold and windy, remained at the house of brother Harmer and wrote to my family.

Sunday, 20th.—Railroad travel being obstructed by drifts of snow, I

visited at Peter Rensimer's; stayed all night and talked to him, his wife
and others, till a late hour.

On the next day wrote a poem on "My Fiftieth Year," which was responded to by John Taylor, both of which were published in *The Mormon* at New York. Returned to Tacony in the evening and repaired to
the house of sister Conrad; the family came together and I taught them
the Gospel. Next day visited with the family, taught them and some of
their friends who came in, the principles of the gospel.

Thursday, 24th.—Bade farewell to my kind friends in Tacony, took
the train for Philadelphia, where I arrived at half past nine. Attended
the Saints' meetings at Washington Hall three times this day; addressed
the people morning and evening; communed with them; heard their testimony in the afternoon. We were blessed through the day with the
Spirit of God and had much joy.

February 1st.—Attended meetings three times in Washington Hall,
Philadelphia. Preached in the morning repentance to the Saints and
preparation for the great restoration. In the evening preached on the
Resurrection to a crowded house, and bid the Saints farewell.

Tuesday, 3d.—Wrote, visited sister Fenton, and there spent the
evening in an agreeable company of some fifteen of the Saints. We sang
and prayed, feasted and rejoiced, and taught them as we were led by the
Spirit. Elder Angus M. Cannon being with me in this and nearly all my
visitings and meetings in this city. A happier companion is seldom
found.

Wednesday, 4th.—Spent the evening at a tea party; at ten o'clock
we sang, "When shall we all meet again?" etc. Knelt down and prayed.
This was my farewell of Philadelphia and the Eastern States. I then took
a final leave of the Saints, and, accompanied by Elder Cannon, started
for the railway. Here I met with brother and sister Beers, and some
others who had come to see me off. I took the train for Pittsburg, where I
safely arrived February 5, at 2:30 P.M. Took the train at three for Mans-
field, Ohio, where I landed safely at 1:30 next morning. Stayed at a
hotel, and on the 6th took train at 12 M. and arrived at Hanover, Huron
County, Ohio, at 4 P.M. Here a neighbor volunteered to carry me half a
mile to my brother, Nelson Pratt's. We were overjoyed to see each other
after twenty-one years' absence. He had a wife and three children living,
viz: a son, Edwin Delano Pratt, aged twenty years; and two daughters,
Helen Orisa, aged fourteen, and Aurelia Fenetto, aged twelve years. Remained and visited with my brother and family; talked, read, reasoned,

etc., until the 11th, when I had a call from a young school teacher named Pratt, perhaps a distant relative, who had a spirit of inquiry and was teachable. We conversed much, and I lent him some books. As he and others were soliciting a meeting, I finally consented to appoint one for Thursday evening at the school house near my brother's. In fulfilment of this appointment I preached to a large congregation in a capacious school house.

Friday, 13th.—At noon took leave of my brother Nelson and his family, who accompanied me to the railroad station, and bid me an affectionate farewell. This night, about eight o'clock, the locomotive ran over and killed a horse, and was thrown off the track with a number of cars, some of which were broken. By this accident we were hindered some six hours, during which time we sat in the cars and slept as best we could. Arrived in Columbus, Ohio, at 4 A.M. Here we stopped and slept at a hotel until 9 A.M. At 1 P.M. started for Cincinnati, where I arrived at dark, and was kindly received by brother Meriweather and family.

Sunday, 15th.—Met with the Saints three times; taught them repentance and reformation of life; stayed at brother Walker's.

Monday, 16th.—In the evening Mr. Alberger and Dr. Darling called to see me, and spent the evening in conversation on the various phenomena of Spiritualism. Mr. Alberger related to me the circumstances of the introduction of a secret order, called the Patriarchal Order, which order, he said, was introduced by spirits in Cincinnati a short time previously by means of a stone, with a new alphabet and a key to read the same. He also made me a present of the stone, or rather a pattern of the same in plaster of Paris, with the alphabet thereon and key to read the same. Also a printed pamphlet containing the ceremonies of the "Patriarchal Order," and the forms of initiation of members into the same, with a request that I would take them to Salt Lake and exhibit them to the Council there.

The following day, wrote an article for the *Cincinnati Gazette*, in defense of Utah. In the evening met with the Saints, and preached at Thos. Shore's. The next day was very rainy; visited at brother Meriweather's, and found brother Geo. A. Smith there, just arrived from Virginia. He had spent some time in Washington City, in company with John Taylor, who was one of the delegation, but as no encouragement was given for the admission of Utah at the present session, the petition was withdrawn.

Friday, 20th.—Wrote for *The Mormon*, visited with brother Smith, etc. My communication to the *Cincinnati Gazette* in defense of Utah, appeared in this day's paper. We mailed several copies of the paper to the members of Congress, and to *The Mormon*.

Sunday, 22d.—Attended at Melodian Hall at 10:30 A.M., and heard an excellent discourse from Elder G. A. Smith. At 2:30 P.M. I preached on first principles, and in the evening met the Saints at brother Shore's, and reorganized the Cincinnati Branch. Elder Joseph Bean was unanimously chosen to preside, and was ordained a High Priest under the hands of G. A. Smith and myself. Brother Benjamin E. Styles was reappointed clerk. At ten o'clock we sung "When shall we all meet again."

We appointed and set apart brother D. O. Ridout to a mission in south-western Virginia. We blessed and administered to several. A man named James Raliston came to us and expressed his faith in the gospel as he had heard us preach it the day before. Many of the Saints now gathered in to see us, and contributed means to help us, and manifested their love in every way that was in their power. We bid them farewell about 2 P.M., and took the train for St. Louis, at which place we arrived safely about midnight.

Tuesday, 24th.—Called and stayed at brother Boardman's. Here, for the first time, heard of the sudden and unexpected death of President J. M. Grant, who died in Salt Lake City, in November last. He was a great and good man, called away in the full vigor of manhood. He has gone to his rest, but we are left to mourn.

Wednesday, 25th.—On repairing to the office found letters from home, also one from sister Ruth Sayers, who crossed the plains with us on our outward trip from Salt Lake City. I also read in the *Western Standard*, a paper published by George Q. Cannon in California, a confirmatory account of the death of President J. M. Grant. We found the Saints in St. Louis well and prosperous. After spending some time in the office in council I repaired to brother Restell's, and was kindly received by sister Restell and sister Pollard. This night I was taken very sick.

March 1st.—I found myself quite well again, and, being Sunday, I met with the Saints three times and had good attendance. I preached in the forenoon, and Erastus Snow and others in the afternoon. We had Sacrament, and the gift of the Holy Ghost was upon us. Brother Snow spake by it in great wisdom.

The spirit of reformation is abroad in the St. Louis branch, but the adversary also has a great hold there.

Monday, 2d.—We met with the Saints and assisted President Snow to confirm twenty-nine souls, who were baptized in the font there. At 7 P. M. the same evening met with the brethren in council.

Much instruction was given to the Elders by Presidents Snow, Smith and myself.

Tuesday, 3d.—Assisted President Snow at the office, on the Deseret alphabet, etc.

The above is the last extract from the journal of President Parley P. Pratt.

Chapter 54

NEW YORK, *January 3d, 1857.*

MY DEAR SON PARLEY: I am well; how are you? Please write and let me know. I long to see and hear from you.

I am getting along very comfortably. You will see by the enclosed how *"Mormonism"* keeps printers and editors busy. Give my best love to all the family, and especially to the children. Remember me to Olivia and Moroni. Do the best you can for me and my family, and try to get a good education; and try by prayer and doing right to cultivate an acquaintance with the Spirit of the Lord.

Read the enclosed letter to the family, and then have it carefully laid away as a part of my history.

Now, my son, farewell.

God bless you. Amen.

Your affectionate father,

P.P. PRATT.

NEW YORK, *January 3d, 1857.*

MY DEAR FAMILY:

A happy New Year to each of you. I am well. I spent Christmas in Philadelphia in a public party of the Saints—say 300 persons—assembled in a large hall neatly furnished and lighted. There were prayers, hymns, songs, recitations, comic, tragic, sublime and ridiculous. There was some music and dancing, merry making, eating and drinking till midnight. I did not dance, but I preached and bore testimony.

On the following Sunday I preached twice in the same hall, some 500 persons being present.

On Wednesday, December 31st, I arrived in this city and put up with President John Taylor. This closed the year 1856.

January 1st, 1857.—I attended a public party of the Saints here from 5 P.M. till midnight. It was like the one in Philadelphia—only there was no dancing. About 400 persons were present. During this party the news arrived of the landing of 220 Saints at Castle Garden direct from Europe, all in good health and spirits. These we visited next day in company with Presidents Taylor, G. A. Smith, and E. Snow, who are here now, and we shall hold a council. The Saints here are mostly emigrants from Europe and very poor. I am now well clothed, and God has opened my way to obtain sufficient funds for traveling expenses.

A letter from my brother Nelson announces that all is well there, and they are overjoyed to hear that I am to visit them. He is trying to sell and go to the valley.

Brother Orson writes to me that all is well with him.

I have gone as far East as I intend to go. I hope soon to commence to return westward, visiting my brother Nelson as I go. The darkness which broods over this country can be felt—it is no place for me. I feel like going to the frontiers and fitting out as soon as grass grows.

The whole country is being overwhelmed with the most abominable lying, mockery, and hatred of the Saints, and with all manner of corruption. The legions of spirits are let loose and are working wonders. All things are ripening for a universal overthrow of all human power in this land.

I am almost an intruder wherever I go. I am a stranger and the world knows me not. There are a few of the Saints and others who will hear us, and not exactly demand a vote of thanks, although some of them would think it a great condescension for which we ought to thank them.

O, God, let me retire from such a generation into dens, caves, deserts, mountains—*anywhere*. But I will say no more about them. I feel for my family and pray for them continually. I hope they with me may have grace to endure to the end, and be saved in the kingdom of God.

My history is mostly completed. It will probably not be published in my day. Should anything happen to me, and the record be preserved, I wish it carefully compiled, copied, and taken care of.

* * * * * * *

My feelings, and the affections of my heart, I will not attempt to describe, but will express them in person when I return. Should I never return, be assured they are as warm and as tender as ever, and I think a little more so.

I hope you will not be cast down or borrow any trouble about me because I admit *an if,* as to my safe return. I have no doubt but that I shall return in safety and live to a good old age. But still I must acknowledge that I do anticipate with a great deal of pleasure the change of worlds. And, every day that I work on my history, I naturally think that the word *finis* will soon be added to the end.　*　*　*　*

Write when you can *via* California and Panama. Now God bless and preserve you all, even to little Mathoni. Amen.

Yours ever,

P. P. PRATT.

To my wife HANNAHETTE *and others.*

MY FIFTIETH YEAR

I AM fifty years old! I have lived to see
Seven times seven and a Jubilee.
That period famed in the days of yore
As a grand release for the humble poor;
When the pledg'd estate was again restor'd,
And the bondman free'd from his tyrant lord.
When man his fellow was bound to forgive,
And begin anew to think and to live.
The nations have hail'd the year of my birth
As a Jubilee to the groaning earth. *
The triumphs of steam over land and sea
Have stamp'd the age of my Jubilee.
I have mark'd its progress at ev'ry stride,
From the day it was launch'd on the Hudson's tide
Till it conquer'd the ocean—grasp'd the land,
And join'd the world in a common band.
I have liv'd to behold the lightnings yield
To the mandate of man, and take the field,
As a servant-runner to bear the news
In an instant, where its lord might choose.

And, scarce less strange, I have liv'd to behold
A *Mormon Sage,* with his wand of gold,
Overturn the world, and toss it up
As a teller of Fortunes would his cup. †
All these are facts; but of little worth,
Compared with a Prophet restored to earth.
I have seen his day and have heard his voice,
Which enraged a world, while the meek rejoice.
I have read the fate of all earthly things:
The end of thrones, and the end of kings.
I have learned that truth alone shall stand,

---

*The first steamboat was launched in 1807, on the Hudson River, by Robert Fulton.
†An American soldier, of the Mormon Battalion, discovered the gold mines in California in 1848.

And the Kingdom of God fill every land.
I have seen that Kingdom rolling along,
And taking its seat 'mid the mountains strong;
While the nations wondered, but could not tell
To what these wondrous things would swell.
I have wandered far, over land and sea,
To proclaim to the world its destiny—
To cry to the nations, repent and live,
And be ready the bridegroom to receive.

I have wandered far—I have wandered wide,
From Maine to the wild Missouri's tide;
And over the Atlantic's sea-girt isles
Full many a weary thousand miles.
I have trampled the desert's burning sands
And the snow-clad mountains of unknown lands.
'Mid the crystal waters of Deseret
I have pulled the oar and cast the net.
I have climbed the steeps 'mid the golden ore,
And roamed o'er the lone Pacific shore.
I have ploughed its bosom many a day
To visit the nations far away.
I have stood on Chili's distant shore,
Where the Polar Star is seen no more.
I have gazed on the Andes' heights of snow,
And roamed 'mid the flowery plains below.

I have toiled with the great in freedom's cause,
And assisted to give to a State its laws.
I have lain in a dungeon, bound in chains,
And been honored in Courts where Justice reigns.
In a thousand joys, and a thousand fears
I have struggled on through my fifty years.
And now, by the law of God, I am free;
I will seek to enjoy my Jubilee.
I will hie me home, to my mountain dell,
And will say to the "Christian" world—farewell!
I have served ye long—; 'twas a thankless task;
To retire in peace is all I ask.

Another fifty years will fully prove
Our message true, and all our motives love.
Then shall an humble world in reverence bow,
And hail the Prophets so rejected now.
Kings shall revere, and nations incense bring

To Zion's temple and to Zion's King.
I shall be there and celebrate the day
'Till twice ten fifties shall have passed away.

A RESPONSE TO P. P. PRATT'S "FIFTIETH YEAR"

BY JOHN TAYLOR

THOU art "fifty years old"—I am glad to see
That thou now canst hope for a Jubilee.
Go rest thee, my friend, for weary and long
Thou hast faithfully striven with a wayward throng;
With a world environed with error's chain
Thou hast wrestled and struggled, but not in vain.
On thy native shore and on foreign land
Thou hast battled for truth with a master hand,
And their cities, and towns, and hamlets have rung
With the sound of truth, with the voice of song;
And thousands in Zion do now rejoice,
Who've read thy works or heard thy voice,
And millions have seen thy bosom swell
With celestial truths thou lov'st so well.

Let drivelling sycophants bow the knee
To that chameleon shrine, popularity,
And with honey'd lips, bound with mammon's spell,
Plaster over the vices they dar'd not tell,
And with wheedling, whining, canting tongue,
Daub o'er the deeds of a hellish throng.
'Twas thine the mask from their loathsome face
To rend, and exhibit their foul disgrace.

Thou hast grappled with sages in error rife,
Thou hast taught to the erring the way of life;
With flaming words and a burning pen
Thou hast bearded gaunt priestcraft in his den,
And said to Baal's grizzly priests, avaunt!
I dare you in your dark, ghastly haunt.
And the canting, craving minions fled
At the truths thou penned and the words thou said.
With Elijah's faith and Elijah's rod,
Thou despised their power and defied their god,
And made the canting hirelings cower
Beneath the truth's keen withering power.
Thou show'd them their systems were doom'd to fall,
That "Upharsin" was written on Babel's wall.

Thou hast spent 'midst their hordes a busy life;
Thou art leaving the den of their Babel strife.
Let others now 'mid the nations roam,
And hie thee away to thy mountain home.

If, sleeping at night, the weary may
Forget the cares and toils of day;
And if by God to man is given
A day of rest in every seven;
If the pledged possession could be restored,
On the grand release by Jehovah's word;
If the debtor's bonds could then be broke,
And the slave be freed from a master's yoke,
And the very land a partaker be
Of the general jubilant Jubilee;
If all bonds were broken on that day,
And chains and manacles thrown away;
If throughout the land, by every tongue,
All joined in the joyous Jubilee song;
If debtors and slaves and earth were free,
Thou oughtest to have a Jubilee.

If a wish from a sincere friendly heart
Can to thee any comfort or joy impart;
If a fervent prayer to the God of grace
Could smooth thy path in thy onward race,
That prayer would be, may grace be given
To wend thy onward course to Heaven.
May'st thou abound in corn and wine,
And the blessings of plenty now be thine;
May thy family all be free from care,
And a husband's and father's plenty share;
May thy sun go down with glory rife,
And dying may'st thou burst into life;
And, when sleeping among the silent dead,
Have the blessings of millions on thy head;
And living with God, may'st thou be free,
And partake of an endless Jubilee.

FINIS

Appendix

Soon after the last extract from his journal, President P. P. Pratt left St. Louis for Arkansas, where he was followed by three bloodthirsty wretches, who had previously declared their intention to kill him. To aid them in their sanguinary designs they preferred fictitious charges against him, from which he was honorably discharged by a United States Court at Van Buren. These assassins then followed him and murdered him in cold blood, near Van Buren, Arkansas, May 13, 1857.

We extract the following, in relation to his death, from *The Mormon* of May 30, published in New York, John Taylor, Ed.:

Assassination of President P. P. Pratt

"Our readers will doubtless be startled with the above announcement; our heart is deeply pained to say it, but we have no reason for doubting the sad intelligence that has reached us, though, as yet, only by the way of the public press. A few days ago we were advised of his apprehension near Fort Gibson; and, close upon the receipt of that information, we learned, by telegraphic despatch, that he had been assassinated near Van Buren, Arkansas, May 13.***

"As we have not the space this week that we require to enter into details, and may, before another issue, receive additional information on the subject, we shall only say, for the benefit of those who are interested, that his assassins followed him some twelve miles from the place of trial, and, taking advantage of his lonely position, shot him.

"Though we deeply deplore the loss to the Church of such a great and upright man, and the bereavement to his family, yet we mourn not. His life has been one of honor and faithfulness; his days have been well spent in the service of his God; his name is revered by thousands and tens of thousands, and will be honored by millions yet unborn; while that of his cowardly assassins, and those who have cheered them on to this damning deed, and who now rejoice over their crime, will be loathsome, and a stink in the nostrils of God and good men."

The following is extracted from the *Millennial Star* of July 4, 1857, and written by his brother, Orson Pratt, who was then Editor of the *Star*:

BIOGRAPHICAL SKETCH OF PARLEY P. PRATT

"This great Apostle and martyr of the nineteenth century was born on the 12th day of April, 1807, in Burlington, Otsego County, State of New York. He was the third son of Jared and Charity Pratt; Jared was the son of Obadiah and Jemima Pratt; Obadiah was the son of Christopher and Sarah Pratt; Christopher was the son of William and Hannah Pratt; William was the son of Joseph Pratt; Joseph was the son of Lieutenant William and Elizabeth Pratt, who were found among the first settlers of Hartford, Connecticut, in the year 1639. They are supposed to have accompanied the Rev. Thomas Hooker and his congregation, about one hundred in number, from Newton, now called Cambridge, Massachusetts, through a dense wilderness, inhabited only by savages and wild beasts, and became the first founders of the colony at Hartford, in June, 1636.

"This ancient pilgrim, William Pratt, was a member of the Legislature for some twenty-five or thirty sessions; and the General Court gave him one hundred acres of land in Saybrook, Connecticut, for service performed as lieutenant in the Pequot war; he was one of the judges of the first Court in New London County. Parley P. Pratt is a lineal descendant, of the seventh generation, from that distinguished pilgrim and humble pioneer to the New World.

"The youthful days of our martyred brother were characterized by the soberness and thoughtfulness of manhood. Though from adverse circumstances his education was extremely limited, yet he displayed, even in youth, an originality of mind seldom exhibited. In September, 1830, he, being led by the Spirit of the Lord from his home in the State of Ohio, came several hundred miles eastward, where he fortunately obtained a copy of one of the most remarkable works of modern times—the Book of Mormon. He read the same, was convinced of its divine authenticity, and traveled in search of the highly favored men of God who had seen angels and heard the voice of the Almighty. He soon succeeded in finding some of them, from whom he learned that about five months previous the first Church of the Latter-day Saints had been organized. He requested baptism, and was immediately after ordained an Elder. The same month he visited Canaan, Columbia County, New York—the county where he had spent many of his youthful days—and after preaching a few times in different neighborhoods, and baptizing Orson Pratt, his brother, he returned to Seneca County.

"Receiving a revelation through Joseph the Prophet, he, in company with three or four others performed a mission, some fifteen hundred miles, to the western boundaries of the State of Missouri, and was among the first of the Saints to stand upon that choice land where the City of Zion is hereafter to be built, preparatory to the second advent of our Savior.

"In the spring of 1831 he returned to the northern part of Ohio, where he met Joseph the Prophet. In the summer he again performed a mission through Ohio, Indiana, Illinois and Missouri, preaching, baptizing and building up the Church.

"In the autumn of 1833 he and about twelve hundred men, women and children were driven by a murderous, furious mob from their own houses and lands in Jackson County, Missouri. Two hundred houses were burned, cattle shot, hay stacks and grain burned, many whipped until their bowels gushed out; others killed, and the afflicted remnant driven across the river into Clay County.

"Soon after this Elder Pratt performed a long journey of about fifteen hundred miles east, preaching repentance and strengthening the Saints.

"In 1834 he again returned to Clay County, Missouri, officiating in his holy calling wherever he went.

"In 1835, having returned to the northern part of Ohio, he was chosen and ordained one of the Twelve Apostles of this last dispensation, and the same year performed a lengthy journey through Pennsylvania, New York, and several of the New England States, and returned again to Ohio.

"In 1836 he visited Canada, and established a large branch of the Church in Toronto, and other branches in adjoining towns.

"In 1837 he visited New York City, where he founded a large branch of the Church.

"In 1838 he removed to Caldwell County, in the western boundaries of Missouri; and in the same year another dreadful persecution commenced against the Saints, and they were for the third time driven from their own houses and inheritances, and their property to the amount of millions was destroyed; some scores of defenseless men, women and children were murdered; scores of others incarcerated in dungeons, among whom was the subject of this memoir; the balance, about fifteen thousand, were exterminated from the State, and found refuge in Illinois. Elder Pratt was kept in prison, *without trial*, about eight months, when, by the kind providence of God, he made his escape; an account of which is published in the *Millennial Star*, Vol. VIII, pages 129, 145 and 161. Immediately after gaining his liberty he published a history of the Missouri persecution, written while in prison. The first edition appeared in Detroit in 1839.

"In 1840 he visited England, and in the town of Manchester commenced the publication of a periodical entitled the *Millennial Star*, which has continued until the present time—this being the nineteenth volume.

"In 1841 he was appointed the President over all the British Conferences, and remained in this high and honorable station until the autumn of 1842, during which he edited the *Star*, superintended the Saints' emigration, and published several small but interesting works. The following winter he returned to Illinois, where he continued laboring in the ministry for one or two years.

"About the beginning of the year 1845 he was appointed the President over all the Churches in the New England and Middle States, his headquarters being at New York City, where he wrote for a periodical entitled *The Prophet*. In the summer he returned to Nauvoo.

"In February, 1846, he was again driven from his home by a ruthless mob. Some fifteen or twenty thousand Saints were also driven from the United States about the same time, with the loss of houses, and lands, and an immense amount of property, which the mob are in the unmolested possession of until the present day. After wading through unparalleled sufferings with his family, he and the suffering Saints succeeded in reaching the Indian country at Council Bluffs, and being called by the Holy Ghost, through the Prophet Brigham Young, to go to England, he left his family upon the broad prairie, without house or scarcely any food, to comply with the word of the Lord. He arrived in England, assisted in setting the Churches in order, and in strengthening the Saints throughout the British islands.

"In the spring of 1847 he returned to his family and brethren; and in the summer and autumn of that year he removed to Great Salt Lake Valley, and suffered incredible hardships until the harvest of 1848.

"He assisted in forming a Constitution for the Provisional Government of Deseret, and was elected a member of the Senate in the General Assembly; and was afterwards elected to the Legislative Council when Utah became a Territory of the United States.

"The year 1851 he was sent on a mission to the Pacific islands and to South America.

"In the summer of 1855 he returned over the Sierra Nevada mountains to his home, and occupied a part of his time in preaching in the various settlements of Utah, and at other times laboring with his own hands in the cultivation of his farm. The following winter he officiated as chaplain in the Legislative Council at the State House in Fillmore City.

"In the autumn of 1856 he accompanied about twenty missionaries across the plains to the States. During the winter and part of the following spring he visited the Saints at St. Louis, Philadelphia, New York and other places, preaching, writing and publishing the glad tidings of the kingdom of God.

"And finally, on the 13th of May, 1857, he fell a noble martyr for the cause of truth, which he had advocated with such untiring perseverance for nearly twenty-seven years. His last great and magnanimous act, in trying to rescue helpless innocence from the fury of their savage persecutors, will be handed down to unborn generations as an imperishable monument to his praise; while his wicked, brutal murderers, and all that gave countenance to the diabolical deed, shall gnaw their tongues for pain, and perish, and be forgotten.

"Among the numerous writings of this martyred Apostle may be mentioned first, the 'Voice of Warning,' printed in New York in 1837, and which has since passed through many editions, and been translated into several foreign languages; second, his 'History of the Missouri Persecutions;' third, his 'Poems;' fourth, his 'Key to Theology;' a masterly production, lately published. 'The History of His Life,' up to near the time of his martyrdom, was written by himself, and is now about ready for the press; this will doubtless prove to be one of the most interesting works proceeding from his pen.

"O, how pleasant is the death of a righteous person! He lays down his body with a sure and certain hope of coming forth from the tomb in the morning of the first resurrection, to reign as a mighty King and Priest of the Most High God, to sit enthroned in eternal glory, ruling with power and dominion for ever and ever.

"O, kind hearted, affectionate brother! How dearly we loved thee in life! How joyous to our soul were the words of life which flowed from thy mouth by the pure spirit of inspiration! How lovely still is our remembrance of thee! We weep not for thy death, for it was glorious! Thou hast left us only for a short moment, and we shall soon embrace thee again! Thy fiftieth year had but just rolled away, and now thy Jubilee has come! Rest in thy Father's house, with all the noble martyrs of the nineteenth century, until the Jubilee of the earth shall also come; then shalt thou return and reign triumphantly with all the redeemed of Adam's race."

From the following letter, written only about four months prior to his martyrdom, he plainly indicates that his pilgrimage and "personal history in this world," were near their close:

"NEW YORK, UNITED STATES,
January 2d, 1857.

"*Dear Brother* ORSON—I received your kind letter on the 30th December, 1856. I was thereby glad to hear from you and of your welfare.

"I am well; I spent about a month in St. Louis; I then came on to Cincinnati and stayed four days, drawing full houses. I arrived in Philadelphia the day before Christmas—was present next day at a grand party in that city, in Washington Hall. It was a fine time. Sunday last I preached three times to a full house.

"I arrived here on Wednesday last; found Presidents Taylor and Smith as well as usual.

"Yesterday I attended a party here, in the Saints' Hall; it was an interesting affair, some four hundred persons being present. We were entertained with songs, prayers, preaching, praying, recitations, eating, drinking, etc.

"In the midst of our evening's enjoyment the news arrived of the arrival of the *Columbia,* with a ship load of Saints from England. Today we accompanied brother Taylor to see them. All well, but a rough passage; no deaths. The weather is mild here, and the winter so far very fine.

"I have not yet seen the Pratt family, of whom you speak, but I think I will visit them in a day or two.

"You ask how long I will stay in the States. I answer, till spring. I will then go home, if God will, if I have to go with a hand cart. This country is no place for me; the darkness is so thick I can literally feel it. I cannot obtain the least assistance here for my family; a tight match to obtain traveling expenses.

"I have heard nothing from home since October 1st, but I hope to hear soon. I congratulate you on the marriage of your first born, and hope you will soon become a grandfather.

"*Now, dear brother Orson, be of good courage—our pilgrimage will soon be over, and our personal history in this world will naturally come to the word* FINIS.

"As to my history, I have it now complete from my birth up to today. It will contain about as much reading as the Book of Mormon. I would publish it, in part or in full, if gold was plentiful. * * *

"I have written to Nelson Pratt and received an answer; he is well. I am going there soon, if all is well.

"I am to start from St. Louis for home just as early in the spring as the weather will permit. Farewell! God bless you.

"I am your own brother,

"P. P. PRATT."

Genealogy

The following correspondence, extracted from a letter from my brother, Orson Pratt, Sen., dated at Washington, D.C., March 10th, 1853, throws a clear light upon our ancestry, back as far as the earliest settlements of the Pilgrim Fathers in Saybrook and Hartford, Conn.

"My *dear brother* PARLEY—I embrace the present opportunity to write a few lines to you.* * *

"It affords me much joy to be able to inform you that I have obtained the names and some knowledge of our ancestors back for many generations.

"The genealogy runs thus: Our father, Jared Pratt, was the son of Obadiah, who was the son of Christopher, who was the son of William Pratt, who was the son of Joseph Pratt, who was the son of Lieutenant William and Elizabeth Pratt, who is supposed to have come with his brother, John Pratt, from Essex County, England, about the year 1633, who were found among the first settlers of Hartford, Connecticut, in the year 1636. They are supposed to have accompanied the Rev. Thomas Hooker and his congregation, about one hundred in number, from Newtown, now called Cambridge, Massachusetts, through a dense wilderness, inhabited only by savages and wild beasts, and became the first founders of the colony at Hartford, Connecticut, in June, 1636, and thence to Saybrook about the year 1645.

"The way I came by this information is as follows: Seeing a short editorial in some of my exchange papers, that there was an attempt being made to search out the lineal descendants of Lieutenant Wm. Pratt, and that the Rev. Frederick W. Chapman, of South Glastenbury, Conn., was engaged in that work, I immediately addressed a letter to him, giving him the names of Jared, Obadiah and Christopher, and asking him for all the information he was in possession of in relation to our ancestors. He immediately sent me a letter and two printed circulars. The following is a copy of the letter:

SOUTH GLASTENBURY, *March 5th,* 1853.

"Dear Sir—I have just received your favor. It affords me pleasure to be able to show you the connecting links between your grandfather, Obadiah Pratt, and the first settler, William Pratt, who came with the company that located at Hartford, Conn. He received a portion of land in the first distribution in February, 1639. He married Elizabeth Clark, daughter of John Clark, of Milford, Connecticut, about the same time. He had eight children. Of these, two were born in Hartford. He removed to Saybrook in 1645. His third child, Joseph Pratt, born at Saybrook, August 1st, 1648.

SECOND GENERATION

Joseph Pratt,
Sarah Chapman,   Married September, 1686.

Thirteen children—five by a former wife. William one of the children.

THIRD GENERATION

William Pratt,
Hannah Hough,   Married October 8, 1700.

Six children, viz:

Joseph . . . . born April 13, 1703
Ephraim . . . . born April 1, 1705
Margaret . . . . born April 1, 1708
Christopher . . . . born Nov. 4, 1712
Elizabeth . . . . born Jan. 20, 1717
Experience . . . . born Sept. 28, 1720

FOURTH GENERATION

Christopher Pratt,
Sarah Pratt,   Married June 14, 1739.

Children:

Stephen . . . . . . .born June 30, 1740, at Saybrook
Obadiah . . . . . .born Sept. 14, 1742,   "
Sarah . . . . . . .born March 28, 1745
Hannah . . . . . .born Aug. 6, 1747
Chalker . . . . . .born Feb. 14, 1750
Samuel . . . . . .

"I want very much to get all the descendants of the last six. Your letter was the first clue to any of them which I have received. It is more difficult to trace the descendants of Joseph than any other of the six children of William Pratt. In fact, they seem to have disappeared from Saybrook about a century ago.

"I have already collected about two thousand of the descendants of William Pratt. There are probably not less than five thousand. Robert Chapman, my ancestor, was married about two years after William Pratt. I have collected over five thousand of his descendants, and the work—a volume of three hundred to three hundred and fifty pages—is nearly ready for the press. I shall be able to collect most of the descendants of William if those whom I address will answer my letters and lend a helping hand.

"May I rely on you to aid me in collecting the descendants of Chrisopher Pratt?

"Is your father living? If so, he may be able to inform you where the brothers and sisters of his grandfather Christopher resided—or, perhaps, give the post office address of one of the descendants of each family.

"He can, of course, give me some account of his uncles and aunts. Please write immediately and inform me. I want the marriage of Stephen, when and to whom—and of Obadiah, when and to whom, and the names of their children—dates of birth; and so of Sarah and the others.

"You can, of course, give me a list of your grandfather's children. Also give the name of your mother, and date of your father's marriage, with a list of all his children.

"I enclose two circulars. There is a Pratt, ex-Governor of Maryland; I know not his address; if you can ascertain, please forward one. Let me hear from you soon. Respectfully yours,

FREDERICK W. CHAPMAN.

"Now, my dear brother Parley, when I received the foregoing letter I wept like a little child; I was so overjoyed that I could not refrain from weeping.

"There are none among all the descendants of our ancestor, Lieutenant William Pratt, who have so deep an interest in searching out his descendants as ourselves. We know that the God of our fathers has had a hand in all this. He it was who brought our ancestor William from England, and established him in this choice land of promise, given to us by virtue of the covenant made with our ancient father, Joseph, the son of Jacob.

"The Lord God of our fathers has multiplied them in this land, and made them almost a nation within a nation. Blessed be the name of our God, for He remembereth his covenants forevermore.

"He has wrought upon the hearts of his servants, our relations, though unknown to them, to inquire out the genealogy and history of our fathers, upon the promised land. Yea, blessed be the name of the Lord God of Joseph and of Israel, for he hath given into our hands the keys of the Priesthood and the doctrines of salvation, that we might stand as saviors upon Mount Zion, in behalf of our ancestors and their lineal descendants. Let us, my dear brother Parley, take hold of this matter in earnest, and assist our kindred in the laudable enterprise which they have undertaken.

"I have no records with me and my memory is weak. Therefore, I hope you will search up all the family records, and all the verbal information within your reach—with names, dates, births, places, marriages and deaths, and forward without delay.

"Does our father's sister, Aunt Lovina Van Cott, or yourself know anything about the descendants of Stephen, Sarah and others, the brothers and sisters to our grandfather, Obadiah? How shall we get a clue to them? Is it possible to find out any descendant of either of the brothers or sisters of Christopher Pratt, of Saybrook, our great-grandfather? Who, and when did our grandfather, Obadiah, marry? How many children had Obadiah? Whom did they marry, and when? How many children had each of our uncles and aunts, the brothers and sisters of our father? And how many children and grandchildren has each of these cousins? In short, all the descendants of our great-grandfather, Christopher, are wanting.

* * * Send all the information you can gather to Mr. Chapman. It might not be amiss to send him your 'History of the Persecution,' your 'Voice of Warning,' and such other works as you may be the author of; and also, if you see proper, a biographical sketch of your life. I have forwarded to him all of my works. * * * I have also sent him all the information in my power concerning our kindred. * * *

"I sent a letter last evening proposing to take some fifty or a hundred dollars' worth of the records as soon as published. These will supply myself and brothers and our rising families. I also proposed to search out, if possible, the ancestors of William Pratt, in England. I expect to visit England in April or May, and shall probably be absent two or three months.

"This from your younger brother,

"ORSON PRATT."

"To Parley P. Pratt.

After receiving the foregoing, I gathered the little information I could, in so new a country as Utah Territory, and adding it to that which I knew myself, the result or summary of the whole is as follows—for a portion of which I am indebted to the family records of my aunt, Lovina Van Cott, and to her memory, she being still living, and near my residence in Salt Lake City.

Our great-grandfather, Christopher Pratt, of Saybrook, Conn., had six children, as follows, viz:

Stephen	born	June 30, 1740, at Saybrook
Obadiah	born	Sept. 14, 1742, "
Sarah	born	March 28, 1745
Hannah	born	Aug. 6, 1747
Chalker	born	Feb. 14, 1750
Samuel		

Our grandfather, Obadiah Pratt, son of Christopher and Sarah Pratt, born in Saybrook, Conn., September 14, 1742, received in marriage Jemina Tolls, born in New Haven, Conn., August 11, 1754. Date of marriage not known. He died in Canaan, Columbia County, New York, March 2, 1797. His wife died in Washington, Dutchess County, New York, November 24, 1812.

Eleven children, as follows:

Jared . .	born in Canaan, Columbia County, N.Y.,					November 25, 1769
Barnabas .	"	"	"	"	"	March 4, 1771
Samuel .	"	"	"	"	"	February 2, 1773
Rhoda . .	"	"	"	"	"	May 30, 1775
William .	"	"	"	"	"	May 21, 1777
Sarah . .	"	"	"	"	"	September 3, 1781
Obadiah .	"	"	"	"	"	July 30, 1784
Lovina . .	"	"	"	"	"	August 6, 1787
Ira	"	"	"	"	"	October 10, 1789
Ellis . . .	Twin sister of Ira, lived five days.					October 10, 1789
Allen . .	born in Canaan, Columbia County, N.Y.,					May 3, 1793

Our father, Jared Pratt, son of Obadiah and Jemima Pratt, received in marriage Mary Carpenter, daughter of Samuel Carpenter, of New Lebanon, New York. She bore him one daughter, named Mary, and afterwards died. This daughter married a Mr. Brown, of New Lebanon, and bore one son, named Jerome Brown. She afterwards lost her husband, and was married to Samuel Bigalow, of New Lebanon; they may be still living at that place.

Our father, Jared, afterwards received in marriage Charity Dickinson, daughter of Samuel Dickinson, of Bolton, New York. I remember seeing him once (Dickinson) when a small boy.

Our father, Jared, died at Detroit, Michigan, of a fever, November 5, 1839, being near seventy years of age. He died in the house of his eldest son, Anson, who buried him some three or four miles north or northeast from Detroit, in Michigan.

Our mother, Charity, died of cholera in the house of her son Anson, at St. Joseph, Missouri, May 20, 1849, and was buried in the graveyard of that town, and a tombstone erected to her memory.

Their children, five in number, were as follows:

Anson, born January 9, 1801, died May 26, 1849.

William D., born September 3, 1802, Town of Wooster, New York, died September 15, 1870, Salt Lake City.

Parley P., born April 12, 1807, in Burlington, Otsego County, New York.

Orson, born September 19, 1811, in Hartford, Washington County, New York.

Nelson, born May 26, 1815.

PARLEY PARKER PRATT'S FAMILY

Married	Children
THANKFUL HALSEY, 9 Sept., 1827 b. 18 Mar., 1797, Canaan, New York d. 25 Mar., 1837, Kirtland, Ohio.	Parley Parker Pratt b. 25 Mar., 1837 d. 26 Aug., 1897 Salt Lake City, Utah
MARY ANN FROST, 9 May, 1837 b. 14 Jan., 1808, Bethel, Oxford, Maine d. 24 Aug., 1891, Pleasant Grove, Utah	Nathan b. 31 Aug., 1838 d. 12 Dec., 1843 Olivia b. 2 June, 1841 d. 12 June, 1906 Susan b. 7 Apr., 1843 d. 28 Aug., 1844 Moroni b. 7 Dec., 1844 d. 18 Apr., 1913
ELIZABETH BROTHERTON, 24 July, 1843 b. 27 Mar., 1817, Manchester, England. d. 9 May, 1897, Salt Lake City, Utah	None
MARY WOOD, 9 Sept., 1844 b. 18 June, 1819, Glasgow, Scotland d. 5 May, 1898, Salt Lake City, Utah	Heleman b. 31 May, 1846 d. 26 Nov., 1910 Cornelia b. 5 Sept., 1848 d. 10 Sept., 1899 Mary b. 14 Sept., 1853 d. 25 Oct., 1911 Mathoni b. 6 July, 1856 d. 1937
HANNAHETTE SNIVELY, 2 Nov., 1844 b. 27 Oct., 1812, Woodstock, Va. d. 21 Feb., 1898, Salt Lake City, Utah	Alma b. 31 July, 1845 d. 13 Nov., 1902

Lucy
   b. 9 Mar., 1848
   d. 26 Feb., 1916
Henriette
   b. 26 Oct., 1851
   d. 18 May, 1918

BELINDA MARDEN, 20 Nov., 1844
   b. 24 Dec., 1820, Chichester, New Hampshire
   d. 19 Feb., 1894, Salt Lake City, Utah

Nephi
   b. 1 Jan., 1846
   d. 29 Apr., 1910
Belinda (Twin)
   b. 8 May, 1848
   d. 10 Dec., 1893
Abinadi (Twin)
   d. Nov., 1914
Lehi
   b. 9 June, 1851
   d. 15 Aug., 1905
Isabella
   b. 1 Sept., 1854
   d. 23 Apr., 1912

Married

SARAH HUSTON, 15 Oct., 1845
   b. 3 Aug., 1822, Stark Co., Ohio
   d. 26 May, 1886, Coyote, Utah

Children

Julia
   b. 1 Apr., 1847
   d. 17 Apr., 1903
Mormon
   b. 8 Jan., 1850
   d. 17 Nov., 1850
Teancum
   b. 15 Nov., 1851
   d. 8 Sept., 1900
Sarah
   b. 31 May, 1856
   d.

PHOEBE SOPHER, 8 Feb., 1846
   b. 8 July, 1823, Hempstead Harbor, N.Y.
   d. 17 Sept., 1887, Provo, Utah

Mosiah
   b. 26 Feb., 1850
   d. 26 Mar., 1850

Omner
  b. 30 Nov., 1851
  d. 7 Jan., 1852
Phoebe
  b. 19 May, 1853
  d. 13 Oct., 1922

MARTHA MONKS, 28 Apr., 1847
  b. 28 Apr., 1825, Raynor, England

Ether
  b. 30 Jan., 1849
  d. 22 Feb., 1849

ANN AGATHA WALKER, 28 Apr., 1847
  b. 11 June, 1829, Leek, England
  d. 25 June, 1908, Ogden, Utah

Agatha
  b. 7 July, 1848
  d. 12 Aug., 1914
Malona
  b. 15 Apr., 1850
  d. 27 Oct., 1913
Marion
  b. 28 Nov., 1851
  d. 6 Oct., 1852
Moroni
  b. 10 Oct., 1853
  d. 28 June, 1911
Eveline
  b. 8 Aug., 1856
  d. 16 Aug., 1917

KEZIAH DOWNES, 27 Dec., 1853
  b. 10 May, 1812, Raynor, England
  d. 11 Jan., 1876, Salt Lake City, Utah

None

ELEANOR J. MCCOMB, 14 Nov., 1855
  b. 9 Dec., 1817, Wheeling, West Va.
  d. 24 Oct., 1874, Salt Lake City, Utah

None

—*Prepared by Una Pratt Giles.*

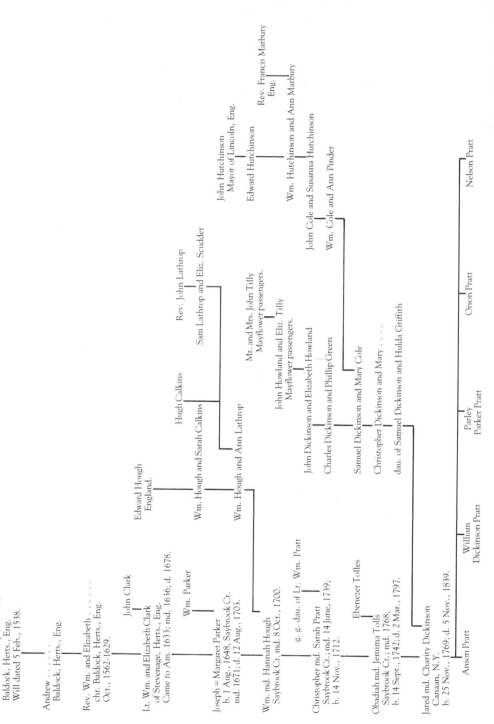

Thomas Pratt md. Joan . . . . .
Baldock, Herts., Eng.
Will dated 5 Feb., 1538.

Andrew . . . . . .
Baldock, Herts., Eng.

Rev. Wm. and Elizabeth . . . . . .
chr. Baldock, Herts., Eng.
Oct., 1562-1629.

John Clark

Lt. Wm. and Elizabeth Clark
of Stevenage, Herts., Eng.
Came to Am. 1633; md. 1636; d. 1678.

Wm. Parker

Edward Hough
England.

Joseph = Margaret Parker
b. 1 Aug., 1648, Saybrook Ct.
md. 1671; d. 12 Aug., 1703.

Wm. md. Hannah Hough
Saybrook Ct. md. 8 Oct., 1700.

g. g. dau. of Lt. Wm. Pratt

Christopher md. Sarah Pratt
Saybrook Ct.; md. 14 June, 1739;
b. 14 Nov., 1712.

Ebenezer Tolles

Obadiah md. Jemima Tolls
Saybrook Ct.; md. 1768;
b. 14 Sept., 1742; d. 2 Mar., 1797.

Jared md. Charity Dickinson
Canaan, N.Y.
b. 25 Nov., 1769; d. 5 Nov., 1839.

Hugh Calkins

Rev. John Lathrop

Sam Lathrop and Eliz. Scudder

Wm. Hough and Sarah Calkins

Wm. Hough and Ann Lathrop

Mr. and Mrs. John Tilly
Mayflower passengers.

John Howland and Eliz. Tilly
Mayflower passengers.

John Dickinson and Elizabeth Howland

Charles Dickinson and Phillip Green

Samuel Dickinson and Mary Cole

Christopher Dickinson and Mary . . . . .

dau. of Samuel Dickinson and Hulda Griffith

John Hutchinson
Mayor of Lincoln, Eng.

Edward Hutchinson

Wm. Hutchinson and Ann Marbury

Rev. Francis Marbury
Eng.

John Cole and Susanna Hutchinson

Wm. Cole and Ann Pinder

Anson Pratt

William
Dickinson Pratt

Parley
Parker Pratt

Orson Pratt

Nelson Pratt

Prepared by Una Pratt Giles.

Index

Index to Illustrations